SECOND EDITION

PERSONNEL LAW

Kenneth L. Sovereign, J.D.

Former Vice President of Industrial Relations
Hoerner Waldorf Corporation
and
Associate Counsel
Champion International Corporation

PRENTICE HALL, Englewood Cliffs, New Jersey 07632

Library of Congress Cataloging-in-Publication Data

Sovereign, Kenneth L.
   Personnel law / Kenneth L. Sovereign. -- 2nd ed.
      p.   cm.
   Includes index.
   ISBN 0-13-658303-2 :
   1. Labor laws and legislation--United States.   I. Title.
KF3455.S68 1989
344.73'01--dc19
[347.3041]   88-27422
                                                  CIP

To my wife, Janet, who tolerates me

Editorial/production supervision: Carole Crouse
Interior design: Joan Stone
Cover design: Edsal Enterprises
Manufacturing buyer: Ed O'Dougherty

© 1989, 1984 by Prentice-Hall, Inc.
A Division of Simon & Schuster
Englewood Cliffs, New Jersey 07632

Printed in the United States of America

10   9   8   7   6   5   4

ISBN 0-13-658303-2

PRENTICE-HALL INTERNATIONAL (UK) LIMITED, *London*
PRENTICE-HALL OF AUSTRALIA PTY. LIMITED, *Sydney*
PRENTICE-HALL CANADA INC., *Toronto*
PRENTICE-HALL HISPANOAMERICANA, S.A., *Mexico*
PRENTICE-HALL OF INDIA PRIVATE LIMITED, *New Delhi*
PRENTICE-HALL OF JAPAN, INC., *Tokyo*
SIMON & SCHUSTER ASIA PTE. LTD., *Singapore*
EDITORA PRENTICE-HALL DO BRASIL, LTDA., *Rio de Janeiro*

CONTENTS

5
WORKING CONDITIONS BASED ON SEX, 80

6
AFFIRMATIVE ACTION AND PERFORMANCE APPRAISALS, 103

7
AGE DISCRIMINATION IN EMPLOYMENT ACT (ADEA), 117

8
REGULATION OF BENEFIT PLANS AND EFFECTIVE USE OF EMPLOYEE AGREEMENTS, 128

9
PRIVACY RIGHTS AND DISCLOSURE OF EMPLOYEE INFORMATION, 145

10
EMPLOYER'S RIGHT TO DISCHARGE, 168

11
POLICIES TO PREVENT WRONGFUL DISCHARGE EXPOSURE, 189

12
PAYMENT OF WAGES UNDER THE FAIR LABOR STANDARDS ACT, 206

13
CONTROL OF UNEMPLOYMENT COMPENSATION COSTS, 222

PREFACE

In all things, success depends upon previous preparation, and without such preparation there is sure to be failure.

CONFUCIUS

Since the 1950s the personnel function has gone through some drastic changes. Each of its many subdivisions has been substantially affected by new federal and state laws plus regulations and local laws. Such common personnel terms as *man, attitude, probationary period, personality defects,* and *old* have different meanings under the law. Past practices not only are obsolete but also are now legally challengeable.

The intrusion of the law into the personnel function has left a knowledge gap, since most managers and personnel practitioners have not had formal training in the application of the new laws to the workplace. This is also true of most lawyers; their training may be in the law as applied to a business relationship, but not to employee relations. It is small wonder that both the manager and the legal counsel become "gun-shy" when facing a personnel law problem.

This "knowledge gap" has not been recognized by institutions of formal education. Most business and law schools do not require the completion of a single course in personnel law but have retained the traditional business law courses. As the late Professor Herb Heneman, Jr., stated in the foreword of the first edition of this book:

It is small wonder that so many managers are uninformed and lack understanding in these areas. It's not too surprising that they resent "government intrusion" into their "right" to manage. These managers seem singularly unaware of where these "rights" came from. . . .
. . . Fortunately, Ken Sovereign's book goes far in removing the barriers of ignorance in relationships between personnel and labor law in the United States.

The text is new and different in that it tells what to do, how to do it, when to do it, and why by an author who both has been a personnel executive corporate counsel who practiced law, and has taught the subject to management personnel since 1980.

The book is designed to be used as a course in colleges and universities, as well as by practitioners. A course in personnel law should be a part of the management and legal curriculum in the same sense as business law. Business failures to a large extent are caused by people problems, and in our "litigation-happy society" a devastating lawsuit with large damages and huge legal fees plays an important part in a business "bottom line." If there is to be a stop to this employee litigation trend, preventive personnel law courses must be offered to students who some day will become managers and lawyers.

The book is written in simple, nonlegal, and practical language in order for the student to understand the marriage between the legal and the personnel concepts. The reader should still maintain an interest in the subject, yet it will send the college student into the real world of management preventive law.

Since the 1960s the law has made a serious attempt to resolve social problems at the work site. Because business success is largely dependent on a good relationship between employees and the organization, the additional rights given to the employee by court interpretation of the law have resulted in a new challenge to management. Some "lay" knowledge of these new rights is necessary if human resources are to be employed in the most economical way. Although the law has entered into all phases of personnel management activity, from recruitment through planning of the economic use of human resources, you don't have to be a lawyer to live with the situation.

With the increasing intrusion of the law into the personnel function in the last decade, there is considerable danger that the present stature and contribution of the personnel function to corporate goals will be replaced by the corporate legal counsel. A strictly legal approach to the solution of an employee relations problem could be devastating to the corporate and individual employees' well-being. The understanding by legal counsel of employee relations consequences and some knowledge of the law on the part of the manager are necessary for organizational survival. If the personnel function ignores the law and the legal counsel ignores the employee relations consequences of a decision, employee litigation is likely to take place.

Since the last edition of this book, two major changes have taken place. The term *Human Resource Manager* has become more popular and personnel law has matured in several areas, but some new problem areas have developed. The term Human Resource Manager is just as inaccurate as the previous terms, such as Industrial Relations Director, Labor Relations Director, Personnel Director, and Employee Relations Manager. Since the generic term *personnel* best relates to people, it will be used throughout this book to include all the various titles of past, present, and future. Rather than being concerned with the latest fad of the proper job title for the personnel function, we will direct our efforts to finding an economical way for the activity to live with its new law partner. Management's "bottom line" will best be protected by preventing exposure to lawsuits through good employee relations and legal practices, regardless of the job title used.

The second major change since the last edition is the maturity of personnel law, which makes it imperative that this book be revised. The first edition was concerned with the substance and application of the social legislation passed in the 1960s and 1970s. The emphasis has now shifted to trying to solve the turmoil in the workplace caused by trying to balance management interests with the newly acquired employee rights.

ACKNOWLEDGMENTS

The author is deeply indebted to his many personnel and legal associates, too numerous to mention, for their encouragement and suggestions in combining the law with the personnel function. To the approximately one thousand lawyers and personnel practitioners who were participants in seminars conducted by the author and sponsored by professional associations and adult educational facilities of colleges and universities, a special thanks for their practical suggestions when field-testing this relatively new subject of personnel law. However, it is only proper that I accept full responsibility for the conclusions, including errors, omissions, and other "goofs" that may occur.

The use of the excellent library facilities of the State of Minnesota Law Library and the University of Minnesota Industrial Relations Reference Library and the cooperation from their component staffs made possible the necessary research and authoritative references contained in the book.

Kenneth L. Sovereign

ABBREVIATIONS USED IN THE TEXT

ADEA	Age Discrimination in Employment Act
ADR	Alternative Dispute Resolution
B.R.	Bankruptcy Reporter (West)
BFOQ	Bona Fide Occupational Qualification
CDC	Centers for Disease Control
CEO	Chief Executive Officer
COBRA	Consolidated Omnibus Budget Reconciliation Act
EEOC	Equal Employment Opportunity Commission
EPA	Equal Pay Act
ERISA	Employee Retirement Income Security Act
et al.	and others
et seq.	First page and section that follows
FLSA	Fair Labor Standards Act
IRCA	Immigration Reform and Control Act
LMRA	Labor Management Relations Act
MBO	Management by Objectives
NIOSH	National Institute for Occupational Safety and Health
NLRA	National Labor Relations Act

NLRB   National Labor Relations Board

OFCC   Office of Federal Contract Compliance

OSHA   Occupational Safety and Health Administration

WAB   Weighted Application Blank

ABBREVIATIONS USED
IN CITATIONS

A.2d	Atlantic Reporter, Second Series
BNA	Bureau of National Affairs—a looseleaf service
CCH	Commerce Clearinghouse—a looseleaf service
CFR	Code of Federal Regulations
Cal.Rptr.	California Reporter
EPD	Employment Practices Decisions (CCH)
F.2d	Federal Reporter, Second Series
FRD	Federal Rule Decisions
F.Supp.	Federal Supplement
FEP Cases	*Federal Employment Practices Cases* (BNA)
LA	Labor Arbitration Reports (BNA)
LRRM	Labor Relations Reference Manual
NLRB	National Labor Relations Board Decisions and Orders
NLRB No.__	National Labor Relations Board Decisions and Orders Advance Citations
N.E.2d	Northeastern Reporter, Second Series
N.W.2d	Northwestern Reporter, Second Series
NYS	New York Supplement
NYS2d	New York Supplement, Second Series

P.2d	Pacific Reporter, Second Series
P.L.	Public Law
RIA	Research Institute of America
S.Ct.	Supreme Court Reporter
S.E.2d	Southeastern Reporter, Second Series
So.2d	Southern Reporter, Second Series
S.W.2d	Southwestern Reporter, Second Series
U.S.	United States Reports (U.S. Supreme Court Reporter)
USC	United States Code
WH	*Wage and Hour Cases* (BNA)

CHAPTER
1
INFLUENCE OF THE LAW
ON THE PERSONNEL FUNCTION

Evolution of Personnel Function
Merging of the Law into the Personnel Function
Federal Laws Most Frequently Encountered in Personnel
Education of Workers as to Their Rights
Relationship of Personnel Problems to Legal Problems
Establishment of Written Policies
Explanation of the Court Structure
Increase in Litigation
Use of Legal Counsel
Making a Risk Analysis

Since the 1960s the law has imposed more restraint on the employee-employer relationship than at any other time. This pressure from regulations has affected traditional personnel policies and practices in two ways. Some personnel practitioners have abandoned all their previous practices for fear of running afoul of the law and have ended up following the letter of the law out of fear.

Another school of personnel practitioners has reacted to law by changing nothing until the law says change and then either complying with it or challenging it.

Neither reaction to the merging of the law into the personnel function is correct. Doing nothing is a disregard for the law that can result in increased employee costs. Waiting for the law to force change in policy will subsequently result in a costly change, one that neither the employer nor the employee may like.

The law's moving into the personnel office has forced the personnel administrator to consider not only the traditional employee relations consequences but also a new problem of legal implications when making an employment decision. That doesn't mean that management is restricted from carrying its function, but it does result in more administrative tasks. This chapter describes how the merging of the law into the personnel function has changed the workday of the personnel practitioner and prepares the reader for a more detailed treatment of the various laws in subsequent chapters.

EVOLUTION OF PERSONNEL FUNCTION

The personnel function as a part of the organization developed from necessity. Somebody was needed to hire employees, process termination, expedite paperwork, administer employee insurance, and act as a liaison between management and the employee. Personnel practitioners were originally semi-professional do-gooders; as organizations became larger, the function grew from an administrative task to one that involved decision making. The personnel director took a place in the "management cabinet" and was largely responsible for people problems. In this intermediate stage of development, personnel was basically a technical function. As more regulations were passed and human resources became more expensive and important to the organization, the personnel director was regarded as a practical but professionally results-oriented person, working closely with the chief executive officer on the people aspects of the business. At this stage of development the law began to merge with the personnel function.[1]

MERGING OF THE LAW INTO THE PERSONNEL FUNCTION

With the enactment of several laws dealing with employee relations in the 1960s and 1970s, the personnel function had another stage of development, whereby the law must be considered in almost every decision made by the personnel practitioner. Employee relations laws have had a profound effect on policies and practices of both large and small organizations. Their policies and practices are now subject to an external audit by a government regulatory agency. In order to pass this external audit, personnel administration must be more objective and develop job-related policies.

Effect of the Merger

It was only a short time ago that the employment manager would hear a familiar phrase from a supervisor: "Don't send me a

---

[1]For references on the personnel function, see George Milkovich and William F. Glueck, *Personnel-Human Resource Management, a Diagnostic Approach* (Plano, TX: Business Publications, Inc., 1985); Herbert G. Heneman III, Donald P. Schwab, John A. Fossum, and Lee D. Dyer, *Personnel Human Resource Management,* 2nd ed. (Homewood, IL: Richard D. Irwin, Inc., 1986); Steward A. Youngblood and Randall S. Schuller, *Effective Personnel Management,* 2nd ed. (St. Paul, MN: West Publishing Co., 1986).

black because I can't fire him." This was a common belief among supervisors when civil rights legislation was first passed. It was a fear caused by a misunderstanding of the application of the antidiscrimination laws to the workplace. No court of law has ever said that you must hire any person who is not, in management's opinion, the best qualified. No court of law has ever said that you must promote somebody who is not qualified or that you can't discharge an employee for poor performance.

When the law entered the personnel function, it did not say that management had to change the standards of performance required of an employee, but it did say that you cannot discriminate in applying those standards to an individual because of race, sex, color, religion, age, and nationality.

Elimination of Pseudo Practices

Management had many "pseudo" practices that not only were discriminatory but also were ineffective personnel practices. When the author was in graduate school, his professor, Dale Yoder, told the class to never use a test unless there is some assurance that it will predict performance on the job. Twenty-five years later the Supreme Court in *Griggs* v. *Duke Power Co.*, 401 U.S. 424(1971) told management the same thing. In the interim, many tests that had no relationship to job performance were used to reject applicants, but the organization was in vogue since it used tests for selection of applicants. Application forms required answers to questions that were not job related. When a regulatory agency asked the purpose of the question, nobody knew, except that it was on the form that was purchased from a professional organization— another pseudo practice. When a worker was retired, the reason was that he or she was 65 and everybody should retire at 65 regardless of performance or knowledge of the job. When a person was discharged and somebody asked the reason, the answer very often would be "poor performance," but

there was no objective measurement of that performance. Often when an employer was questioned under oath how performance was measured, the answer would be that it couldn't be measured except by subjective observation.

When the law moved into the personnel function, these practices were externally audited and management came to realize that maybe some demands of the regulatory agency to comply with the law were also good personnel practices. For many years the personnel practitioner was frustrated because there was no professionalization of personnel practitioners. The law moving into the personnel function made great strides in professionalizing this area of management activity, where other efforts have failed. The law forced objectivity. What is wrong in forcing a test to predict success on the job? Why is it wrong for a question on an application form to be job related or to reject subjectivity in the measurement of performance?

Management Resistance

In the following chapters managers and personnel practitioners will be shown how the law often aided in making the personnel function more efficient and useful. The law does not interfere with good management, but it does require a change in practices, and it increases the administrative work load of the personnel function. It is understandable that management often would be hostile to changes necessary to comply with regulatory decisions. This is a normal reaction. Management also resisted the National Labor Relations Act when it became effective in 1938. The feeling of being overwhelmed by all the new laws will disappear when personnel law is better understood.

The philosophy of top management or its belief of the reasonableness of the particular law often influences management's decision on whether the law should be challenged. Often the value of the law is overlooked because of management resistance. Management in the decision-making process seeks legal counsel, but lawyers also differ on the

EXHIBIT 1-1

HMO
ERISA
Equal Pay Act
National Labor Relations Act
Fair Labor Standards Act—State Codes
The Employee Polygraph Protection Act
Immigration Reform and Control Act of 1986
Consolidated Omnibus Budget Reconcillation Act
Antidiscrimination Laws—Executive Order 11246—State Laws
Rehabilitation Act of 1973—Vietnam Veterans Rehabilitation Act

application of the law to a given set of facts unless there is a well-settled principle of law involved. Since legal counsel is seldom asked to consider the employee relations consequences of a legal decision, the input of the personnel practitioner at this stage of the decision-making process is highly important.

The practitioner must not only point out the employee relations consequences but also make cost comparisons, within and outside of the industry. This entry of the law into the personnel function does not mean that personnel administrators must be lawyers, but they must be aware of possible legal implications and permissible activities. Because contemporary personnel administration must consider the legal implications before action is taken, more knowledge of the law is required than in the past.

FEDERAL LAWS MOST FREQUENTLY ENCOUNTERED IN PERSONNEL

The merging of the laws into the personnel function was a gradual process, accelerated by enforcement of discrimination laws, federal control of pension plans and welfare problems, and safety regulations, all of which seemed to come into focus in the middle 1970s.

Manager's Burden

Exhibit 1-1 illustrates the manager's burden of the various laws that she or he must be concerned with when managing people. At the outset, this may seem like an impossible burden, but as will be shown in later chapters, none of these laws will prevent the organization from being a profitable operation.

EDUCATION OF WORKERS AS TO THEIR RIGHTS

The legal problems that the contemporary personnel practitioner faces today are so much greater than those of two decades ago that often it is difficult for top management to realize it.

The change is caused not only by the existence of regulations and laws but also by the worker's being better educated about his or her rights and obligations. Most laws and regulations promote communication to the employee by requiring the employer to post official notices of employee rights. Many states also have similar posting requirements where federal laws do not apply. Most statutes require the regulatory agency to impose a penalty or fine for failure to meet the posting requirements. The regulatory agency will usually supply the poster on request. Posting provisions generally require that the notice be posted in a conspicuous place so as to permit ready observance. For some laws both applicants and employees must be communicated with; accordingly, the employment or personnel office is the logical place for the postings. The employer who posts by the time clock or at an exit complies with the requirements of a conspicuous place, but the posting is seldom read. Communications to employees should be placed where the employee will take time to read them, such as in the lunchroom. An entrance, an exit, or a time clock is not usually one of those places.

Worker Education Programs

In addition to communication via government posters, the labor unions have publicized the workers' rights under the laws and regulations in their periodicals and at meetings.[2] They also hold training seminars for their members and leaders on the law and give information on how to exercise their rights. Labor education centers on university campuses work with labor organizations to provide educational opportunities to union members. (Most of these universities also have management education centers.) These labor education centers have a full-time staff who work with an advisory committee of union leaders. They develop a curriculum and course material in a wide variety of subjects. The centers are usually supported in part by the university budget, the remainder coming from tuition.

Some of the subjects taught in labor education courses are Labor-Management Cooperation, Economics of Concession Bargaining, Labor Law, Advance Grievance Handling, Arbitration, and Health Care Costs.[3]

A function of labor education centers at universities is to communicate to the union membership what their rights are under the law. Each school year 200 to 300 members will attend these classes on a given campus.

Legal Advertising

Since the Supreme Court in 1977[4] held that lawyers could not be prevented from advertising, there has been a rise in the use of the media to encourage the public to see a lawyer about any problem from personal injury to a fight with one's spouse. Before 1983 13 percent of the lawyers advertised; by 1986 24 percent were advertising. An additional 18 percent stated in the survey that they intend to advertise in the near future.[5] Lawyers who don't advertise state that it is unprofessional, but as more do it some observers believe all law firms will be forced into it.

The rapid increase in advertising of legal services indicates that it must work. If any employee hears over the radio or on television that he or she can consult a lawyer about any problem without paying a fee, this will increase the exposure to lawsuits. In the past, employees who had claims of potential employer liability would often refrain from

---

[2]*1987–88 Union Leadership Academy Course Information,* Labor Education Service, University of Minnesota.

[3]Labor unions are beginning to represent workers in nontraditional areas. See "The Changing Situation of Workers and Their Unions (report by AFL-CIO Committee on the Evolution of Work, February 1985), p. 18.

[4]*Bates* v. *State Bar of Arizona,* 97 S.Ct. 2691, 433 U.S. 384 (1977).

[5]Lauren R. Raskin, "Law Poll," *ABA Journal* (May 1986), p. 44.

seeing a lawyer because they were not sure how good a case they had. Therefore, they didn't want to pay an unknown fee to the lawyer for talking about it. With the advent of advertising free legal assessment of the case, the employer is especially vulnerable to being sued.

The media, notice-posting requirements, legal advertising, labor education centers, and the high level of education among the workers have contributed to making contemporary employees well educated on procedures and remedies when their rights are violated. An employee who knows his or her rights and obligations is more likely to use those rights against an employer than the less-educated employee of the past, although some of the statutes granting those rights have existed for many years.

RELATIONSHIP OF PERSONNEL PROBLEMS TO LEGAL PROBLEMS

Problems Encountered in Personnel Administration

Although the personnel practitioner may be aware of the legal consequences of an employment decision, often other members of management are not. Management is sometimes hostile to the changes necessary to comply with government regulations and interference with employment decisions. It becomes the duty of the personnel practitioner to make management aware of the consequences of the regulations and applicable laws, to assess policies and practices in relation to developments in the law, and to obtain legal counsel when necessary. As the personnel function of management attempts to solve legal problems, solutions must be weighed in light of employee relations consequences. The hypothetical situations shown on page 7 point out the dilemma of the personnel practitioner since the law has entered into the function.

Whether the solutions of these problems should be based on legal considerations or employee relations considerations or both depends on several factors:

1. Do the facts fit into a well-established principle of law, or is this a gray area, where there is a choice?
2. Is the employee relations consequence so severe that it is worth the cost of challenging the law to get a court interpretation?
3. What are the indirect and direct costs of compliance as compared to challenging the law through the courts?
4. What are the problems if the employer complied with an unsettled area of law?

In the past, determinations in employment decisions were made on instinct and had no basis except a certainty by the decision maker, which would be accepted by management, that it was right. The above examples point out that such decisions can, and often do, have legal consequences. When such a decision was made in the past, only management reviewed it. Now there is an external audit of policies and procedures.

Employee relations consequences are a consideration only if there is uncertainty about the interpretation of the statute or regulation. Management is responsible for compliance where there is no doubt about interpretation. The reasonableness of the statute or regulation also affects top management's decision on whether to challenge the law. The personnel practitioner's opinion of whether the law can be lived with often has a bearing on the decision to challenge the law. The efficient employment of human resources will demand that solutions to employee relations problems are found that do not result in exposure to lawsuits.

Living Economically with the Law

The employer must prevent exposure to lawsuits by putting policies and practices legally in place so the employee is discouraged from starting a lawsuit. Once the lawsuit is started it is too late, since management time and legal fees have already occurred.

Today's personnel administrator must find

A Personnel Administrator's Day

Situation	Wife of an employee is a qualified over-the-road driver and applies for an opening as a driving partner of a married over-the-road driver.
Legal Considerations	If one refuses to hire is it sex discrimination? What is job-related reason? Are moral considerations valid for disqualification under Title VII?
Employee Relations Considerations	This can cause domestic problems that will reflect on performance, and stability of employment of both male and female employees.
Situation	Employee has been off work and ill for 14 weeks (sick benefits expired) and returns with a doctor's slip stating that she can perform only "light work." Supervisor says he does not have light work and sends her to personnel office.
Legal Considerations	Under most handicap laws (both state and federal), must make reasonable effort to accommodate. If there is no light work, what data are available as to the physical requirements of all the jobs? Can you transfer to make room for handicapped worker?
Employee Relations Considerations	Past practice is to give light work to employees with an industrial accident to avoid loss of time for safety record purposes and loss of income for insurance purposes. What is the medical definition of light work; what is the employer's definition?
Situation	White male employee who had a better performance appraisal rating than a black female wants to know why he was not promoted instead of the black female.
Legal Considerations	Affirmative action goals are being satisfied, but was white male discriminated against to the extent that there will be a reverse discrimination charge?
Employee Relations Considerations	How valid is the performance appraisal program? It is subject to legal scrutiny. It has been the criterion used for promotions in the past although never validated.
Situation	Personnel practitioner attends meeting with office supervisor who wants to terminate an employee who was a leader in a meeting with other employees about the length of their coffee break periods and a salary increase policy (office is nonunion).
Legal Considerations	Is this kind of action protected by the National Labor Relations Act although no union? Can one employee act collectively without a union? Is one meeting collective action under the law?
Employee Relations Considerations	This is a disruptive incident. Employer must maintain order in the office, cannot have employees getting together every time they are dissatisfied. Leader could cause problems, even promote a union if demands are not met.
Situation	Personnel administrator receives a call from supervisor that National Guard reservist wants six-month leave to go to officer's training school for the National Guard reservist.
Legal Considerations	Must give leave of absence for military duty but is this a voluntary assignment for which a leave of absence can be denied? Not sure, little case law on it.
Employee Relations Considerations	Too long a leave. Employee must be replaced by training a new person.

EXHIBIT 1-2

Statute → Enforcement agency → Agency guideline → The challenge by management → of Enforcement agency to comply with statute

a way to communicate to operating management that it may not have a full range of choices about how it deals with employees but is not prevented from acting in the best interests of the business.

Changing Personnel Practices

The use of such terms as *probationary period, permanent employee, merit increases, annual salary* in a job offer, and *personality problems* on the termination form now causes serious exposure to a lawsuit. The use of these terms never did fit into good professional human resource management and now the law is questioning their meaning.

Personnel administrators are increasingly faced with correlating a number of seemingly conflicting legal and employee relations implications. Therefore, they must have enough knowledge of the law to be aware of the legal implications and when to seek legal counsel.

A vital part of personnel administration involves advising management of the consequences of failure to apply the law as interpreted by a regulatory agency. As new laws have been enacted and government agencies created to enforce them, gray areas have erupted.

The many uncertainties in the law have resulted from regulatory agencies issuing guidelines or interpretative bulletins that sometimes exceed the original intent of a law, as shown in Exhibit 1-2.

The extent of compliance with new laws and guidelines that are not yet judicially interpreted is a business decision. The personnel administrator with the assistance of legal counsel must advise management of the alternatives so that the company can make a sound business decision, to comply with or challenge the enforcement procedures of the regulatory agency or the courts.

Exposure to a Lawsuit

Throughout this book the text will refer to *exposure* to a lawsuit. Nothing can stop an employee from seeking a lawyer to represent him or her in a lawsuit. However, if the facts of the case show that the employee has a good chance of winning, the lawyer will take the case on a contingency (usually one third of what is collected). If the facts show it will be a difficult case to win, the lawyer either will refuse to take the case or will demand an up-front fee before taking it. *Exposure* as used in this book means that the employer's actions have developed facts that give the employee a good chance of winning, the lawyer will take it on a contingency fee, and it costs the employee nothing to sue.

If the policies and procedures of the employer are legally in place and there is little chance of winning, which causes the lawyer to demand a fee, there probably won't be a lawsuit because the employee will not take the risk of losing and paying a fee. This is common in discharge cases where the employee's income has stopped. The only employer that wins a lawsuit is the one who avoids the suit.

ESTABLISHMENT OF WRITTEN POLICIES

When the law merged with the personnel function, there was a need for personnel administration to become more legally aware. The law demanded more exactness than that which is necessary when dealing with people. The best policy is no policy at all, but unfortunately this is no longer advisable or realistic. The legal approach is seldom the best approach when solving people problems. Our society, however, demands that we become more legal and have more policy. This is essential if the employer is to be protected from lawsuits.

When management reads of the large jury awards to employees against other employers, the first reaction is to have more policy, but this is not always the answer. It is just as bad, legally, to have too much policy as too little. However, in our litigation-happy society we must have more policy if we are to avoid lawsuits. There are some areas, such as sexual harassment, drug testing, control of pilferage, and discharge, that demand policies regardless of the size of the organization if liability is to be avoided. A small organization may need very little policy, but at some point the cherished informal approach to dealing with employees becomes too difficult and the style of management must become more formal. The policy manual should be drafted only when it becomes necessary because of the increased number or frequency of people problems.

How Much or How Little Policy?

The first objective in reviewing existing policies or writing new ones is to make them as short and simple as possible. These criteria are important from both legal and employee relations standpoints. If you include too much, the policy will not be followed by even the most conscientious of your managers and you will run the very risk of lawsuits that you wanted to avoid. If you have too little detail, you may also invite litigation to interpret the meaning of the statement. It is not uncommon for managers to use policy to justify a position or course of action that has already been decided upon or to ignore policy that they do not like. Neither approach should be encouraged.

As a practical matter the statements in a policy manual should be limited to those employment situations where uniform administration is necessary to avoid lawsuits. For example, when one department requires employees to sign out when leaving the facility during meal periods and another department in the same organization does not, the

consequences may be minimal. However, if one department has a different leave of absence policy from that of another—possibly because the decision has been left up to the supervisors—the exposure to litigation under the discrimination laws may be serious. This leads to the first axiom of policy making:

- Make written policy only for those procedures that involve substantial legal exposure and can be uniformly administered throughout your organization.

First decide what you want the policy to accomplish. Is it intended to outline standard operating procedures? Is it an aid to managers in solving people problems or handling interdepartmental relationships? Or is it a communication from management about what must be done in certain situations? Most statements can do no more than one of these things. The reason may become clear from the second axiom:

- Policies affecting people can be relatively general, but others must be procedure oriented.

Many personnel practitioners believe that statements in policy manuals should be limited to those relating to people and that all other matters should be covered by statements on internal procedures. From a legal point of view this approach has many desirable features.

A common mistake of some practitioners is to go to a seminar or purchase a "how to" book and then proceed to write policies because they understand that it is the thing to do. Those with such an inclination might look at the apparent inverse correlation between the number of policies and the success of the organization. Policies that are not uniformly administered, or that are used in place of alert and intelligent management, are worse than no policies at all. Those who have the responsibility for writing policy manuals must be aware of these possibilities, but the drafting committee or the approving authority cannot know how the policy will work. This is the reason for the next axiom:

- Make the proposed policy an internal guideline before stating it as policy and communicating it to the employees.

The legal difference between an internal guideline and a policy is that an internal guideline tells management what they should do about a problem while a policy, after it is communicated, tells employees what they can expect management to do. When management tells employees something, the employees have a legal right to depend upon management to follow through. When management makes a statement, it becomes a condition of employment that the employee considers when deciding to seek employment elsewhere or to remain with the present employer.

From the time when John Marshall was Chief Justice of the Supreme Court (1801), our judicial system has been attempting to fit the Constitution and the various laws passed by Congress into contemporary economic and social situations. This is a momentous task for the courts, yet it is no more difficult than that faced by management in trying to write policies that will fit all employees. The policy often does not fit the case of the individual employee or the facts surrounding the specific situation. As a result personnel practitioners are always bumping the employee's head on the policy doorway as they attempt to push through. Better to keep policies in line with the next axiom:

- Make every policy as flexible as possible and provide an escape hatch as wide as possible while staying within the legal limits and organizational objectives.

This statement might sound like double-talk at first, and an example might help in clarification. Suppose that a supervisor decides to do something about the poor quality of the output of his or her section. The supervisor announces a policy of progressive discipline. The first offense will result in a written warning, the second in a lay-off, and the third in discharge. Af-

ter the warning and discipline, an employee turns in a poor-quality product for the third time. The policy calls for discharge, but the supervisor faces a situation where one operator is ill and another is on vacation, and if the employee is discharged—as the policy requires—no one will be available to run a machine to meet the deadline for an important customer. The dilemma could have been avoided if the statement had been more flexible for the third offense, and had stated that severe disciplinary action would be given up to and including discharge.

Personnel practitioners who are strict constructionists might say that this statement is not definite enough and that such a policy would not stand up under judicial scrutiny. The courts would not agree. In *Hamilton* v. *General Motors Corp.,* 606 F.2d 576 21 FEP Cases 521 (5th Cir. 1979), the court said that subjectivity is not illegal per se if objective standards are involved. Where people often go astray in writing policies is in attempting to find easy ways to solve people problems. Too often the result is that some time after the policy is written, they find that there is no easy way to avoid people problems and still be legally sound.

Essential Policies to Avoid Exposure to Lawsuits

The real test for deciding whether you should have a policy in a given area is whether you can give an affirmative answer to two questions.

1. Is the policy absolutely necessary for the smooth and efficient operation of the organization?
2. Are you seriously exposed to lawsuits or frequent employee relations problems if you do not have a policy?

The first question can be answered on the basis of past problems that arose because of the lack of policy.

The answer to the second question is not as simple. An element of uncertainty always surrounds dealing with possible legal consequences as well as employee relations problems. A key question here is the willingness of management to enforce the policy. Management must make a conscious decision that it is going to do so. The first step in enforceability is a clear statement from top management. All too often, this statement has a tone that seems to ask for co-operation rather than one of giving direction and indicating an intention of enforcement. For example, one statement from a CEO read as follows:

This manual contains the most recent operating and staff policies for ABC company. I urge you to review them so that if you have any questions you can put them through the proper channels. I hope you will find this policy manual useful in carrying out your responsibilities.

This statement from the CEO does not imply that management will enforce the policies. Instead it seems to allow the managers to enforce the policies if they wish to do so, which creates the greatest possible exposure to lawsuits. The managers who do enforce the policies expose those who do not. A manual with this type of statement from the CEO is merely a guideline and should not be communicated to the employees involved. Doing so opens the possibility that the manual will be considered a contract.[6]

To avoid violations of antidiscrimination laws does not necessarily require a written policy. Any employer can follow a nondiscriminatory course without one. Policies that cannot—or will not—be enforced should not be communicated to employees. Management may wish to establish internal procedures that managers may follow or not depending upon the circumstances and the direction of their superiors. These procedures may be written, and inevitably some of them may come into the hands of employees other than the managers for whom they were intended. The important point is that employees would not be permitted to depend upon them as conditions of employment. In one typical case the discharge of the employee was unquestionably justified, but the written policy in the handbook was not followed and as a result the employee was awarded damages.[7]

To avoid litigation in certain areas, only a few policies are needed.[8]

Unless a compelling operating need or a state statute requires it, most organizations will not require much more than a few specific policies to avoid lawsuits. However, specific policies may be necessary for certain job categories, such as antitrust violation restrictions for sales-related jobs, and conflict of interest policies for certain other positions.

Often the policy manual becomes the repository for statements in other fields such as employee benefits, vacation, and severance pay. These are benefits that tell employees what they have a right to expect. They belong in a separate book—not in the policy manual. In determining what should be communicated to employees, management should keep in mind the fact that once the communication is issued, management relinquishes flexibility in that field. In the future, the employees have a right to depend upon the statement. This is not to say that policy cannot be changed, but change must come before the fact. One employer included a discussion of severance pay in a policy manual drafted in 1962. In 1971, the manual was changed. The court held the obligation did not cease upon the modification in 1971 but that severance pay accrued on a different basis from 1971 on.[9]

This case also illustrates the danger of having a policy on severance pay. Why not give severance pay as the occasion arises? That procedure allows management to retain its flexibility. Some employee relations

---

[6]See *Kinoshita* v. *Canadian Pacific Airlines, Ltd.,* 803 F.2d 471 (9th Cir. 1986).

[7]*Pine River State Bank* v. *Richard F. Mettille Sr.,* 333 N.W. 2d 622 (Minn. 1983).

[8]For importance of policy to avoid litigation, see "An Ounce of Prevention," *Inc.* (October 1984), p. 153.

[9]*Johnson* v. *Allied Stores Corp.,* 679 P.2d 640 (Idaho 1984).

points may be lost in not telling the employees what a fine organization they are working for and lack of a policy statement may cause some difficulty in recruiting. But other ways can be found to emphasize good working conditions without granting the employee a right that can be the basis for a lawsuit later. A policy on a matter such as severance pay should not be put in writing unless no other alternative exists and management is willing to accept pitfalls that may result.

Recommendations for Drafting Policies

When consideration is being given to whether an organization should have a policy manual or statements of organizational positions on particular subjects, the starting assumption should always be that the best policy is no policy at all. The flexibility and informality of unwritten personnel policies is still to be preferred. Recent developments, however, may make such an approach not in the best interest of the organization. If, for example, the organization is threatened with unionization, it legally is too late to communicate changes after the union activity commences. To comply with the various discrimination laws and with the Federal Wage-Hour Law, certain written policies are necessary. Present practices may be in conflict with various state or local laws. Finally, the organization may have grown to the point where managers and supervisors need guidance to ensure uniform administration of procedures in dealing with employees. Some recommendations are

1. Keep the language simple and nonlegal. Such terms as "we have the right to" when you already have the right raise a question about whether you are giving away part of the right or retaining part of it. Similarly if you state that "exceptions may be made for," you raise unnecessary questions. In the absence of a statement that "there will be no exceptions," you imply that you can make them. If exceptions are necessary, you do not need a policy to make them. Do it, but say why.

2. Clear, concise, and straightforward wording with few syllables is essential if all persons the policy affects are to understand it. Nothing is more damaging to effectiveness than a disagreement over what the statement says or means.

3. Indicate that the authority is coming from top management and that the policy is not giving it up. When you start telling what management will do, you open exposure to lawsuits when for some reason management does not do what is stated. A policy statement is not a union contract. Always state that as laws change and experience dictates, policies will have to be changed or modified and that employees will be given sufficient notice of any changes.

Once the few policies are drafted, they should be reviewed by top management and then revised on the basis of the comments received. The second draft should be reviewed at the next level of management and again revised. The process should be repeated on a step-by-step basis until everyone from top management to the first-line supervisors have had an opportunity to review and contribute to the policies.

The next step is to "field-test" the statements for a period of time as guidelines before they are finally adopted as policy. This development process is often necessary to make sure that they have as much acceptance as possible. During the entire review and testing, the substance of the statements as decided by top management will probably not be changed although the wording may be. If you have only those policies that are absolutely necessary, going through the democratic process of review is unlikely to change the substance.

Revision of Present Policies

In many cases policies already exist in some form, but since the merger of the personnel function with the law, revision is necessary. Present policies may be in conflict with state or federal laws, the company may have been organized by a union since the last policy was written, or the organizational structure may have changed. Whatever the reason, the important point to remember is that the change should not become effective for a period of time. The employee should be allowed enough time to look for a new job if he or she does not like the new conditions imposed by the revision. (Where there is a union, employees have a right to challenge the reasonableness of the policy, but they do not have to until it affects an employee.) Although the law does not interfere with the end result of effective personnel administration, it does require some extra caution in many areas. The drafting or revision of policies is one of them.

EXPLANATION OF THE COURT STRUCTURE

One of the problems created when the law moved into the personnel function is the overreaction of management when it is reported in the news media that a company of 50 employees had to pay a million dollars in damages for a wrongful discharge. The CEO immediately calls his lawyer and wants some guidance to be certain the company is not exposed to any liability but will still be permitted to discharge undesirable employees. The mistake the CEO makes is that this is only a decision of a lower court (unless it is a Supreme Court decision) and there are two more chances that the decision will be reversed on appeal.

Whether a decision is in favor of the employer or the employee, nothing should be done until the time for appeal has expired. Knowledge of how the court system works will be helpful in preventing costly management mistakes when reading about a court decision in the news media.

Structure of the Federal Courts

Our federal courts are structured at three levels: district court, appellate courts, and Supreme Court. The district court is where the case starts. All the evidence is recorded, witnesses testify, and in certain cases the jury will participate while in other cases the judge

makes the decision. The federal district court decisions are cited in this text as West's Federal Supplement Reports. An example of the citation would be 560 F.Supp. 820 (D.C. Mont. 1987). 560 is the volume number, F.Supp. is Federal Supplement Reports, and 820 is the page number. D.C. Mont. is the district court of Montana where the case was decided, and 1987 is the year of the decision.

Although district court decisions are important, they are not considered precedent setting and if not appealed only apply to the area where the court has jurisdiction. The employer must decide, after consulting an attorney, whether the decision necessitates changing a policy.

Within a certain time after a decision is rendered (usually 30 days), either party may appeal the decision to the next higher court. This court must consider the appeal. It is called the appellate court and considers whether the decision of the lower court was proper as to the law and the facts presented. The appellate court will usually not hear new evidence. These cases are cited in this text as _____F.2d_____ (5th Cir. 1987). The F.2d stands for West's Publishing Federal Reporter 2d series, and the 5th circuit is where the case was decided. There are 12 circuit courts of appeal in the United States, which are divided into geographic areas. Most lawyers respect circuit court opinions because about 18 percent are appealed to the U.S. Supreme Court (the highest court in the system), which hears a little over 1 percent of the appeals filed.

The Supreme Court doesn't have to grant review of the appellate court decision (the petition for review is called a Writ of Certiorari). If the Supreme Court refuses to review, the decision of the appellate court becomes the law in the circuit where it was decided. The Supreme Court will not hear any new evidence but will make its decision based on the oral argument, legal reasoning of the appellate court, and evidence presented in the district court. Both the appellate court and the Supreme Court review whether the rules of procedure were followed in the district court.

All federal judges are appointed for life by the president with the consent of the senate. Presidents tend to appoint judges of their own political philosophy, so one president in office may appoint most of the judges in a certain court and another president of a different philosophy may appoint those in a higher court. Often the philosophy influences the interpretation of the law and as a result upper courts will reverse lower courts.

Most state courts have basically the same structure as the federal, only they interpret the state laws. The court where the case starts is the district court, then there is the appellate court and the Supreme Court. As in the federal system, the appellate court must consider the appeals from the district court, but the Supreme Court can decide what cases they will hear.

Explanation of Legal Documents

The personnel executive should become familiar with the basics of legal terms because often the servicing of court proceedings against the company is made to the persons in the personnel office when the matter involves employees. Most legal documents have a time limit in which they have to be acted on; it is highly important that the documents are expedited promptly. Failure to act within the time limits can result in liability by default or other serious legal consequences. In most legal documents the time limits are clearly stated, and the court serving the papers and the attorneys involved are clearly stated on the documents.

Interrogatories. Interrogatories are a set or series of written questions served on one party in a proceeding for the purpose of a factual examination of a prospective witness. They are used mostly in pretrial discovery to obtain information to aid the attorney in preparing the case and selecting witnesses.

The personnel practitioner will sometimes receive the interrogatories from an opposing attorney to obtain information about employees. An attorney should always review the information before it is mailed. Answers to interrogatory questions are not done under oath but are often used as a basis for questions that are answered under oath. Answers can also determine how the attorney will try the case. The request for interrogatories comes directly from the attorney requesting them; they do not need court approval unless objected to by the opposing party.

Exhibit 1-3 is an interrogatory served on a company where the personnel department would supply the answers. In the interest of brevity, only enough questions are included to show a typical interrogatory.

Deposition. The deposition is a pretrial discovery procedure whereby the testimony of a witness is taken outside of open court, pursuant to permission by the court to take testimony from a witness. Most questions are based on, but not restricted to, the interrogatories. A deposition differs from interrogatories in that it is under oath and it is used under certain conditions in court proceedings for questioning the witness. When a deposition is taken, it is contemplated that the person will be a witness in the trial, but this is not always the case.

When an employee is requested to give a deposition, often there is a sense of insecurity; although the other attorneys may be present, the employee requests the legal counsel from the company to be present. This is a policy matter for management and legal counsel to determine. Some companies consider it good employee relations to give legal security to an employee when giving a deposition; others feel that the presence of one attorney representing the employee's interest is enough.

Subpoena. The subpoena is an order directed to a person to testify as a witness at a particular time and place.[10] The most common subpoena in the personnel department is to appear and bring all documents and written materials related to the subject mat-

---

[10]*Black's Law Dictionary,* 5th ed. (St. Paul, MN: West Publishing Co., 1979).

STATE OF _____   DISTRICT COURT

COUNTY OF _____   SECOND JUDICIAL DISTRICT

LEO SMITH,)

              Plantiff,   )

      v.   )   INTERROGATORIES

ABC COMPANY   )

          Defendant.   )

TO: DEFENDANT ABC COMPANY AND ITS ATTORNEY JOHN ROE, (ATTORNEY'S ADDRESS)

PLEASE TAKE NOTICE that Plaintiff, Leo Smith, requests, pursuant to Rule 33 of the Rules of Civil Procedure, that the Defendant ABC Company answer the following Interrogatories within the time prescribed by law. These Interrogatories shall be deemed continuing in nature and should the answers require modification or supplementation it is demanded that you so advise Plaintiff and his attorney.

DEFINITIONS

Unless conclusively altered by the context of a specific Interrogatory, the following definitions are to be considered to apply to all the Interrogatories contained herein.

A.   You and Your means ABC Company, present and former directors, officers, employees, attorneys, agents, representatives, and any and all other persons, firms, corporations, or entities acting or purporting to act on behalf of ABC Company.

B.   Identify or Identification

    1.   When used in reference to a person, means her or his:

        a.   Full name

        b.   Present or last known residence address

        c.   Position and job description at the time in question

INTERROGATORIES

1. Describe the nature of the supervision of your premises employed to maintain control over employees on the job, in the cafeterias, and in any other areas of the premises to which the employees have access.
2. Had you received any complaints in 1975 by nonunion workers that they were being harassed by union workers?
3. If the answer to interrogatory No. 2 is yes, identify all persons who made such complaints.
4. Did any security unit, the foreman, or any other of your employees investigate such complaints?

                     LAW OFFICES OF RICHARD ANDERSON

          By _____

             Richard Anderson

             (Address)

Dated _____   (Telephone)

ter of the case. This is called a subpoena duces tecum. Often the records are all that the attorney wants, and production of the records satisfies the subpoena; it is not necessary for the person in charge of the records to testify. However, permission from the attorney signing the subpoena not to appear is required. When receiving a subpoena duces tecum, the attorney requesting the documents should always be asked whether only the records are wanted or does the person subpoenaed have to testify. A lot of time will be saved if documents only must be produced. Also, it is not advisable for the personnel practitioner to appear in the courtroom and be called as a witness subject to cross examination. Any personnel document marked confidential, as between company counsel and the employee, need not be produced.

Exhibit 1-4 is a typical subpoena duces tecum, often received in workers compensation, divorce and other civil suits, and government proceedings. Subpoena duces tecum is also used in criminal proceedings.

Summons. A summons is an order served on the defendant to appear in court and to give an answer within a specified time to the suit that has begun against the person. The nature of the lawsuit is stated in the complaint.

It is important to note the time and date when the summons is received as the answer must be within a specified time, usually 20 or 30 days. As soon as a summons is received, legal counsel should be notified. Exhibit 1-5 is an example of a summons used in a civil case.

Complaint. A complaint in a civil proceeding is the first or initial pleading by the plaintiff. It asks the court for legal redress of an alleged wrong. The complaint is usually received with the summons. Under the rules of civil procedure of the courts it must contain certain information about the case such as the alleged wrong, the names of the parties, county and name of the court where the action is brought, and relief sought. The complaint also states why the defendant is

being sued, and the relief requested by the plaintiff.

Exhibit 1-6 is an example of a complaint. It was filed by a person owning a semi-trailer who is suing for injuries caused by improper loading of the trailer by employees of the defendant. The personnel department should not in any way respond to a complaint but refer it to legal counsel. For the purposes of brevity, only the essential elements of the complaint are shown in Exhibit 1-6.

The essential elements of the complaint should be noted. Paragraph I tells what the defendant did. Paragraph II describes the wrong committed by the defendant. Paragraphs III and IV state the result of that wrong, and paragraph V states the relief or remedy requested by the plaintiff.

INCREASE IN LITIGATION

The entry of the law into the management function is not a phenomenon particular to personnel, but it is indicative of the growth of law in all business and social activities. Beginning in the early 1970s there was a growing concern for people to be protected legally from every problem, even from their own gullibility. Litigation has been growing so fast that it is difficult to know the total number of pending cases on the dockets of the courts. The unfriendly stigma of a lawsuit has almost disappeared. Doctors are sued by patients, lawyers by clients, parents by their children; brothers sue brothers and sellers sue their customers. As the mother said to the father, "If I make Johnny eat his spinach, he will sue us." Social legislation such as antidiscrimination laws, the Occupational Safety and Health Act, the Employee Retirement Insurance Act, the Immigration Reform and Control Act, Consolidated Omnibus Budget Reconciliation Act, and various environmental laws has given added legal opportunities to individuals never before experienced in judicial history. The alphabet-soup of government regulatory agencies creates a thriving climate for the litigation-happy individual.

EXHIBIT 1-4

No. 3073—Subpoena Duces Tecum. (Rev. 1953)

State of Minnesota,   **DISTRICT COURT**

County of .... Smithson ....   1st ....*Judicial District*

.... John Doe ....
                                                      ⎫
.... ⎬
                            vs.   *Plaintiff* ..... ⎬   **SUBPOENA**
.... Homer Smith ....   ⎬   **DUCES TECUM**
                                                      ⎭
....

                            Defendant ....

THE STATE OF MINNESOTA TO .... ABC Corp., Milltown, Minnesota .... :

You are hereby commanded to appear in the above named court at the Court House, in the

County ....*of* .... Smithson .... *, on the* 22nd

day of .... August ...., 19 82 , *at* .... 9:00 .... *o'clock* .... fore .... *noon, then and*

there to testify on behalf of .... John Doe .... *in*

above entitled proceeding.

You are further directed and commanded to bring with you the following papers and documents

now in your possession or under your control, viz.:

    All Personnel Records, including wages paid during the last two years,

    days absent during said period, all medical records and work performance

    records and appraisals.

WITNESS, The Honorable .... RONALD E. HACH .... *Judge of said*

Court, and the seal thereof this .... 2nd .... *day of* .... July ...., 19 82

                            HAZEL G. ART
                                                      ....
                                                         Clerk

                            By ~~Walter Meadow~~
                                                         Deputy

State of Minnesota,

County of .... Smithson ....

I hereby certify and return that I served the within Subpoena on the within named

.... Personnel Director ....

....*by reading the same to him and delivering to him*

a true copy thereof, at .... ABC Corp., 415 Jones St., Milltown, Minnesota

in said County and State, on this .... 15 .... *day of* .... Aug. ...., 19 82

SHERIFF'S FEES: Arnold Anderson
                                                      ....
    Service, ... 15.00   *Sheriff of said County*

    Mileage, $ .... 12.00   *By* ~~M. Johnson~~

(All names and places are fictitious)

EXHIBIT 1-5

STATE OF _____   DISTRICT COURT
COUNTY OF _____   SECOND JUDICIAL DISTRICT

LEO SMITH,   )
)
              Plantiff,   )
)
       v.   )   <u>SUMMONS</u>
)
ABC COMPANY   )
)
              Defendant.   )

THE STATE OF MINNESOTA TO THE ABOVE-NAMED DEFENDANT:
     You are hereby summoned and required to serve upon Plaintiff's Attorney an Answer to the Complaint which is herewith served upon you within twenty (20) days after the service of this Summons upon you, exclusive of the day of such service. If you fail to do so, judgment by default will be taken against you for the relief demanded in the Complaint.

                                              _____
                                              John Roe
                                              Attorney for the Plaintiff
                                              (Address)
                                              (Telephone)

When to Use Legal Counsel

When legal documents are received that require an answer, they should be referred to legal counsel. Sometimes these documents can be interpreted as admitting liability, which should never be admitted without advice of counsel. Once liability is admitted or implied, there is nothing left to mitigate and the person is at the mercy of the court or regulatory agency.

Written agreements that can be interpreted as enforceable contracts should be either drafted or reviewed by an attorney. When a lay person drafts a contract, it is more likely to be challenged. In the event of latent liability, the drafter is protected if the contract is reviewed by an attorney. No document should be signed without understanding the terms or having it explained by counsel. When the corporation is involved, there should be some control on who has authority to sign, because any member of management can bind the corporation if there is reason to believe that the person signing has authority to do so.

Since the erosion of the at-will doctrine, many astute employers have legal counsel review all discharges to determine whether there is a possible exposure to a lawsuit. This is a good procedure when there is any doubt. Voluntary quits in some

EXHIBIT 1-6

STATE OF _____	DISTRICT COURT
COUNTY OF _____	SECOND JUDICIAL DISTRICT

LEO SMITH,   )
)
      Plantiff,   )
)
     v.   )   <u>COMPLAINT</u>
)
ABC COMPANY,   )
)
      Defendant.)

Plaintiff, for his cause of action against the above Defendant, alleges as follows:

I.

That some time prior to May 25, 1976, Plaintiff, Leo Smith, at that time an independent trucker, pursuant to a Contract of Employment, picked up a semitrailer at the business place of Defendant at 2334 Oakdale Avenue, Milltown, Mill County, Minnesota, which trailer had been loaded by Defendant's agents, servants, or employees, with large rolls of foil for transport to Defendant's facility in Chicago, Illinois.

II.

That at said time and place, Defendant, through its agents, servants, or employees, acted in a careless, negligent, and unlawful manner by failing to secure properly, block, or insure otherwise that said rolls of foil, when loaded in said trailer, could not come loose and roll off said trailer and injure persons in the vicinity thereof.

III.

On May 25, 1976, at Defendant's facility in Chicago, Illinois, while said trailer was being unloaded by Defendant's agents, servants, or employees, a roll of foil fell on Plaintiff, thereby crushing his body.

IV.

That said injuries were as a direct result of the negligence, carelessness, and unlawful behavior by Defendant, through its agents, servants or employees, in failing to secure properly or block said rolls and thereby preventing them from rolling off the trailer.

V.

WHEREFORE, Plaintiff demands judgment against the Defendant in the amount of One Million Dollars ($1,000,000), together with costs and disbursements herein.

_____
John Roe
Attorney for Plaintiff
(Address)
(Telephone)

situations can be constructive discharge, and if that possibility exists, it should be reviewed by counsel.

A Litigation-Happy Society

To illustrate how people are suing each other at a rapid rate, in 1960 there were 59,284 civil cases filed in federal district courts. By 1986 this figure had increased to 254,828, an increase of over 200 percent when the population was increased by 25 percent. In 1986 there were 34,292 cases filed in federal appeals courts and there were 25,276 cases waiting to be decided. Each year the number of pending cases increases. The courts simply cannot keep up with the caseload.[11]

Although many of these cases are not charges by employees against their employers, these charges do account for a large proportion of the increase. In fiscal year 1986 the EEOC had 68,882 cases filed, down slightly from the 1985 figure of 72,000, but state agencies had an increase of 3,000 for the same period. The total of the state and federal agency discrimination charges for 1986 was an amazing 122,623. Like the courts, the EEOC gets further behind each year. In 1986 they had 63,446 closures and received 68,882 cases.[12]

Some social scientists fear that the willingness to sue is destroying the personal relationships and trust between individuals that has made our society so pleasant.

Growth of Legal Profession

The increase in litigation has created a demand for more attorneys, and once the trend has started it is difficult to stop. When the demand is there everybody enters law

school, and there has been no sincere attempt to limit the number of students. As long as a shortage existed and students could meet the standards, they were admitted. Many became lawyers four years later, however, when the field was already overcrowded. In 1988 there is one lawyer for every 345 persons; in 1958 there was one lawyer for every 1879 persons in the United States.[13]

The increase in litigation caused an increase in attorneys, and now, with the surplus, the number of attorneys has caused an increase in litigation. This is evident by the amount of advertising they now do. In 1977 the U.S. Supreme Court in *Bates* v. *State Bar of Arizona,* 97 S.Ct. 2691 (1977), held that attorneys could not be denied the right to advertise. This started a trend of lawyers encouraging people to come in and discuss their rights free of charge. As the slogan goes, "Know your rights; come and see us; there is no charge for consultation." Many lawyers feel it is not professional to advertise, but this is rapidly changing. In 1983 only 13 percent of the lawyers advertised and by 1985 this had increased to 24 percent.[14]

Economic Use of Legal Counsel

There has been a growing dependency of the personnel function on the legal counsel. The social legislation of the late 1960s, 1970s, and 1980s increased employee rights to the extent that the law has become an external auditor of the personnel function. The personnel practitioner must have enough knowledge of the law to make a determination of when legal advice is necessary. Managers and personnel practitioners must find an economical way to obtain this advice.

[11]1986 Annual Report of Director of Administrative Office of U.S. Courts (Washington, DC: U.S. Government Printing Office). See also *1987 Lawyers Almanac,* Prentice-Hall Law and Business, 855 Valley Rd., Clifton, NJ 07013.

[12]*Equal Times* (March 1987), an EEOC internal newsletter publication.

[13]American Bar Association and Bureau of the Census, "Population Estimates and Projection" (Department of Commerce, July 1988).

[14]Raskin, "Law Poll," *ABA Journal* (April 1986), p. 44.

It is too expensive for the practitioner to be educated by the legal counsel in the basics of the legal process or for the practitioner to educate the attorney on the personnel aspects of a problem. Although both disciplines are at times needed, it is not necessary or advisable for the person carrying out the personnel function to be a lawyer, or for the lawyer to have expertise in personnel. The legal approach to personnel problems is rarely the best approach.

It is often said that the only thing an attorney has to sell is his or her time.[15] So when using legal counsel, the objective is to take the least time possible and still get the information and guidance that is necessary. Before calling, review what you are going to ask. Organize the references that you think you will need and have them in front of you. It is expensive to go to the file and find a document while the attorney is holding the line.

Be prompt in supplying information. Tell the attorney all the facts. There is nothing more expensive than for the attorney to find out the bad facts after he or she has prepared the case. If the bad facts come out through the opposing attorney while in court, it is very damaging to the case. Sometimes the attorney will ask for a continuance and prepare the case all over again with new pleadings and witnesses if he or she did not have all the facts before preparing the case. If in your reading you come across a certain case and you want to talk to your attorney about it, get the citation if it is available. Before the issue can be considered, the attorney has to look up the case, and it often takes a great deal of time to find the citation, especially if one of the names of the parties to the case is spelled wrong.

---

[15] A client once asked a lady in a law office to get him a cup of coffee. When she returned she asked him what she could do for him. Realizing he had mistaken his attorney for a secretary, he apologized. She said she didn't mind taking her time at $100 an hour. The cup of coffee cost him $25.

The more you can do to help the attorney the less time it will take for him or her to give an opinion, and that saves money. It is no reflection on your ability as a practitioner to seek legal advice, but when it becomes unnecessarily expensive then it will be avoided at times when it is needed. It is not unprofessional to question an attorney's fees statement. You should request that it be itemized as to the fee hours charged, who performed the service, and what the time charge was for those individuals. A statement that says "for services rendered" should not be accepted. The statement should be detailed enough to allow, if necessary, another attorney to assess the reasonableness of the charges.

The practitioner must learn how to use legal counsel economically, because whether she or he likes it or not, the law has now become a partner in the personnel function.

USE OF LEGAL COUNSEL

One of the most common errors of managers is not seeking legal advice early enough in the decision-making process. The counsel should be asked: What are the legal consequences of my decision? What are the legal alternatives? What can I do to prevent my decision from being challenged in the courts? Where there are no alternatives within the law, that should be determined after every possible avenue is explored. After legal advice is received it then becomes a business decision whether to take the exposure to a lawsuit or comply (often at a high cost) and eliminate all possible chance of a lawsuit, even though legally it may be right. Whether to take the adventurous approach or the conservative one depends upon management philosophy, how much the regulation interferes with economic operation of the enterprise, and what are the chances of prevailing.

Legal counsel should be expected to give an uncompromised legal opinion, which may not satisfy the person seeking it. The practitioner should give all the facts and be able to distinguish between a legal opinion and a personal prejudice toward the problem. Often managers will not ask legal counsel, because of the fear that the answer will be no. If this situation exists the legal counsel is failing in its assigned tasks of advising management. Managers do not want to know what they cannot do but what they can do and still be legal. If they decide to be contrary to the established law then this is a business risk for top management to make.

Distinction between Personnel and Legal Function

When the personnel function obtained top management status, it became exposed to an avalanche of government regulations that brought the lawyers into an area with which they were often unfamiliar. The lawyer looks at a personnel problem in a legal context; decisions are based solely upon what the lawyer believes the law says one must do or not do. The personnel director must consider the consequences of a decision and the conflicting considerations between a personnel decision and legal decision. For example, it is a legal determination that only those employees who filed a claim for disability pay due to pregnancy should be paid when the court determines that the state law was violated; it is an employee relations consideration whether to pay all employees who became disabled from pregnancy whether they filed a claim or not.

The legal counsel determines only what is required under the law while the personnel practitioner in considering the employee relations consequences may go beyond what the law requires. In another example, the courts have stated that a safety inspector from the Department of Labor cannot enter an employer's premises without a search warrant unless the employer agrees.[16] It is a policy decision whether the employer wants to require a warrant.

Relationship of Legal Counsel to Employees

When there is an in-house counsel or a law firm that the company has designated as legal counsel, the relationship of counsel to the employees should be explained to the employee when she or he becomes involved in a legal problem. When an attorney is acting on behalf of a corporation on a legal matter involving an employee, the attorney-client relationship is between the attorney and the corporation. There is no attorney-client relationship with the employee unless the employee obtains a different attorney to represent his or her interests.

Information that an attorney obtains when acting for the corporation belongs to the corporation and is confidential to the corporation. The employee as an individual has no right to see the information or to use it.[17] It is immaterial whether the employee gave the information to the attorney representing the corporation at the direction of a superior or obtained the information elsewhere, as long as the information was obtained while performing a function on behalf of the corporation and is relevant to the case.[18]

A corporation has a right to any information that the employee obtained in the course of employment that is job related; the employee can be disciplined or discharged for refusing to disclose it. However, it is good employee relations to inform the employee how the information is being used, but the employee has no constitutional right under the Fourth or Fifth Amendment to take immunity when the employer requests information.[19] Corporate counsel also can look at all the files

---

[16]*Marshall* v. *Barlow's, Inc.*, 436 U.S. 307 (1978).

[17]Some states have statutes requiring the employer to show the employee his or her own records.

[18]*Diversified Industries* v. *Meredith*, 572 F.2d 596 (8th Cir. 1977).

[19]*U.S.* v. *Solomon*, 509 F.2d 863 (2nd Cir. 1975).

concerning the employee; the employee has no remedy under the law to prevent it.

Often employees seek personal advice of the in-house counsel or company attorney. The corporation, as a matter of policy, must determine whether the attorneys should be used to give advice to employees when they have personal problems. Some personnel practitioners take the position that one hires the whole person; therefore the employee's legal problems are company problems and the company should give them initial aid in the same manner that the company nurse does when an employee has a head cold.

Other practitioners take the position that getting too involved legally in an employee's personal problems can have an adverse effect if that advice is followed and the results are unfavorable to the employee. A policy followed by many companies is to refuse legal advice to employees on matters not related to their job duties. This may require an initial conference to determine whether the legal problem is job related. If it is determined that it is not job related, the employees are advised to seek their own lawyer. It is advisable not to assess the merits of the case in this situation as the employee's lawyer may have a different opinion.

Some companies will permit the in-house counsel to do so-called first echelon legal work. Legal counsel will look over a deed for an employee buying a house, for example, or give advice on an automobile accident as to alternatives and the court procedure and assess and recommend a local attorney. Companies that use their in-house counsel in this manner believe that it is good employee relations as long as their counsel does not get involved in the employee's personal legal problems to the extent of representing the employee against the other party or giving advice for which the company may be responsible in the event of adverse consequences. This is a good policy for companies with in-house counsel if it is restricted to nonunion management personnel. The benefit to the company outweighs the adverse results as long as discretion is used.[20]

Obtaining Legal Opinions

The opinion of counsel can be valuable to the practitioner, depending on how it is obtained and used. An option should be requested before taking any questionable legal action that may result in legal implications.

The outside legal counsel or the law department should get the problem as early as possible. The more lead time before the legal opinion must be rendered, the more time for research and the more complete is the opinion. Often a considerable amount of research is necessary: A half-page memo or letter may be the result of eight hours of research.

Since opinions are expensive, when an opinion is requested the problem should be properly framed. Asking further questions takes time, which increases the cost of legal services. When requesting an opinion, the personnel executive should

1. Give the attorney all known facts. Facts should not be condensed or digested. Do not be reluctant to disclose all the facts, even those that are damaging.[21]

2. When giving the facts, be prepared to provide documents such as memos, letters, or other written support.

3. Always identify assumptions and state those separately from the facts.

4. Be prompt in returning information requested. When the attorney must call twice for the same information, the company is usually charged for two telephone calls.

5. When calling for advice, have all the documents available and think out the questions beforehand.

---

[20]Those benefits could include saving management time of the employee seeing a lawyer or employee satisfaction. A troubled employee is often a poor producer, and you hire all his or her problems.

[21]In this author's experience as an in-house counsel, failure to disclose damaging facts was a common practice among managers.

Sometimes a person will receive two different legal opinions on the same issue or problem. There are several reasons why legal opinions differ:

1. A slight difference in the facts or circumstances may have a different legal result.
2. There may be some changes in the laws between the time the first opinion and the second opinion are received.
3. Different lawyers may come to different conclusions when they weigh various facts and interpret statutes or court decisions. Experience, background, and personal beliefs often affect the interpretation of the law.
4. In gray areas of the law there are legal risks that cannot be avoided. Different attorneys may give different advice. Some attorneys will be more adventurous than others in assessing a legal problem.

Oral versus Written Opinions

Because of the expediency of the situation, many practitioners telephone legal counsel and ask for an immediate oral opinion. An oral opinion has many pitfalls and should not be used to solve important legal problems. This is especially true where legal counsel is not familiar with the subject matter. Even where the counsel is considered an expert, oral opinions can be misleading and should be used only when the problem is routine and an immediate answer is essential. The pitfalls of an oral opinion are that

1. The attorney has to remember the facts and apply them to the law with little thought.
2. There is a danger that the recipient of the opinion may misunderstand it.

3. There is no record of the opinion. If the consequences are adverse, there is always a question of what facts were given and the content of the opinion.
4. Since oral opinions lack research, they may not reflect the most current law.

Written opinions take longer, are more costly, but have fewer misunderstandings and can be retained in the file for future reference. However, when using a written opinion in another situation, care must be taken that the facts are the same.

Information that an attorney receives or gives a company employee is privileged information that cannot be used by a third party or subpoenaed.[22] It is important to identify that the information was received through the attorney as an employee of the company and to classify it as confidential in the file. One way to do this is to have an attorney mark all legal opinions confidential. An example of how documents should be marked when received from an attorney is shown in Exhibit 1-7.

A statement similar to this should be marked on all documents given to the counsel, as shown in Exhibit 1-8. Usually the counsel will do so, but if not, then the person sending them should do it.

MAKING A RISK ANALYSIS

When management is considering whether to challenge a law or to comply, it should have a conference with legal counsel and a

---

[22]*Upjohn* v. *U.S.*, 101 S.Ct. 677 (1981).

EXHIBIT 1-7

> *The enclosed matters are communicated to you in confidence and constitute or contain legal services given to you by legal counsel. There are to be no duplications distributed or otherwise disclosed except through the attorney rendering them.*

EXHIBIT 1-8

> *This document contains legal matters that is given to an attorney for his or her own use and is not to be disclosed to other persons unless upon the advice of the attorney receiving it.*

number of risk considerations should be explored:

1. Is the desired course of action likely to bring a lawsuit?
2. Can the company financially risk the lawsuit or is compliance less expensive?
3. What consequences may result from the desired course of action—in the marketplace, with corporate goodwill, on employee relations, on corporate objectives and priorities?
4. Is the company in line with other companies in the industry?

The next consideration is the approximate cost of the case. In determining the cost it should be decided how far the company will appeal the case. Then the company budgets for attorney's and witness cost at the first level of the hearing, the cost of appeal to the next court until a final determination. When considering the attorney's costs, these cannot be exact figures; an attorney can only estimate the time involved. For example, in research sometimes an attorney can find a case that serves as authority for the client's position in an hour or two; at other times research may require half the day. Because all the attorney has to sell is time, a two-page opinion can cost $900 or $200 depending on the time for the research and drafting. When considering the cost of a case, the company should always ask the price per hour of the attorney's time, plus an estimate of what the case will cost and, if anybody else will be involved in the case, that person's hourly cost. Also when considering the cost, management time must be considered. Litigating a lawsuit involves the time of manage-

ment personnel; cost as well as management time availability must be considered.

Cost Compared to Importance of Issue

Once the cost of the case is determined, an assessment should be made of winning. There is never a sure case; the parties must look at the strengths and weaknesses of both the plaintiff and the defendant and be prepared for a surprise decision. The role of the legal counsel in assessing the chances of winning is to consider the facts in light of research or expertise on the subject and advise the client; the final decision on whether to take the risk belongs to the client.

Once it is decided to take the matter to court, a management representative should be assigned to the case and become involved as much as possible. A lot of the attorney's time can be saved by client availability. Another reason to be involved closely is that settlement is always a possibility at any stage of the proceedings and counsel cannot settle without the consent of the client. Sometimes settlement possibilities exist only for a short time; if the management representative is not available, that opportunity is lost.

When assessing whether to litigate or settle, the economic considerations must be weighed with the employee relations or operational consequences. Where a testing program is being challenged by EEOC and management is convinced that because of the low educational level of the local labor market, tests must be given in order to select qualified applicants, then the cost of litigation must be considered against the operational consequences if the test is eliminated as a selection tool.

Statistics show that society is litigation happy; everybody is suing and there is no end in sight. The increase in litigation of all types, including employee relations cases, means that legal implications of employment decisions will not go away and the personnel executive must become involved with legal concepts.

If the personnel executive develops policies and procedures that consider legal implications, the marriage of the law with the personnel function will not be a costly one. The most economical relationship will allow the organization to continue to function without having to restrict legal advice in areas where it is needed to prevent exposure to lawsuits.

2

DISCRIMINATION UNDER CIVIL RIGHTS ACT OF 1866 AND TITLE VII

Application and Coverage of Civil Rights Act of 1866 and Its Amendments
Discrimination under Title VII
Out-of-Court Settlements

Chapter 1 described how the law moved into the personnel function and drastically changed personnel management. These traditional practices of adopting attitudes, beliefs, and ideas about political or ethnic background for an employment decision are now restricted by antidiscrimination laws.

Many of these well-accepted practices and policies are no longer advisable. A key reason has been the impact of antidiscrimination legislation that outlaws policies and practices that result in disparate treatment of or disparate impact on any protected class of applicants or employees.

State and federal antidiscrimination statutes affect all phases of the employment process, from initial advertising of a job vacancy through hiring, promotion, discipline, discharge, and retirement of the employee.

Title VII was the first major antidiscrimination legislation that drastically affected employment decisions. If the employment decisions resulted in a person's being treated differently because of race, color, religion, sex, or national origin, Title VII would cause the employer to change its position and restore the employee to his or her original status, including reimbursement for any monetary losses.

Although Title VII had the greatest impact on the employment relationship, it was not the first antidiscrimination statute passed by Congress. In 1866 Congress passed a civil rights act that prohibited discrimination because of race. In 1870 and 1871 the act was amended to plug the loopholes in the 1866 statute. This statute was not applied to the employment relationship until 1971, but it is now used in discrimination cases as much as Title VII.

This chapter will discuss the application of Title VII and 1866 statutes (as amended) to the employment relationship. Many of the legal principles established under these two statutes also apply to other antidiscrimination statutes, such as those on age discrimination and discrimination against handicapped workers. These subjects will be given consideration in subsequent chapters.

APPLICATION AND COVERAGE OF CIVIL RIGHTS ACT OF 1866 AND ITS AMENDMENTS

The original statute was passed shortly after the Civil War to support the Thirteenth Amendment. It gave blacks the same rights under the law as whites. Since it did not cover all activities, such as right to sell, purchase, lease, or inherit real and personal property where the state has jurisdiction, the act had to be amended. The 1871 amendment, which is presently the most widely used, asserts that when acting under the "color of the state" (any local, state, or federal governmental units) all persons must be given the same rights.[1] The Supreme Court has interpreted *persons* to mean all ethnic groups, not only blacks.[2] The 1871 amendment made the employer or the employee acting in behalf of the employer personally liable for violating the act.

Personal Liability

In *Vinard* v. *King*, 728 F.2d 428 (10th Cir. 1984), the director of a municipal-owned hospital discharged an employee without a hearing, contrary to the procedure in the handbook. The court held the director personally liable but not the hospital, since it was part of the municipality, which couldn't be sued. Even if it could be sued, the city could be liable only if an employee's action is based on policy that is unconstitutional. This makes it much harder for employees who have been wrongfully discharged to sue the city.[3] When a prison guard placed an inmate in a cell with another inmate whom he knew to be dangerous and the plaintiff was assaulted, the guard was held personally liable.[4]

---

[1]Text for statutes can be found in 42 USC Sect. 1981–83.

[2]*St. Francis College* v. *Al-Khaziaji*, 107 S.Ct. 2022 (1987).

[3]See *St. Louis* v. *Praprotnik*, 108 S.Ct. 915 (1988).

[4]*Smith* v. *Wade*, 103 S.Ct. 1625 (1983).

This personal liability extends to judges of state courts who in an administrative action violate the statute.[5]

The courts strictly follow the requirement that the defendant must be acting under the authority of the state. In *McCarthy* v. *KFC Corp.*, 607 F.Supp. 343 (D.C. Ky 1985), the court would not accept the argument that since the defendant used the name Kentucky Fried Chicken it was under the authority of the state and therefore an individual could be sued for the wrong.[6]

Differences from Other Antidiscrimination Laws

Besides individual liability, one of the differences from Title VII is that the plaintiff must show an intent to violate the act.[7] This is often difficult to do, and since it is not necessary under Title VII, the plaintiff's attorney will often use both statutes. If intent cannot be shown, she or he can always fall back on Title VII.

Another difference between the 1866 statute and most other antidiscrimination statutes is that there is no limitation on retroactivity. The act goes back to the date of the incident.

Another distinction is that it is an exclusive remedy,[8] so if you do not want to go through the Equal Employment Opportunity Commission (EEOC) or other administrative agencies, you can go directly into court. This is sometimes a great advantage when the plaintiff wants to get the case adjudicated quickly. Since it is exclusive remedy, if the plaintiff fails under other antidiscrimination statutes, he or she can still bring an action under the 1866 statute.

The 1866 statute does not cover sex discrimination. This is a major difference, since sex discrimination charges are very common.

Another major advantage of the Civil Rights Act of 1866 over most other antidiscrimination statutes is the right of jury trial. If possible the employee will always choose jury trial over a judge's decision. Juries are more sympathetic to employees (most of them are employees or have been at one time) than a judge who must follow the law more closely and is not as emotionally influenced as a jury.

The right of jury trial and ability to make an individual personally liable are two great incentives for the plaintiff to sue under the 1866 act, if legally possible, rather than under other antidiscrimination statutes.

DISCRIMINATION UNDER TITLE VII

The broadest antidiscrimination statute is the 1964 Civil Rights Act (commonly called Title VII). It is the principal source of antibias rules for employment practices. The act prohibits discrimination in all employment decisions on the basis of race, color, religion, national origin, or sex, including pregnancy, childbirth, or abortion. Title VII applies to employers, labor unions, apprenticeship committees, employment agencies, and state and local governments. It covers all employees from the part-time office boy to the chief executive officer. Before a business is subject to the act, it must affect interstate commerce and employ 15 or more individuals for at least 20 weeks during the current or preceding calendar year.[9]

The Equal Employment Opportunity Commission enforces the objectives of the act. All charges under Title VII must begin

---

[5]*Forrester* v. *White*, 108 S.Ct. 538 (1988).

[6]Personal liability under other laws will be discussed in Chapter 18.

[7]*General Building Contractor's Assn.* v. *Pennsylvania*, 102 S.Ct. 3141 (1982).

[8]*Patsy* v. *Florida Int'l. University*, 102 S.Ct. 2557 (1982).

[9]If an employer is not covered by federal law, state or municipal laws fill in the void. Employers should not seek jurisdictional shelter under federal law because some other law will cover them.

with the EEOC or a state referral agency, whose decision is not binding on the EEOC.

Definition of Discrimination

Title VII did not define discrimination. The first task of the courts was to define it. Discrimination exists, according to the Supreme Court in the landmark case of *Griggs* v. *Duke Power,* 401 U.S. 424 (1971), if there was disparate treatment of the protected class.

If an employment policy treated one class of employees or individuals within the class differently from another class or had the effect of eliminating employment opportunities of a protected class, the courts defined this as a disparate impact that is unlawful unless a business necessity could be shown. In order for an employer to determine whether employment practices would result in an adverse impact on a member of the protected class, the EEOC issued guidelines that would enable the employer to determine mathematically whether a disparate impact on a certain class of employees existed. This formula is not a statutory definition of a violation but only evidence of violation. When a disparate impact is found, the employer must give a nondiscriminatory reason why it exists. Exhibit 2-1 illustrates how an employer can determine whether a disparate impact exists.

If the selection rate for minorities is less than 80 percent of the selection rate for the remaining applicants, a disparate impact is demonstrated. To make this computation, divide the selection rate for the minorities (or covered group) by the selection rate for

the remaining applicants and compare the result to 80 percent. If the selection rate for minorities is less than 80 percent of the selection rate for the remaining applicants, a disparate impact is demonstrated. In this example 67 percent is below 80 percent; therefore a disparate impact would exist.[10]

When the term *disparate treatment* is used, it is in a case where an employee alleges that she or he has been treated less favorably than others because of sex, race, and so on by policy or action of the employer. Sometimes the term *disparate impact* is used in place of the term disparate treatment, but the meaning is not the same. Disparate treatment is a term used by employees when the employer has treated one person differently from another because of membership in a protected class. The disparate treatment complaints are individual cases, and the plaintiff must show that the employer had an unlawful motive or intended to discriminate. The basis for a violation under this theory can be found in *Furnco Construction Co.* v. *Waters,* 438 U.S. 567 (1978), and *Texas Community Affairs* v. *Burdine,* 450 U.S. 248 (1981). Disparate impact is a term used when the plaintiff challenges the policies of management as being discriminatory toward a group of employees who are members of the protected class, regardless of the employer's intent to discriminate. The disparate impact theory was defined in *Griggs* v. *Duke Power Co.,* 401 U.S. 424 (1971).

-----

[10] The court in *Albemarle Paper Co.* v. *Moody,* 422 U.S. 405 (1975) gave judicial approval to the formula.

EXHIBIT 2-1

Applicants 100	Number of Minority Rejected 53	Number of Nonminority Rejected 30

Rate of selection = 100 − rate of rejection

$$\frac{\text{Selection rate for minorities (47\%)}}{\text{Selection rate for nonminorities (70\%)}} = 67\% \; < 80\%$$

The distinction is important to employers because if the complaint is disparate treatment and only one person is involved, intent or unlawful motive must be shown. Often employers become concerned about treating one employee differently from another. These concerns are not well founded because many times the person involved is not a member of a protected class. Even if he or she is, if a nondiscriminatory reason can be shown and there is no intent to discriminate, the action is legal.

Under disparate impact, although the plaintiff does have to show intent, it must be shown by statistical evidence that the policy or procedure had the effect of discriminating against several members of the protected class. In *Watson* v. *Fort Worth Bank & Trust,* 108 S.Ct. 2777 (1988), the court held that although there may have been disparate treatment of a black female (who was refused four promotions by subjective decisions of white males), the plaintiff failed because she brought the suit under the disparate impact theory and could not prove that a protected class was unintentionally affected by an employer's policy since in fact the employer had no policy. However, under the disparate treatment theory she would have had a strong case for individually being treated differently because she was a member of a protected class, but she would have had to show intent and the employer could then have rebutted with a nondiscriminatory reason. It must be remembered that an employer can always treat a member of the protected class differently (although it may be disparate treatment) as long as there is no intent to discriminate and a nondiscriminatory reason can be shown.

Prima Facie Evidence

It is a legal principle that before a person can go to court, it must be shown that a wrong has been committed by stating certain facts. In discrimination lawsuits this is called a prima facie case (will establish a fact until rebutted). In alleging discrimination in employment the

Supreme Court said that the charging party must establish a prima facie case by showing the following:[11]

1. The applicant is a member of a class protected by the statute alleged to be violated (sex, race, national origin, age, and so on).

2. The applicant applied for the vacancy and is qualified to perform the job. (Where the employer requested specific questions be answered in a resume and the applicant refused to answer those questions, the court held that the plaintiff had not completed the application process and therefore was not an applicant and failed to establish a prima facie case.)[12]

3. Although qualified the applicant was rejected.

4. After rejection, the job vacancy remained and the employer continued to seek applications from persons of equal qualifications. (If the employer rejects a minority but hires another equally qualified minority, this is not a defense to rebut the requirement that there was no rejection of the first applicant.)

Distinction between Equal Employment and Equal Opportunity

It is a common belief among managers that there is no discrimination when a minority is rejected and another minority is accepted. This was considered in *Connecticut* v. *Teal,* 102 S.Ct. 2525 (1982). The court stated that Title VII is designed not only to protect groups but to protect individuals as well. In this particular case, the selection procedures show no adverse impact upon the group, but individuals are denied equal opportunity employment because of an identifiable pass/fail barrier. Those individuals are entitled to protection under Title VII. If individuals are deprived of employment opportunities or if their status is affected because of race, religion, or nationality, Title VII is violated. The law guarantees members of the protected classes

---

[11]*McDonnell Douglas Corp.* v. *Green,* 411 U.S. 792 (1973).

[12]*Tagupa* v. *Board of Directors Research Corp., U. of Hawaii,* 633 F.2d 1309 (9th Cir. 1980).

the opportunity to compete equally on the basis of job-related criteria. The fact that others were not discriminated against in the hiring process does not mean that certain individuals have not been wronged.

It was clear in this decision that there is a difference between equal employment and equal opportunity. Title VII requires that an employee be given an equal opportunity to be employed. Prior to the Teal decision, employers could review their hiring and promotion procedures according to the end result. The procedures would pass scrutiny by EEOC if the final result did not show a disparate impact. The courts and EEOC did not inquire into the disparate impact or disparate treatment of the component parts of the process. The Supreme Court in the Teal decision stated that the "bottom-line" approach is not a defense if in the process individuals have been adversely affected. In this case certain individuals were disqualified for promotion because they failed to pass a test that had not been validated. The results of the test had a disparate impact, therefore business necessity had to be shown by validating the test to show that it was job related. The fact that the final selection rate did not show a disparate impact was immaterial. The Teal decision clearly establishes the difference between equal employment and equal opportunity to be employed.

Discrimination can take place at any step in the employment process. The individual must be given an opportunity to show that she or he is qualified. Elimination from consideration for a promotion or to fill a vacancy for non job related reasons denies the opportunity to be considered according to qualifications. An equal opportunity employer is one who gives the opportunity to become employed. Any barrier that is not job related or a business necessity is discrimination under Title VII.[13]

---

[13]In *Bell* v. *Birmingham Linen Service*, 715 F.2d 1552 (11th Cir. 1983), a sexist remark by the supervisor responsible for filling a vacancy was enough to show that the employee's sex was a barrier to the promotion.

Protection from Retaliation

Many statutes that grant certain rights to employees have a provision that prohibits the employer from retaliating against an employee who attempts to aid in the enforcement of the statute. The legislative purpose of the provision is to encourage the employee to use the protection of the statute by reporting a violation and enhancing its enforcement.

Title VII has a similar retaliation provision as in other statutes.[14] Retaliation is defined by the courts as an unlawful practice of an employer whereby the employer discriminates against the employee for participating in the enforcement of a statute.

The application of these principles can be found in *Donnellon* v. *Fruehauf Corp.*, 796 F.2d 598 (11th Cir. 1986). The employee filed a discrimination complaint with the EEOC alleging that she was denied the sales representative position because of her sex. Three weeks later she was discharged. Four days after her discharge she filed an additional charge with the EEOC alleging that she was discharged in retaliation for filing her original claim. The court held that there was no sex discrimination but that she was discharged in retaliation for filing a claim.

In order to get into court for a retaliation case (prima facie proof of retaliation), the employee must show

1. That she or he has engaged in statutorily protected activity.
2. That the employer has taken an adverse employment action.
3. That there is a causal connection between the protected activity and adverse action.
4. That the employer would not have taken the adverse action, "but for" the employee's good faith belief that the practice under the law was wrongful, and he or she was seeking to enforce it.

---

[14]42 USC Sect. 2000(e)(3) provides that an employer cannot discriminate against an employee "because he has opposed any practice made an unlawful employment practice by this subchapter or because he has made a charge, testified, assisted, or participated in any manner in an investigation or hearing under this chapter."

It is up to the employer to show that the adverse action had nothing to do with the filing of the charge. If the employee's conduct was unlawful, excessively disloyal, hostile, disruptive, or damaging to the employer's business, then she or he cannot claim protection under the statute's discrimination clause.

In Donnellon there was no question that the plaintiff could meet the requirements to get into court. It then became a question of why she was discharged. The employer, according to the court, could not give an articulated, clear, and consistent reason for the discharge. Each witness gave a different reason (an inconsistent reason is always damaging in any discharge case). The court put great weight on the fact that she was discharged a month after filing the sex discrimination charge. In *Reeder-Baker* v. *Lincoln National Corp.*, 649 F.Supp. 647 (N.D. Ind. 1986), the court found retaliation because no event occurred between filing the charge and the employees' discharge. Sometimes the employer will give clear reasons for discharge but they are not very persuasive. Such reasons as "generally poor work performance," "failure to cooperate," or "gross insubordination" usually will not be accepted by the court as legitimate, nondiscriminatory reasons, but will be considered a pretext to the retaliation.[15]

The reason for the discharge must stand on its own. If the employee would not have been discharged for the offenses committed or other employees committed the same offenses and were not discharged, then the courts conclude it was retaliation.[16]

The retaliation on the part of the employer must be intentional, showing that the employer treated the plaintiff differently from the way the firm would have treated other employees under similar circumstances.[17] The most important element in the defense of retaliation cases is that the discipline or employment decision is applied to all employees when the situation is the same. The mistake that employers often make is to treat a person who has filed a charge either more leniently or more strictly; then retaliation charges are filed. Either policy is troublesome in retaliation charges. The more lenient policy reaches the point of no return; when enforcement takes place, retaliation is alleged. The overly strict policy will cause almost indefensible retaliation charges.

The establishment of proper procedures for discharge as discussed under wrongful discharges in Chapter 11 and the employee complaint procedure as discussed in Chapter 15 are the best defenses to retaliation charges. If the employer's discipline, grievance, and discharge procedures are uniformly applied, violation of statutory retaliation provision will seldom be found.[18]

Role of Trade Unions under Title VII

A labor organization is defined, for coverage purposes under Title VII, as any organization, agency, or employee representation committee that exists to deal with the employer as to grievances, labor disputes, and conditions of employment. Any conference or joint board that is subordinate to a national or international labor organization is also subject to the act. The labor organization must have at least 15 members for coverage under Title VII. The labor organization cannot exclude from membership or otherwise discriminate against members because of race, color, religion, sex, or national origin, or age, nor can it cause the employer

---

[15]In *Wrighten* v. *Metropolitan Hospitals, Inc.*, 726 F.2d 1346 (9th Cir. 1984), a black nurse was discharged for complaining at a news conference about the treatment of black patients. The court found that the discharge was retaliation under Title VII.

[16]In *Hochstadt* v. *Worcester Foundation for Experimental Biology*, 545 F.2d 222 (1st Cir. 1976), the employee's behavior over a long period of time was such that other employees were quitting. She gave out confidential information, was disloyal, and was uncooperative. This caused the discharge, not filing the discrimination charge.

[17]*Monteiro* v. *Poole Silver Co.*, 615 F.2d 4 (1st Cir. 1980).

[18]See *EEOC Compliance Manual*, Sect. 1.89, Part III.

to discriminate against an individual. It cannot maintain segregated locals or discriminate as to referrals for acceptance in apprenticeship training programs.

Labor unions have a special duty under Title VII to represent fairly all employees apart from the requirements of the National Labor Relations Act. They must attempt to eradicate any discriminatory practices and process grievances within the scope of their bargaining agreement or power to negotiate a change.

For more than 30 years the National Labor Relations Act was the only legislation concerned with labor management relationships except for some occasional disputes under the Fair Labor Standards Act.

In 1972, when Title VII was amended, a third party entered the relationship. EEOC could sue both the union and the employer for discrimination. The problem immediately arises who has jurisdiction, the board or EEOC, especially when procedures are different. If the union discriminates, does the board still hold a representation election under the act? What happens to the employee's right to strike over discriminatory practices of both the company and the union?

For the purpose of this section it is important only to review a few basic principles concerning the role of the union in discrimination cases.

1. The Supreme Court, long before Title VII, held that where the union entered into a collective bargaining agreement with the employer that discriminated against blacks, this is a violation of the duty of fair representation because under the act all classes of employees must be represented.[19] Based on this decision the courts refuse to enforce an unfair labor practice against a union where it discriminates.[20]

2. Since the employees have elected the union to be their bargaining representative, they cannot

discuss discrimination matters directly with the employer but must go through the union. If there is evidence that the union approves of employer discriminatory practices, the employees must still go to the union before going to EEOC. Where the employees went out on strike over discriminatory practices without going through the grievance procedure, it is not a protected activity; therefore, discharging the employees is not an unfair labor practice.[21] (Discharge because of strike activity is otherwise unlawful.) The court said that although employees have a right to be free from discrimination under Title VII, the right cannot be pursued at the expense of orderly collective bargaining.

When employees are represented by a union, the employer should not entertain complaints about discrimination unless they are discussed with the union first. The National Labor Relations Board and the courts strictly hold the employer to the rule that regardless of whether the union is discriminating, the employees are represented by the union and therefore they must act through their representative.

Business Necessity as a Reason for Discrimination

Business necessity is a term that originated with the Supreme Court.[22] In the Griggs case the court stated that business necessity is justification for a policy that discriminates against a member of a protected class. Business necessity has been defined as "that which is reasonably necessary to the safe and efficient operation of the business."[23] Business necessity has not been as useful as a defense to the employers as it might appear because of the narrow interpretation by the courts of what is efficient (or normal) and safe operation of the business.

The courts have held that business necessity cannot be used as a defense unless there

---

[19]*Steele* v. *Louisville & Nashville Co.,* 323 U.S. 192 (1944).

[20]*NLRB* v. *Mansion House Center Management,* 473 F.2d 471 (8th Cir. 1973).

[21]*Emporium Capwell Co. & Western Addition Community Organization* v. *NLRB,* 420 U.S. 50 (1975).

[22]*Griggs* v. *Duke Power,* 401 U.S. 424 (1971).

[23]This was first defined in *Robinson* v. *Lorillard Corp.,* 444 F.2d 791 at 798 (4th Cir. 1971), cert. denied, 404 U.S. 950.

is a showing of no other acceptable alternative that will serve the employer equally well and has a lesser impact on members of protected groups.[24] With a defense of business necessity, the employer admits discrimination but argues that there is a reason for it.

Bona fide occupational qualification (BFOQ) differs from business necessity in that it is defined by 703(e) of Title VII and originally referred only to sex. Section 703(e) states that sex discrimination is valid in certain circumstances where sex is "a bona fide occupational qualification reasonably necessary to meet the normal operation of that particular business or enterprise." As a practical matter there is very little difference between the two and often they are interchanged when used as a defense for discrimination in an employment decision.

The courts usually reject the employer's perception of business necessity when it is not supported by objective data that show that the discriminatory action is necessary for the efficient operation of the business. The courts demand evidence that the traditional qualifications used by an employer are necessary to the safe and efficient performance of the job.

The employer often fails to sustain this burden because of subjective beliefs of what is necessary for the safe and efficient operation of the business.

Where the employer alleged business necessity in promoting a white over a black because the white had supervisory experience, the court found that the need for supervisory experience in order to perform the job was subjective.[25]

The one area in which the employer has been able to show business necessity is where the safety of the employee or safety of others is involved. In the Hayes case cited in note 24 the court was quick to approve a fetal protection program that the employer had for X-ray technicians who became pregnant. Business necessity has been accepted as a good reason for discrimination in airline cases where flight attendants become pregnant and are removed from duty. In *Levin* v. *Delta Airlines,* 730 F.2d 994 (5th Cir. 1984), the court had little trouble in holding that removal of the flight attendants as soon as it was known that they were pregnant was a business necessity. However, the employees argued that there was available a less-discriminatory alternative that would cushion the adverse consequences of the discriminatory policy. The court held that the employer need only adopt the alternative when it is a customary practice in similar situations and that failure to use the customary alternative indicates that the policy was not a pretext.

Other than for the safety factor, business necessity is very difficult to prove. Where customers in South America would not deal with a female sales representative and the employer removed her, the court said as a matter of law that the reason was insufficient defense of business necessity for the sex discrimination.[26] Since discrimination is admitted when using business necessity, the employer should not use it unless there are very strong facts to support the defense.

A Nondiscriminatory Reason for the Employment Decision

It is well-settled law that when an employee alleges that she or he has been discriminated against, the employee must establish a prima facie case as previously defined in this chapter. Once that is accepted by the court, the employer has to show a nondis-

---

[24]In *Hayes* v. *Shelby Memorial Hosp.,* 726 F.2d 1543 (11th Cir. 1984), the employer proved business necessity but failed to offer an alternative for a transfer and therefore was held for retaliation. Failure to offer a transfer indicated that the employer was retaliating for filing a charge.

[25]*Walker* v. *Jefferson Co. Home,* 726 F.2d 1554 (11th Cir. 1984). See also *Hawkins* v. *Bounds,* 752 F.2d 500 (10th Cir. 1985), where the employer required supervisory experience for the promotion but didn't give blacks the opportunity to train.

---

[26]*Fernandes* v. *Wynn Oil Co.,* 653 F.2d 1275 (9th Cir. 1982).

criminatory reason for the employment decision. This principle was established by the Supreme Court in two landmark decisions.

In the first situation, *Furnco Construction Corp.* v. *Waters,* 438 U.S. 567 (1978), the employer had to defend what appeared to be a discriminatory action of refusing to hire three black bricklayers who were fully qualified. The firm had a policy of hiring only bricklayers known to be experienced and competent or recommended by other contractors as skilled workers. The evidence showed that this policy was consistently followed with all applicants. Under this policy some blacks were hired. The court held that the employer had to only give a legitimate nondiscriminatory reason for not hiring the blacks and that there is no requirement for the hiring procedure to maximize the hiring of minorities.

In the second case a female alleged that she was discharged because of her sex and a male was hired in her place.[27] The issue before the court was what kind of proof was necessary to prove to the court that the action was nondiscriminatory. The court held that once a prima facie case was established the employer had to articulate a nondiscriminatory reason for the action. The employee could rebut the reason as being a pretext (not the real reason), but it must be by strong evidence that discrimination was the real reason. It then became a question of fact for the trial court to decide. The court in Burdine said there was no burden on the employer to persuade the court that the reason was not a pretext. This was up to the employee to do.

Under court decisions a statistical imbalance in a certain job category assumes that the employer discriminated either in the hiring or in the promotion policy. The absence of members of the protected class in certain job categories establishes the prima facie case. However, the employer can rebut the assumption by giving nondiscriminatory reasons why the condition exists (for example, recruiting was broadly based, few minorities applied for the jobs, and there were few minorities unemployed in the labor market area).

It is now well-settled law that in any situation where the employer's action is alleged to be discriminatory it can be defended by showing a nondiscriminatory reason, and the burden is on the employee to show it was discrimination. To prevent exposure to lawsuits under Title VII or any other antidiscrimination statute, the employer should always ask the question: Was the reason for the action a nondiscriminatory one? If the answer is in the affirmative, then there is good defense in the event it is challenged as being discriminatory.

OUT-OF-COURT SETTLEMENTS

When an employer receives a discrimination charge, there are three approaches to take. One is to adopt an aggressive, adversarial advocacy and take the offensive. The second approach is to adopt a passive but adversarial position. The approach is a defensive one where the employer lets the employee be the aggressor. The third approach is to pursue settlement as soon as possible[28] (over 90 percent of all claims are settled without a trial or any other hearing). None of these approaches is proper until several factors are considered.

Factors to Be Reviewed

1. The problems created by administrative and/or judicial proceedings: the length of time it takes to get a decision, the necessity to have witnesses who later have to work with employees, the emotional stress for some management members, and the management time the process takes (this is a hidden cost of litigation).

---

[27]*Texas Department of Community Affairs* v. *Burdine,* 450 U.S. 248 (1981).

[28]The author once knew a manager who would immediately offer to settle the case, regardless of the facts, for the cost of transportation for a corporate Equal Opportunity Office representative to investigate the charge.

2. The chances of prevailing. This is a judgment factor that is better determined by legal counsel, who can only make an educated guess. Some cases that should never be lost *are* lost, and sometimes all the facts point to losing and the case is won. If there are "gray areas" in the law it becomes more difficult to assess the case.

3. The out-of-pocket cost of taking the charge through the judicial process. In discrimination cases if the employer loses he or she must pay the employee's attorney's fees, which are sometimes more than the damages.

These factors should be considered in the early stages of the case. As the case progresses, these factors become less important, and if the case is settled "on the courtroom steps," most of the economic advantages of settlement are gone. One approach that has increasing popularity, in the early stages of the dispute, is a process called the Alternative Dispute Resolution, commonly referred to as "ADR." The parties can select a mediation process, nonbinding arbitration or binding arbitration, as an alternative to a full-blown trial. ADR is effective when the parties have not communicated to each other the reasons for their disagreement. Sometimes the parties are in agreement but they do not know it, or there is a minor disagreement that somehow got expanded. In these situations ADR could be helpful. Some attorneys and practitioners believe that it weakens a case to make an approach to settle, but if ADR is suggested as an alternative to an expensive trial, it is difficult to see how this would weaken the case.

The Settlement Process

When it appears that both parties want to settle, no final agreement should be reached until a settlement agreement is drafted. The terms of the settlement agreement are as important as the award agreed upon. This agreement should be reviewed by an attorney. When the attorney drafts the agreement the practitioner should be certain that it contains certain elements, including the following:

1. The charging party or regulatory agency (if involved) should release any and all rights it has to further pursue the case, including participating in a class action. In some cases the parties involved may want to get releases from other possible members of the class.

2. The parties should agree to keep the terms of the settlement confidential.

3. There should be no determination of who is right or wrong.

4. Payment of the charging party's attorney's fees should be agreed upon. A settlement agreement does not prevent the charging party from later collecting attorney's fees unless there is previous agreement.[29]

5. In regard to conduct after the case is closed, the employer should agree to take steps so the situation will not be repeated. However, nothing should be agreed upon that will interfere with the economical operation of the business or that is administratively burdensome.

6. Since retaliation is always a possibility, there should be a clause that states that settlement terms will not prevent the employer from treating the charging party any differently from other employees.

Unreasonable provisions can be prevented by hard negotiations; usually the parties will agree rather than not settle when there is disagreement over language. It is the amount of the award and demands for reinstatement that often prevent a settlement.

Considerations for Out-of-Court Settlements

Considerations as to out-of-court settlements should contain legal as well as employee relations consequences. Another consideration is that a settlement does not prevent a retaliation charge if the employee were reinstated. Neither will a court order to reinstate prevent retaliation charges. Therefore, in the settlement negotiations, whether reinstatement is a "must position of the em-

---

[29]*Miller v. Staats*, 706 F.2d 336 (D.C. Cir. 1983).

ployee" has considerable influence on the decision. The employee will often propose reinstatement along with full back pay, but that is sometimes a starting point for negotiations.

As to employee relations considerations, the first problem is with the supervisor involved. Any monetary settlement implies discrimination regardless of the settlement agreement. With some managers and supervisors, this stigma is difficult to overcome, especially in a sex discrimination case when their wives are active in feminist movements. If any member of management feels that settlement is admission of guilt and the facts show that actually there was no discrimination, settlement for economic reasons is often a mistake, unless management determines that economic considerations override all other considerations.

Also in consideration of employee rela-
tions consequences of a settlement, the effect of lump-sum payment on other employees is important. It has little effect unless the employee is reinstated. If reinstated, the exposure to adverse employee relations is present, but it does not always have an adverse effect on employee relations. One way to mitigate an adverse effect on employee relations is to prohibit disclosure of the terms in the settlement agreement.

Settling a case where there is little evidence of discrimination is not advisable when consideration is given to the long-range economic and employee relations consequences. In situations where the legal assessment of winning in the courts is better than 50 percent, the long-range economic and employee relations benefits are worth risking a court decision, although the immediate cost may not justify it.

CHAPTER
3

SELECTING QUALIFIED APPLICANTS WITHIN TITLE VII

Preemployment Procedures
Selection Process
National Origin Discrimination
Immigration Reform and Control Act of 1986 (IRCA)
The Selection Audit

PREEMPLOYMENT PROCEDURES

The antidiscrimination laws described in Chapter 2 have considerable impact on the entire management function. One of personnel's major areas of activity is the recruitment and selection of qualified applicants. These areas were especially affected by antidiscrimination laws. The selection process deeply involves all members of management who interview job candidates and make decisions on selection. Members of management must be aware of the exposure to costly and time-consuming charges of discrimination even though they may be acting in good faith.

The antidiscrimination statutes do not specifically state what type of recruitment or selection is in compliance. We must look to court decisions, policies, and agency guidelines for direction.

This chapter is designed to alert every person in the organization to the problems caused by federal and state antidiscrimination laws in the selection of the most qualified person for the job. An employer should always check both state and federal laws before making an employment policy decision.

Recruitment

The recruitment procedure is the preliminary step to the selection procedure; unless designed properly, it will have a devastating effect on the selection of qualified applicants. The place to prevent disparate impact in selection is in the recruitment procedure. Some employers have said that it is not possible to select a qualified candidate because of the restrictions of antidiscrimination laws. This statement simply is not true. The supervisor who says, "Don't send me a minority or a female because I cannot refuse to hire them," does not understand the purpose and objective of the antidiscrimination laws.

Recruitment is a two-step process. First, the employer must announce a job opening to a labor market area that contains applicants capable of responding. Second, those capable of responding must become aware of and be encouraged to answer the announcement.

Where only one or two sources of recruitment are relied upon, state and federal agencies will attack the method as not being broad enough to attract all segments of the labor market. It is essential that a broad recruiting base be used.

The key question in all recruitment procedures is whether the method limits the non-job-related characteristics of the person who may apply. There are certain inquiries that may have sex limitations, with such gender-base terminology as busboy, bartender, directress, or pressman.[1] These have all been popular terms in the past, but now they can cause problems with the regulatory agencies. This type of ad limits the number of persons applying for the vacancy and could result in an adverse impact in the selection process.

In a study of 42,343 advertisements in 14 national newspapers, it was found that more than 2 percent of the ads would be called overtly discriminatory.[2]

Perhaps a more serious effect of an ad that limits the number of persons replying is that the ad is not serving the legitimate business reason of seeking the best-qualified applicants available. Even if one were to disregard the legal restrictions of a gender-based ad, it still is not a sound recruitment practice.[3]

Another common recruiting method is word of mouth (sometimes called an informal contact or employee referral). Many employment managers rightfully believe this

---

[1]*Brennan* v. *Approved Personnel Services, Inc.,* 729 F.2d 760 (4th Cir. 1975).

[2]John P. Kohl, David B. Stephens, and Gerald McCaulley, "Questionable Advertising Practices by Business Firms: Result of a National Survey of 'Help Wanted' Ads," *Labor Law Journal,* 37, no. 9 (Sept. 1986), pp. 660–67.

[3]For use of ads in recruitment see Elizabeth S. Palkowitz and Michelle M. Mueller, "Agencies Foresee Change in Advertising's Future," *Personnel Journal* (May 1987), p. 124.

to be the best source of qualified applicants. Courts closely examine this procedure because experience indicates that one worker will rarely refer another of a different race, nationality, religion, and so on. As a result, a "built-in headwind" limits the hiring of minorities if this is the sole source of applicants.[4] If the employee referral approach to recruiting is accompanied by an affirmative action program to encourage minorities and females to apply, the package would probably be acceptable to the courts.[5]

An affirmative action program to encourage minorities and females to apply would be to seek applicants actively from such sources as the Urban League, minority-oriented media, local Spanish-American organizations, women's organizations, and schools with large minority populations.

Recruitment procedures that require listing all new job openings with state employment agencies and advertising in media with an adequate minority and female audience will have little or no chance of EEOC challenges.

If the employer chooses word-of-mouth or walk-in as the sole method of recruiting or any other single method of recruitment, the procedure will not be questioned unless the work force has a statistical imbalance. Only when there is an imbalance in the work force and there is evidence of disparate impact in the selection process is a recruitment procedure questioned by the courts and regulatory agencies.

The traditional methods of recruiting should not be eliminated because of anti-discrimination laws; the same resources should be used for protected classes in the same manner as other employees. However, the employer should be alert to possible disparate impact. If several sources are used, a disparate impact would be unlikely.

Preemployment Inquiries on Application Forms

The application form is an important document from which hiring decisions are made, but it presents potential discrimination problems and can form the basis for successful lawsuits.

There is nothing in the federal statutes, guidelines, or court decisions that prevents making preemployment inquiries either on the application forms or orally except for garnishments or arrests. The only limitation is that inquiries are required to have a job-related purpose and the information must not be used for discriminatory purposes.

Where apprenticeship applications asked for race and no Mexican-Americans were considered, the court held the inquiry was used for discriminatory purposes.[6]

If the application form has a disparate impact upon the hiring process, then it will be considered wrongful and will be challenged. These challenges will be indefensible where it can be shown that few applicants are placed after information is received and such information does not have a real business purpose in selecting qualified employees, as was the situation in the Inspiration Consolidated Copper Co. case.

Unstructured preemployment inquiries such as "What do you expect in salary in five years?" present the greatest exposure to liability in the selection process.[7] Unless such inquiries have a purpose, the regulatory agencies or the courts may require the employer to show that no discriminatory

---

[4]In *EEOC* v. *Detroit Edison Co.*, 512 F.2d 301 (6th Cir. 1975), the court concluded that employee referrals would perpetually imbalance the work force in favor of white males that already existed at the facility.

[5]*Diggs* v. *Western Electric*, 587 F.2d 1070 (10th Cir. 1978); *United States* v. *Georgia Power Co.*, 474 F.2d 906 (5th Cir. 1973).

[6]*U.S.* v. *Inspiration Consolidated Copper Co.*, 6 CCH Employment Practices Decisions, Para. 8918 (D.C. Ariz. 1973).

[7]The author once knew of a manager who would ask when "the War of 1812 was fought?" If the applicant didn't know, he would reject the applicant.

purpose exists. The absence of a business purpose is taken as an indication of discriminatory intent. Specific areas where questions may lead to liability include

Arrest and Conviction. One court held that questions about arrest are absolutely barred.[8] Questions about conviction should include a statement that the organization will consider the nature of the conviction, offense, age committed, and the like.

Age. Questions are not illegal per se but one should be prepared to give a good reason for asking.

Height and Weight. It is claimed that this tends to screen out females and Americans of Asian and Spanish descent. This is difficult to defend if disparate impact is found unless height and weight are specific requirements of the job, for example, police and prison guards.[9]

Marital Status. This is illegal per se if asked only of women. (Unless prohibited by state law, some states such as Minnesota and California make married persons a protected group.) If asked of both sexes, this is legal if there is a no-spouse hiring rule, which is permissible under federal law.[10]

Physical Characteristics. When asking about physical characteristics of the applicant, it must be factually determined what physical requirements are necessary for the job. If similar positions have different requirements, it is questionable whether the physical requirements are job related. Where females cannot wear glasses but males can and jobs are similar, this is held an unlawful requirement.[11]

---

[8]*Gregory* v. *Litton Systems,* 472 F.2d 671 (9th Cir. 1972).

[9]*Dothard* v. *Rawlinson,* 433 U.S. 321 (1977).

[10]*Harper* v. *TWA,* 525 F.2d 409 (8th Cir. 1975).

[11]*Laffey* v. *Northwest Airlines,* 567 F.2d 429 (D.C. Cir. 1976), cert.denied, 434 U.S. 1086 (1978).

Although the application form may comply with federal law, more stringent state laws often could make the application form illegal. Employers should always check state laws before being comfortable that their application form is legally sound.

The Use of the Weighted Application Blank

One of the problems that employers have with regulatory agencies is that the application form has questions that are not job related. When asked why a question is on the form, employers cannot give a business-related answer. The law doesn't restrict any question as long as it has a business purpose and the information is for a nondiscriminatory purpose. If the questions asked have a job-related purpose, they are seldom challenged as being discriminatory. One way to be sure the application form is not discriminatory is to use a technique called the Weighted Application Blank (WAB).

This is a technique that for many years was used to control turnover by the selection of job applicants according to defined personal history factors. WAB is more accurately defined as structured method for determining which characteristics and other variables found in a job applicant are important for success on certain specified jobs.[12]

The concept on which this method was developed is that certain quantitative and objective information is found in each applicant that will determine behavior for a particular job category. For many years employment managers and supervisors have subjectively determined that a certain type of person will or will not succeed in a certain job (for example, a supervisor who believed that all persons from Wisconsin were lazy). This was usually based on limited experience that employees who lived far away, had high wages on previous jobs, did not

---

[12]"Development and Use of Weighted Application Blanks," rev. ed., no. 55 (Industrial Relations Center, University of Minnesota, Minneapolis, 1971).

have a car, were divorced, either quit or were discharged from the previous job, were all turnover applicants for some reason. The WAB seeks to establish a profile by the use of statistical techniques and analysis that with some degree of accuracy predicts whether certain factors have any influence on job tenure.[13]

Exhibit 3-1 shows some of these factors. The data are taken from a sample of employees on the payroll for a period of three months or less and from another group of employees with one or more years of service. The purpose of this study was to control turnover in the unskilled and semiskilled job categories.[14]

The original list of factors was based on the opinions of the employment manager and over 30 supervisors on what characteristics determine the ideal employee. Of 16 original factors, only 9 were found to differentiate between active groups and terminee groups. This is illustrative of what regulatory agencies are referring to when they insist that a question on the application

---

[13]Although there is not an absolute correlation between tenure and success on the job, for the purpose of WAB analysis, tenure of one or more years on the job is predictive of some degree of success based on the assumption that if an employee lasts one year or longer, performance has been rated as acceptable.

[14]The WAB technique assumes that there is an opportunity to select from the labor market. In a tight labor market, as in some areas during the Korean War, the employer moved the employment office upstairs; if applicants could walk up the stairs, they were hired.

EXHIBIT 3-1

The following factors were used in a weighted application blank survey of the paper stock division:

1. Location
2. Age hired
3. Weight
4. Height
5. Marital status
6. Number of children
7. Friends or relatives employed here
8. Referred by
9. Prior job injury
10. Military service
11. Education
12. Length of last job
13. Number of jobs in last three years
14. Reasons for leaving last job
15. Wages before hire
16. Type of last job

The factors numbered 2, 4, 6, 9, 10, 14, and 16 were discarded as they did not differentiate between the active group and the terminee group.

EXHIBIT 3-2

The ideal employee in the paper stock division had the following characteristics at the time of hire:

1. Is from local or labor market area of approximately 20 miles of plant site
2. Weighs between 151 and 170 pounds
3. Is married
4. Has friends or relatives who work here
5. Was a walk-in
6. Has education of 8 years or less or is a high school graduate
7. Last job was 12 to 23 months in duration
8. Had 1 to 2 jobs in the last 3 years
9. Wages before hire were less than or equal to employer's starting rate

A cutoff score of 11 or better was arrived at by using the greatest differentiation between the active group and the terminee group. This would mean that 72 percent of the actives would have been hired and 4 percent of the terminees would have been hired.

Source: All exhibits relating to the WAB method are from personnel files of Hoerner Waldorf Corporation, St. Paul, Minnesota, 1969–1970.

form have a business purpose rather than reflecting subjective thinking of the employer. Exhibit 3-2 shows the ideal employee for the paper stock division.

Exhibit 3-3 shows the work sheet to establish a hiring profile for the paper stock division. This calculation is the correlation of the personal histories with the tenure on the job. It is a mathematical formula that provides relative weighing of each significant independent characteristic. The characteristics are given a point value, and a cutting score is developed by drawing a line between the number that shows where the most terminees would be eliminated and the most actives would have hired.

Exhibit 3-4 shows in graphic form that for the paper stock division a cutting score of 11 would be effective in eliminating hires who will be terminated within a year. In this study of actives and terminations, no data were compiled as to the reason for termination except that an applicant with certain (point value) characteristics of less than 11 would be more likely to be terminated than an applicant above 11.

The WAB is most effective in the factory and office semiskilled jobs. There is little or no use for the higher skilled jobs or managerial jobs because factors other than personal characteristics, such as job assignment, supervision, training, and work experience, would outweigh the personal characteristics used in WAB. Most personnel practitioners can develop the WAB to fit their needs with some research and a little training. More sophisticated WABs can be found in the literature, and study of this literature may be advisable.[15]

_____

[15]Daniel G. Lawrence, Barbara L. Salsbury, John G. Dawson, and Zachary D. Fasman, "Design and Use of Weighted Application Blank," *Personnel Administrator,* 27, no. 3 (1982), 47; "Study in Predicting Voluntary Labor Turnover with Weighted Application Blank," *Marquette Business Review,* 21, no. 1 (Spring 1977). See also note 12.

EXHIBIT 3-3 *Paper Stock Distribution of Weighted Scores*

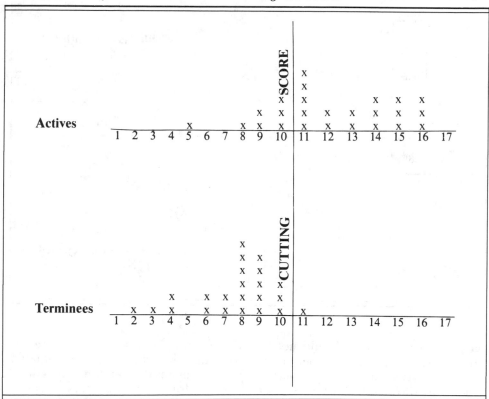

The system described in this chapter is a simplified one that works; if a method works, it should be used without becoming too academic.

WAB as Defense to Questions Asked

The WAB replaces the possible subjective interviewer's biases, which are often artificial barriers in the selection and promotion of the protected classes. It is certainly more defensible in showing nondiscriminatory reasons than the less objective measures used by many interviewers. Like any other selection device, it should first be determined whether the WAB has any adverse impact in the selection of protected classes; if so, then the method used to develop it should be tuned up to be sufficient for validation

purposes. The experience of those who use WAB has been that there is no disparate impact provided that the characteristics used and sample come from all classes of employees. If the present work force that is used as a sample has a statistical imbalance, then WAB would probably be challenged as perpetuating discrimination. The WAB also serves to establish reasons for asking certain questions in the interview that have been found to be predictive of tenure and success on the job. Affirmative action compliance officers and EEOC have consistently stated that there must be a legitimate purpose for asking questions in the interview. Questions to determine characteristics used to score the WAB would have a legitimate nondiscriminatory purpose.

The WAB should be used in the initial screening interview; if the applicant fails at

EXHIBIT 3-4   *Paper Stock Division (Differentiation by %)*

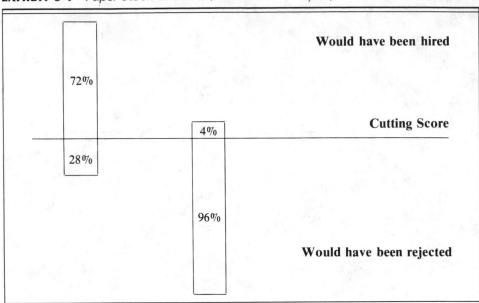

this level, further interviews would not be necessary. This would eliminate the opportunity for supervisor and manager bias at the second level of the hiring process.

For several years practitioners have been using the weighted application technique as an effective way to predict turnover. The requirements of the antidiscrimination laws also make it an effective tool in eliminating bias in the selection process.

Application Form Audit

It is advisable for the employer to audit the application form and other preemployment inquiries and ask:

1. For what purpose is this question being asked?
2. Could it be proven that it is job related?
3. Is the question important enough to trigger a possible investigation by EEOC or the state agency?

If all these questions can be answered in the affirmative, then the employer should continue to ask them. If there is no real reason for a question, it should be eliminated.

To be assured that interviewers do not use answers for a discriminatory purpose, it is recommended to put a statement on the application form as follows:

Information obtained from the questions asked on this application form or orally requested will not be used for discriminatory purposes.

Another method to assure that the application form complies with antidiscrimination laws is to have the applicant answer only job-related questions and those necessary for employment processing. Exhibit 3-5 is a form where the particular boxes are checked for answers relating to the job being applied for.

Application forms have, in the past, contained many questions unnecessary to the selection of qualified applicants, and personnel practitioners seldom audit the form. Antidiscrimination laws have caused a substantial improvement in the application form because the practitioner is forced to audit

EXHIBIT 3-5   *Protection of Information on Application Forms from Being Interpreted as Discriminatory*

After general information is requested and there is need for special information the following section could be inserted.

The information requested below is needed for certain job assignment or for other nondiscriminatory reasons. Since this information is only necessary for certain jobs, answer only those questions where the box is checked. The remaining questions do not apply to the job(s) you are applying for.

- ☐ Marital status, date of marriage, or divorced if any
- ☐ What was your previous address?
- ☐ How long did you live at your previous address?
- ☐ How long at your present address?
- ☐ Weight
- ☐ Height
- ☐ Age
- ☐ Have you been convicted of a crime in the last ten years?
- ☐ Name of all relatives working here
- ☐ Do you have any known defects that will prevent you from performing the job(s) you are applying for? If yes, describe.

- ☐ Occupation of father
- ☐ Method of transportation to get to work

(Questions included above should have reference to the requirements of at least one job.)

the questions so they relate to the job being applied for.[16]

Preemployment Testing

The most significant change in the selection process as a result of antidiscrimination laws is in the area of preemployment testing.[17] The field of industrial testing grew substantially after World War II to the ex-

tent that it was considered by many personnel practitioners a necessity in the selection process. The increased use of tests was often without an indication that it was an effective selection tool except that the personnel manager was not in vogue unless tests were used. Most testing programs were instituted with little or no knowledge of the jobs for which the selection tests were given. Often the tests determined only whether the applicant was an average American. Testing programs, whether valid or invalid, became popular because they afforded a crutch for the selection of an applicant. It was an easy way for the nonprofessional interviewer to screen and select applicants.

For more than three decades professors were advising their students not to use a test

---

[16]See Joseph J. Famularo, *Handbook of Personnel Forms, Records and Reports* (New York: McGraw-Hill Book Company, 1982).

[17]For additional information on legal aspects of testing see Richard D. Arvey, *Fairness in Selecting Employees* (Reading, MA: Addison-Wesley Publishing Co., Inc., 1979).

as a selection tool unless it was validated to determine whether the test could predict job performance.[18] However, this pseudo-psychological method of selecting applicants continued with increasing popularity. The failure of personnel practitioners to validate tests was contrary to sound selection practice and was doomed to fall under the ax of antidiscrimination laws. When the ax did fall, many employers abandoned tests altogether.[19] This result was unfortunate because a properly validated test is one of the least discriminatory means of selecting employees. It reduces the need to rely on the unconscious, illegal, subjective judgment of the interviewer.

Restrictions on Testing

Although antidiscrimination laws do not prohibit the use of tests in the selection process, they do limit their use. Some employers feel that the requirement of antidiscrimination laws for validation and the risk of being in violation are too great compared to the accuracy of predicting success on the job. For this reason many small employers have chosen not to use the test as a selection tool, or if they do use it the scores are a very small part of the decision-making process.

Judicial requirements for valid testing can be found in the leading and most-quoted case in antidiscrimination law, *Griggs* v. *Duke Power Co.*, 401 U.S. 424, decided by the Supreme Court in 1971. The selection test used by Duke Power Co. was the Purdue Vocational Test form B for initial testing and form A for retesting purposes. The time limits were disregarded, and it was considered a work test. Applicants protected by Title VII were affected adversely as shown in Exhibit 3-6.

Fifty-two percent of Caucasians tested were enrolled in a training program, but only 13 percent of blacks and 5 percent Spanish-

Americans. The Griggs case stands for the following principles in preemployment testing:

1. A test must be job related. If verbal ability is not required to perform functions of the job, one should not test for it.
2. An employer's intent not to discriminate is irrelevant. This is applicable only to Title VII; other statutes require intent.
3. If a practice (training school in Griggs) is fair in form but discriminatory in operation, it will not be upheld.
4. The defense for any existing program that has adverse impact is *business necessity*. Business necessity was not defined by the court.
5. Title VII does not forbid testing, only tests that do not measure job performance.
6. The test must measure the person for the job and not the person in the abstract.
7. Less-qualified applicants should not be hired over those better qualified because of minority origins. There is no requirement to hire unqualified persons.

Where the test has an identifiable pass/fail score that denies an employment opportunity to a disproportionately large number of the protected class and prevents an individual from proceding to the next step in the selection process, this would be in violation of Title VII.[20]

In determining whether the procedure has an adverse impact, statistical evidence should be considered; however, a statistically unbalanced work force (disproportionate number of nonminorities or females) does not necessarily mean that the selection procedure is in violation. The reason for the condition may not be the selection procedure but a characteristic of the labor market.

Validation of Tests

If a test has an adverse impact on the selection process as was the case in Griggs, it must be validated as to whether it is

1. Job related
2. Predictive of performance
3. Necessary because no less-discriminatory

---

[18]D. Yoder, *Personnel and Labor Relations* (Englewood Cliffs, NJ: Prentice-Hall, Inc., 1938).

[19]In a survey in 1963, 90 percent of employers were using tests; in 1971 only 55 percent used tests of one kind or another. "Personnel Testing," *Bulletin to Management*, ASPA-BNA Survey no. 12 (Washington, DC: Bureau of National Affairs, 1971).

[20]*Connecticut* v. *Teal*, 102 S.Ct. 2525 (1982).

EXHIBIT 3-6

Number Tested	Mean Score	Race	Enrolled in Training School
108	38.75	Caucasian	52
41	24.92	Negro	13
1	—	Oriental	1
1	—	American Indian	0
14	29.53	Spanish-American	5

Source: Court records, *Griggs* v. *Duke Power,* 401 U.S. 424 (1971).

methods are available; then business necessity is required

Good faith effort or neutrality in placing applicants is irrelevant if an adverse impact results. The court in Griggs did not say how the test should be validated, but at the time of the Griggs' decision *Albemarle Paper Co.* v. *Moody,* 422 U.S. 405, was working its way through the lower courts. In June 1975 the Supreme Court put to rest the question of what constituted the proper validation of a preemployment test as well as the back-pay issue.

In 1963 Albemarle Paper Co. adopted the Wonderlic Test A and B series as a screening program for selection of employees. General population norms were used to set cutoff scores until the Griggs decision; after that Albemarle hired an expert in industrial psychology to validate the test. He used ratings of job performance from three different supervisors, which were correlated with test scores. After the validation 96 percent of the white applicants passed the test and 64 percent of the blacks. The test scores were primarily used to select and place employees in 11 separate departments where 17 training lines of progression were established.

Exhibit 3-7[21] shows the placement of em-

---

[21]Term used in Appendix of *Albemarle Paper Co.* v. *Moody,* No. 74-389, is "negro." It is used in the Exhibits 3-7 and 3-8 referring to that case in its historic context. The term is now considered improper in antidiscrimination documents. The preferred term now is "blacks."

ployees in the wood yard, which is an unskilled job category.

The skilled lines of progression were in the paper mill. To be placed in this line of progression it was necessary to have a certain score in the Wonderlic test as shown in Exhibit 3-8. Note the adverse impact.

The court in Albemarle said that because the tests had an adverse impact on "hiring," the company must validate the tests. The validation of the tests by Albemarle was improper to show business necessity because

1. The validation process used was not related to the job being applied for. Subjective supervisors' ratings were compared to test scores. The study focused on experienced employees in upper level jobs; high scores of that group are not predictive of qualifications for new workers to perform lower-level jobs.
2. The supervisors rated older whites and experienced workers, whereas tests were given to job applicants who were younger, unexperienced, and nonwhite.

Particular attention has been paid to these two cases because a substantial part of the 1978 EEOC Employee Selection Procedures Guidelines as related to testing had their origin in the Griggs and Albemarle cases. These guidelines have had little change in subsequent years.

EXHIBIT 3-7

A. Wood Yard Department	Negro	White
Yard Crew		
Crane Operator (Large)	0	9
Long Log Operator	0	4
Log Stacker Operator	0	4
Small Equipment Operator	0	4
Bulldozer Operator	0	1
Oiler	0	4
Chip Unloader	1	3
Chain Operator	0	4
Chipper Operator No. 2		
Chipper Operator No. 1	4	0
Tractor Operator	5	0
Chip Bin Operator	4	0
Laborers	12	0
Service Crew		
Dempster-Dumpster	1	0
Winch Truck Operator	3	0
Winch Truck Operator Helper	1	0
Laborer	6	0

Source: Appendix to brief of appellants, *Albemarle Paper* v. *Moody*, No. 74-389.

EXHIBIT 3-8

C. A Paper Mill Department	Negro	White
Paper Machine Line of Progression		
Machine Tender No. 1	0	4
Machine Tender No. 2	0	4
Back Tender No. 1	0	4
Third Hand No. 1	0	4
Third Hand No. 2	0	4
Fourth Hand No. 1	0	4
Fourth Hand No. 2	0	4
Front Plugger No. 1	0	4
Back Plugger No. 1	1	4
Back Plugger No. 2	0	4
Beaterman	0	4
1st Helper	0	4
Brokeman	4	0
Stock Puller	0	0
Laborer	1	0

Source: Appendix to appellant's brief, *Albemarle Paper* v. *Moody*, No. 74-389.

Types of Test Validation

There are three types of test validation that are stated in the EEOC guidelines and have been judicially accepted.

1. *Criterion-related validity.* This is a collection of data that measure job performance and establish statistical relationships between measures of job performance and test scores. This is the traditional method of validation of preemployment tests, which has been used for more than 30 years. Supervisor ratings must be objective or will fail to meet the criteria in the Albemarle case.

2. *Content validity.* This correlates certain aspects of the job performance with test scores to measure job performance. This differs from the criterion validation in that the job performance is measured in the specific job for which the applicant is being tested. This method of validation relies heavily on job analysis methods alluded to by the appellate court in the Albemarle case.[22]

3. *Construct validation.* This is a psychological method of validation based on research whereby a psychological trait is identified as essential to the successful performance of the job and develops a selection procedure to measure the presence and degree of that trait. Examples of a trait would be leadership ability and ability to work under pressure.

An important requirement of the EEOC guidelines that has been judicially accepted is found in Section 5(I), where it is stated that procedures to select for a higher-skilled job than the original job of the applicant would not be appropriate if three conditions existed:

1. The majority of the applicants selected do not progress to a higher-level job within a short time after being placed on lower-level job.[23]

---

[22]Job analysis as used by the court is a statement that provides basic information about job requirements and characteristics of persons who can successfully perform the job.

[23]Five years would be considered too long until it is tested in the courts; a short period is a matter of judgment of the enforcement agency. The length of time would be somewhat related to the degree of skill required.

2. There is no real distinction between the higher- and lower-level jobs or if selection procedures measure skills not necessary to perform the higher-level job.

3. Knowledge could be acquired on the higher-level job without the employee's being trained on the lower-level job.

The validation process is expensive and time consuming and even when completed may not be accepted by the courts. In view of this lack of certainty in judicial acceptance, the employer should seriously consider whether testing is necessary to predict job performance. Testing is especially subject to exposure if it has an adverse impact.

Preemployment Physicals

Questions about physical ability to perform the job being applied for can lead into questions about medical history and preemployment physical examinations. Many preemployment physical examinations given by employers are not related to the physical requirements of the job.

An audit of company preemployment physical examinations is advisable in light of the requirement that any prerequisite to hiring must be job related. The first step in determining an applicant's physical condition is to ask. Asking the applicant about physical conditions should be the starting point of determining whether the applicant can perform the job applied for. This can be done formally by a premedical questionnaire designed by the company physician. Exhibit 3-9 is a suggested form that would determine the type of preemployment physical examination to be given or whether an examination is needed at all.

The questions in Exhibit 3-9 should be adapted to the particular operations and job categories. It may not be job related to ask about diabetes unless diabetes is related to job performance. In many cases diabetes can be treated so it will not interfere with the job. Some of the questions may not relate to the job but would

EXHIBIT 3-9 *Preemployment Medical History*

DATE _____

(Suggested form to determine the type of preemployment physical examination or whether an examination is needed.)

Full Name _____

Address _____

Date _____ Social Security No. _____

Date of last doctor visit _____ Doctor's name and address _____

_____

Name and address of family physician if not same as above _____

_____

Circle illnesses or conditions you have had and give approximate year of diagnosis and recovery date. (Note: delete those that are not job-related.)

Diabetes	Glaucoma	Heart trouble
Cancer	Asthma	Jaundice
Tuberculosis	Alcoholism	Kidney disease
Venereal disease	Rheumatic fever	Vein trouble
Allergy	High blood pressure	Bleeding tendency
Drug addiction	Nervous disorder	(internal or external)

Other illnesses or physical conditions not mentioned above (give year of diagnosis

and recovery date) _____

_____

_____

_____

Are you allergic or sensitive to any medicines or other substances? _____

Please describe _____

_____

List operations you have had, giving approximate dates, hospitals, and names and

addresses of surgeons _____

_____

_____

EXHIBIT 3-9   *(Continued)*

List serious injuries, broken bones, and so on, giving approximate dates _____

_____

_____

List any permanent disability as a result of injuries and illnesses

_____

Name or otherwise identify medicines you are now using or have used within the

last six months _____

Do you use tobacco now? _____In the past, when stopped? _____

If yes, what type and the daily amount? _____

How long have you been using tobacco? _____

Do you use alcoholic beverages? _____Type _____

Weekly amount _____How long have you been using them? _____

Do you have any known disabilities that may prevent you from physically performing

the job(s) you are applying for? _____

_____

NOTE: This exhibit is for the purpose of example only and not to be construed to
provide professional medical advice. The questionnaire should not be used
without professional consultation. Some questions may violate a state handicap law and should be checked.

be important information for emergency treatment at the job site by a company nurse or first-aid specialist. Other questions may relate to co-worker problems, such as smoking. The last question, whether you have any disabilities to prevent you from performing the job, is the most important and should be asked of all applicants even if a formal questionnaire is not used. It is important not only for job placement but also to determine whether the applicant has any handicaps and therefore may come under the federal or state statute.

One might wonder if the applicant would tend to falsify the information. This tendency always exists, but there is less likelihood of falsification when a written form is provided than if it is an oral, unstructured inquiry of the applicant's physical condition. Further, the courts will almost always support discharge for falsifying information when applying for work.[24]

----

[24]See *Fiber Glass System, Inc.* v. *NLRB*, 807 F.2d 461 (5th Cir. 1987), where it was shown that the employer would not have hired the applicant if he had told the truth.

The next important step in making a preemployment physical job related is to be assured that the doctor has knowledge of the physical requirements of the job. Often this is difficult as either the doctor does not want to take the time to study the job or the job content changes so rapidly that it makes the study obsolete in a short time. It is best for the doctor to observe the various jobs. If this is not possible, a good job description will be sufficient. In the job description the physical requirements of the job should be noted; when the job is changed, the job description should be updated and communicated to the doctor. Preemployment inquiries as to the applicant's physical condition can be justified in determining job placement or, if the applicant is handicapped, in meeting the employer's obligation to accommodate through job placement.[25]

Although questions about medical history and physical or mental disabilities are not specifically prohibited by the law, they are hazardous unless a specific business purpose can be shown. Often the same information can be obtained without a discriminatory emphasis that may trigger an investigation or a complaint. For example, as has been noted, instead of asking whether an applicant has any disabilities, one should ask whether any disabilities would interfere with the ability to perform the job for which application is being made. If an applicant does not know, further inquiry as to the physical condition is justified. However, to protect the applicant's right to privacy, disclosure of medical information should be only to persons who have a need to know.

This discussion on preemployment inquiries has been directed to those involved in screening applicants; however, as a practical matter interviews are conducted on all levels of management. To avoid exposure to discrimination and to eliminate prejudice by management personnel, those who interview should not be allowed the discretion of the past. Written guidelines to standardize preemployment inquiries are helpful. All preemployment inquiries should have the specific purpose of determining the qualifications of the individual applicant as required by the job and not necessarily what the interviewer believes will make a good employee.

SELECTION PROCESS

The advent of Title VII caused changes in the selection of applicants for many organizations. The key new element was that the evaluation of the applicant must be objective. The practice of selecting candidates by the instincts of the supervisor, prejudices—often based on a single experience—or other subjective criteria will no longer withstand judicial scrutiny. It is questionable whether these subjective methods were ever effective in selecting the best-qualified person. (The author knew a supervisor who would not accept applicants who were too fat because he believed that they were all lazy!) The day of the supervisor who said that he could determine the physical strength of applicants by looking at the applicant is over. As one court said, an "eyeball test" is not valid for determining the strength of an applicant.[26] These may be extreme examples but many other equally ridiculous ones could be given by employment managers.

If the selection procedure is to fulfill its major objective of hiring qualified applicants, it is necessary to establish appropriate job specifications and structure at least part of the interview. Before antidiscrimination laws, employers were not required to establish job specifications. If they did, their validity or accuracy was never questioned by anyone except internal management, which often aided in drafting them. Under antidiscrimination laws the selection procedure is subject to the EEOC Employment Guide-

---

[25]Treatment of handicapped workers is found in Chapter 4.

[26]*EEOC* v. *Spokane Concrete Products,* 534 F.Supp. 518 (E.D. Wash. 1982).

lines, enforcement agencies, and scrutiny of the courts. Selection procedures must be modified to eliminate exposure but still be effective in selection of the best-qualified applicant.

Establishing Criteria for Selection

Most companies either formally or informally establish some criteria for selection. When establishing these criteria the labor market conditions must be taken into consideration. When the criteria are not supported by the labor market conditions, the employer must either lower the criteria for selection or not be able to fill the vacancy. What usually happens is that the criteria are lowered. For example, the employer establishes a qualification of a college degree in chemistry and four years of experience for the position of a chemist. When nobody can be found on the labor market with those qualifications, the standards are lowered to three years of college and three years of experience. A white male applies with those qualifications and gets the job. One week previous to filling the vacancy a black female with three years of college and four years of experience was turned down because she did not meet the criteria. She finds out that the white male with less experience was hired and files a charge under Title VII. The employer now has an extremely difficult defense. This practice of lowering the standards and not notifying the turn-downs is common and can result in a lawsuit, not because the employer intended to discriminate but because the selection procedure did not consider the discriminatory problem when standards were lowered.

When a particular job category is short in supply and the manager is forced to go without help for a period of time, she or he becomes desperate and crisis hiring results. The case history on page 56 illustrates this point.

Use of Job Descriptions and Job Analysis

Qualifications for the job are determined by job analysis from current job descriptions.

What has caused these techniques to be subject to judicial suspicion is that many times they are developed for ad hoc purposes, as a method to justify the wage and salary or promotion decisions. An audit of the job analysis and job descriptions often discloses that any resemblance between what the employee is doing and what the job analysis or job description states is purely coincidental. Often job descriptions are valuable for exhibits in EEOC hearings or disputes under the Fair Labor Standards Act; however, they can be damaging when they are not kept up to date or are developed to get an employee a raise or to otherwise upgrade the job content on paper. Actual observance of job content for purposes of job analysis and job descriptions is necessary if they are to be used as a basis for employment decisions. When the job analysis and job descriptions are developed by objective methods, the employer is then in a position to establish an applicant pool of qualified candidates.[27]

Use of Applicant Pool to Eliminate Crisis Hiring

The applicant pool is a technique by which the employment manager has made an attempt to have available qualified candidates to fill future vacancies. It is developed by predicting job vacancies in the next six-month period (or whatever period is appropriate) in certain job categories. After determining the need or size of the pool, the employment manager immediately recruits and selects the best-qualified applicants for that job category. When all the candidates are selected for the anticipated vacancies, recruiting and selection stops until job offers are made to those placed in the applicant pool.

In selecting candidates for the applicant pool, those selected are told that when a va-

---

[27]Job analysis and job descriptions should be developed by persons who are not supervisors or members of the personnel staff. In the author's experience, industrial engineers or outside consultants are persons most likely to develop unbiased job analyses and job descriptions.

Crisis Hiring—A Case History

The department head requests a quality control supervisor. The market for experienced quality control supervisors is extremely tight. A month goes by and the department head completely discredits the personnel department to the CEO for failure to fill the vacancy. The CEO calls in the vice president of personnel, who relieves the pressure by agreeing to recruit a quality control supervisor, since the employment manager has been unable to do so and if anybody is to be accountable it must be the department head. Another two weeks pass, and top management continues to apply the pressure. A well-dressed, fast-talking person (wearing a tie with ducks on it) applies for the job. The vice president of personnel interviews him and gives him the standard skill reading rule test that is given to all machine operators. His answer to a $2\frac{3}{4}$-inch measurement is "2 inches one big mark, and one small one." The intelligence test score shows the mind of an eight-year-old. The personnel vice president sends him to the production manager, who, after shooting thousands of ducks through conversation with the applicant, hires him. The vice president of personnel, out of professional pride, tells the production manager that the person he has hired can neither read a rule nor come up to the intelligence level of a high school education, which is one of the qualifying requirements of the job. His answer is "He can learn by my training."

This type of crisis hiring will later cause problems when "the duck-hunting trip is over" and the production manager is faced with the problem of too many rejects.

---

cancy occurs they will be hired; if they are not available when a vacancy occurs, other candidates in the pool will be selected according to their qualifications and the order in which they were accepted in the pool.[28]

The courts often require quotas to correct discriminatory practices. An offer of a job that is refused is the same as a hire to satisfy quota requirements.[29] This concept is reinforced by the Supreme Court, where it held that a job offer after discriminatory refusal to hire stops liability even though retroactive seniority of six years was not included in the

job offer.[30] In view of the rule in the courts that a job offer is the same as a hire, one criticism of the applicant pool is eliminated, that is, that once placed in the pool the best qualified will not be available when the vacancy occurs and the underutilized category is not filled. Whether the vacancy is filled or not, as long as the offer is made, the good faith effort has been made to correct the underutilization under the court rule.

The applicant pool gives almost zero exposure to affirmative action problems and still allows the employer to hire the best-qualified applicant. The applicant pool must be properly structured to include qualified persons of all classes. Where the employer established an applicant pool that had a height requirement that excluded more women than men, the court held that although some women were not discriminated against, others were by the requirement.[31]

---

[28]The practice of telling applicants that their application blank will be kept on file and if a vacancy occurs they will be called for an interview is troublesome because all too often they are not called and a less-qualified person is hired through normal recruiting sources.

[29]A remedy for a statistical imbalance caused by discriminatory practices is to require the employer to hire a certain percentage of the protected class discriminated against. The employer therefore must take the best qualified within those classes to comply with court order. *Contractor's Association of Eastern Pa.* v. *Secy. of Labor*, 442 F.2d 159 (3rd Cir. 1971).

[30]*Ford Motor Co.* v. *EEOC*, 102 S.Ct. 3057 (1982).

[31]*Costa* v. *Markey*, 677 F.2d 1582 (1st Cir. 1982).

Where an employer had a labor pool that had a majority of whites and of 234 clerical staff hires only 7 whites were hired, the court held discrimination against whites.[32] The establishment of an applicant pool does not protect the employer unless selection is made from that pool. In the Craig case the applicant pool was properly structured with whites but there was a disparate impact in selecting only blacks from the pool.[33]

NATIONAL ORIGIN DISCRIMINATION

Unlawful discrimination occurs when an employment decision is based on the national origin of the person adversely affected by that decision. Although national origin discrimination under Title VII has not been popular and case law is scarce, compared to other protected classes such as race, religion, and sex, it can be troublesome if totally ignored. National origin bias is unlawful in hiring and promotion, the same as in race, religion, and sex. However, it has one additional feature: where the employee cannot speak English. To require the employee to do so can be violative of Title VII if knowledge of English is not required for successful performance of the job. Where Spanish-Americans were not provided with translated tests for carpentry jobs, there was no violation because English was a requirement for the job.[34] Employers can require a bilingual employee to speak English on the job.[35] Labor unions may be required to publish collective bargaining agreements in a foreign language in order to ensure adequate representation of their members when a large proportion of the membership speak only a foreign language.

Discrimination because of national origin is unlawful if physical requirements such as height tend to exclude certain nationalities, unless business necessity can be shown.

National origin under Title VII has nothing to do with citizen status: The employer may refuse to hire noncitizens provided it is applied to noncitizens of all national origins.

Dress and Grooming Codes

Prohibition of dress and grooming customs can be a violation of national origin if native appearance does not interfere with the job. However, the courts give very liberal interpretation to this section of the act. Employers can prescribe any dress code that doesn't show intentional discrimination because of nationality or sex. This is true whether it be requiring males to wear neckties and not females,[36] prohibiting males from wearing earrings, requiring males to shave off a beard, or specifying hair lengths.[37] Company requirements on grooming and dress must be stated as a job necessity and should not be adopted for the sake of appearance. This is the position of most courts. See *Bhatia* v. *Chevron USA, Inc.,* 724 F.2d 1382 (9th Cir. 1984).

Title VII was originally interpreted to mean that many dress and grooming codes were discriminatory, but subsequent court decisions changed this.

National origin discrimination is also a violation of the Immigration Reform and Control Act, discussed in the next section. Many observers believe that there is greater potential of exposure under this act than under Title VII.

---

[32]*Craig* v. *Alabama State University,* 451 F.Supp. 1207 (Ala. 1978).

[33]For further information on the applicant pool concept, see Justice Powell's appendix opinion in *Regents of University of California v. Bakke,* 438 U.S. 265 (1978). In *Johnson* v. *Transportation Agency,* 107 S.Ct. 1442 (1987), the court in approving the applicant pool concept stated that an affirmative plan that requires all applicants in the pool to compete with all other applicants is acceptable.

[34]*Frontera* v. *Sindell,* 522 F.2d 1215 (6th Cir. 1975).

[35]*Garcia* v. *Gloor,* 609 F.2d 156 (5th Cir. 1980).

---

[36]*Fountain* v. *Safeway Stores,* 555 F.2d 753 (9th Cir. 1977).

[37]*Miller* v. *Missouri Pacific Ry.,* 410 F.Supp. 533 (D.C. Mo. 1976).

IMMIGRATION REFORM AND CONTROL ACT OF 1986 (IRCA)

This act [8 USC 1324(a)] substantially changes the employer's right to hire undocumented or illegal aliens.[38] Previous to the act it was not considered illegal to knowingly hire an undocumented alien. Congress, in all its wisdom, concluded that the only way to stop illegal entry into the United States was to prevent the employer from hiring undocumented aliens. For this reason there is a substantial burden on the employer to know whether an applicant is legally qualified to work in the United States.

The act imposes sanctions not only on the employer but also on the individual within the company who knowingly hires an unauthorized alien without complying with the statute. It is also unlawful to knowingly continue to employ an alien. The Immigration and Naturalization Service (INS), which is responsible for enforcement, has issued regulations implementing the act [8 CFR Sect. 274a (2)]. It is important that the employer has a copy of these regulations because they are a good guide for compliance.

The IRCA is not violated by a simple mistake in hiring. The employer must have known that the alien hired was not authorized to work in this country. However, there is an obligation to verify that each person hired is eligible to be employed, and the employer must make a sworn statement that all applicants were verified. Since these requirements are administratively burdensome, it appears that there will be some relaxation of them. It isn't practical that the president would have to verify when hiring his son or daughter.

Verification of Employability

The employer must have sufficient documentation, before hiring, that the applicant is authorized to work in the United States. The documentation must reasonably appear to be genuine. A passport, certificate of citizenship, naturalization or resident card (green card), valid work authorization card, or birth certificate would establish employment authorization. However, a driver's license or a state-issued ID card would only establish identity, and further documentation of authorization to work, such as an unexpired work permit or a Social Security card, would be required. Both the applicant and the employer are required to fill out an I-9 form. The employer is required to inspect the applicant's part and make certain that the questions answered on the I-9 form appear to be accurate. Verification is required for all applicants, not just those believed to be aliens. Hiring without verification may constitute harboring an alien and be in violation. Verification requirements if not followed have an exposure to a fine under the terms of the statute.

Penalties

Penalties are in the form of a fine ranging from $250 to $2000 per illegal alien hired. If there is a second violation the fines are increased from $250 to $3000. A pattern practice or a complete disregard for the act would result in a criminal violation, which permits up to $10,000 in fines and six months in prison.

The employer is required to retain employment records for three years or one year after termination, whichever is sooner. Failure to do so carries a fine of $1000.[39] The wording of the statute indicates that the enforcement provisions leave little room for discretion.

Discrimination Provisions

The statute (Sect. 102) provides for a remedy when discriminating because of

---

[38]See "Employees Wary of Immigration Law," *ABA Journal* (February 1987), p. 29.

[39]This is an unusual provision. Most statutes requiring record keeping do not provide for a penalty when the statute is violated.

nationality in the same manner as Title VII, but it is broader, since it covers employers with 3 or more employees. (Title VII covers 15 or more.) The employer is prohibited from using nationality as a factor in hiring when the applicant is documented. When requiring identity, the employer under the terms of the statute must be cautious not to appear to use nationality as a factor in the hiring decision. The employer, under specific provisions, may not favor one nationality over another but may give preference to U.S. citizens.[40] If the INS adopted the EEOC position, verification requirements would force the employer to justify the reason for asking certain questions. "Where born" was a "red flag" under EEOC rules, but maybe it was necessary for verification under the statute.

Although the statute was passed in November 1986, penalties did not become effective until June 1988, so there are many gray areas to be cleared up by the courts. One of the gray areas is whether an undocumented alien is protected by other statutes.[41] One thing is certain: To avoid violation, the employer should verify all applicants, and also if any of the present employees are suspect, the employer must have complete documentation or a showing of good faith effort to determine the employee's status. It is essential that the employer keep records for three years, perform the additional paperwork required by the act, and have a statement from CEO to all management personnel that the statute will be complied with.

Because the IRCA covers employers employing three or more persons and the remedies are severe fines, rather than reinstatement with back pay as under Title VII, and will be enforced by the Justice Department, many scholars and practitioners fear that national origin discrimination will cause the next wave of lawsuits. The fears that foreign-looking applicants and those with accents will not be hired are real when you consider that there has been very little national origin enforcement since Title VII was passed.[42]

To avoid national origin lawsuits the employer should do the following:

1. Review the recruiting and selection procedures. The emphasis in the past has been on other forms of discrimination and nationality has often been overlooked.
2. Audit supervisors' practices to be assured that they are not treating one ethnic group differently from another. Many individuals have prejudices against an ethnic group that are often based on past experience.
3. Tolerate an accent unless it interferes with the job. Sometimes an accent will cause prejudices that result in discrimination charges.
4. Have a broad harassment policy that includes all members in the protected class, not just related to sex.
5. Require employees to speak English only when necessary.
6. Be sure height and weight requirements are necessary for the job.
7. Treat lawful aliens who are in process to become U.S. citizens the same as U.S. citizens.
8. Permit nationality discrimination allegations in your complaint procedure. If it is properly established, an employee will use it rather than a regulatory agency if he or she believes it is fair.

THE SELECTION AUDIT

In order to avoid exposure to lawsuits or a lengthy administrative hearing before a reg-

---

[40] In *Esponoza* v. *Farah Mfg. Co.*, 414 U.S. 811 (1973), the court held that it was proper to require U.S. citizenship, but if its purpose was to determine nationality it was in violation of Title VII.

[41] In *Patel* v. *Quality Inn South*, 846 F.2d 700 (11th Cir. 1988), the court held that an undocumented alien had the protection of the Fair Labor Standards Act. Although this is only one circuit, the decision was very logical and may start a trend in other circuits.

[42] Under Justice rules 28 CFR Section 44.200(a), intent and knowledge are required for discrimination. In this respect IRCA differs from Title VII. The rule will have to be challenged in the courts to establish a true difference between IRCA and Title VII.

ulatory agency, it is advisable to conduct an internal yearly analysis of the total selection process. It would start with the recruiting efforts to find qualified candidates, followed by the various stages of the selection process. Then a determination should be made of whether the entire procedure results in an adverse impact on members of the protected class. The selection audit should also include the IRCA. The audit would determine whether the regulations were being followed in the preemployment stage.

Recruiting Practices

The most important element in a recruiting audit is to make sure that more than one source is used. There are a variety of methods used to inform the market that a vacancy exists. The source contact and the referrals must include recruitment sources that the protected classes normally use. Information on the race and sex composite of these sources can be obtained from governmental agencies.

"Help wanted" advertisements should be reviewed to determine whether the wording would exclude members of the protected class. The use of different advertising channels for different job classifications is good evidence that a sincere effort is being made to notify the entire labor market of the job openings. The factor in determining whether recruiting methods are effective is the applicant flow, which should be reviewed with labor market population statistics on minorities and sex.

Application Review

The next step in the selection audit is to analyze the application form. The most important element is whether it contains job-related questions. The applicant should be requested not to answer questions that are not job-related. The form cannot in any way indicate that the information would be used for discriminatory purposes. If there has been any change in policy since the last audit, such as to include an employment-at-will state-

ment or a release to obtain medical information, the audit would verify that it was properly worded in the application form.

The important element in the audit of the application form is to determine for what purpose each question is being asked and how the information will be used. If there is a discriminatory purpose for any question, then business necessity must be shown.

Interviewing

The two main items to audit in the interview process are whether there is some degree of standardization in the questions asked by each interviewer and whether the criteria established for the job are being uniformly applied. Another practice to audit would be to determine whether previous rejects were reconsidered in the event the criteria were later changed. It would also be important to investigate whether the criteria for a higher job were being used for a lower-level job when there was no possibility that the applicant would progress to the higher job in the foreseeable future. The interview policy may be clear but often it is not followed, especially at the second and third interview level. It is very important that all interviewers have some degree of standardization. The entire selection process should be reviewed to determine whether there are any "disqualifiers," such as arrest records, tests, or being handicapped. As we saw in *Connecticut v. Teal*,[43] (see p. 31) the law requires an equal opportunity to be employed and if there are disqualifiers, business necessity must be shown if the disqualifier has an adverse impact on members of the protected class. It should also be determined whether members of the protected classes apply and, if not, some investigation should be made to determine the cause. Sometimes there exists some element in the employer's policy that has a "chilling effect" on certain applicants.

The audit need not be as detailed as outlined above but must be sufficient to deter-

---

[43]*Connecticut v. Teal,* 102 S.Ct. 2525 (1982).

mine whether a disparate impact exists. If one is found, a step investigation is necessary to correct it.

Determination of Adverse Impact Threshold

The EEOC Uniform Guidelines (which have judicial acceptance) use a "4/5 or 80 percent" test to determine whether an adverse impact exists. The adverse impact threshold for females is therefore 0.8 times ($\times$) the selection rate for males. For minority applicants, the adverse impact threshold is 0.8 times ($\times$) the selection rate for nonminority applicants. This formula could be safely used for any protected class. However, it would not work if the job class contained only a small number of employees. Where the class is too small to apply the formula, there is little exposure of the selection process for that protected group. If there is no adverse impact in the selection process, the audit can be very brief. It is only when one is found that a step investigation is necessary.

Compared to other aspects of personnel law, selection has very few legally uncertain areas left. The employer's selection policy should have little exposure to lawsuits. The greatest error the employer can make is to select applicants who are not the best qualified because it is believed that the law must be complied with. In the area of selection, it is clear the employer can hire the best-qualified applicant without interference by the law.

CHAPTER 4

ACCOMMODATION FOR RELIGION AND PHYSICAL HABITUAL HANDICAPS

Accommodation for Religious Beliefs
Accommodation for Physical Handicaps
Habitual Handicaps
Drug and Alcohol Problems
Dealing with AIDS in the Workplace

Most antidiscrimination statutes require the employer not to take race, sex, national origin, or color into account when making an employment decision. The goal is to achieve a work environment where discrimination is not present. The requirement of Title VII is that all individuals are to be treated alike. In the handicap and religious section, the law requires equal employment opportunity plus giving special treatment to an employee with a disability or religious belief by requiring accommodation.

The issue in most handicap and religious discrimination situations is whether, and to what extent, the employer can take an employee's disability or religious belief into consideration in making employment decisions. It is in this respect that disability and religious discrimination differ from race or sex discrimination. The existence of a disability or religious belief causes or is perceived to have caused an interference with work performance, according to opponents of the law.

The law recognizes that the existence of these conditions may sometimes interfere with performance, and yet these impairments or religious beliefs should be accommodated in the workplace. Legislatures, Congress, and the courts have also recognized that there are limits to the measures which employers have to take if such conditions interfere with performance. The law terms this as *undue hardship* and will not require the employer to make adjustments. It is because of the conflict between disability or religious beliefs and the legitimate requirements of the employers that the courts have developed the concept of *reasonable accommodation.*

The discussion in this chapter will be different from chapters where other antidiscrimination laws are discussed. In this chapter we recognize that the religious and handicapped employee must be treated differently; the only issue is to what extent. Accommodation is required for both religious beliefs and disability, but the degree of the duty to accommodate may be different. In religious beliefs the employee can subjectively choose whether or not his or her beliefs will take precedence over conflicting employ-

ment requirements, where the disabled employee does not have that choice.[1] As we shall see in the sections on accommodations for the religious and the handicapped, the courts recognize the similarity but take choice into account when considering the degree of accommodation that is required.

ACCOMMODATION FOR RELIGIOUS BELIEFS

Title VII states that it is unlawful to discriminate because of religion. The statute does not require complete religious freedom in an employment situation; in many situations this would interfere with the normal conduct of the business. A nonprofit religious organization can discriminate on the basis of religion when making an employment decision.[2] What Title VII does require of other employers or labor unions is to make reasonable efforts to accommodate the religious beliefs of the employees or applicants. This duty to accommodate includes religious observance as well as religious beliefs. Teaching a Bible class at night, being a lay preacher, or going to summer Bible camp would be some of the activities that would require an attempt to accommodate.[3] However, the religious observance is not unlimited. A lay Sunday school teacher left work on December 24 before the end of the shift to decorate the church and prepare her church hall for religious school students to stage a Christmas play. The court held that this did not constitute religious observance protected by Title VII but instead was a social and family obligation.[4]

---

[1]See Scott H. Nichols, "Iowa's Law Prohibiting Disability Discrimination in Employment: An Overview," *Drake Law Review* 32 (1982–83), 273, 382.

[2]*Corp. of Presiding Bishops* v. *Amos,* 107 S.Ct. 2862 (1987).

[3]For complete reference on religious discrimination, see James G. Frierson, "Religion in the Workplace," *Personnel Journal* (July 1988), p. 61.

[4]*Wessling* v. *Kroger Co.,* 554 F.Supp. 548 (E.D. Mich. 1982).

The Concept of Accommodation

The concept of accommodation is rooted in the case law on religious discrimination as a violation of Title VII and the Constitution. Title VII allows the employer to discriminate on the basis of religious beliefs if "it is unable to reasonably accommodate to an employee's religious observance or practice without undue hardship on the conduct of the employer's business."[5]

The extent to which the employer must disrupt the business to accommodate for religious observance was decided by the Supreme Court in the leading case of *Hardison* v. *TWA,* 432 U.S. 63 (1977). The court required the employer to show reasonable efforts to accommodate. If rescheduling work assignments caused seniority to be violated, co-worker rights to be infringed upon, or other changes in normal operations that would cause increased costs in order to accommodate, it would not be religious discrimination to refuse to do so. Under Hardison the court said that the employer only had to bear de minimus cost to accommodate; otherwise it would be discriminating against other employees for whom no similar expenses are made to allow them time off from work. But where the employer failed to show that rescheduling Saturday work was an additional cost and further evidence revealed that other employees volunteered to work, accommodation would not be undue hardship.[6]

Duty to Make Reasonable Effort to Accommodate

If accommodation will reasonably preserve the employee's job (that is, compensation, terms and conditions of employment, and no adverse consequences to the employer) then the employer should accommodate.[7] Where the employer would have to either excuse the employee for Saturday work, permit make-up, or get volunteers, this would be a burdensome administrative task and could increase costs and undue hardship under the act.[8] This reasonable accommodation may extend to more than allowing the worker to trade shifts. In *Smith* v. *Pyro Mining Co.,* 827 F.2d 1081 (6th Cir. 1987), the court held that inasmuch as the employee had religious objections to asking others to work for him on Sunday, reasonable accommodation required the employer to do so.

Although only de minimus accommodation is required, a good effort is still the rule. In *Proctor* v. *Consolidated Freightways Corp. of Delaware,* 795 F.2d 1472 (9th Cir. 1986), the employee was told at the time of hiring that she would be required to work on Saturdays, but this did not relieve the employer of the duty to make a reasonable effort to accommodate. If the employer has a workable system for employees who are absent on Saturdays, it would not be unreasonable to give assurance that the nature of the position was such that being absent on Saturdays did not affect the employer's interests. But it was not failure to accommodate to refuse to guarantee the employee that she would not have to work on Saturdays.[9] This duty to accommodate would extend to the situation where the employee after working for a period of time joined a church that prohibited working on Saturdays or where Sunday was voluntary but later became necessary [*EEOC* v. *Ithaca Industries, Inc.,* 847 F.2d 116 (8th Cir. 1988)].

Alternative Accommodations

Although in almost every situation the employer has a duty to make a good faith

---

[5]For a good discussion on accommodation, see Thomas D. Brierton, "Religious Discrimination in the Workplace: Who's Accommodating Who," *Labor Law Journal* (May 1988), p. 299. Also see Douglas Massengill and Donald J. Peterson, "Job Requirements and Religious Practices: Conflict and Accommodation," *Labor Law Journal* (July 1988), p. 402.

[6]*Brown* v. *General Motors Corp.,* 601 F.2d 956 (8th Cir. 1979).

[7]*American Postal Workers Union* v. *Postmaster General,* 781 F.2d 772 (9th Cir. 1986).

[8]*Wisner* v. *Saunder Leasing Systems,* 784 F.2d 1571 (11th Cir. 1986).

[9]*Protos* v. *Volkswagen of America,* 797 F.2d 129 (3rd Cir. 1986).

effort to accommodate, once this effort is made the requirements of the statute are satisfied. In *Ansonia Board of Education* v. *Philbrook*, 107 S.Ct. 376 (1986), the employee, after six years of being employed as a school teacher, joined a church that prohibited members from working on certain holy days, a practice which caused him to miss six school days a year. The board policy was to grant three days for sick leave and three days for personal business leave. The employee wanted to take the six days in this manner and the school board offered leave without pay and several other alternatives to accommodate, but it rejected the employee's request that he be permitted to use personal business leave for religious purposes. The Court held that where there are several possible alternatives the employer need not grant the one the employee prefers and the employer does not have to show that each of the employee's alternative accommodations would result in undue hardship. All the employer has to do is offer a reasonable accommodation, and an unpaid leave is reasonable unless a personal business leave is allowed for all other purposes except religious ones.

Accommodation for Union Dues

One of the most common situations under religious discrimination is where under the labor agreement all employees must pay dues to the labor union, and an employee, because of religious beliefs, refuses to do so. The union demands termination under the terms of the labor agreement; the employer refuses. Courts who have considered this question have held that if the employee pays the amount of the dues to charity, this is reasonable accommodation of the employee's religious beliefs by both the union and the employer.[10]

Employees' or applicants' religious observance and beliefs should not be a problem to the employer since the Hardison case. When an applicant is hired and there is some indication that religious beliefs will interfere with the employment situation, the employer should not refuse to hire the applicant, since that would be discrimination because of religion. The applicant, however, should be informed that an attempt will be made to accommodate; if that is not always possible, the applicant must decide whether to accept the job or from time to time not be able to observe religious beliefs.

It is extremely important for the employer to attempt to accommodate when requested to do so because of religious beliefs. Failure to make a reasonable attempt will invariably result in violation even though it can be shown in retrospect that accommodation was not possible.

ACCOMMODATION FOR PHYSICAL HANDICAPS

Contrary to common belief, no federal law covering private employers similar to Title VII makes it unlawful to discriminate in hiring or promotion of handicapped persons.[11] The Rehabilitation Act of 1973 requires federal contractors to take affirmative action to hire or promote qualified handicapped individuals.[12] The affirmative action required of government contractors and employers receiving federal assistance is similar to that required under Executive Order 11246 (discussed in Chapter 6) with one exception; by definition a handicapped worker is not as qualified as a nonhandicapped worker for all job assignments. Therefore, there is a duty of the employer to accommodate the handicapped worker by making a good faith effort to place the applicant or employee in a job that the person is qualified to perform

---

[10]*Tooley* v. *Martin Marietta Corp.*, 648 F.2d 1239 (9th Cir. 1981); *Nottelson* v. *Smith Steel Workers*, 643 F.2d 445 (7th Cir. 1981).

[11]Approximately 41 states have antidiscrimination laws for the handicapped. These laws supplement or fill the void of federal law. (Congress has a federal law under consideration.)

[12]87 Stat. 355, 29 USC Sect. 701–94.

with the same competency as a nonhandi-capped worker.

Definition of a Handicapped Person

The Rehabilitation Act of 1973, Section 503, requires any business that has a contract of $2500 or more and provides services or personal property to any agency of the federal government to take affirmative action to employ handicapped workers. This requirement also applies to subcontractors. This means that virtually every employer that sells or provides services directly or indirectly to the federal government, or all public sector employers, are covered under the act. If the employer has government contracts that exceed $50,000, a written affirmative action program must be developed.

The statute defines a handicapped person as "any person who has a physical or mental impairment which substantially limits one or more of such person's major life activities and has a record of such an impairment, or is regarded as having such an impairment."[13]

Many of the issues that courts have to decide under the act concern the definition of a handicapped person. The statute provides that "no otherwise qualified handicapped individual shall, solely by reason of his handicap, be discriminated against." Any allegation of discrimination immediately raises the issue of whether the person is in fact handicapped. The law in this area seems to be developing on a case-by-case basis with only general guidance from the courts.

Judicial Definition of a Handicapped Employee

The definition of a handicapped employee is found in *Southeastern Community College* v. *Davis,* 442 U.S. 397 (1979). The plaintiff in Davis was a deaf applicant to a nursing school who could not understand speech without lip reading. The school refused to admit her on the grounds that her hearing disability would make it unsafe for her to be a nurse. The Court said that under Section 504 of the Rehabilitation Act of 1973, an "otherwise qualified person means one who is able to meet all of the program's requirements in spite of the handicap."

The courts have stated that although certain physical conditions like height, weight, and strength may render the employee incapable of performing the duties of the job, they are not impairments that substantially limit one or more major life activities.[14] Where the job required working at certain heights and the employee could not work at those heights, the court stated that being physically incapable of doing the job doesn't mean it is physical impairment.[15]

The Supreme Court in *School Board of Nassau County* v. *Arline,* 107 S.Ct. 1123 (1987), had to decide whether an elementary school teacher with active tuberculosis was a handicapped person under the act. The Court decided that a person suffering from a contagious disease is a handicapped individual within the meaning of the Rehabilitation Act and the employer may not discriminate because the employee suffers from the disease. The Court recognized that the employee must be qualified and if the disease poses a serious health threat to co-workers, she or he may not be qualified. The Court said that whether there is a serious health threat to others must be decided on an individual basis, but this does justify excluding from coverage under the act all persons with an actual or a perceived contagious disease.

Many states do not consider a medical condition a handicap, while others, such as New York and California, do. Most state courts are following the federal courts in in-

---

[13]Sect. 7 of Rehabilitation Act of 1973, 29 USC Sect. 706(6).

[14]*Jasany* v. *U.S. Postal Service,* 755 F.2d 1244 (6th Cir. 1985).

[15]*Forrisi* v. *Bowen* 794 F.2d 931 (4th Cir. 1986).

terpreting their handicapped laws by deciding on a case-by-case basis. Since it is the custom for the states to follow the Supreme Court, it appears that since Arline a contagious disease will be considered a handicap in the state courts, unless there is a serious health threat to others.

Accommodation for Handicapped Persons

The extent to which a covered employer must accommodate a handicapped worker depends upon the applicable section of the law. Under Section 504 (dealing with recipients of federal financial assistance) the employer is merely obligated to treat equally handicapped and nonhandicapped individuals. Under Sections 501 and 503 federal employers and contractors are obligated to take affirmative action to employ and advance in employment qualified handicapped individuals. This distinction puts more of a burden on federal employers and contractors than on employers who merely receive federal assistance. What is reasonable for federal assistance agency may not be for a federal contractor. However, most of the case law has been developed for federal assistance programs, and the only conclusion to be drawn is that it may take a little more effort to accommodate for the government contractor. How much more would be determined by the facts of the case. One court said that the legislative history of Section 501 (29 USC 791) demonstrates that Congress intended that the federal government be a model employer of the handicapped.[16] The court went on to say that reasonable accommodation means some workplace modifications, some work schedule adjustments, and even some acquisition of special equipment. This is a minority view.

Regardless of whether an employer is covered by Section 501 or 504 or by a state law, there still exists a duty to make reasonable accommodation. The courts have struggled with the requirement of reasonable accommodation, not only because employers have different degrees of obligations depending upon what section of law they are under or whether they have state law but also because there is an absence of a federal or state statutory definition of accommodation.

In order for a court to reach the reasonable accommodation question, there must be a job available. The Rehabilitation Act of 1973 is not a "make work" public employment statute but an attempt to prohibit the discriminatory placement of existing positions.[17]

The guideline for reasonable accommodation is found in *Southeastern Community College* v. *Davis*, 442 U.S. 397 (1979). (The facts are discussed on page 66). The plaintiff, being deaf, could not meet all the requirements of the program unless the standards were substantially lowered and Section 504 does not impose this obligation upon an educational institution.

In *Stutts* v. *Freeman*, 694 F.2d 666 (11th Cir. 1983), the applicant could perform all the duties of the job but could not pass the aptitude test. It was not necessary to pass the test to perform the essential functions of the job. The court held that refusal to try the plaintiff on the job was a failure to accommodate.

Some courts have liberally interpreted the Stutts decision in favor of the handicapped person and required the employer to make some modifications, such as transfers, or modifying a vehicle so a handicapped person can drive it.[18] Other courts consider the Davis decision as not requiring any modifications in the program, as was held in *Strathie* v. *Department of Transportation*, 716 F.2d 227 (3rd Cir. 1983).[19] This is the majority rule in the circuit courts.

---

[16]*Gardner* v. *Morris*, 752 F.2d 1271 (8th Cir. 1985).

[17]*Sisson* v. *Helms*, 752 F.2d 991 (9th Cir. 1985).

[18]*Simon* v. *St. Louis County, Mo.*, 656 F.2d 316 (8th Cir. 1981).

[19]Also see *Carter* v. *Bennett*, 840 F.2d 63 (D.C. Cir. 1988).

BFOQ as Applied to Accommodation

One factual situation that often arises is where the employer feels that although the person can perform the essential functions of the job, he or she would not be able to perform it safely and therefore this would be a Bona Fide Occupational Qualification (BFOQ) exception. The standard for BFOQ was established in *Weeks* v. *Southern Bell Telephone and Telegraph Co.,* 408 F.2d 228 (5th Cir. 1959), and followed in most state and federal jurisdictions. The Court in Weeks said that in order to establish a BFOQ for sex discrimination, the employer "must show that all or substantially all members of the class would not be able to perform safely and efficiently the duties of the job." This is often difficult to show. It would have to be obvious, such as 20/40 vision for a bus driver.[20]

Although cases turning upon the question of reasonable accommodation are decided upon a case-by-case basis, one common thread running through all the decisions is that the employer must make a bona fide attempt to accommodate. The problem that the personnel practitioner or manager often has is that supervision has a subjective notion that the handicapped worker cannot perform the job and refuses to give him or her a chance. The reason often given is the risk of future injury. Unless there are objective facts to substantiate the reason, it will not stand judicial scrutiny.[21]

Bona Fide Effort to Accommodate

To avoid liability for discrimination for religious beliefs and for handicaps, the employer must make a good faith effort to accommodate. Often supervisors will give a subjective reason for not making an attempt. The courts in any area of discrimination will no longer tolerate management perception. The statutory duty to accommodate does not require the employer to prejudice the safety of the co-worker or interfere with business objectives, change methods of doing business, or in any way increase costs. What the courts and Congress are telling the employer is that he or she must make a bona fide attempt to accommodate. When making this attempt, failure to accommodate is not culpable as long as the effort was made in good faith without intent to discriminate. The court will seldom say that the reason why it cannot be done is not a good business practice or that is is uncommon in business. They leave the determination of good business reasons up to management as long as they are non-discriminatory.

Any reasonable offer of accommodation satisfies the statute. The Supreme Court made it clear in the Philbrook case that the employee does not choose the accommodation. She or he must take what the employer offers as long as it is reasonable. From the case law it is safe to say that it is better to make any offer of accommodation than not to attempt to accommodate and make no offer at all.

HABITUAL HANDICAPS

Smoking Problems in the Workplace

Smoking in the workplace is a twofold problem for the employer. Studies show that there is a marked difference in costs of keeping a smoker and a nonsmoker on the payroll.[22] The second problem is the contention of co-workers that passive smoke creates an unhealthy environment. They argue that the employer is not providing a safe place to work or they are handicapped because they cannot tolerate passive smoke.

To solve this problem employers have formulated various policies from smoking in

---

[20]*Lewis* v. *Metropolitan Transit Commission,* 320 N.W.2d 426 (Minn. 1982).

[21]*Maine Human Rights Comm.* v. *Canadian Pac. Ltd.,* 58 A.2d 1125 (Me. 1983).

[22]W. L. Weis, "Can You Afford to Hire Smokers?" *Personnel Administrator* (May 1981), pp. 358–81; M. M. Kristen, "How Much Can Business Expect to Profit from Smoking Cessation?" *Preventive Medicine* (1983), pp. 71–78.

designated areas only (sometimes these areas are selected to discourage smoking) to a complete ban even during nonwork hours and at home. (United States Gypsum announced such a policy in January 1986 and started enforcing it later that year.)[23] Subsequent case law indicates this is enforceable if job related. The problem has also entered the political arena, and states are passing statutes with increasing frequency restricting smoking both in public and in the workplace. These statutes vary as to the degree of restrictions. Most of them require separation of the smokers and nonsmokers by requiring designated areas. They are carefully worded to protect the rights of both the smokers and the nonsmokers.[24]

Legal Rights of Smokers and Nonsmokers

There have been relatively few legal battles between smokers and nonsmokers. One reason is that the state enforcement agencies first attempt voluntary compliance and have been very careful not to push enforcement and risk the chance of bad case law. As a result the statutes have been effective and where resisted the agency has not pursued them unless the smoker or nonsmoker files a complaint. As one lower court put it as dictum, "the desire of employees who wish to smoke cannot be disregarded, but where people must work with a smoker there is a rational basis for prohibiting smoking."

Nonsmokers often cite the landmark case of *Shimp* v. *New Jersey Bell Telephone Co.,* 368 A.2d 408 (N.J. S.Ct. 1976), to show they have

---

[23]"Banning Employee Smoking Beyond the Company Gates," *Insight,* March 2, 1987, pp. 40–41; "Company Prohibits Smoking at Work and at Home," *American Medical News* (February 1987), p. 12.

[24]Generally these statutes have been upheld by the courts. See *Rossie* v. *Wisconsin State Department of Revenue,* 395 N.W.2d 801 (Wis. App. 1986), where the court said that a statute requiring the employer to designate certain areas for smoking does not unconstitutionally deny a smoker equal protection. The employee had been a pipe smoker for 18 years and argued that the statute was protecting nonsmokers by prohibiting smoking in certain areas.

some rights. In this case the employee, while working as a secretary, had for several years suffered from other employees' smoking. She had occasional nosebleeds as well as severe throat irritation. The court held that smoke was an unnecessary toxic in the workplace and the employer had failed to provide a safe place to work. The court was particularly concerned about the company policy of no smoking around certain machinery in order to prevent damage but not around employees who may be damaged permanently.

Although this case has been frequently cited for the rule that nonsmokers can win in the courts, the nonsmoker has not prevailed in other cases. Most courts hold, as in *Smith* v. *Western Electric Corp.,* 643 S.W.2d 10 (Mo. 1982), that the employee must show serious physical reaction from smoke in the workplace. In this case the employee had blackouts from passive smoke, which was a sufficient physical condition to find that the employer failed to provide a safe place to work. In *Gordon* v. *Raven System Research Corp.,* 462 A.2d 10 (D.C. App. 1983), the court rejected the argument that the employee who was supersensitive to smoke had a cause of action. It must be more than a nuisance or a discomfort. There was no duty to provide a safe place to work for a supersensitive person. Also in *Kensell* v. *State of Oklahoma,* 716 F.2d 1350 (10th Cir. 1983), the court concluded that there is no general duty to provide smoke-free areas when there is no severe physical reaction.

In *McCarthy* v. *Washington Department of Social and Health Services,* 759 P.2d 351 (Wash. 1988), the employee alleged that she developed pulmonary disease from exposure to passive smoke. The court held that an employer has a common law duty to provide a safe place to work. This case is significant because if the employer doesn't act on a complaint of smoke in the workplace, there is an exposure to a lawsuit.

Since it is difficult for a nonsmoker to show that by permitting smoking the employer failed to provide a safe place to work, some employees are alleging that they are handicapped because they are sensitive to passive smoke. They seek protection under the Rehabilitation Act of 1973. The case most often cited for this legal theory is *Vickers* v. *Veterans Administration,* 549 F.Supp. 85 (D.C. Wash. 1982), where the employee was supersensitive to passive cigarette smoke and the court took the minority view and held that she was a handicapped person under the Rehabilitation Act of 1973, but reasonable accommodation was made. This theory was also supported in *Parodic* v. *Merit System Protection Board,* 690 F.2d. 731 (9th Cir. 1982), where the employee was able to show that smoke caused chest pains, congestion, and breathing trouble when she was transferred into a room where employees smoked. When removed from the areas where employees smoked, her condition improved. The court held that the employer had to either transfer her to a smoke-free area or make disability payments. Courts have not found that persons sensitive to passive smoke are handicapped under either federal or state law unless they have severe physical reaction. However, the *Parodic* case comes close.

One nonsmoker alleged that the employer breached the employment contract when he failed to provide a smoke-free environment, since he knew that she quit her former job because of the smoking in the office. The court held that there was no obligation to provide a smoke-free environment based on knowledge that the employee quit her former job because of smoking. Such a provision would have to be expressly stated in an employment agreement or promise made at the time of hiring. The court also rejected the argument that there was a duty to protect employees by providing a smoke-free environment.[25]

Some smokers have been successful in collecting workers compensation when their physical condition is the result of their smoking both on and off the job. An employee was a smoker since age 15 and worked for the employer 33 years, during which time he suffered from bronchitis and allergic asthma. Over a period of time he was told by his doctor to quit smoking, but he didn't. He was medically determined to be totally disabled as the result of bronchitis. He filed for workers compensation and the court held that even though his bronchitis was caused by smoking, job conditions aggravated the preexisting condition and the employer was liable.[26]

The Arnold case is illustrative of the exposure the employer has, whether it is from smokers or nonsmokers. The nonsmokers are saying, "We are exposed to passive smoke and this creates an unhealthy environment under which we have to work." The smokers are saying, "We were able to smoke when we were hired, there is no law against smoking in the workplace, and therefore we have the same rights as the nonsmokers." The employer has exposure to employee relations problems and lawsuits because of smoking unless nonsmokers are hired and a smoke-free environment is maintained.

Recommendations for a Smoking Policy

In the interest of reducing cost of operations and exposure to lawsuits, the employer should control smoking at the workplace before legal costs are incurred and the conflict between smokers and nonsmokers becomes a major personnel problem. There are several ways to do this.

1. The employer should consider the implications of recruiting if a policy were initiated to hire nonsmokers only. This is legal, since nonsmokers are not a protected class.

2. Prohibiting smoking in the workplace is certainly a possibility where there is a union that consents. If there is no union and ample notice is given, there may be a slight exposure to a lawsuit but more of an exposure to "political suicide" if the CEO or other top management personnel smoke. A complete ban on smoking

---

[25]*Bernard* v. *Cameron & Colby Co.,* 397 Mass. 320 (Mass. 1986).

[26]*Arnold* v. *Firestone Tire & Rubber Co.,* 686 S.W.2d 65 (Tenn. 1984).

is becoming more popular among adventurous employers. A ban on all smoking, both at home and at the workplace, is worth considering in certain industries.

3. Establishing designated areas is a compromise solution in the conflict between nonsmokers and smokers and is the most common method to restrict smoking at the workplace but not necessarily the best. This is what most state and local statutes require and is a political solution.

4. When a smoker and a nonsmoker are located in the same area, it becomes a personnel problem to decide which one should be relocated. If the employees can't agree on this, some companies relocate the smoker while an equal number relocate the nonsmoker. Case law dictates that the nonsmoker must be relocated, if the employer is to provide a safe place to work or accommodate for the handicapped.

5. Incentive plans to encourage smokers to quit have been successful in large companies. Whatever works should be continued. To increase wages for employees who quit smoking appears to be rewarding the wrong people. A better plan would be to pay less to those who do smoke. It is well established that smokers are the more expensive employees; therefore, their wages or other benefits should offset the higher costs (U.S. Department of Health and Human Services, "The Health Consequences of Involuntary Smoking," a report of the Surgeon General, 1986).

6. Employers should provide treatment programs for smokers in the same manner they do for alcoholics.

7. Until a completely smoke-free environment is achieved, smoking should be allowed in those areas that do not physically affect other employees (unless the employer is required by statute to designate areas). To voluntarily designate areas for smoking does not create a smoke-free environment and only increases hidden costs. Enforcement is a constant problem both in keeping nonsmokers out and in making smokers take time out from their duties to idly smoke. It is comparable to coffee breaks in cafeterias which have always caused an enforcement problem.

The employer should have a long-term objective of a smoke-free workplace. This can be achieved by one of several methods, but all have their faults. Presently it is more of a personnel problem than a legal one. Apart from any personnel problems, which only the employer can assess, for a smoke-free environment in the workplace it is recommended that the employer

1. Hire only nonsmokers
2. Offer treatment to smokers presently on the payroll
3. Give some extra benefits to nonsmokers
4. Set a realistic date for achieving a smoke-free workplace, not to exceed three years or when the CEO who smokes retires

DRUG AND ALCOHOL PROBLEMS

One of the most common problems relating to physical conditions facing the employer, other than back problems, is that of drug and alcohol abuse.[27] The problem is serious, not only because of its high cost in workers compensation, absenteeism, production loss, and poor quality,[28] but also because there is no complete solution without possible exposure to litigation.

Need for a Policy

No matter how large or small the company, a policy should be written even if a substance abuse condition does not presently exist. According to the various reports of the U.S. Department of Health and Human Services, more than 9 percent of the population over 18 years of age are substance abusers. The possibility of the employer's having the problem is rather high. The existence of a policy with the proper communication may prevent a substance

---

[27]Thomas E. Geidt, "Drugs and Alcohol Abuse in the Workplace: Balancing Employer and Employee Rights," *Employee Relations Law Journal*, 11, no. 2 (Autumn 1985), 181–205.

[28]See "Drugs and Alcohol in the Workplace: Costs, Controls and Controversies," Bureau of National Affairs, Washington, D.C., 1986; John Krizay and Edward Carels, "The Fifty Billion Drain; Alcohol, Drugs and the High Cost of Insurance," *CompCare Publications* (1986).

abuse condition from developing in the workplace. Another reason for having a policy is that some states by statute require a written policy before any testing can be performed and then a great deal of freedom is given for testing.[29]

The existence of a policy will prevent exposure to a claim of invasion of privacy since the employee is forewarned that the policy will be enforced and violation of it will result in severe disciplinary action up to and including discharge. If the employee objects to the policy, he or she will have an opportunity to find another job. For this reason all policies should have a time period before they become effective. Some courts will hold that continued employment after the policy is announced is implied consent to its terms and therefore the policy is not an invasion of privacy.[30]

Essential Elements of a Policy

The purpose of the policy should be clearly stated in order to discourage the use of drugs and alcohol. Discharge should be the last resort for the violation of the policy.

The policy should not be a "canned one" that some other company has adopted but should fit the needs and environment of the company where it will be enforced. The policy for the public sector should be different from the policy for private sector employees, since the public sector employee has the protection of the Fourth Amendment of the Constitution. The policy should apply to present employees, since there is less restriction on preemployment procedures. The type of industry may also warrant different procedures. There would be more latitude for enforcement in jobs involving significant risks of injury to co-workers, the public, or those who have security responsibility.

The policy should define a substance abuser, a definition that may not always agree with that of the state or federal statute. The

Rehabilitation Act of 1973 [Sect. 706(7)(b)] states that alcohol or drug abuse is not under the act if the substance use threatens the safety of others or interferes with job performance. The act is silent on whether a person in treatment is a handicapped person. There is some indication, however, that a person in treatment could be considered handicapped under the statute.[31] Although there may be some question under a state or federal statute as to whether a particular condition constitutes a handicap, there should be no question under the policy if the term is properly defined. Using his or her own definition, the employer can always make a policy more strict or more clear than a statute and enforce it as a policy rather than relying upon a statute.

The policy should be divided into two sections, one dealing with drug abuse and one with alcoholism. The two substance abuses have to be treated and enforced differently. One distinction is that many state laws consider alcoholism as an illness or a handicap while drug use is considered an antisocial, intolerable, and illegal activity. Often a person using drugs is selling drugs illegally to acquire more money to satisfy the habit, while an alcoholic can buy legally all the liquor she or he wants and doesn't inflict the habit upon others. For this reason there is more tolerance in treatment of an alcoholic than of a drug abuser. Other reasons for treating the two differently depend on job category or type of industry.

Surveillance for Presence of Drugs

In any surveillance issue, the law considers the balance between the employee's privacy rights and the employer's need to protect property and the safety of others.

---

[29]See Minnesota Statutes, 181.94–181.97.

[30]*United States* v. *Sihler*, 562 F.2d 349 (5th Cir. 1977).

[31]In *Healy* v. *Bergman*, 609 F.Supp. 1448 (D.C. Mass. 1985) the court held that an employee in treatment may be considered handicapped because treatment doesn't prevent him from doing his job. In *Ferguson* v. *U.S. Dept. of Commerce*, 680 F.Supp. 1514 (M.D., Fla. 1988), the court said the employer should have taken steps to diagnose the condition so treatment could be offered.

The most reliable surveillance for drug abuse is observation on the job. The policy could be written to require any person who observes the use or possession of drugs in the workplace to report it to management or be subject to discipline for failure to do so. There are many warnings of drug abuse in the workplace that management can detect. Absenteeism, difficulty in concentration, spasmodic work patterns, generally lower job efficiency, relationship with co-workers, deterioration of personal appearance, frequent use of breath purifiers, and so on are all indications to management that make the employee a suspect, and the condition should be further investigated to determine the cause.

Often observance on the job comes in the advanced stages of drug use and the employer may want to correct the problem sooner. For this reason testing has become the most popular method of surveillance.[32] A surveillance method should not be used unless there is some reason to believe that the employee may be using drugs.[33] The reason can be somewhat subjective, but it should be objective enough to show that testing is not at random. In *BMWE Lodge 16* v. *Burlington Northern Ry.*, 802 F.2d 1016 (8th Cir. 1986), the court upheld testing where an employee was involved in or associated with an accident, committed a human error, or returned to work after a furlough or similar leave of absence. Other circuit courts have rejected the right of the employer to test. The issue will eventually have to be settled by the U.S. Supreme Court (several cases).

Testing Procedure for Drug Abuse

1. Prior to testing, the employee should be given a chance to list any drugs taken in the last month and under what circumstances.
2. When requested to take a test, the employee will be informed why the test is necessary, and if there is any other way to get the facts the company will use it first.
3. If the first test is positive, the employee will be suspended. Further testing by a licensed laboratory will be required before any further action is taken or the results released.
4. Test results will be disclosed only to those persons who have a need to know for job-related decisions. Any further disclosure must be with the employee's consent.
5. Upon receipt of final test results and if positive, the employer will give the employee an opportunity to explain or challenge the results before taking disciplinary action.

Other methods of surveillance that could be used, depending upon the state law, would be T.V. surveillance and the use of electronic eavesdropping devices (about half of the states prohibit this). Undercover investigation is also permitted in many states. When any method of surveillance is used, it should be stated in the policy that the employer will from time to time use a test or other methods of surveillance when it is necessary to get the facts. If a polygraph test is used, considerable care should be taken in its administration, since this could be found to be an invasion of privacy. It should be administered by a professional and the employee should sign a statement before seeing the results that the questions asked were job related and reasonable. If she or he refuses to answer questions she or he should be asked the reason.[34]

Regulation of Off-Duty Drug Abuse Activity

A positive drug test may be the result of off-duty use. To take action on the use of drugs away from the workplace, the employer must show that off-duty con-

---

[32]"Drugs in the Workplace," *NIDA Capsules*, National Institute on Drug Abuse (March 1986).

[33]Drug and alcohol testing are mandatory subjects of bargaining under NLRB guidelines (Memorandum GC87-5, September 1987).

[34]In *O'Brien* v. *Papa Gino's of America*, 780 F.2d 1067 (1st Cir. 1986), the court held that the discharge was not wrongful when the polygraph test revealed he was using drugs, but upheld a jury award of $400,000 for invasion of privacy because the administrator went beyond permissible bounds in questioning.

duct affects the job or the employer's business. If an employee is arrested or convicted on a drug charge, the arrest or conviction must render the employee unable to perform his or her job satisfactorily or result in excessive absenteeism or affect the employer's business before he or she is discharged.

Correction of Drug Abuse by Employer

When the employer is positive that the employee is a drug abuser, the matter should be handled internally without the help of law enforcement authorities. The policy should make it clear that discharge will be delayed if the employee will voluntarily enter into treatment. (Some employers believe that treatment is too late after using drugs on the job and termination is the best solution. This is legally sound in most states, but may not be the best employee relations policy.) If the employee has undergone treatment and reverts to drug use, then termination is the only alternative. The termination should be for violation of the policy for the use of drugs that affects performance or the safety of others, and no mention should be made of any illegal activity.

Policy on Alcohol Abuse

Although there is some similarity between drug and alcohol abuse, such as treatment, high costs to employer in health care, loss of production, and causes of death and disability from auto accidents,[35] the problems should be treated differently. The problem of alcohol is often more an employee relations problem than a legal one. Many states consider it an illness, while others consider

it a handicap.[36] The techniques used for detection in alcoholism are not as legally restrictive as in the case of drugs. The use of alcohol is a legal activity and the danger of defamation is not as great.

Surveillance for Alcohol Abuse

The method of surveillance for alcohol abuse is practically unrestricted. Observation and undercover methods are the most effective and have as their objective to get the employee to seek help. Undercover methods often involve the use of treated alcoholics to detect abuse among fellow workers and then an attempt to get the problem drinker to seek help.

Another effective method is the use of assessment centers located in most large cities. The assessment center will determine whether the problem is caused by alcohol and if so whether the person is addicted to it and needs treatment. Often the problem might be alcohol, but the person is not an alcoholic but uses poor judgment in drinking too much at a particular time, which caused a problem. This is common in driving-while-drunk situations.

The policy on alcoholism should not have as its objective to discourage the use of alcohol unless its use cannot be controlled. In this respect it differs from drug abuse. The employee must recognize that she or he has the problem and needs help. If the employee doesn't realize this and fails to seek help and the problem continues, then the only recourse for the employer is to terminate.[37] The policy should therefore include a step-by-step procedure to correct the problem insofar as uncontrolled use of alcohol affects the work of the employee. A policy on alcoholism should state:

---

[35]H. J. Harwood, D. M. Napolitano, P. L. Kristiansen, and J. J. Collins, "Economic Costs to Society of Alcohol and Drug Abuse and Mental Illness," Research Triangle Park, NC, Research Triangle Institute, 1984; Fifth Special Report to Congress on Alcohol and Health, Washington DC, U.S. Dept. of Health and Human Services, 1983.

[36]*Connecticut Life Insurance* v. *Department of Industry, Labor and Human Relations,* 273 N.W.2d 207 (Wis. 1979); *Clowes* v. *Terminix International, Inc.,* 528 A.2d 794 (N.J. 1988).

[37]In *Whitlock* v. *Donovan,* 598 F.Supp. 126 (D.D.C. 1984), the court stated that the employee must be given a firm choice between rehabilitation and discipline soon after discovery.

1. After the employee admits that he or she needs help, the employee should be referred to an assessment center. If the employee refuses and alcohol is suspected to be the cause of the work-related problem, then termination is the only alternative and the policy should clearly state that the options are to take treatment or quit.

2. Once the employee agrees to seek help, treatment should be offered and medical leave without pay granted. Most companies cover this under their health care and sick leave policy. (A few states require it.)

3. While in treatment the employee should maintain his or her employee status and the employer's policy should determine what benefits he or she should have; however, they should be the same as for other illnesses or handicapped persons.

4. Only after the employee refuses treatment or treatment fails should the employee be terminated, not for alcoholism but for the work-related problems caused by the use of alcohol.

It must be remembered that, unlike drug abuse, alcoholism does not usually affect the co-workers' performance. The alcohol abuser also can be tolerated longer than the drug abuser because the effect normally is not as devastating to the job or on the co-workers and its effect is not as immediate. The objective of a policy on alcohol is to eliminate the job-related problem, and the policy for drug abuse is to eliminate the use or possession of drugs.

Preemployment Procedures in Substance Abuse

Any reasonable substance abuse program can be started in preemployment procedures to determine whether the applicant is an abuser. Preemployment tests have been permitted in almost every state. The employer can set about any nondiscriminatory criteria for rejecting or requiring treatment before considering the applicant. However, in some states where substance abuse is considered a handicap, there have been some court decisions that require the offer of treatment at the applicant's expense before

total rejection. The application must be reconsidered after the applicant has been successfully treated.

Policy Needed to Avoid Lawsuits

The problem of substance abuse is not going to disappear. The employer must educate management personnel to cope with it. A policy that is judicially sound and considers employee relations consequences in its enforcement must be communicated to management personnel and all employees. The purpose of the policy is to discourage substance abuse in the workplace and inform the employee of what action the employer will take when it is violated. The policy should be sensitive to the employee's expectations of privacy, the rights of co-workers to have a safe place to work, and the necessity to have an efficient operation. It should offer an alternative of treatment or refusal to hire once it is determined that the applicant is an abuser. Reasonable means to determine facts, including testing, are judicially acceptable.

The courts have never interfered with an employer to correct a problem that affects the business and safety of others. In this respect the rights of the employer are greater than those of the employee. Substance abuse is no exception. There is no interference from the law, provided the employer has as an objective to correct substance abuse in the workplace and not correction for the good of society.

Employer Third Party Liability for Inebriated Employees

When employees become inebriated at company-sponsored events or when employees are sent home after drinking at work, most courts hold that the company is not liable unless negligence can be shown. In some states, even where negligence is shown the courts have held that the states' "Dram Shop" law does not apply. In *Meany* v. *Newett*, 367 N.W.2d 472 (Minn. 1985), the court refused to apply the "Dram Shop" statute to the employer. It was shown that the employer was negligent in serving the inebriated employee at a company-sponsored event who later injured another person in an accident when driving while drunk. Decisions from the highest courts of New York, Maine, and Kansas as well as Minnesota have held that employers should not be held liable to third parties for the actions of the employees who become intoxicated at company-sponsored events.

In *Meyers* v. *Grubaugh*, 750 P.2d 1031 (Kans. Ct. 1988), the employee drank beer before going off duty. While going home he was involved in an accident that caused injury to the plaintiff. The court held that the employer is not liable for off-duty conduct of the employees although the condition was caused while on duty. This is the majority rule, but courts in some states such as Texas and New Jersey would hold otherwise.

Although the law in most states protects the employer from third party liability when an employee becomes inebriated at an employer-sponsored event or while on duty, this does not mean that the employer should let an employee become intoxicated. There is always an exposure to lawsuit, and to some extent there is a moral obligation to control employees at a company-sponsored event such as a Christmas party.

The employer can avoid a possible lawsuit either by having a cash bar or by controlling the period of time that a free bar is open. One way to do this is to start serving the food after a short refreshment period. If an employee comes to the event intoxicated, she or he should be sent home so others can have a good time.

DEALING WITH AIDS IN THE WORKPLACE

In order to properly solve the problem of AIDS in the workplace, the employer should have a basic understanding of the nature of the disease, modes of transmission, testing

and disclosure of results, and the nature of the disability that results from the disease.[38] The best strategy for the employer is to have a planned program on the "back burner" to be used when the problem presents itself. In addition, the employer should be currently educated on all aspects of the disease. The purpose of this section on AIDS as distinguished from the section on drugs and alcohol is not to recommend a policy but to prepare the employer to cope with the problem when it exists.

Basic Understanding of the Disease

According to the U.S. Centers for Disease Control (CDC),[39] AIDS is reliably diagnosed as a disease that renders the human immune system incapable of fending off certain otherwise rare and fatal illnesses. It is a virus; its shorthand name is HIV virus. Medical science doesn't expect to find a cure until after 1990. It is predicted that the disease will spread rapidly until a cure is found.

The HIV virus infects persons in various stages:

1. In the first stage a person is exposed to the virus but has no physical symptoms. Medical science is not sure whether persons in this category can transmit the disease or what percentage will develop AIDS.

2. In the next stage a person gets mild warnings such as weight loss, abnormal fatigue, and swollen lymph nodes. This stage is sometimes called "AIDS-Related Complex." At this stage the victim may have moderate illness that affects the job but for the most part is able to work. Approximately 25 percent of this group will develop AIDS.

3. In the next stage the person will develop AIDS

---

[38]For detailed information on AIDS, see "Facts about Aids," U.S. Department of Health and Human Services, Public Health Services, August 1985; "Focus: AIDS in the Workplace," Prentice-Hall Personnel Management Series, Old Tappan, NJ 07675; "AIDS What Everyone Should Know," American College Assn. Rockville, MD 20855.

[39]*Morbidity and Mortality Weekly Report*, 34, no. 45 (1985) 682–94; see also no. 221 (1986) as to guidelines for health care workers.

from the previous stage. He or she will contract such rare diseases as Kaposi's sarcoma and certain types of rare pneumonia. This individual often will be able to work but will be absent due to illnesses more often than normal.[40]

4. In the final stage of AIDS a person is in the advanced stage of an illness. She or he requires extended hospitalization and is most likely unable to work. It is at this stage that death will come.

Transmission of the Disease

Medical data are in agreement that AIDS can be transmitted only through intimate sexual contact, intermingling of blood or blood products, and perinatal transmission from infected mothers to their offspring. All epidemiological evidence indicates that only blood and semen are the proven media of transmission.[41] There is no known case in which AIDS has been transmitted by any other means. Employees who claim that they can contract AIDS by sharing a restroom or a drinking fountain, washing in the same sink, sharing a desk or a chair, using the same telephone, eating at the same table, wearing the same protective clothing, or talking at a meeting have no medical data, and their position can be termed irrational and emotional. AIDS is hard to get; in fact, you have to go out of your way to get it.[42]

Statutory Protection of AIDS

Many employers are prohibited under federal, state, and local laws from discriminating against a handicapped person. The trend in various states and the courts is to consider AIDS as a handicap.[43] For the employer to take any other position than that the AIDS victim is handicapped would result in legal exposure unless a high court some time in the future holds otherwise. However, there are a number of factors determining whether an AIDS victim is handicapped, such as specific statutory coverage, job requirements, the employee's current medical condition, and the state of the medical knowledge about AIDS.

Tests for AIDS

In view of the available medical information, the employer has no demonstrable interest that would justify testing applicants or employees for AIDS. The reliability of the tests is questionable. If the test is positive the information is of little value to the employer, since the mere presence of AIDS does not affect the job. Since a test has no job-related purpose there is no justification for testing either applicants or present employees. In the case of applicants, they would create more job risk as to turnover, absenteeism, and medical care costs than an applicant without AIDS, but under most state laws this is not a reason for rejecting an applicant who is considered handicapped.

Knowledge of the presence of AIDS should be received only from the employee or when his or her physical condition interferes with the job relationship. AIDS may be the cause of absenteeism or poor performance, but the employment decision should be made on the job-related effect and not on the cause. When considering testing, one question should be asked: Why do I want to know? If you do know that an employee has AIDS, what use is the information, other than to expose confidentiality to those who do not have a need to know?

Problems with Co-workers of AIDS Victims

Legally there is nothing an employer can do when a co-worker refuses to work with an AIDS victim. The largest exposure comes

---

[40]Estimates for health care costs for this stage range from $91,000 to $140,000.

[41]*Morbidity and Mortality Weekly Report,* 34, no. 45 (1985), 682.

[42]See *Morbidity and Mortality Weekly Report,* 34, no. 45 (1985), 682.

[43]In *Mantolete* v. *Bolger,* 791 F.2d 784 (9th Cir. 1985), the court held that an AIDS victim was handicapped under Section 503 of the Rehabilitation Act.

from the employer's discharging or transferring the person with AIDS. If the employer wants to do something with the person who has AIDS, there are several good business reasons to take action. However, few of them will stand judicial review. Such defenses as that AIDS can be transmitted by casual contact, that the cost is too high on health insurance premiums, that the disease is fatal so it is useless to train because training costs will be too high, and that all employee with AIDS is more accident prone may sound logical to the employer, but the court will seldom agree. The defense of customer or co-worker rejection has been rejected in other areas, such as sex and race discrimination.[44]

The only answer to the co-worker who objects to working with a person with AIDS is education at all levels of the organization.[45] It is advisable to have a doctor as well as a supervisor present the information. One thing that can be done when an employee objects to working with a person with AIDS is to transfer him or her if possible and if the objecting employee will agree.

This policy of education or transferring is easily stated, but often it is not the solution to an all-too-frequent employee relations problem. Suppose an employee is suspected of being a "gay" who has recently had an extended period of absences and while at work looks flushed and weak. A group of employees approach the supervisor and state that they represent the concerns of all the employees in the department, who believe this person has AIDS. They demand that the employer test the employee and put him or her on an extended leave of absence until the test results are known. They express fear for their own health and that of their families. (This is the same problem as schools sometimes experience with students when a known AIDS victim is attending the same class.) The employees threaten that the whole department will refuse to work unless their demands are met or the employer can prove that the suspected employee does not have AIDS.

This puts the employer "between the rock and the hard place." The employees under the National Labor Relations Act have the right to withhold their services because of adverse working conditions.[46] If the employer concedes to the demands, there is a statute in most states that defines AIDS as a handicap and accommodation is necessary. Also the question of invasion of privacy when testing and releasing the results will be present unless there is a real reason to suspect. Transferring to another department would only create the problem with another group. Suppose the employee admits she or he has AIDS? This doesn't mean other employees can be affected unless through intimate sexual relations or contact with the affected blood, neither of which are job related, except in the health care industry, where precautions are taken. Legally the employer cannot do much about avoiding the exposure to a lawsuit.

The solution to this problem is not found in the literature or from legal counsel. The employer must probe for the solution. Try to convince the employees that their reservations are without medical authority; talk to the suspected employee and get his or her reaction and ask for help. If several alternatives are explored and none of them offers a solution, then the employer must "take the bull by the horns" and decide what is best for the organization. Either tell the complaining employees "to walk" or quit and get replacements or deal with the suspected employee in the best possible way to prevent a

---

[44]*Sprogis* v. *United Airlines, Inc.*, 44 F.2d 1194, 1199 (7th Cir. 1971) cert. denied; *Diaz* v. *Pan American Airways, Inc.*, 442 F.2d 389 (5th Cir. 1970) cert. denied; *Wigginess* v. *Fruchtman*, 482 F.Supp. 681 (S.D., N.Y. 1979), cert. denied.

[45]See "The Workplace and AIDS: A Guide to Services and Information, Part II," *Personnel Journal* (February 1988), p. 101, for a complete directory of organizations, education programs, consultants, and articles focusing on AIDS in the workplace.

[46]*NLRB* v. *Washington Aluminum Co.*, 370 U.S. 9 (1962).

lawsuit. The next time the problem comes up the solution may be entirely different, depending upon the employees involved.

Recommendations for Dealing with AIDS

1. AIDS should be treated like any other disability that is covered by state or federal laws against discrimination (more than three quarters of the states have such laws).
2. Educate co-workers about AIDS before an actual case presents itself. How it is transmitted and why it is not a work-related condition should be stressed.
3. Maintain confidentiality of all medical records.
4. Do not in any way discriminate against a person with AIDS. Be able to document any discipline as nondiscriminatory.
5. Do not exclude AIDS victims from training or consideration for promotion.
6. Accommodate or make a good effort to accommodate the AIDS victim by offering a transfer to a similar job or by any other reasonable action.
7. Don't test for AIDS, whether it be an applicant or a current employee.
8. Don't formulate a special policy for AIDS.

The employee with AIDS should not be terminated any more than an employee with heart disease or any other physical condition that may in the future cause the employer problems and additional expenses.

5

WORKING CONDITIONS BASED ON SEX

HISTORICAL DOMINANCE OF THE MALE IN THE WORKPLACE

One of the most difficult provisions of Title VII for some employers to accept is the requirement that persons of equal qualifications be given equal employment opportunities regardless of sex. The social norm that a woman's role is that of a housekeeper and child rearer is often the controlling factor. The norm permits the female to enter the labor market only from economic necessity or when men are not available. During World War II women were encouraged to enter the labor market as a contribution to the war effort. When G.I. Joe returned to the labor market after the war, "Rosie the Riveter" simply did not have the physical strength to do a man's job.[1] This thinking that the woman's place is in the home and not in the workplace was accepted in the courts as well as in social institutions. In the often-quoted case of *Muller* v. *State of Oregon*,[2] Supreme Court Justice Bremer at page 421 stated that "History disclosed the fact that woman has been dependent upon man. He established his control at the outset by superior physical strength and this control in various forms with diminishing intensity has continued to the present."

This stereotyped thinking among males was still in the Congress when Title VII was passed. Congressman Howard Smith of Virginia, as opposition to the act, reasoned that if sex were included as an amendment to Title VII, it would not pass.[3] Although this maneuver failed, members of Congress expressed their skepticism about women in the workplace by stating in Section 703(a)(e)(1) of Title VII that "where sex is a bona fide occupational qualification, reasonably necessary to the normal operation of the business, it would not be unlawful to discriminate on the basis of sex."

The enactment of Title VII did not suddenly change the patterns of sex discrimination that had been around for a hundred years. A start can be made by the law, but the remainder will have to be done by the courts, the economics of operating a business or enterprise, and a change in the reluctance on the part of women to bring a lawsuit.

Even though affirmative action programs are in place and working, they cannot undo in 15 years a practice that existed for over a hundred years. Behavior is derived more from social, traditional, cultural value than from legislation. Women in the workplace may be treated in a polite and proper way in the social context, but in the subconscious thinking of the decision maker such treatment is inappropriate for good business.

Many managers believe that it would be awkward to offer a single woman travel opportunities because a single woman should not be traveling alone or with a male co-worker; or they believe family priorities take precedence over the job and therefore transfers should not be offered. These inherited biases often create unintentional discriminatory behavior.

This chapter highlights some of the employment problems under Title VII and the Equal Pay Act that are particular to women in the workplace and are not as common with the other members of protected classes. There are different problems for the employer in the administration of equal employment opportunity for a minority, or for a Seventh Day Adventist than for a woman being harassed by a male. Sex discrimination in employment benefits is treated in Chapter 8.

TITLE VII RESTRICTIONS ON SEX DISCRIMINATION

Title VII states that an employee cannot be treated differently because of sex unless sex

---

[1]"Rosie the Riveter" was the working girl in World War II. The song was written to eulogize the part women were playing in replacing men in the war effort industries.

[2]208 U.S. 412 (1908).

[3]*Congressional Record*, Vol. 110, pp. 2577–84 (1964).

is a bona fide occupational qualification (BFOQ).[4]

In some early cases the only issue before the courts was whether women were treated differently from men and, if so, was there a BFOQ that justified such treatment. When a company refused to hire a woman with preschool children but hired men with preschool children, women were treated differently. The Supreme Court declared such a policy unlawful and remanded the matter to the lower court to determine whether a BFOQ existed.[5] What the court was really saying is that different treatment between males and females based solely on gender raises the issue of BFOQ.

The best example of whether the discrimination is gender based is found in those cases where pregnancy disability payments are excluded from health insurance plans but payments are included for men who become ill or disabled. In one situation the Supreme Court said that since men are not given disability for pregnancy, there is no benefit that men are given that women are not.[6] This case was decided under the Equal Protection Clause of the Fourteenth Amendment. The next question was: Would the same reasoning apply to a case under Title VII? Two years later the court said that it did. The court reasoned that there is no doubt that Congress did not intend to change the Constitution when Title VII was passed; in order to be in violation of Title VII, it must be gender based.[7]

Grooming and Dress Code as Preferential Treatment

Whenever a question of discrimination because of sex comes before the court, the issue is: "But for" the employee's sex would there have been different treatment? If management requires a dress code for women different from that for men, this would be discriminating unless a BFOQ could be shown.

A hospital required women to wear full uniform but allowed men to wear street clothes under their white laboratory coats. This is discriminatory on its face and when the court rejected the employer's argument that patients are used to seeing men dressed like doctors and women like nurses as a BFOQ, back pay was awarded to those who were discharged when they refused to wear the white uniforms.[8]

Another common discriminatory dress code is one that requires women to wear provocative clothing but that does not require men to do so. This is most common in bars and restaurants where the employer often argues that this is necessary for business reasons. However, this BFOQ argument is seldom accepted by the courts.

A leading case on dress is one in which the employer required the receptionist to wear provocative clothing but didn't require the men to do so. The court found this discriminatory.[9] Under present case law this could have been argued under harassment, since the Supreme Court has held that dress can be evidence of a hostile environment.[10]

Dress and grooming codes can be a violation of the race and nationality section of Title VII, and in these areas the courts are more apt to find BFOQ than where sex is involved.

BFOQ as a Defense in Sex Discrimination

Section 703(a)(e)(1) of Title VII specifically states that sex discrimination is lawful

---

[4]Although *bona fide occupational qualification* (BFOQ) is a statutory term defined in Title VII and *business necessity* was defined by the courts, the two items are often used simultaneously and are given the same strict interpretation.

[5]*Phillips* v. *Martin Marietta Corp.,* 400 U.S. 542 (1971).

[6]*Geduldig* v. *Aiello,* 417 U.S. 484 (1974).

[7]*General Electric* v. *Gilbert,* 429 U.S. 125 (1976). This ruling was voided by the Pregnancy Discrimination Act, as discussed in Chapter 8.

[8]*Cornell* v. *Sparrow Hospital Assn.,* 377 N.W.2d 755(Mich. 1985).

[9]*EEOC* v. *Sage Realty Corp.,* 507 F.Supp. 599 (S.D., N.Y. 1981).

[10]*Meritor Savings Bank, FSB* v. *Vinson,* 106 S.Ct. 2399 (1986).

if BFOQ can be shown. In race, religion, color, and national groups such an exception is conspicuously absent in the statute (although the courts have allowed the BFOQ defense in cases concerning these protected classes). When BFOQ is used as a defense, the employer automatically admits sex discrimination under the terms of the statute.

EEOC guidelines construe the exception narrowly, and the courts have followed. Where an airline alleged that females were an essential BFOQ for flight attendants, the court said that "discrimination based on sex is valid only when the essence of the business operation would be undermined by not hiring members of one sex exclusively."[11] The Supreme Court in upholding a BFOQ for an Alabama Statute that required minimum height and weight (which excluded 33 percent of the women and only 1 percent of the men) stated that the prison system warranted the exclusion of women. The court was careful to point out that the exception to individual capacity is "extremely narrow."[12]

From the cases decided since Dothard, it appears the BFOQ will be decided very narrowly on a case-by-case basis and a narrow interpretation will be given. There are few guidelines for BFOQ except that if the employer had reasonable factual basis to believe that substantially all women would be unable to perform safely and efficiently the assigned duties of the job, sex discrimination would be legal.

Often it is the employer's perception that females are not qualified for the job. In *U.S. v. Gregory*, 818 F.2d 1114 (4th Cir. 1987), the county sheriff refused to hire female correctional officers for an all-male county jail. He argued that this would infringe upon the privacy of inmates and guards because of the personal contact required by the job. The court ruled that the county failed to show that gender was a BFOQ for correctional officers. According to the court, the employer could not demonstrate "why it could not accommodate, through reasonable modification of the facility and job functions, female corrections officers." This is an example of where the job title and the fact that it was an all-male jail would indicate that sex would be a BFOQ for correctional officers. However, the court looked into the job content and held that sex would not prevent women from performing the duties of the job.

As in other discrimination situations, there is no substitute (if at all feasible) for giving the employee an opportunity to perform before using BFOQ as a defense. Job assignment based on sex cannot be defended except in rare cases such as safety or privacy consideration. Normally customer preference is not considered as BFOQ. When an employer stated that foreign customers are prejudiced against women, the court said that sex discrimination for salespersons is invalid as a matter of law.[13]

Discrimination because of Marriage

The presence of the historical social norm that the workplace is not for women makes it appropriate that when women get married they should be encouraged to leave the labor market. Airlines for years had a no-marriage rule for stewardesses. The federal postal services in 1913 decided that married women should not hold a classified position.[14] The Economy Act of 1932 (Section 213) stated that married women in the federal service would be retained only if they were more efficient than their husbands.[15]

Title VII declares a no-marriage rule un-

---

[11]*Diaz* v. *Pan American World Airways, Inc.*, 442 F.2d 385 (5th Cir. 1971).

[12]*Dothard* v. *Rawlinson*, 433 U.S. 321 (1977). However, usually weight requirements are not considered a BFOQ, as in *Weeks* v. *Southern Bell Telephone and Telegraph Co.*, 408 F.2d 228 (5th Cir. 1969).

[13]*Fernandez* v. *Wynn Oil Co.*, 653 F.2d 1275 (9th Cir. 1981).

[14]U.S. Civil Service Commission, *Women in the Federal Service*, 2nd ed. (Washington, DC: Government Printing Office, 1938).

[15]U.S. Civil Service Commission, *Women*, 1938.

lawful when it does not apply to both sexes equally,[16] but it does allow the application of BFOQ as provided in Section 703(e). What this means to the struggling personnel practitioner is that if two employees get married, a rule could require that one must go but the rule could not state which one, unless on some basis other than sex. The rule also means that if one had a superior-subordinate relationship, BFOQ could be a defense on a showing that the spouse relationship interfered with the efficient operation of the business.

The leading decision pertaining to a no-spouse rule was a case where there was statistical evidence that because of a no-spouse rule, a disparate impact in hiring females resulted (73 female applicants were rejected compared to 3 males).[17] The court found what most personnel practitioners know, problems between married employees lead to grief for employers, and BFOQ permits the no-spouse rule. The court also said that married couples working together could cause emotional problems that would affect their work performance. If one spouse has a dispute with the employer or co-worker, the other spouse may become involved.

The Yuhas decision has been followed by other courts to the extent that if the no-spouse rule is administered properly, it is not sex discrimination although there may be a disparate impact.

The rule has been extended to unmarried couples living together. The courts will not make a distinction and hold that an employer is not in violation for refusing to hire or continue to employ a person living with another employee.[18] However, some states include marriage as a protected class in their discrimination laws,[19] and in those states it would be a violation to discriminate against employees who are not married. In *State by Johnson* v. *Porter Farms, Inc.*, 382 N.W.2d 543 (Minn. App. 1986), the court held that termination of an unmarried employee for living with a person of the opposite sex violated the provision on marital status,[20] since married persons live together.

In those states that have statutes protecting the marital status discrimination for hiring and promotion, the employer is permitted to prevent a superior-subordinate relationship between spouses by transfers or in the hiring process. The employer usually can show BFOQ in this situation.[21]

Sex Discrimination in Work Assignments

It is a well-established principle in anti-discrimination law that one cannot determine categorically that all females are incapable of performing certain tasks.

When considering qualifications for promotion under a labor agreement, labor relations practitioners discovered early in their careers that unless the applicant is given an opportunity to perform, it is difficult to win in arbitration. In some cases a legitimate reason can be shown for not giving the opportunity to perform other than subjective reasons such as safety or exposure to property damage; then the failure to give the opportunity would not be a damaging factor to the case.

In work assignments for females it is advisable to permit performance before rejection unless there is substantial, objective evidence why they cannot do the job or the safety of others would be jeopardized if they

---

[16]42 USC Sect. 2000(d) et al.

[17]*Yuhas* v. *Libbey Owen Ford Co.*, 562 F.2d 496 (7th Cir. 1977), cert. denied.

[18]*Espinoza* v. *Thomas*, 580 F.2d 346 (8th Cir. 1978).

[19]Michigan, Minnesota, Montana, Rhode Island, and Washington, to name a few.

[20]See also *Slohoda* v. *United Parcel Serv., Inc.*, 475 A.2d 618 (N.J. Super. A.D. 1984) where an employee was discharged for having sexual intercourse out of wedlock when he was married. The court allowed a cause of action because the policy did not prevent an unmarried person from having sexual intercourse.

[21]For further information on marital discrimination, see Leonard Bierman and Cynthia D. Fisher, "Anti-Nepotism Rules Applied to Spouses; Business and Legal Viewpoints," *Labor Law Journal*, 35, no. 10 (October 1984), 634.

are permitted to perform. Courts that have considered the issue of female work assignments have held that the employer cannot determine employment opportunities on the basis of physical capabilities and endurance of women as a group. Where it was required to lift heavy objects, the job could not be denied the employee because she was a female.[22]

In another heavy-object-lifting case the employer rejected a female because it was alleged that she did not have the physical ability to perform the job. The court said that the applicant must be given a reasonable opportunity to demonstrate her ability to perform the duties.[23] In the Long case the court also applied the same rule when a job was refused because of race. The employer who denies work assignments to females because of alleged limitations of females needs to be reminded of the song about Rosie the Riveter.

SEXUAL HARASSMENT— DEFINITION AND CONTROL

Harassment in the workplace is a violation of Title VII when a member of the protected group is treated differently from other persons. The act does not have a specific provision prohibiting harassment as such, but the courts[24] and later the EEOC have so interpreted the statute. Racial harassment would be a case in which a black would be subject to racial slurs and pranks or other bigoted acts of employees or supervisors.[25]

A nationality harassment situation involved a supervisor who, in order to communicate a no-smoking rule to a single

violator (who was German), posted a no-smoking sign in German. Harassment was admitted but the employee did not subsequently violate the no-smoking rule. (The relief requested was removal of the sign.)

Most harassment situations involve sexual harassment. It is difficult to determine what came first in the workplace: sexual relations or sexual harassment. Until recently, management did not have to contend with the sexual relations between employees either within or outside the working relationship as long as they did not interfere with work performance or it did not occur on company time.[26] If management were aware of sexual advances, it would ignore them as a normal result of the attraction between the sexes and something that would be worked out between the parties involved. If in extreme cases correction were needed, the matter was handled on a confidential and individual basis. The typical manager reasoned (and many still do) that because of the personal nature of sexual harassment, dealing with it openly would sometimes create more problems than it would solve. Another reason for management's reluctance is that sexual advances are often difficult to define. Acquiescence and encouragement are always possibilities. Also, female employees are frequently reluctant to bring the matter to the attention of the employer for fear of embarrassment or because of creating an adverse condition with the supervisor or co-worker and uncertainty about what action management will take.[27]

Several surveys have been made to determine whether sexual harassment in the workplace is common. In general these surveys found that unwanted sexual harassment existed for more than 40 percent of the employees reporting; 1 to 2 percent reported being coerced into sexual relations,

---

[22]*Rosefeld* v. *Southern Pacific Co.*, 444 F.2d 1219 (9th Cir. 1971).

[23]*Long* v. *Sapp*, 502 F.2d 34 (5th Cir. 1974).

[24]Harassment received its first formal judicial recognition in *Williams* v. *Saxbe*, 413 F.Supp. 654 (D.C. D.C. 1976), where the court held that Title VII's prohibition on sex discrimination includes a prohibition on sexual harassment.

[25]*Hamilton* v. *Rodgers*, 783 F.2d 1306 (5th Cir. 1986).

[26]Rules about no sexual relations at the workplace are difficult to enforce because they are a rarity to witness.

[27]For further reading, see Paula M. Popovich and Betty Jo Licata, "Role Model Approach to Sexual Harassment," *Journal of Management*, 13, no. 1 (Spring 1987), 149–61.

which is the most extreme form of sexual harassment. The 1 or 2 percent may not seem large but if the figures are accurate, based on the number of women employed, about 400,000 working women a year have unwanted sexual relations, which could be called employment rape.[28]

These surveys may not be entirely reliable because there is no legal definition of sexual harassment. It means different things to different employees.

Legal Basis for Sexual Harassment

Sexual harassment is a form of sex discrimination, but it is distinguishable in that the conduct involves sexual favors or the creation of an environment that tolerates unwelcome sexual advances or language. Where discrimination because of an employee's sex involves an adverse employment decision, this violates Title VII. Also sex discrimination and sexual harassment can be distinguished in that sex discrimination is usually a single act, while sexual harassment usually involves continual conduct.[29]

The EEOC guidelines were issued in 1980 and codified the court decisions of the previous four years. Certain parts of these guidelines (Sect. 1604.11) have judicial acceptance. 29 CFR Section 1604.11 states:

Harassment on the basis of sex is a violation of §703 of Title VII. Unwelcome sexual advances, request for sexual favors, and other verbal or physical conduct of a sexual nature constitutes sexual harassment when: (1) submission to such conduct is made either explicitly or implicitly a term or condition of an individual's employment, (2) submission to or rejection of such conduct by an individual is used as the basis for employment decisions affecting such individual, or (3) such conduct has the purpose or effect of unreasonably interfering with an individual's work performance or creating an intimidating, hostile, or offensive working environment.

The reason sexual harassment is unlawful is that Title VII prevents one sex from being favored over another; where a male favors a female and not other males, there is a violation. By the same principle a male could be sexually harassed by a female and the courts have so held. A male sexually harassing a male is unlawful because females are not given the same attention;[30] however, a bisexual cannot be guilty of harassment because no favors are shown to either sex.

Using the same reasoning, a transsexual would not be protected by Title VII since it is yet to be determined medically which sex is being favored.[31] Where a transsexual was denied use of female restroom facilities, claiming to be a female at the time of applying for a job, and the employer discharged for misrepresentation since the plaintiff was a male in the employer's opinion, the court said discharge was not a violation of Title VII as the act is not intended to cover transsexualism.[32]

If the harassment would not have occurred "but for" the employee's sex, it is harassment because it constitutes an unequal condition of employment.[33] However, the

---

[28]"Sexual Harassment in Federal Government—An Update," U.S. Merit Systems Protection Board, Washington, DC, July 1988. Also see Susan E. Martin, "Sexual Harassment: The Link Between Gender, Stratification, Sexuality and Women's Economic Status," in Jo Freeman (ed.), *Women: A Feminist Perspective* (Mountain View, CA: Mayfield, 1984).

[29]In *Shore* v. *Federal Express*, 777 F.2d 1155 (6th Cir. 1985), a female employee was involved in an intimate relationship with a male. The male was promoted to an executive position and, as a supervisor, terminated the female because the relationship interfered with office operations. This was sex discrimination but not harassment, since the conduct did not involve favors and was not continual, and since an unpleasant, sexually unacceptable working environment was not created. Also see *De Cintio* v. *Westchester County Medical Center*, 807 F.2d 304 (2nd Cir. 1986).

[30]*Wright* v. *Methodist Youth Services*, 511 F.Supp. 307 (Ill. 1981); *Joyner* v. *AAA Cooper Transportation*, 597 F.Supp. 537 (Ala. 1983).

[31]A transsexual is described as an individual who is mentally of one sex but physically of another. 63 ALR3d 1199 (1975).

[32]*Sommers* v. *Budget Marketing, Inc.*, 667 F.2d 748 (8th Cir. 1982).

[33]*McKinney* v. *Dole*, 765 F.2d 1129 (D.C. Cir. 1985).

conduct must be sufficiently persuasive to alter the conditions of employment.[34] In deciding whether there has been sexual harassment, the EEOC and the courts will look at the facts as a whole and the totality of the circumstances. Some courts will consider evidence of the complainant's sex life to determine whether the conduct constitutes sexual harassment.[35]

Reverse Sexual Harassment

The EEOC guidelines [296FR Sect. 1604.11] also deal with what might be called sexual harassment in reverse. In this type of case an employee climbs the corporate ladder, at the expense of other qualified persons, by giving sexual favors to the supervisor. The qualified employees passed over have a claim for sexual discrimination. One court that has considered this situation [*Toscano* v. *Nimmo*, 570 F.Supp. 1197 (D.C. Del. 1983)] has upheld EEOC guidelines stating that when a less-qualified employee is promoted because of sexual favors, the more-qualified employee not promoted was sexually harrassed when refused the promotion.

Normally a third party does not have a cause of action. In *Blaw-Knox Foundry and Mill* v. *NLRB*, 646 F.2d 113 (4th Cir. 1981), the court stated that employee action in protecting a female cousin from a supervisor was not a protected activity. However, where a supervisor supported the employee's protest of sexual harassment and was discharged, the court held a protected activity [*NLRB* v. *Downslopes Industries*, 676 F.2d 1114 (6th Cir. 1981)].

Sexual Harassment as Common Law Tort

Sexual harassment may also be grounds for common law tort claims such as as-

sault, battery, intentional infliction of emotional distress, intentional interference with contract, negligent supervision or negligent dismissal, and invasion of privacy.[36] If there is a legal basis for doing so, the employee will bring an action under the common law rather than under Title VII because there would be a jury trial and punitive damages would be allowed rather than back pay and reinstatement as under Title VII. This type of case is on the increase, and it makes sexual harassment more of an exposure. Since the 11th, 8th, 7th Circuit Courts of Appeals and several states have already allowed punitive damages for sexual harassment, there is no reason to believe that it will not continue.[37] In *Lucas* v. *Brown and Root, Inc.*, 736 F.2d 1202 (8th Cir. 1984), the court said that the employee's having to give her body to keep her job amounted to prostitution, and a supervisor status doesn't give the power to damage the employee.

When the employer has knowledge and fails to do anything about it, the courts in almost every case have held the employer liable under Title VII.[38] However, if they find a blatant example of inaction they will allow a negligence action before a jury and allow them to find punitive damages, as was the situation in *Ambrose* v. *U.S. Steel* 38 EPD para. 3564 (CCH) (D.C. Calif. 1985), where management did nothing about vulgar and offensive epithets.

State of the Law—Meritor Case

Many questions about what is or is not sexual harassment were cleared up in the first case on the subject to come before the Supreme Court. In the landmark case of *Meritor Savings Bank, FSB* v. *Vinson* (herein-

---

[34]*Downes* v. *FAA*, 775 F.2d 288(D.C. Cir. 1985).

[35]See *Laudenslager* v. *Covert*, 415 N.W.2d 254 (Mich. App. 1987).

[36]This type of tort will be discussed in more detail in Chapter 17 on malpractice.

[37]*Phillips* v. *Smalley Maintenance Services*, 711 F.2d 1524 (11th Cir. 1983); *Bell* v. *Crackin Good Bakers*, 777 F. 2d 1497 (7th Cir. 1986).

[38]*Katz* v. *Dole*, 709 F.2d 251 (4th Cir. 1983).

after called Meritor), 106 S.Ct. 2399 (1986),[39] Ms. Vinson alleged that Taylor, who was a vice president of the bank, had asked for sexual relations with her. At first she refused, but later yielded out of fear of losing her job. She testified that she had sexual relations with the manager from 40 to 50 times in the previous four years both during and after business hours but that she never reported her action to any of the manager's supervisors nor did she attempt to use the complaint procedure that the employer had established. She also alleged that Taylor fondled her in front of other employees and followed her into the women's restroom when she went there alone, exposed himself to her, and even on occasion forcibly raped her. These activities ceased after she started going with a steady boyfriend. About a year later she took sick leave for an indefinite period. Three months later the employer fired her for excessive sick leave.

She brought suit alleging sexual harassment during the four years of employment. The district court held that she was not subjected to sexual harassment but merely was involved in a broken love affair. The appellate court reversed the decision, holding that the action was a violation of Title VII even though no job opportunities were involved. The court imputed notice to the employer since the manager obviously knew about the harassment. Since the manager was the representative of the employer, the employer knew or should have known.

The Supreme Court in a unanimous decision held that a violation of Title VII is predicated on two types of harassment:

1. Those involving economic benefits
2. Those where a hostile environment is created

The provocative dress and speech of the alleged victim and voluntary participation in sexual affairs do not preclude a finding that the episodes were unwanted and therefore unlawful. The Court said that the employer is not relieved of liability in all situations where there is an announced policy against sexual harassment or by the failure of the victim to utilize existing grievance procedure. (In this specific case the grievance procedure required the employee to complain to her immediate supervisor—the person she wanted to complain about.)

The Court majority was not willing to impute knowledge in all cases in which a supervisor was involved as had been ruled by the appellate court and the EEOC guidelines. It was stated that the facts and circumstances in each case should determine whether the employer had notice, but that the absence of notice did not necessarily insulate the employer from liability. Many state courts impute knowledge.

This decision summarizes all previous appellate court decisions on sexual harassment and clearly defines sexual harassment as unwelcome but goes further in saying that voluntary participation does not necessarily mean that the approach is welcome. The Court invalidated the EEOC guidelines that state that you can impute knowledge where the supervisor is involved at least where no job opportunities are related to the activity. The Court thus reversed several appellate court decisions that have upheld the guidelines. The employer can be liable even though there was no knowledge and established grievance procedure was not used, but it depends upon the facts of each case. Knowledge is not automatic because the supervisor is involved, as stated in EEOC guidelines.

This landmark decision stated that in order to find sexual harassment there must be three elements:

1. It must be unwelcomed.
2. The employer must have knowledge, either actual or imputed.
3. Either job opportunities must be involved or a hostile environment created.

The Meritor decision cleared up many conflicting standards previously developed by

---

[39]This case attracted considerable attention from the media and scholars. See Richard Greene, "Pattern of Fornication," *Forbes*, 137, no. 16 (June 1986), 770.

the courts and EEOC in each of these elements. The decision must be read in detail to aid the employer in policy development.

Unwelcomed Harassment

The court recognized that a person may be the victim of sexual harassment even though she participated in or condoned acts of a sexual nature. It is difficult for an employer to know whether an intimate relationship is "unwelcomed" or at what point it will be welcomed. It appears the only way the employer will know is for the employee to say that advances or an environment are presently unwelcomed. The ruling on admissibility of evidence concerning the complainant's sexual behavior will help, since the employer can argue that because of the behavior a reasonable person would believe that the conditions were not entirely unwelcomed.

Job Opportunities or Hostile Environment[40]

There are two types of sexual harassment: quid pro quo harassment and hostile environment. Quid pro quo is defined as being forced to choose between acquiescence to a superior's sexual demands or forfeiting an employment benefit (for example, promotion, wage increase, leave of absence, or continued employment). The common situation is where the employee is terminated for refusing sexual demands of the supervisor. Since this type is easily identified by its objectivity, there is little problem with it.

Hostile environment claims are more difficult to prove because it is more subjective in that it does not involve a specific employment benefit and can involve a co-worker. It is defined by the EEOC guidelines as an interference with the employee's work behavior or a creation of an offensive work environment.[41] The Meritor case merely reaffirmed the appellate court's position that hostile environment is a violation of Title VII and that provocative dress requirements and verbal statements could constitute hostile environment. It did not specifically define hostile environment. The plaintiff in Meritor was not required or asked to give sexual favors as a condition of promotion. From the testimony, her promotions were based upon merit, the employer liability was therefore based on hostile environment and not quid pro quo harassment. The court held in this situation that the manager's behavior of exposure, fondling, and having sex relations on and off the job 40 to 50 times in the last four years constituted a hostile environment.

Since Meritor, the sixth circuit in *Rabidue* v. *Osceola Refining Co.,* 805 F.2d 611 (6th Cir. 1986), established standards of proof for sexual harassment based on hostile environment under Meritor. This was a situation in which a co-worker often made obscene comments and directed vulgar remarks at the plaintiff. The management was aware of the co-worker's vulgarity but was unsuccessful in its attempts to curb his offensive behavior. (There was no evidence of discipline.) Also other male employees sometimes displayed pictures or posters of a sexual nature in work areas that the plaintiff and other female employees frequented.[42] The plaintiff was ultimately discharged for just cause and sued for sexual harassment under Title VII.

The court held that in order to find hostile environment the employment conditions must interfere with work performance and affect the psychological well-being of a reasonable person in a similar environment. The plaintiff must show that she suffered some injury or was actually offended by such con-

---

[40]For a more complete discussion, see Robert K. Robinson, Delaney J. Kirk, and Elvis C. Stephens, "Hostile Environment: A Review of the Implications of *Meritor Savings Bank* v. *Vinson,*" *Labor Law Journal,* 38, no. 3 (March 1987), 179–83.

[41]29 CFR 16.011 (A).

[42]In *Klink* v. *Ramsey County,* 397 N.W.2d 894 (Minn. App. 1986), the court said it takes more than photos to create a hostile environment. An employer is not required to maintain a "pristine work environment."

duct as a result of the abusive work environment. The court, in considering whether there is a hostile environment, must evaluate the conditions existing before the plaintiff was hired, the background and experience of the plaintiff, her co-workers and supervisors, and the totality of the physical environment.

Whether a hostile environment exists must be evaluated on a case-by-case basis. The court in Rabidue noted that in some work environments sexual jokes and vulgarity are extremely common and that Title VII was not meant to bring about "a transformation in the social mores of American workers." The remarks may be annoying, but if they are not so offensive as to have seriously affected the plaintiff there is no hostile environment.

This is the first case after Meritor to define hostile environment, and some other jurisdictions may not interpret Meritor so conservatively. They may follow the dissent in this case, wherein it was stated that this was an antifemale environment and the reasonable-person test fails to account for the wide divergence between most women's view and that of men. The definition of a hostile environment will be before the courts again, and it is a business decision whether the Rabidue case or the dissent should be followed and whether the employer should consider the Rabidue environment as hostile. However, in sixth circuit Rabidue is law.

Knowledge Imputed to Employer—State of the Law

This is one of the cloudiest areas of the Meritor decision. Surveys show that only a small percentage of employees who are being harassed will report it to the employer. The EEOC guidelines[43] explicitly state that employers are responsible for all acts of sexual harassment in the workplace where the supervisor is involved, unless it can be shown that the employer took immediate action to correct. The Supreme Court was widely split

on whether they should adopt the guidelines,[44] but the majority held that employers are not absolutely liable for acts of supervisors. Most appellate courts who have considered the issue state that knowledge is imputed to the employer where the supervisor is involved and when such harassment is quid pro quo.[45] Some lower court cases after Meritor have indicated that this will be extended to the hostile environment situation. In Meritor the court had no trouble in finding that knowledge was imputed, since the grievance procedure required the plaintiff to go to the person involved, and since the employee was not encouraged to complain, the court imputed knowledge. From the dictum in the case, the court indicates that if there was a grievance procedure and a policy, knowledge would not be imputed, but we cannot be sure.

The Meritor case cleared up many issues, such as that hostile environment is a violation under Title VII; that sexual harassment must be unwelcomed and acquiescence doesn't always mean that it is welcome; and that unless the employee can report to some other member of management than the person involved, knowledge will be imputed. However, whether there is hostile environment without specific proof that work performance is affected and whether proof is required that the employee is actually offended by the environment are still open questions.

Control of Harassment

Although the Meritor case did not specifically define what is unwelcome, when knowledge is imputed, or what is meant by hostile environment, the employer can define these elements with an enforceable policy. The employer can recognize that there are some gray areas and by policy can go further than the law and still not be contrary,

---

[43]CFR Sect. 1604.11(d).

[44]The court was unanimous on all other issues but split five to four on this issue.

[45]See *Miller* v. *Bank of America* 600 F.2d 211 (9th Cir. 1979); *Horn* v. *Duke Homes,* 755 F.2d 599 (6th Cir. 1985).

which would prevent exposure and still not interrupt the operation. It is then the policy that is violated rather than depending on an uncertain area in the law. The law recognizes that the employer may from time to time have difficulty in eradicating sexual harassment since it is difficult to define, but what the court will not recognize is the failure to draft a clear, concise policy.

If the employee complains about being harassed, don't call your lawyer but investigate immediately. In *Swentek* v. *U.S. Air, Inc.*, 830 F.2d 552 (4th Cir. 1987), the court held that prompt investigation and a written warning relieved the employer of liability. The employer took steps to remedy the charge and it was adequate.

If the employee has a bona fide belief that she or he is being harassed, this should be recognized by the employer regardless of whether the initial thought is that it is meritless. Through separate interviews with both the person involved and the complainant, the employer can determine how to relieve the situation and eliminate exposure to a lawsuit. At this point it is an employee relations problem and not a legal question. Whether the facts come within the Meritor case or whether there is a gray area is immaterial for policy enforcement. The legal issue does not arise until a complaint is filed and an adverse relationship is created. However, immediately doing something about the complaint will usually avoid a complaint and the legal fees that follow.

Need for Immediate Investigation

Whether or not an investigation is immediate is determined on a case-by-case basis. Some of the considerations are:

1. What is the harassment complained of? (Sexual favors for job opportunities would demand quicker investigation than a hostile environment.)
2. What is the size of the company? (A large company with a bureaucracy of management would take longer to start than a small company where everybody reports to the CEO.)
3. How well does the company know the employees involved or how much investigation is needed to get both sides of the facts before the complaint can be evaluated?[46]

When making a decision as to whether harassment exists, it is essential not to falsely accuse an employee of harassment, because this is just as serious as not doing anything with an employee who is guilty of harassment. Some employers have an outside source do the investigation; this makes it more impartial.

Necessary Ingredients for Policy

In the Meritor case the Supreme Court said that in order to bring an action for sexual harassment it must be shown that it is unwelcome, the employer has knowledge or there is reason to impute knowledge, there are job opportunities involved, or there is hostile environment. How the courts subsequently define these elements is not important if the employer drafts the proper policy, which will be internally enforced, and each of these ingredients is defined by the policy, although they may be gray for the courts.

1. The policy should prohibit both quid pro quo and environmental harassment.
2. As to knowledge, the policy should require the employee to report any unwelcome event or condition. A failure to report will indicate a welcome relationship or environment.
3. The hostile environment should be defined as containing sexual advances, innuendos, vulgar statements, and so on that the employee considers hostile or objects to. Although the law doesn't consider isolated instances as a hostile environment, the employer can do so for investigation purposes.
4. The policy should warn the employee that once it is established beyond a doubt that the policy (not necessarily the law) has been violated, swift and severe action will be taken.
5. If substantial facts cannot be established, it should be explained to the complaining party

---

[46]*Dornheckler* v. *Malibu Grand Prix Corp.*, 828 F.2d 307 (5th Cir. 1987).

that the situation will be monitored for a period of time.

This policy should clearly define an unwelcomed sexual relationship under the policy. It is unwelcomed when the employee says so. Any unwelcomed advances or sexual statements of any kind will be investigated once they are reported or otherwise become known to the employer.

Reporting Procedure for Policy

An environment is hostile for purposes of investigation and action when the employees say so or the management using the "reasonable-person" test considers it hostile. As in other necessary elements for sexual harassment, the policy puts the responsibility on the employee to define harassment; the law steps in only after the employee complains and the employer disagrees and does nothing about it. Inasmuch as the policy stresses reporting, a procedure should be included in the policy or otherwise communicated to supervisors and employees. The essential elements of a reporting procedure are these:

1. State that a complaint of sexual conduct can be reported to any member of management, but the name of the person (or persons) involved must be disclosed.
2. State the method of investigation and the appropriate time limits. (Time limits should be very short.)
3. If the complaint is valid under the facts, take immediate action.
4. Give assurance that the information will be confidential and there will be no retaliation whatsoever.
5. Clearly state the company's position on failure to report: that in this case it means that it is a welcome relationship and the employee doesn't consider the environment hostile. State that fear of loss of a job is not a reason for not reporting to some member of management.

The existence of a policy doesn't relieve the employer of liability unless it requires reporting. In the Meritor case the policy was of little help since the employee had to report to the immediate supervisor, who was the person involved. In *Yates* v. *Avco Corp.,* 819 F.2d 630 (6th Cir. 1987), the court stated that although a policy existed it was not effective in encouraging the employee to report; therefore knowledge was imputed and the employer was held liable.

The exhibits that follow will help the employer get started on a policy to control sexual harassment in the workplace.

This recommended policy goes further than most companies are willing to go.[47] However, in view of the appellate courts' imputing knowledge when supervision is in-

---

[47]"Sexual Harassment: Employer Policies and Problems," PPF Survey no. 144 (Washington, DC: Bureau of National Affairs, 1987).

EXHIBIT 5-1   *Procedure for Investigating a Complaint*

1. Both complainant and person involved will be separately interviewed.
2. The interview will take place within ＿＿ days after management has knowledge of the unwelcome incident or condition.
3. If facts are in dispute no action will be taken until, in the opinion of independent investigators, the facts are established.
4. Both the complainant and the person involved will be told of the results of the investigation and their legal rights will be explained in writing.
5. No action will be taken unless there is more than one incident of harassment.
6. Discipline will be given according to the facts of each case, but the matter will immediately be corrected where necessary.

EXHIBIT 5-2   *Harassment Notice*

DATE _____

For many years the management of this company has by policy and to the public stated that it is an equal opportunity employer. All management employees have, without exception, been instructed to strictly adhere to this policy. There are, however, rare instances of unwelcomed harassment of minorities, nationalities, and persons because of their sex, age, or religion. Any type of discriminatory action or harassment of one employee against another because of race, age, religion, sex, or national origin that interferes with good working conditions or job opportunities is a violation of company policy and employees responsible will be subject to severe disciplinary action. Our commitment as an equal opportunity employer applies to all employees including members of management, and we intend to enforce it by immediately investigating all known incidents or complaints of employees and taking necessary disciplinary action where incidents are found to be in violation of company policy. Employees who are subjected to harassment of any type are required to report to any member of management any violations of the above policy. The report will be confidential, given to only those persons who have a need to know. Failure to report any type of harassment will be considered by management to indicate an acceptable relationship or that the incidents do not create unreasonable working conditions. You can be assured there will be no retaliation for reporting. The company also recognizes that false accusation of harassment can have serious effects upon the accused. Therefore, false accusations will result in the same severe disciplinary action applicable to one found guilty of harassment.

volved and the five to four split in the Supreme Court, the employer must find some way to have the matter reported. Forcing the employee to report appears to be the only solution.

Sexual harassment conduct is not any different from any other undesirable conduct with which the employer must cope in the workplace. Enforcement of house rules is always a problem; prohibition of sexual harassment is just another rule that must be enforced.

Sexual harassment in the workplace is a difficult problem to control. History reveals that sexual behavior has caused persons to give up kingdoms, ruined political and religious careers, and caused business careers to fail. This will not change because of the existence of a policy. Employees, supervisors, and managers will continue to risk their jobs, reputation, and family structure for sexual activity. Employers who think that the problem will go away or will not become one of the major consequences will realize their mistake only after they have paid large monetary sums in damages or have adverse public and employee reaction because of their failure to respond to employee harassment complaints.

An effective policy and procedure may cause the activity to go underground, but the employer will be relieved of liability if the policy is effective. The key to control of sexual harassment is to have employees report it, which forces the person involved to define it as unwelcome.

OFF-DUTY CONDUCT AND SEX DISCRIMINATION UNDER TITLE VII

Off-duty conduct begs the question of where the employee's right to privacy ends and the employer's right to interfere begins. Compared to other areas such as drugs, moonlighting with competition, and arbitration under the labor agreement, the area where the personnel practitioner has the most frustrating problem is where the male-female relationship enters the workplace. The problem is not new, but the increase of women in the work force, the advent of Title VII, and the assertiveness of women's rights require a new discipline for the personnel management function.[48] [In 1945, 3 of every 10 women were in the work force. In 1988, 7 of every 10 women were working (*Monthly Labor Review*, U.S. Dept. of Labor, March 1988).]

It is rare when a social relationship does not become work related, because there is a "built-in" connection. Unintentional promotions, pay increases, job assignments, giving time off, and excusing tardiness because of sexual favors are often the result of an off-duty relationship that at the outset is none of the employer's business.

Control of Social Relationships

When the off-duty relationship ceases or one of the persons involved terminates or is promoted, the problem is created and it is very difficult to defend any employer's decision. In *Hunt* v. *Mid-American Employees Credit Union,* 384 N.W.2d 853 (Minn. 1986), there existed an intimate relationship between a secretary and a sales manager. The two went on a business trip and upon their return the employer discharged the secretary.[49] She immediately filed a sex discrimination charge. The sales manager objected so strenuously that there was a question of his loyalty, so he was also discharged. He filed a wrongful discharge suit based on the handbook. The

employer successfully defended both charges but lost two good employees and incurred large legal costs as the result of off-duty conduct that originally was none of the company's business.

Social relationships should be discouraged at the very beginning, but care should be taken not to interfere with privacy rights. The employees should be informed of the hazard both to themselves and to the company. Education and the hard sell is the best approach. The relationship should not be discouraged, only the problem created when the two people are working for the same employer.

If the education and "hard sell" approach does not work, the employer may want to consider stopping the relationship, as was the case in *Patton* v. *J.C. Penney,* 719 P.2d 854 (Ore. 1986), where the employee refused to stop dating a co-worker and was discharged. The court held, in stating that the employer's interest outweighs the employee's right of privacy, that this was not a violation of public policy or an invasion of privacy.

Discipline for Off-Duty Conduct

When considering whether off-duty conduct can be just cause for discipline, the courts and arbitrators are influenced by the following factors:

1. The damage to the employer's business or reputation
2. The effect on co-workers of off-duty relationships or conduct
3. The effect the off-duty relationship or conduct may have on the employee's on-duty performance and on an efficient work force

In all these factors the main element is that there must be a connection between off-duty activity and a detriment to the work relationship.[50] One way to avoid exposure to lit-

---

[48]See Robert C. Ford, "Should Cupid Come to the Workplace," *Personnel Administrator,* 32, no. 10 (October 1987).

[49]In a graduate school course, the professor gave his class what was later realized to be the best advice this author has ever received in college: "Never have an affair with your secretary." That advice is more appropriate now than it was 40 years ago.

[50]For further reference on this subject, see Marvin Hill, Jr. and Donald Dawson, "Discharge for Off-Duty Misconduct in Private and Public Sectors," *The Arbitration Journal,* 40, no. 2 (June 1985), 24; also, Adolph Koven and Susan Smith, *Just Cause: The Seven Tests* (Dubuque, IA: Kendall/Hunt, 1985), pp. 104–9.

igation is to communicate by policy or rules at the outset that the company will not permit an off-duty social relationship between male and female. (This could also include a sexual relationship between two males or two females.)

AN OVERVIEW OF EQUAL PAY ACT

The first interference by the federal government in the payment of wages was in 1938, when the Fair Labor Standards Act was passed and employers were told that they had to pay a minimum wage and overtime premium to their employees. For the next 25 years there was no further interference with employers' right to determine wages of their employees. By 1962 the percentage of women in the work force increased from 25 percent to about 35 percent; earnings of women average 60 percent to 70 percent those of men for year-round full-time work.[51]

Congress considered this a social problem in the same manner as minimum wage legislation. In 1963 it amended Section 6 of the Fair Labor Standards Act, and called the amendment the Equal Pay Act (EPA).[52] EPA simply states that no employer shall discriminate in the payment of wages within a facility on the basis of sex for equal work on jobs that require equal skill, equal effort, and equal responsibility and are performed under similar working conditions, unless the differential is based on seniority,[53] a merit system, an incentive pay system, or any factor other than sex.

The EPA statute is easily defined but can cause problems in wage and salary systems. Many employers have depended on loopholes and other defensive provisions for the survival of their wage and salary systems. Since 1979 vigorous enforcement by EEOC has jeopardized such a policy.

Definition of Equal Work

Management often has a bona fide belief that there is a difference in skills, responsibility, and effort and that is the reason for the difference in wages. This is usually a misconception and is the reason for the exposure under the EPA.

The first opportunity that the courts had to answer these questions was in *Schultz* v. *Wheaton Glass Co.*, where male selector packers were receiving $.21 per hour more than female selector packers.[54] They performed substantially the same work, which was inspection work, except that approximately 18 percent of the time the male selectors did materials handling tasks.[55] Females were not permitted to perform these tasks because they were restricted from lifting anything over 35 pounds. The court, in a landmark opinion on the interpretation of EPA, established a legal principle in finding a violation of EPA; it has been followed by other courts in many decisions. In view of the refusal of the Supreme Court to review the decision, these principles can be considered as controlling. These principles are sometimes called the "equal work standard."

1. The equal work standard requires only that the jobs be substantially equal and not identical. Small differences will not make them unequal.
2. When a wage differential exists between men and women doing substantially equal work,

[51]"Economic Indicators Relating to Equal Pay," U.S. Department of Labor, Women's Bureau, Pamphlet no. 9 (Washington, DC: Government Printing Office, 1962); also Earl F. Mellor, "Investigating the Difference between Men and Women," *Monthly Labor Review*, 107 (June 1984).

[52]29 USC 206 et seq.

[53]In *Henry v. Lennox Industries, Inc.*, 768 F.2d 746 (6th Cir. 1985), the court upheld a differential based on seniority and not job content.

[54]421 F.2d 259 (3rd Cir. 1970), cert. denied, 398 U.S. 905 (1970).

[55]Right after the enactment of EPA, the first loophole that employers conceived in EPA was to change the job content to include tasks that women did not normally perform. The author in 1965 spent a great deal of time writing "compliance job descriptions."

the burden is on the employer to show that the differential is for some reason other than sex.

3. Where some but not all members of one sex performed extra duties in their jobs, these extra duties do not justify giving all members of that sex extra pay.

4. That men can perform extra duties does not justify extra pay unless women are also offered the opportunity to perform these jobs.

5. Job titles and job descriptions are not material in showing that work is unequal unless they accurately reflect actual job content.[56]

What is a substantially different job is decided on a case-by-case basis. Where there is a substantial difference in effort, skill, or responsibility, the courts permit a pay differential between the sexes. The principle that job content, not job titles or job descriptions, is what determines whether jobs are equal was also followed in the Eighth Circuit.[57]

Another justification for a wage differential between men and women on which the employer relied was shift work. Where all men worked the night shift and women the day shift, it was argued by employers that the differential was justified because they were not similar working conditions. In one of the few EPA cases to reach the Supreme Court, it was held that working conditions as used in EPA do not refer to the time of day when work was performed and different shifts do not justify a pay differential.[58]

This case also established the rule that equal pay violations could be remedied only by raising the women's wages, not reducing the men's, but left open the question of whether changes in job content could remedy the violation. Often employers attempted to justify pay differentials between

men and women by arguing that working conditions were not similar, that the jobs performed by males were more hazardous tasks than ones performed by females. There are situations where this might be a defense. However, such a defense should be used with extreme caution. Statistics show that 70 percent to 85 percent of all industrial accidents are not caused by physical conditions but by unsafe acts of the employee. Under these statistics hazardous working conditions would not justify the differential if accidents are caused by the employee and not the hazardous conditions.

Measurement of Equal Skills

When considering skills such factors as experience, training, education, and ability are taken into account. Any one of these factors can justify a differential.[59] Possessing a skill is not enough; the person must also use that skill on the job.[60]

A common "equal skill" situation that courts have struck down is where the employer trains men for promotional purposes but does not offer to train women who for some reason are not considered in the promotion plans; when the jobs are compared, the trained men have more skills than women.[61]

Where male tellers were paid more than female tellers, the employer argued that the males were being trained in all aspects of banking to replace senior officers; because they were in a bona fide training program, the differential was justified. The court said that mere recognition by management of the ability to be promoted does not constitute a bona fide job-training program. Subjective evaluation of potential for promotion stand-

---

[56]In the author's experience, they may be accurate for a short time in reflecting job content but if a woman could do the job, the supervisor would let her do it and the job description would become obsolete; the jobs would become equal, but the pay would be unequal.

[57]*Katz* v. *School Dist. of Clayton Missouri*, 557 F.2d 153 (8th Cir. 1977).

[58]*Corning Glass Works* v. *Brennan*, 417 U.S. 188 (1974).

[59]In *EEOC* v. *McCarthy*, 768 F.2d 1 (1st Cir. 1985) the court held ability to be more important.

[60]In *Hein* v. *Oregon College of Education*, 718 F.2d 910 (9th Cir. 1983), the court said that a female not using her skills couldn't be compared with a male who used his skills.

[61]*Schultz* v. *First Victoria Bank*, 420 F.2d 648 (5th Cir. 1969).

ing alone cannot justify pay differentials under EPA.[62]

In order to justify pay differentials under EPA through a bona fide training program (1) it must be open to both sexes, (2) employees must be notified of the training opportunities, (3) there must be a defined beginning and ending of the training program, and (4) a definite course of study and advancement opportunities upon completion are essential. It is also advisable to put the program in writing.

Job Responsibility to Justify a Differential

The defense of a difference in responsibility to justify unequal pay occurs mostly in administrative, professional, and executive jobs, where before the 1972 amendment these employees were excluded from coverage under EPA.

One of the first cases under the responsibility defense was where the employer claimed that men had to make decisions that women did not have to make. The court found that although men did make decisions that women did not, such decisions were subject to review by supervisors. Therefore, the differential was not justified under the responsibility defense.[63]

Often the employer justifies a pay differential between sexes in the same job categories by claiming that one type of work is more difficult than another. Where the employer claimed that management of soft-line departments such as clothing, usually managed by women, had less responsibility than hard-line departments as sporting goods, usually managed by men, the court held that there is no substantial difference to justify less pay for women than for men.[64] In *EEOC* v. *Madison Community Unit School District No.*

12, 816 F.2d 577 (7th Cir. 1987), the court held that paying female coaches of girls' track and tennis teams less than male coaches of male track and tennis teams is a violation of the Equal Pay Act. An important point in the case was the fact that the school district discouraged women from applying for positions of coaching boys' teams. In all Equal Pay cases whether or not females had an opportunity to do or train for the work of the males is a very important factor.

Misuse of Term "Merit Pay"

One of the factors that will justify differentials is where a properly communicated bona fide merit system is applied without regard to sex. All too often the term *merit pay* is used to include cost-of-living increases, longevity increases, and other, general, across-the-board increases that have no relationship to meritorious performance.[65] The purpose of a merit pay plan is to motivate performance, not to justify pay increases. Merit increases that will survive judicial review under EPA are individual increases in pay related to the job performance of that individual. A bona fide merit policy is a pat on the back with dollar bills in the palm of the hand.

Determining a wage level on some factor other than performance is the major fault with merit pay plans and why they do not stand judicial scrutiny. In an inflationary period the employer wants to keep earnings in line with the labor market conditions, yet does not want to set a precedent by implying that pay increases are automatic or based on labor market conditions. Rationalization sets in and any believable reason is given. In *Brock*

---

[62]*Marshall* v. *Security Bank & Trust Co.*, 572 F.2d 276 (10th Cir. 1978).

[63]*Hodgson* v. *Fairmont Supply Co.*, 454 F.2d 490 (4th Cir. 1972).

[64]*Brennan* v. *T.M. Fields, Inc.*, 488 F.2d 443 (5th Cir. 1973).

---

[65]This usually happens when the employer does not want to set a precedent of granting cost-of-living increases or longevity increases; thus it is called merit. The misuse of the term becomes evident in EEO cases where a merit increase is given one month and an employee is discharged the next month for poor performance. Often merit raise surveys are made, but they are in reality market surveys. See "1989 Compensation Planning Survey," Gibson and Company, Inc., 212 Carnegie Center, Princeton, NJ 08540, 1988.

v. *Georgia S.W. College,* 765 F.2d 1026 (11th Cir. 1985), the employer argued that wage difference was due to a merit system. The court found that the ratings were based on subjective personal judgment, that they were ad hoc, and that in many cases the raters were ill informed.

In order for a compensation plan to be based truly on merit, it should be given at a time when some significant performance has been completed. For administrative purposes, that could be done by periods, provided that the waiting period is not too long to chill motivation. In production incentive plans for factory workers, merit pay for the previous three-month period should be the maximum waiting period and paid separately within two weeks after the end of the merit rating period.

Necessary Elements for a Bona Fide Merit Plan

In order for a merit pay plan to be bona fide under the various statutes, it should be in writing and contain all or most of the following elements.[66]

1. The employee must believe that good performance will result in additional compensation.[67]
2. There should be a direct correlation between the amount of pay and the exceptional performance, without any upper limits. Upper limits tend to dampen the motivation of certain workers.
3. The employee should understand the merit plan before it is adopted so that there are no surprises at evaluation time. (The author can recall working with the most motivated incen-

tive worker he has ever known. She was asked at 10:30 A.M. how much incentive pay she had earned so far that day and she knew. This employee understood the incentive plan.)
4. The performance should be accurately measured either by objective performance appraisals or by standards of performance with which the employee agrees. If agreement cannot be accomplished, the employer should be sure that it is right and adopt it. Sometimes employees have to work with the plan before they are convinced they can earn additional money.
5. The base pay should not be reduced because an employee is on a merit system. Merit pay should be given when performance is above the average worker's base pay.
6. The merit system must be updated periodically. Job content affects the performance; if not current, either the company or employee is unfairly affected.
7. Managers must believe in the system and be trained to properly administer it.
8. Follow-up procedures are necessary to prevent bias and leniency. Nothing can defeat a merit plan faster than leniency or bias.[68]

Factors Other Than Sex to Justify a Differential

Wage and salary plans based on seniority are not in violation of EPA if there is a direct correlation between seniority and pay levels and it is otherwise a bona fide seniority plan. Most seniority plans fail under EPA because they are not applied to males and females in a like manner. Departmental seniority that excludes females is a good example.

Another factor, other than sex, that employers tested in the courts is the area of employee fringe benefits. In order to justify a pay differential under the Equal Pay Act, the reason for the difference in benefits must

---

[66]In *EEOC* v. *Aetna Insurance Co.,* 616 F.2d 719 (4th Cir. 1980), and *Brennan* v. *Victoria Bank & Trust Co.,* 493 F.2d 896 (5th Cir. 1974), the courts allowed discrimination when a merit plan contained these elements.

[67]A prominent industrial engineer once told the author that an incentive plan is 10 percent technical knowledge and 90 percent selling it to the employees involved.

---

[68]For further reading, see James E. Brennan, "Compensation: The Myth and the Reality of Pay for Performance," *Personnel Journal,* 64, no. 3 (March 1985), 73–75; Arthur A. Geis, "Making Merit Pay Work," *Personnel,* 64, no. 1 (January 1987), pp. 52–60; Berry Wilson and Dennis Patzig, "Does Your Organization Have the Right Climate for Merit?" *Public Personnel Management,* 16, no. 2 (Summer 1987), p. 127.

be based on a factor other than sex. The employer argued that requiring a greater pension contribution for females than for males because women live longer was a factor other than sex. The Supreme Court adopted the lower court's position that actuarial distinctions based entirely on sex could not qualify as an exception based on any factor other than sex.[69] In a situation where a deferred compensation plan with optional contributions and optional method of receiving benefits, one of which was an insured annuity plan, under the plan women would receive less benefits for the same contribution than men because of use of sex-segregated actuarial tables. The Court said that this was not a factor other than sex, that is, longevity of life would not justify a differential under the Equal Pay Act.[70]

An example of valid factors other than sex according to the Labor Department's opinion (not reversed by EEOC since it obtained jurisdiction in 1979) is temporary or permanent assignments made to a lower-rated job with the employee retaining the rate of the old job (sometimes called a red circle rate), which is greater than for the female doing the same work. A bona fide training program as discussed in this chapter could be a factor other than sex.

One factor other than sex that has not been judicially reviewed is part-time work. Such review is unlikely unless EEOC brings it to court. The Department of Labor has taken the position that part-time employment (under 20 hours per week) is a factor other than sex to justify a pay differential.

EEOC Regulations Interpreting Equal Pay Act

In August of 1986 the EEOC issued new regulations interpreting the EPA (29 CFR

Part 1620—2 and 51 CFR 24716), which made some modifications as to their position on certain issues. Although the regulations for the most part adopted the Department of Labor regulations and court interpretations, certain aspects of the changed regulations are worth noting.

The meaning of the term *establishment* was expanded to include two or more distinct physical portions of the business as one establishment as long as they are located in the same physical place of business.

There was some change in fringe benefits, but for the most part they adopted judicial interpretations. That is, employers must make the same benefits available to females as they do to males without regard to cost or actuarial studies.

Probably the biggest change was in the definition of "equal work." The EEOC takes the position that if employers pay a higher rate to a new male employee than they do to a former or a present female employee, that is a violation. (This is certain to be tested in the courts.) This definition assumes that the higher rate was based on sex and doesn't consider market conditions. Another significant change in the new regulations is that EEOC is going to consider any violation as a continuing violation, and therefore any violations beyond the statutory period will be counted.

The new "regs" will disallow two of the former defenses and closely scrutinize two others. They will not allow a wage difference between the average cost of one group of one sex and that of the opposite sex as a group. This is contrary to the majority of court decisions that state that market conditions must be considered. This is certain to be challenged. They also state that they will not allow unequal rates established by a collective bargaining agreement. This was formerly allowed under 29 CFR Section 1620.23.

The EEOC said they will closely scrutinize any situation where additional duties are added to justify unequal pay. They will determine if it is bona fide. The former posi-

---

[69]*City of Los Angeles* v. *Manhart*, 435 U.S. 702 (U.S. S.Ct. 1978).

[70]*Arizona Governing Committee for Tax Deferred Annuity and Deferred Compensation Plans, Etc., et al.* v. *Nathalie Norris Etc.*, 103 S.Ct. 3492 (1983).

tion of the agency that head of household will justify a difference will also be watched with a questionable eye.

The old defenses of merit, seniority, quantity, quality, and any other factor, other than sex, were left untouched by the new regulations. However, the EEOC will no longer depend on job evaluations systems to justify the difference. This is the death of the comparable worth theory under the EPA. Some changes are in order if the employer is to get along with the EEOC. Of course, any of these changes can be challenged in the courts.

Failure of EPA to Correct Differentials between Sexes

From the outset EPA did not correct wage differences that existed before the act. The employer took the position that existing wage and salary systems did give equal pay for equal work; thus there was no need to change the policy of determining wages by job evaluation, market conditions, profitability, or competitive practices. The determination of wages by market conditions and job evaluation were found by researchers to have built-in sex bias.[71]

Starting salaries in job categories that are predominantly female are traditionally lower and will stay that way, as long as the supply of labor is adequate. Over the years study after study has confirmed that the average compensation of women is from 59 to 64 percent of men.[72]

If starting salaries for the same work are different between the sexes, the differential continues as salary increases are granted. The justification usually given by employers is that the jobs are not the same. The law permits pay discrimination as long as the employers give legally acceptable reasons. If these reasons are not challenged by the employee or by the enforcement agency, it is never determined whether they are legally acceptable. Where violations are found under EPA, the correction is made only within the specific job categories. The basic wage and salary procedures are not considered by the courts nor will the courts require the employers to change them. Often within a short time due to changes in job assignments, the violations recur and remain that way unless another complaint is filed.

This section has shown why present wage and salary procedures have failed to eliminate wage differentials between the sexes. It would be presumptuous to assume that the factors that determined wages and salaries in the past will be abandoned by employers. Such considerations as employee qualifications, job content, union membership, labor market conditions, employee work behavior and contribution, local practices, profitability, and competition will continue to determine the compensation level unless the courts or Congress intervenes. As long as these factors determine compensation, there will be continual exposure to violations of EPA.

Audit of EPA Compliance

Most employers are in violation of the Equal Pay Act, and when an employer is challenged, a lengthy and expensive lawsuit results. The factors mentioned previously, although valid, offer very little defense. For this reason it is good insurance to audit your compensation plan to determine the extent of noncompliance. Where it is found that there are serious compliance problems, the corrections can be made gradually and often without anyone knowing a violation ever existed. This is much better than an equal pay

---

[71]"Women, Work, and Wages; Equal Pay for Jobs of Equal Value," National Academy of Sciences Committee on Occupational Classification and Analysis, Washington, DC, 1981.

[72]*The Earnings Gap between Women and Men,* Women's Bureau, U.S. Department of Labor, Washington, DC, 1979; Donald J. Treiman and Heidi L. Hartman, *Women, Work, and Wages: Equal Pay for Jobs of Equal Value,* National Academy of Sciences, Washington, DC, 1981; James P. Smith and Michael P. Ward, *Women's Wages and Work in the Twentieth Century* (Santa Monica, CA: The Rand Corporation, 1984); Lester C. Thurow, "Sixty-Two Cents to the Dollar," *Working Mother* (October 1984), pp. 42–46.

complaint by the EEOC where the employer is being accused of taking compensation from the employees in violation of the law. Necessary procedures for EPA audit are as follows:

1. Determine the distribution of pay increase percentages within each job category and whether there is any relationship with performance.
2. Calculate the average pay increase within each job category by race and sex.
3. Determine the average pay increase given by each supervisor within each job category.
4. Review the performance ratings and history of promoted employees.
5. Correlate the relationship between pay increases and turnover.
6. Determine the relationship of the current year's increase with that of the previous year.

These various procedures are necessary to determine whether there is any logic to the company's compensation system. If there is some logic to the compensation system, it is much easier to defend when an equal pay charge is made by the EEOC.

In summary, management should do three things:

1. Have a rational reason for its compensation levels
2. Explain to the employees how their wages are determined
3. As much as possible, correct wage differentials between sexes, rather than trying to justify them

Although the failure of employers to abandon traditional methods of determining pay levels and pressures of the labor market conditions make compliance with EPA difficult, that does not mean that the statute should be ignored. Programs and procedures that show good faith efforts to eliminate differences between sexes will minimize exposure to litigation. They are also an effective defense in the event a lawsuit is started.

COMPARABLE PAY FOR COMPARABLE WORTH

Comparable worth is a theory of determining wages by requiring equal pay for employees whose work is of comparable worth even if the job content is totally different. The proponents of the theory state that the Equal Pay Act, Title VII, and Executive Order 11246 require its application. The concept was first developed by the Classification Act of 1923, which required equal pay for equal work in the executive branch of the federal government. Later the National War Labor Board issued General Order No. 16 (November 1942), which allowed adjustment between male and female rates based on comparable quality and quantity of work on the same or similar operations in a wage and price controlled economy.[73] As the increase of women in the work force continued (it doubled from 1960 to 1983) the pressure to do something about the difference in earnings increased. Since the Equal Pay Act failed in other respects there was hope that the revival of the theory would be legally supported by new interpretation of the Equal Pay Act or Title VII. The concept was called the "women's issue of the 80s" and became a very controversial equal employment issue.[74]

It didn't take long for the issue to get into the courts. After several jurisdictions decided that there could not be a claim of comparable worth under the EPA, the issue went before the Supreme Court, who stated in *County of Washington* v. *Gunther,* 101 S.Ct. 2242 (1981), that the four defenses under

[73]Sean DeForest, "How Can Comparable Worth Be Achieved," *Personnel,* 61 (September-October 1984), 6; Merrill J. Collett, "Comparable Worth: An Overview," *Public Personnel Management Journal,* 12 (1983), 326.

[74]Victor V. Veysey, "Comparable Worth: What Is Management Doing?" *SAM Advanced Management Journal* (Summer 1985); Marvine J. Levine, "Comparable Worth in the 1980's: Will Collective Bargaining Supplant Legislative Initiatives and Judicial Interpretations?" *Labor Law Journal,* 38, no. 6 (June 1987), 323.

the EPA applied when there was an issue of whether Title VII or EPA could be used, that the Bennett Amendment required the EPA defenses to be used when there was conflict between EPA and Title VII. Therefore, the plaintiffs could not apply the "equal work" standard under EPA. However, the court stated that this didn't preclude the plaintiffs from starting an action under Title VII alleging disparate treatment and sex discrimination. The court was careful to state that the comparable worth issue was not before them. The plaintiffs in Gunther brought action because female guard jobs were 95 percent equal in job content to those of males but were receiving only 70 percent pay. Women's advocate groups then began to sue under Title VII using the disparate treatment argument but applying the comparable work theory.

Legal Death of Comparable Worth Theory

Although several circuits had previously held that it is not up to the courts to determine the worth of an employee,[75] the issue was settled in *State of Washington* v. *Am. Federal, State and County and Municipal Employees,* 770 F.2d 1401 (9th Cir. 1985), where the court held that Congress did not intend Title VII to interfere with the law of supply and demand or prevent employees from competing in the labor market. The court made it clear that under Title VII the plaintiff must show that the differential existed because of sex and not other factors such as the market

conditions. Since it was not appealed, this case legally eliminated the comparable worth theory under Title VII and affirmed the position of the courts in other jurisdictions.[76] Search of case law reveals that there is not a single court opinion upholding the concept of comparable worth under EPA or Title VII. The theory judicially died as quickly as it was born.

It is unlikely that Congress will pass legislation adopting the comparable worth theory, and those states that have passed statutes have not really applied the theory but have merely brought female rates up to those of males, using various criteria to do so. There is no feasible method to apply the theory unless you start from zero for all classifications and then agree upon criteria to set the differentials. This is politically and economically infeasible. Although there is no practical way to solve the wage inequity problem through the comparable worth theory, the comparable worth theory as an academic concept was an attempt to correct the wage differences between sexes. It has had a value in that it is telling the employer that the social problem of unequal pay for equal work must be solved. No one sweeping method or theory will achieve this, but this doesn't relieve the employer from trying. The market conditions must be considered, but the laws of supply and demand can be influenced by management policy. Where the employer accepts laws of supply and demand, without an attempt to integrate the jobs and apply equal pay for equal work, litigation under the Equal Pay Act on a case-by-case basis will be the only solution.

---

[75]*Lemons* v. *City and County of Denver,* 620 F.2d 228 (10th Cir. 1980), cert. denied, 449 U.S. 888 (1980); *Christenson* v. *Iowa,* 563 F.2d 353 (8th Cir. 1977); *Spaulding* v. *University of Washington,* 740 F.2d 686 (9th Cir. 1984), cert. denied, 105 S.Ct. 511 (1984).

---

[76]*Plemer* v. *Parson's Gilbane,* 713 F.2d 1127 (5th Cir. 1983); *Power* v. *Barry County,* 539 F.Supp. 721 (D.C. Mich. 1982); *Christensen* v. *University of Iowa,* 563 F.2d 353 (8th Cir. 1977).

6

AFFIRMATIVE ACTION AND PERFORMANCE APPRAISALS

Scope and Purpose of Affirmative Action
Reverse Discrimination and Affirmative Action
Seniority and Antidiscrimination Laws
Exposure of Performance Appraisal Plans

The basic theory of all affirmative action executive orders, starting with those unenforced orders of President Franklin D. Roosevelt in the early 1940s, is that if you are to receive government funds or do business with the government, certain conditions can be imposed. One of these conditions is that you must adopt an affirmative action program to employ and promote members of the protected class.[1] Affirmative action means different things to different people.[2] Some believe that, within reason, a preference should be given to those members of the protected class who have in the past been discriminated against although the individuals within the class may not be the victims of the discrimination. This group believes that there should be a set-aside goal or preference quotas to correct the past discrimination.

Others believe that affirmative action should not favor one class over another, since in doing so you are granting benefits to groups who may not be as well qualified. The opponents argue that the effort will fail to improve the economic position of the very groups that the executive order was designed to protect. This school of thought believes that affirmative action should not be used to remedy the effects of either actual or historical discrimination that benefits the nonvictims to the detriment of the nonprotected classes. They argue that only those who have actually been discriminated against should be given a remedy through affirmative action preference.[3]

The Supreme Court has had this issue before it nine times in an eight-year period and has failed to set a clear and concise policy to follow. At one time it appeared that the court had established some principles to guide employers on what to do in hiring, crew reduction, and promotions to stay within the law and still correct past discrimination. However, recent decisions have, in some respects, confused the employer to the point where we cannot be certain whether a particular program will stand judicial scrutiny and we must depend upon case-by-case decisions for guidance.

This chapter will review the cases in the areas of hiring, promotion, layoffs, and voluntary programs to correct past discrimination. Considering the state of the law, some recommendations will be given on how to stay out of court when using an affirmative action program to comply with various executive orders (11246 covers most employers in the private sector).

Many of the Supreme Court decisions involve the public sector, but the same principles apply to the private sector; therefore, this chapter will not make a distinction between the two.

SCOPE AND PURPOSE OF AFFIRMATIVE ACTION

Approximately 80 percent of the work force is covered under Title VII, the Age in Discrimination and Equal Pay Act.[4] State and federal equal employment opportunity legislation extends to all but the smallest employer. The employer who has 1 or 100 employees cannot afford to disregard the national, state, or local policy that every person shall have a right to employment without regard to race, color, religion, sex, national origin, or age. It is good personnel policy to have an affirmative action program; whether it is voluntary or forced on the employer by the government should not be a factor in

---

[1] See Affirmative Action Guidelines, EEOC, Federal Register, Vol. 44, January 19, 1979.

[2] See Buddy Robert S. Silverman, "A Litmus Test for EEOC Philosophies," *Personnel Journal* (May 1987), p. 143.

[3] For this point of view see Peter G. Kilgore, "Goals, Preferences, and Set Asides: An Appropriate Affirmative Action Response to Discrimination," *Labor Law Journal*, 36, no. 7 (July 1985), 410.

---

[4] *Employment and Earnings*, vol. 35, no. 7 (Washington, DC: Bureau of Labor Statistics, July, 1988). This publication reports a total civilian labor force of 118,834,000 in 1987 of which over 88,000,000 are in protected classes, as compiled from employment status tables by sex, age, and race.

adopting a policy. If the employer is to select and train the best-qualified applicants available, 80 percent of the labor force cannot be ignored. It is also difficult for the personnel director to explain to the sales manager why a government contract was lost because of the failure to adopt an affirmative action program that is neither a cost consideration nor impossible to institute.

The lack of affirmative action policies for minorities, female, and handicapped also has legal implications when a discrimination charge is filed against the employer, and the regulatory agency discovers that the employer did not have an affirmative action program. The employer's defense to a discrimination charge is badly shattered when the absence of an affirmative action program is discovered at some point in the proceedings. Usually the plaintiff's attorney will do so when cross examining the employer's witness, but often the agency will discover it.

The scope of affirmative action is as broad as making the first sale and hiring the first person. The concept of affirmative action is a remedial concept that requests employers and labor unions to take positive steps voluntarily to improve the work opportunities of women, racial and ethnic minorities, handicapped workers, and Vietnam veterans who have been deprived of job opportunities. If the employer chooses not to have a program, the government may choose not to do business with that employer. There is nothing in Executive Order 11246 that requires the employer to hire or promote a person who is not the best-qualified for the job, but just make a good faith effort to find qualified applicants among the members of the protected groups.

Although the purpose of an affirmative action program is to encourage the employer to improve job opportunities for the protected classes, the Office of Federal Contract Compliance (OFCC) is not prevented from reporting any violations of Title VII to the Justice Department or EEOC for enforcement under Title VII of a discriminatory practice.

The objective of an affirmative action program has been accomplished if there is a measurable improvement in hiring, training, and promoting minorities or females in those job categories that show underutilization of the protected class.

Basic Elements of an Affirmative Action Plan

An affirmative action plan has six basic elements:

1. An Equal Employment Opportunity Policy Statement [41 CFR SS 60–2.13(a) and 60–2.20]. This is usually a statement from the CEO.
2. Procedures for internal and external dissemination of the policy [41 CFR S 60–2.13(b) and 60–2.21]. Include the union, if any, large customers, and employee groups, as well as all employees.
3. Specific allocation of responsibilities for implementation of the AAP. See 41 CFR S 60–2.13(c) and 60–2.22 for details. It is advisable to include a job description of the person assigned.
4. A work force analysis of all job titles [41 CFR S 60–2.11(a)]. This is a must element. It determines what is needed to correct past discrimination.
5. Plan of action [41 CFR S 60–2.13(f) and 60–2.24]. An action program should be developed to eliminate any identified problem areas or to show improvement.
6. Internal audit and reporting system [41 CFR S 60–2.13(g) and 60–2.25]. This should be a record of what you are doing.

Implementation of the Plan

The first step in determining whether one can improve employment opportunities is to determine whether there will be any employment or promotion opportunities in a given period on which to improve. The next step is to determine whether there has been a denial of job opportunities or there is another reason why there are no members of the protected class in that job category. If there is a possibility to improve a job category as to employment or promotion of a member of the protected class, then it is considered an under-utilized job category that can be improved on, and an affirmative action objective can be established. Affirmative action does not demand that underutilization be corrected immediately, but that a good faith effort be made to improve the number of the protected class in a certain job category.

It has been judicially determined that a labor market is defined for purposes of compliance to Title VII as an area where the employer has been recruiting.[5] However, new areas should be considered in affirmative action recruiting if the old method is not bringing results.

The implementation of an affirmative action program to increase job opportunities where they have been denied overlaps with the requirements of Title VII in the recruitment and selection process. A good affirmative action program will comply with requirements of Title VII when a charge is filed for discrimination in hiring.[6]

REVERSE DISCRIMINATION AND AFFIRMATIVE ACTION

The exposure to reverse discrimination charges is created when the employer wishes to reduce the work force, make temporary lay-offs, or promote and still comply with the affirmative action plan that was previously agreed to and communicated.

The Supreme Court justices over the years have had difficulty in agreeing how this should be done. In most of the decisions relating to the problem of reverse discrimination and correcting past discrimination by affirmative action, the court has been widely split. The first case was decided by a

five to four vote, and even though there were two changes in the court membership (O'Connor and Scalia), subsequent decisions were by a split vote, also mostly five to four.

Affirmative Action in Selection

In *Regents of the University of California* v. *Bakke,* 438 U.S. 265 (1978), the majority court held that where the medical school admissions program favored blacks over whites to correct an imbalance of whites over blacks it was a violation of the Equal Protection clause of the Fourteenth Amendment and Title VII. This case stood for the principle that you could not correct socialite discrimination by an affirmative action policy that favored one race over another.

One year later, again by a five to four majority, the court gave its approval to an affirmative action program when it held in *Kaiser Aluminum and Chemical Corporation* v. *Weber,* 443 U.S. 193 (1979), that an apprenticeship program for an all-white maintenance department that reserved 50 percent of the openings for black applicants (although they may be junior to white employees) was not a violation of Title VII. The court reasoned that since it was agreed upon by the employees (union in this case), it was temporary until racial imbalance was achieved and the whites were given the same opportunity as the blacks to compete for 50 percent of the job openings. Therefore, the program was not in violation. The courts in subsequent cases allowed past discrimination to be corrected by affirmative action as long as the conditions in Weber existed; otherwise they would revert to Bakke and find reverse discrimination.

Affirmative Action when Reducing Work Force

The issue again came before the court in *Firefighters Local Union No. 1784* v. *Stotts,* 467 U.S. 561 (1984), where the municipality laid off according to a court-approved voluntary affirmative action plan that was the result of a discrimination charge alleging that the department was discriminating against blacks.

---

[5]*Hazelwood School District* v. *United States,* 433 U.S. 299 (1977).

[6]The distinction between enforcement of Title VII and Executive Order 11246 is that Title VII deals with individual or affected class complaints alleging that discrimination has taken place. Order 11246 is concerned with programs to correct past discrimination without reference to any specific complaint by an individual.

The lay-off violated the seniority provisions of the collective bargaining agreement but maintained the balance of the court-approved affirmative action program. (51 cities had similar programs.) The court held that the seniority provisions of the collective bargaining agreement couldn't be ignored (the court will usually protect seniority regardless of how it affects discrimination) and the plan was inconsistent with the spirit and the letter of the antidiscrimination laws unless a court first ruled that discrimination existed. In Stotts, the lower court, without a trial, had determined that discrimination exists but didn't provide a remedy since a voluntary agreement was reached.

In the similar case of *Wygant* v. *Jackson Board of Education,* 106 S.Ct. 1842 (1986), the court majority found that socialite discrimination alone is insufficient cause to justify racial preference. It held that in order for a lay-off procedure under an affirmative action plan to favor one race over another, there must be convincing evidence of prior discrimination as determined by a court.[7]

The Wygant decision was very narrow, as the court in *Sheetmetal Workers Local Number 93* v. *City of Cleveland,* 106 S.Ct. 3063 (1986), said an employer may develop an affirmative action plan in hiring and promotion in the settlement of an employment discrimination charge. Here the employer and union had violated the statute and entered into a court-approved settlement agreement to remedy the violation. The union also violated the settlement agreement. The Court said this was identical to a private out-of-court settlement, thus following the Weber case. However, in another case the Court held that only those employees who were directly affected could receive race-conscious relief.[8]

At this point it appears that unless there was a judicial determination that past discrimination existed and there was a court-

ordered remedy, an affirmative action plan that discriminated against one class to the benefit of another in hiring and lay-offs will be in violation of the Fourteenth Amendment and Title VII. An exception would be if the conditions existed as found in Weber.[9]

Affirmative Action in Promotion

The proper determination of whom to promote is a keystone in the successful management of any organization. It is a commonly accepted personnel doctrine that one determines promotion on the basis of ability to perform the job. No other criteria should be used, with the exception of seniority, which is a determining factor only after candidates are in every other respect equally qualified to perform the job.

In 1972 a lower court found the State of Alabama guilty of systematically excluding blacks from state trooper jobs. They were ordered to follow a quota for hiring and promotion. By 1979 no black had been promoted to the upper ranks. The court then approved a program whereby the state would develop a program within one year for promotion of blacks to the rank of corporal and to comply with EEOC guidelines in all other respects. Two more years passed and no black had been promoted. The department then agreed to develop a test, which proved to have an adverse impact on minorities. The court then ordered the state to promote 50 percent blacks to existing vacancies in the rank of corporal. The state challenged that order.

The Supreme Court in *United States* v. *Paradise et al.,* 107 S.Ct. 1063 (1987), by a five to four vote affirmed the lower court's order, stating that the court had wide discretion in ordering remedies where discrimination had been found, that the plan was temporary and whites had an equal chance to be promoted. The Court to some extent

---

[7]In *J. A. Crossman* v. *Richmond,* 106 S.Ct. 3327 (1986), the court struck down a city minority set-aside award for public contract, following Wygant.

[8]*Local 24 of Sheetmetal Workers* v. *EEOC,* 106 S.Ct. 301 (1986).

[9]Congress by statute can constitutionally favor one race over another: *Fullilove* v. *Klutznick,* 444 U.S. 448 (1980).

followed Weber, City of Cleveland, and Fullilove in affirming that racial preference can be given under certain conditions.

The real uncertainty of affirmative action programs that result in reverse discrimination was created by *Johnson* v. *Transportation Agency, Santa Clara County*, 107 S.Ct. 1442 (1987), where the facts lacked the requirements of previous decisions that upheld racial preference to correct past discrimination in affirmative action plans. There was no previous court determination of discrimination, there was no record of past discrimination against women (although an imbalance existed), the plan was permanent, and the plan did not have the approval of the employees or any employee representative). The plan did not set aside a specific number of positions for women, but it did expressly authorize that race and sex were factors when evaluating qualified candidates in areas where these groups were not proportionally represented.

In Johnson both a male and a female had been rated as qualified, although the male was two points higher in the interview evaluation. The male was the unanimous choice of the evaluators among nine candidates, but because of the fact that 36 percent of the labor market were women and of the 238 employees in the department none was a woman, the female was selected by the agency director. Sex was one of numerous factors taken into account, and the facts indicate that it was the major factor.

The court in a six to three decision held that Title VII permits the employer the right to voluntarily rectify a manifest imbalance in the work force by an affirmative action program. The Court didn't overrule the previous cases of Bakke, Wygant, or Stotts but relied heavily upon Weber. According to the Court, the facts were similar to Weber, but many students of affirmative action believe that only the result was similar. The plan was permanent and allowed whites to be excluded who were better qualified. The holding in the case is that a bona fide affirmative action plan can use race, sex, or ethnic background as a factor

in hiring or promotion. How much of a factor is uncertain.[10]

One thing certain is that this case will not avoid further litigation, since reverse discrimination has been dealt a serious blow that will not be allowed to stand. Employers cannot live with promoting people who are not qualified and later being challenged when they are removed from the job because of poor performance. However, it is predicted that most courts will put qualifications first where there is a big difference between the two candidates.

In promotions there is some certainty that affirmative action plans will be upheld that use reverse discrimination to correct an imbalance, as indicated in the Johnson case. However, because of the confusion in previous cases, we cannot be absolutely safe from exposure. To be safe, an employer would be wise to have a procedure whereby all employees would be informed of a vacancy and be given consideration if they had an interest. Although supervision may object to this policy, it not only would eliminate some exposure but also would be a good personnel practice. As in recruiting, unless everybody that has an interest is considered, it is difficult to say that the best-qualified person receives the promotion. Exhibit 6-1 is a suggested form that could be used.

Recommendations for an Acceptable Plan

At the beginning of this chapter, we stated that every employer should have an affirmative action program as defense for discrimination charges. The case law review has not changed this; in fact, it appears from the Johnson case that affirmative action plans can be used as defense for reverse discrimination. To what extent these defenses can be used is an uncertainty. It also appears from the Johnson case that an employer now has less exposure than previously to reverse discrimination charges. We must remember that re-

---

[10]This is difficult to reconcile with Bakke (1979), where the court said you cannot correct socialite discrimination by affirmative action.

EXHIBIT 6-1 *Position Opportunities Announcement*

	DATE OF ANNOUNCEMENT	REMOVE DATE
JOB TITLE	DIVISION/DEPARTMENT	
SUPERVISOR	SALARY CLASSIFICATION	
REQUIREMENTS		
DUTIES		
IF YOU WISH TO BE CONSIDERED FOR THIS POSITION, PLEASE CONTACT		
WE ARE AN EQUAL OPPORTUNITY EMPLOYER		

verse discrimination charges had a degree of certainty under Bakke in 1978, lost it under Weber in 1979, regained it under Stotts and Wygant in 1986, but lost it again in 1987 under Johnson.

In order to avoid exposure to litigation for reverse discrimination, the employer should do the following.

1. Step up recruiting and encourage qualified employees in the protected class to go into positions not commonly held by protected groups.
2. Continue to hire or promote the most-qualified person for the position based on criteria established by the employer.[11] To do

otherwise will only postpone litigation to when the employer has to terminate the marginal worker.

3. Change affirmative action plans only if they are not achieving the desired results. If after a long period of time there still remains a statistical imbalance in certain jobs, a documented nondiscriminatory reason is essential to the survival of the plan.

4. Adopt an affirmative action plan that promotes the objective of the business. If such a plan causes an exposure to litigation, then the employer must decide whether to change the plan or risk exposure to reverse discrimination. Any plan that excludes members of the protected class from consideration will cause an exposure.

5. State specifically in the plan that one class will not be favored over another in achieving a balanced work force but an imbalanced work force will be a consideration when promoting.

---

[11]Being overqualified is not a reason for rejection. In *Bishop* v. *D.C.*, 778 F.2d 781 (D.C. Cir. 1986), the court held that not selecting a white over a black because he was too qualified is a pretext for not selecting the white.

Employer Posture in a Compliance Review

If the employer is a government prime contractor of $10,000 or more, it is likely that a compliance review will be conducted to determine adequacy and implementation of an affirmative action policy. If in the opinion of the compliance officer the program is not effective, then recommendations are made to change it. If the employer refuses the changes, the compliance review officer can recommend cancellation of an existing contract or bar future contracts. Contract bar is effective only after a hearing. The final decision is made by the OFCC, subject to judicial review. When the agency cancelled a contract and issued a bar to future contracts and the employer appealed, the court held that the action was unreasonable because the affirmative action program was adequate.[12]

In order to avoid a dispute over the affirmative action program, the employer, after receiving notice from the review agency, should make preparation for compliance reviews. Proper preparation will enable the review officer to obtain all the pertinent facts about the program in the shortest possible time. It will also show an attitude of cooperation. Records such as applicant flow data, hiring records, and EEO-1 report and number of promotions and demotions should be readily available. Employees are often interviewed, so it is advisable to have some names in mind if asked by the compliance officer what employees that employer would like to be interviewed. One should be prepared to give a business reason for underutilized categories and other implications of discrimination or lack of good faith effort. Cooperation with the compliance officer is advisable, but it should not extend to those areas where the employer feels the compliance officer is on a fishing expedition, which may be an unreasonable burden to keep or supply irrelevant records.

SENIORITY AND ANTIDISCRIMINATION LAWS

The original method to eliminate subjectivity was to make decisions based on seniority. For many years seniority has been used to eliminate prejudice or subjective decisions, not only in labor agreements but also in the judicial system and many other social institutions. In the federal court system the chief judge of a district or appellate court is usually the senior judge. The U.S. Supreme Court and the legislative branch of the government rely heavily on seniority in many of their administrative procedures and customs.

Seniority System That Perpetuates Discrimination

Seniority systems that discriminated against minorities and females were common before the antidiscrimination laws. Unions had segregated locals, employers had separate seniority lists for males and females and for blacks and whites, and many companies had segregated facilities. Since discriminatory seniority systems were established many years before antidiscrimination laws, they would accordingly perpetuate discrimination toward minority or female workers. This problem was dealt with by the Supreme Court regarding the Teamsters Union, which had two separate seniority lists—one for city drivers and one for over-the-road drivers. The system had an adverse impact because there were no minorities on the over-the-road seniority list and there was no practical way for minorities to be put on the list. There was no question that this situation would continue for a considerable period. The Supreme Court held that as long as the system was instituted before Title VII and it was neutral on its face, the seniority system did not violate Title VII although it perpetuated discrimination.[13]

---

[12]*Firestone Synthetic Rubber Co.* v. *Marshall*, 507 F.Supp. 1330 (D.C. Tex. 1981).

[13]*International Brotherhood of Teamsters* v. *United States*, 431 U.S. 324 (1977).

Seniority as a Defense

The Supreme Court made it clear in a later case that if there were any evidence of intentional discrimination, such a system would be invalid.[14] In 1982 the court carried the Teamsters case one step further and stated that although the system was instituted after Title VII and had an adverse impact that perpetuated discrimination, it was still valid unless intent to discriminate could be shown.[15]

From these cases a legal principle has emerged that unless intent to discriminate can be shown, a seniority system that has an adverse impact and perpetuates discrimination is valid.

EXPOSURE OF PERFORMANCE APPRAISAL PLANS

Personnel literature is abundant on what is an effective performance appraisal plan to improve employee effectiveness.[16] We are told that appraisals should motivate employees to perform at their highest levels. Various methods and goals to achieve these results often evaluate work behaviors, while others focus on personality traits. Some academic writers and practitioners tell what management is doing wrong to cause performance appraisals to be ineffective, while others take a positive approach and tell how to make them effective.[17]

This section will be concerned with the legal aspects of performance appraisals. As a personnel technique, performance appraisal can be effective as a training device in improving performance, but if used to make an employment decision on a member of the protected class it must be a valid system or it will be challenged in the courts. All too often management fails to realize that evaluating performance is subject to external audit in the same manner as selection, promotion, or discharge.

In some organizations the same basic performance appraisal systems have been in use for many years—so many in fact that they are seldom audited as to their usefulness. Criteria for employee performance were originally developed around the personality characteristics of white males. Very few female or minority employees were at organizational levels that merited performance reviews. Since the advent of discrimination laws, this reliance on obsolete standards and practices is particularly dangerous when organizations use the results in the selection of candidates for promotion and in granting wage increases.

Under present court decisions a rating system that depends upon subjective criteria and measures personality traits rather than behavior is worse than having no performance appraisal at all. When allegations are made that a rating system is discriminatory and therefore violates Title VII, the employer must defend the methods used and— if they prove to be subjective—that defense becomes very difficult. An example of what can happen is the case of a black engineer who filed a class action suit against General Motors alleging that GM has a discriminatory performance appraisal system that is used for selecting candidates for promotion. The complaint asked that a nondiscriminatory program be instituted and an injunction be issued against further use of the present system.[18] The court action emphasizes the point that failure to correct the faults in a subjec-

---

[14]*Pullman Standard* v. *Swint,* 102 S.Ct. 1781 (1982).

[15]*American Tobacco Company* v. *Patterson,* 102 S.Ct. 1534 (1982).

[16]A survey showed that only 30 percent of the managers and employees believed that performance appraisals were effective in improving performance. Opinion Research, Inc., Princeton, N.J., 1984.

[17]See Terry R. Lowe, "Eight Ways to Ruin a Performance Appraisal," *Personnel Journal,* 65, no. 1 (January 1986), 60; Tom G. Cummings, "Improving the Value of Performance Appraisals," *SAM Advance Management Journal* (Spring 1986), p. 19; C. E. Schneir and L. S. Beaty, *The Performance Management Source Book* (Amherst, MA: Human Resource Development, 1987).

[18]This case was settled out of court for a large sum in back pay and an agreement by GM to revise the performance appraisal system.

tive system invites litigation and possible penalties.

Reasons for Failure of Appraisal Systems

Most appraisal systems fail because the rater is not trained and

1. Rates all performance on one impressive performance on a job
2. Has a dislike for one particular trait
3. Stays away from extreme ratings, never excellent or unacceptable
4. Relies on recent events instead of performance for the whole period
5. Avoids conflict or justification by giving a good appraisal
6. Compares ratee with self and how performance affected his or her own situation
7. Does not inform ratee what part of performance is being appraised and how it will be measured
8. Does not rate results or behavior but uses subjective measurements
9. Fails to give proper feedback

Judicial Review of Performance Appraisals

It took judicial action to force management to review their performance appraisals and to question whether they accurately measured performance on the job. For years the courts have considered performance appraisals a legitimate management right and function. With the advent of the antidiscrimination laws, the courts were forced to review the function. What they found were subjective appraisals, and any resemblance between actual performance on the job and what the appraisal said was coincidental.

One of the first appellate courts to scrutinize performance appraisals was the Fifth Circuit in New Orleans. The employer's appraisal methods did not relate to performance on the job but to trait characteristics. The court said that where the appraisal is used to make an employment decision or an adverse impact is shown, the appraisal methods must be validated with performance.[19] In this case, transfers were dependent almost entirely on favorable recommendation of the immediate supervisor, who used subjective evaluations of job performance as a basis for promotion. Subjective evaluations permitted the supervisor to exercise race discrimination in the promotion process.

One year later another court, in *Brito et al.* v. *Zia Company*, 428 F.2d 1200 (10th Cir. 1973), held that the Zia Company discriminated against Spanish-American workers when it used an invalid performance appraisal for promotion purposes. In that case the court said that the Zia Company used an invalid test according to EEOC guidelines because the test was correlated with an invalid performance appraisal. Therefore, the promotion procedure was invalid as a result. At Zia Company only a few evaluators kept any records. Some supervisors evaluated employees not directly under their supervision while other evaluators were present in the plant only half of the time; in some instances evaluation was done when the evaluator had not been in the plant for months.

It was clear that the evaluations were based on best judgments and opinions, with no evidence of identifiable criteria of job performance. In the Zia case the court relied heavily on EEOC guidelines.

The courts are quick to reject appraisal systems that are subjective and not related to job performance.[20] A subjective appraisal by its nature uses different criteria for different job categories and for different persons and therefore gets the attention of the courts, just as other subjective decisions.

In one case the court said that unless there are written guidelines for the raters and they are otherwise trained in the standardized method of appraisal, the process is invalid.[21]

---

[19]*Rowe* v. *General Motors*, 457 F.2d 348 (5th Cir. 1972).

[20]*Wade* v. *Mississippi Cooperative Extension Service*, 529 F.2d 508 (5th Cir. 1976).

[21]In *Bohrer* v. *Hanes Corp.*, 715 F.2d 213 (5th Cir. 1985) the court found objective standards and dismissed an age discrimination charge.

Although the courts hold that subjective methods arc unlawful, they continue in many organizations; when challenged, the courts will almost always declare the method in violation of Title VII.[22]

In Jackson, the court said performance evaluations were impermissibly subjective and used unarticulated standards to judge job performance. There is little disagreement among the courts that subjective appraisal methods are in violation of Title VII;[23] however, an appraisal method is bound to have some subjectivity and this is recognized by the courts. The courts have approved subjective methods in hiring if they include objective standards. Where the subjective oral interview was given to applicants for an electrician's job but there was a requirement that the applicant meet certain tests or have eight years of journeyman experience, the court said that the subjective oral interview is not discriminatory as long as objective criteria of certain skill tests or experiences are also used.[24] It would appear from the rationale of this case that if an objective standard for performance were established and subjective reasons were stated why that performance standard was not met, the appraisal method would be valid.

Need to Change Performance Appraisals

Many progressive employers have changed their performance appraisal methods and have adopted the use of management by objectives (MBO) as a basis for their performance systems. Where performance appraisal uses MBO, it must be an ongoing procedure between the supervisor and the subordinate, not just a meeting every six months during which only the most recent data are used. Those who

have been successful with an MBO approach have insisted on the classical form of quantitative and measurable objectives rather than the more subjective type used by some companies.

If the employer does not validate performance appraisals, the courts will on a case-by-case basis. In *Allen* v. *City of Mobile*, 466 F.2d 1245 (5th Cir. 1972), cert. denied, 411 U.S. 909 (1973), the court said that the performance rating system was discriminatory and prescribed another performance rating system. There is no assurance that the judicially prescribed method of appraisal has any more validity or would serve a more useful purpose for promotion than the employer's system; however, the method prescribed by the court is the legal, valid method for those employers within the jurisdiction of the 5th Circuit Court of Appeals.

Another court followed the Allen case and ordered a rating system that would ensure that minorities and nonminorities would be equally graded. The federal district court prescribed the performance appraisal as an alternative to the one that it struck down, but it was not a validation method that could be applied to other factual situations.[25]

The problem of performance appraisal systems as related to court decisions was studied by Feild and Holley of Auburn University. These investigators found that the courts consistently rejected appraisal systems as invalid when no specific instructions were given to the raters, appraisals were trait oriented rather than behavior oriented, and job analysis was not used in developing the content of the rating form.[26]

The need for validation of performance appraisal systems cannot be overempha-

[22]*Jackson* v. *Ebasco Services*, 634 F.Supp. 1565 (D.C.N.Y. 1986).

[23]If there is no rating system, creditable supervisor testimony is acceptable. See *Cova* v. *Coca-Cola Bottling of St. Louis*, 574 F.2d 576 (6th Cir. 1978).

[24]*Hamilton* v. *General Motors Corp.*, 606 F.2d 576 (5th Cir. 1979).

[25]*Harper* v. *Mayor City Council of Baltimore*, 359 F.Supp. 1187 (D.C. Md. 1973).

[26]Hubert S. Feild and William H. Holley, "The Relationship of Performance Appraisal Systems Characteristics to Verdicts in Selected Employment Discrimination Cases," research paper (Auburn, AL: Auburn University, 1980).

sized. If the organization does not review its system, the courts may on a case-by-case basis. The court-prescribed system may not be any better than—indeed, it may not be as good as—the one struck down, but its use will be required to free the employer from liability in discrimination cases.

Recommendations for Validating Appraisal Plans

The first step in the validation of a performance appraisal procedure is to eliminate—as far as possible—all criteria based on personality traits. The next step is to determine whether any relationship exists between what the appraisal procedure measures and job performance. If the correlation is not good, start with a new procedure. The next thing to do is to develop a new system that utilizes some of the court decisions in discrimination cases.

At this point it many be a good idea to reevaluate the purpose of the rating procedure. Is the purpose to improve performance (a training function)? Do you want a basis for wage and salary determinations or for promotion decisions? If you decide that the main use is for training, then the procedure—minus the subjective elements—may meet the validation requirements of the courts. If the purpose is to determine wage and salary levels or to establish eligibility for promotion, it is imperative that the method relate clearly to job performance. Key considerations in your validation review should include

1. The level of performance expected of the employee expressed in quantitative terms to the extent possible
2. Criteria that will determine whether the employee met the expectations of the job
3. An audit of the effectiveness of training of those doing the rating
4. The use of standardized rating methods

Removing Subjectivity from Appraisal Results

The courts are saying that unless performance appraisals are objective, they cannot be used to make employment decisions when members of the protected class are involved. A performance appraisal program is objective if it contains the following elements.

1. The rater states what is expected of the employee in the form of job standards based on assigned responsibilities. The employee must understand what part of the job is being appraised.
2. The rater evaluates and discusses the performance informally during the appraisal period. The employee must be told how she or he is doing and not be surprised at appraisal time.
3. Written ratings are supported by specific examples or observations of behavior related to the job. These observations should be made by the rater.[27]
4. Where the rater cannot observe continually, the opinion of others who use the employee's services can be used.
5. The rater appraises results, not effort or personal characteristics. The only proper subject for performance appraisal is productive behavior that produces results.[28]

Suggestion for a Judicially Acceptable Appraisal Plan

What type of form the rater is required to use depends a great deal upon the job category and the purpose for which the rating is to be used. Exhibit 6-2 is a suggested form that considers all the decisions of the courts and at the same time would serve to evaluate performance and improve the effectiveness of the ratee.

---

[27]For a small company, observation is probably better than a formal rating system. However, the observation must be communicated to the ratee.

[28]A consultant was once asked by a client to speak to the client organization and "motivate them to communicate." "What aren't they doing?" asked the consultant. "They aren't getting their reports in on time," replied the client. "Well, I have a suggestion for you," said the consultant. "Call them together and tell them 'Get your reports in on time or you are likely to be fired.' You will get your reports." It is sometimes helpful to remember that your system should concentrate on measuring what you want employees to do, not on what you want them to be.

EXHIBIT 6-2 *Valid Performance Appraisal Procedure*

Steps in Developing a Valid Procedure

1. Rater meets with ratee to discuss
   a. Job responsibilities
   b. Improvements to be achieved during the rating period
   c. A work plan to achieve those improvements, which concentrates on results and behavior
   d. The method used to evaluate performance under the work plan
   e. The standardized form to be used in the evaluation process
   f. How the evaluation results will be used (salary review, for promotion or for training only, and so on)
2. Ratee makes a self-assessment of strengths and weaknesses and what he or she feels is needed to achieve the improvements. (This is not communicated to anyone except that it was done.)
3. Rater does periodic monitoring of the progress during the review period, communicating to ratee unacceptable performance, praising superior performance, and modifying the work plan if necessary. This is an ongoing procedure that communicates to the ratee the progress toward achieving the improvements.
4. Rater states the reason for conclusions on the form and analyzes the ratee performance as to why the expected improvements were exceeded or not met. Rater prepares for meeting with ratee.
5. Rater meets with ratee and discusses his or her evaluation of the ratee's performance and develops a plan for improvement through formal training or on-the-job exposure if appropriate. (The evaluation should be no surprise to ratee if progress reports were made.)
6. Rater explains to ratee how the results are going to be used according to what was discussed in the initial meeting at beginning of review period.
7. Rater has the next level of supervision review the process; this eliminates the charge of bias and fixes responsibility for compliance.

Drafting a Performance Appraisal Plan

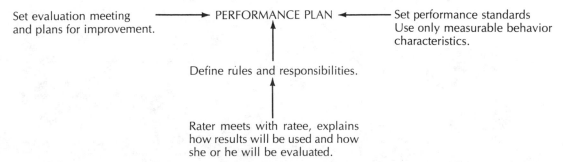

Set evaluation meeting and plans for improvement. ——→ PERFORMANCE PLAN ←—— Set performance standards. Use only measurable behavior characteristics.

↑

Define rules and responsibilities.

↑

Rater meets with ratee, explains how results will be used and how she or he will be evaluated.

Although most court decisions have not made it a requirement, it may be advisable to provide an opportunity in the plan for the employee to make a self-assessment of his or her strengths and weaknesses in achieving the expectations of the job. This self-analysis may then be used for comparison with the rater's report and discussion of differences of perception. Self-assessment not only is a training exercise but also may eliminate serious differences between the rater and the person being rated. Of considerable importance is the fact that the procedure is less likely to be challenged in the courts.

Performance appraisals have enjoyed extensive application in both public and private employment, but the decisions of the courts have placed the system in a precarious position. Employers must undertake research as to validation of performance appraisals. Basically, the objection to them is that they do not measure actual job performance. The courts are in complete agreement that—where a member of a protected class is involved—a subjective, unstandardized system cannot be used as a nondiscriminatory reason for not promoting one person over another.

CHAPTER

7

AGE DISCRIMINATION IN EMPLOYMENT ACT (ADEA)

The problem of what to do with the older worker has haunted employers for many years. There seemed to be no easy solution to the problem of the marginal worker who has been with the company for 30 years and has substandard performance for 25 of the 30 years. Like many other personnel problems, the solution was an arbitrary one: compulsory retirement at age 65 for all employees, except the board of directors and chief executive officer. This solution was destined to meet with social and political opposition for two reasons. One, many employees were still productive at age 65;[1] physical and mental ability and attitude toward retirement are an individual matter, not one that can be categorized. Second, there is no medical or other authority for age 65 as the time when most employees cease to be productive.[2]

The compulsory retirement at 65 became almost universal in American business as well as in other organizations. In a survey of 400 companies in 1977, 2 of 3 companies had compulsory retirement, typically at age 65. The usual reason given was to create job opportunities for younger persons.[3] When almost all employers have a policy with social and economic implications, political forces will usually step in to correct it. As members of Congress have so often said about employer practices, "You correct it yourself or we will do it for you" (when it becomes politically advisable). As for the older worker, compulsory retirement, demotion, or discharge to make room for a younger person was an easy solution until Congress stopped it in 1978.

AN OVERVIEW OF ADEA

The purpose of the Age Discrimination in Employment Act (ADEA)[4] is to promote employment of older persons based on their ability to perform and to prohibit compulsory retirement.

The act and its amendments contain the following basic provisions:

1. It forbids employers with 20 or more employees, including public employers, employment agencies, and labor organizations (with 25 or more members), to make employment decisions based on a person's age when that person is over 40. This is interpreted to mean that preference cannot be shown within the protected group. An employer could not express preference of a 45- to 55-year-old person as this would discriminate because of age. The Tax Equity and Fiscal Responsibility Act of 1982 amended ADEA to require the same benefits between age 65 and 69 as granted employees below that age group.[5]

2. The act invalidates compulsory retirement in pension plans in the private and public sectors. If inability to perform the job can be shown, or if an executive in a policy-making position, or if the person has a pension above $44,000 without Social Security, the employee could be subjected to compulsory retirement.

3. The act authorizes jury trial of any issue of fact.

4. The act expressly authorizes employers to treat older employees differently in certain circumstances:

    a. If age is a bona fide occupational qualification

    b. If different treatment of older workers is based on reasonable factors other than age

    c. If the decision is the result of a bona fide seniority system

    d. If discharge is for just cause, age cannot be used as a discriminating reason.

5. The law is enforced by EEOC; however, because of right of jury trial the commission has more legal clout than in other antidiscrimination laws.

---

[1]In 1985 11 percent of the work force was over 65. Donald G. Fowles, comp., "A Profile of Older Americans: 1986," American Association of Retired Persons, Washington, DC 20049.

[2]The basis that a 65-year-old worker was so old as to warrant compulsory retirement came from German Chancellor Otto von Bismarck in 1887 as the age when the German social security system should start. Life expectancy is twice what it was in 1887. Further, Bismarck was neither a doctor nor an entrepreneur but an army general.

[3]William W. Mercer, Inc., "Employer Attitudes toward Mandatory Retirement" (New York: June 1977).

[4]29 USC Sect. 613 et seq.

[5]29 USCA 623(g)(1), Sect. 116 P.L. 97–248 96 Stat. 353 (1982).

Exemptions under ADEA

The ADEA provides that if an employee has been employed for two years preceding the retirement date in a "high policy-making position" this employee would be exempt from the compulsory retirement restrictions of the ADEA.[6] The issue in all these cases is what is considered a high policy-making position. Although this exemption may be used by a large number of employers, few cases ever reach the courts. Either the disputes are settled out of court (often a voluntary retirement arrangement is worked out) or the employee who has a claim chooses not to sue. From the few court decisions we do have, a high policy-making position is defined as that held by the person who actually performs the policy-making duties for the two-year period.

This definition was challenged in *Whittlesey* v. *Union Carbide Corp.*, 742 F.2d 724 (2nd Cir. 1984), where the court held that a chief labor counsel was not a bona fide executive within the meaning of ADEA. The plaintiff was one of six attorneys who reported to an assistant general counsel; the assistant general counsel reported to the general counsel, who reported to the president of Union Carbide. It was argued by the company that since the plaintiff was highly compensated he was an executive for the purposes of the act. The court held that the level of salary is not determinative of whether a position comes within the exemption of the act. The exemption is one of function, not pay. Here there were minimal supervisory duties and Union Carbide did not encourage or invite its house lawyers to participate in a dynamic policy-making role; they were employed to do legal work, not executive work.

Another case that considered the question of a bona fide executive exemption was *Colby* v. *Graniteville Co.*, 635 F.Supp. 381 (S.D. N.Y. 1986). The plaintiff's primary duty in this case consisted of the management of a department or subdivision of the company. His title was Senior Vice President of Administration of a sales division in New York. He reported only to the president of the company. The managers of accounting, administrative services and office service, the administrator of financial analysis, and the administrator of credit all reported to the plaintiff. He was a member of several operating and administrative committees, including the Executive Compensation Plan. He was the only employee in the New York office who had a car and a country club membership provided by the company. The court said that high pay accompanied by the nature of the responsibilities given to only a few individuals in the company made him a bona fide executive, and therefore he could be forced to retire at age 65.

The facts in these two cases are in sharp contrast in that the reporting relationship, the number of employees, supervision, and almost all the job responsibilities are different. The employee in the Colby case not only had the responsibilities of an executive but also was treated like one when given a country club membership, a company car, and participation in executive committee activities.

When considering whether or not an executive can be retired at age 65, the employer must consider the job content, the reporting relationship, and whether or not the employee participated in policy-making decisions.

Problems in Defending Employment Decisions

Since ADEA is concerned with workers who are over 40, many unique problems are created that are not found in other antidiscrimination laws. In 1985 36 percent of the work force was over 40 and there were over 16,000 cases filed with the EEOC.[7] This was a 52-percent increase since 1982. In 1986 26,349 cases were filed with EEOC (last fig-

---

[6]29 USCA Sect. 631(c).

[7]Nicholas J. Mathys, Helen La Van, and Frederick Schwerdtner, "Learning the Lessons of Age Discrimination Cases," *Personnel Journal* (June 1984), p. 30.

ures available). With the baby boom generation coming under the act in the late 1980s and early 1990s, employees over 40 will be the largest protected class under anti-discrimination laws.

ADEA is the only antidiscrimination law that allows jury trial. Since the average age of people selected to serve on a jury is over 40 and almost all jurors are now or were at one time employees, there isn't much sympathy for the employer.[8] It is also "human" for a judge to sympathize with the older worker since his or her age is usually over 40.

The employer has another "built-in headwind" when dealing with the older worker. Due to the length of service, the worker's salary is usually higher than the market price for the same skills. When the labor costs have to be reduced, the older worker can be replaced by a younger person (who is probably as well qualified) at less cost. ADEA inhibits management's desire to perpetuate the company by training and promoting younger workers if older workers cannot be replaced until they retire. At one time the older worker could be retired at 70 so at least there was some room to move up the younger worker, but with the age 70 limitation removed management must now prove poor performance before the older worker can be replaced. This is often difficult to do with a worker of 30 years of service and subjective performance appraisals that are judicially unacceptable as a rationale for employment decisions.[9] It is no wonder that management loses over 50 percent of the ADEA cases that go to court, not to mention the vast, unrecorded majority that are settled out of court.

---

[8]Jury trial is permitted in ADEA cases even though other forms of relief are available, such as arbitration or contractual remedies.

[9]In a 1987 American Society for Personnel Administration survey, 22 percent of the respondents were using personal traits to measure performance and 75 percent said their appraisal systems were useful in making decisions involving older workers. Since courts do not accept personal traits as a valid method to measure performance, it is not surprising that age lawsuits have increased more than any other discrimination cases.

AGE AS A FACTOR IN MAKING A DECISION

The ADEA affects every employment decision where the employee involved is over 40. The courts have interpreted the act to mean that age need not be the only factor but must be the determining or significant factor. If there is a finding that there are significant and compelling factors involved in making the decision, other than age, the plaintiff will not have established a prima facie case and the action will fail.[10]

Factors other than age may include discharge for just cause. Where a 56-year-old repeatedly ignored specific directions of his supervisors, the court held that discharge was not because of age but for insubordination.[11] By the same reasoning, where discharge of an employee was bad faith and violation by the employer of covenant of fair dealing under the state law, the court awarded the major share of punitive damages for violation of implied covenant and not violation of ADEA.[12]

The inability to perform satisfactorily the particular job and incompetence are factors other than age that could justify a discharge or transfer; however, performance and incompetency determinations are often subjective. Therefore the burden of proof is greater than in traditional misconduct situations where objective facts are more easily obtainable. It is advisable in incompetency situations to have objective measurements of unsatisfactory performance before a decision involving an older worker's performance. When an employee is not performing satisfactorily, the company has to either transfer or terminate. It is difficult for the employee to admit poor performance, and if there is protection under ADEA very often the employee will allege that if it wasn't for

---

[10]*Loeb* v. *Textron,* 600 F.2d 1003 (1st Cir. 1979); *Spagnuolo* v. *Whirlpool Corp.,* 641 F.2d 1109 (4th Cir. 1981).

[11]*Havelick* v. *Julius Wile & Sons, Inc.,* 445 F.Supp. 919 (S.D. N.Y. 1978).

[12]*Cancellier* v. *Federated Department Stores, dba I. Magnin,* 672 F.2d 1312 (9th Cir. 1982).

his or her age, the decision would not have been made.

In *Huhn* v. *Koehring Co.*, 718 F.2d 239 (7th Cir. 1983), the employee had 30 years of service as a sales representative. The company terminated him for poor performance. They stated that they were not satisfied with his sales record in his sales territory. The employee contended that the termination was because of his age. The court in granting a motion for summary judgment stated that the company can make a decision to terminate even if it is unjust. As long as it can be shown that the decision was not based on age, there is no violation. The court went on to say that the issue was not whether there was satisfactory performance, since the company determines this, but whether age was a factor in making the decision. Since the plaintiff could not show that age was a factor, the complaint was dismissed.

Where the employer can show that the decision to terminate was not based on age, it can be defended even where a subjective performance is used. *Cova* v. *Coca-Cola Bottling Co. of St. Louis*, 574 F.2d. 958 (8th Cir. 1978), so held. Evidence that there were attempts to improve performance and that the plaintiff was warned about unsatisfactory performance is a strong defense to rebut the employee's contention that the decision was based on age. In *Bohrer* v. *Hanes Corp.*, 715 F.2d 213 (5th Cir. 1985), the plaintiff had been a salesman for 20 years. He was moderately successful in meeting his sales quotas but according to the company was deficient in other aspects of his job. The company gave subjective evidence that he did not institute merchandising techniques with his customers and would not follow any management policy or instructions if he disagreed with them. The evidence showed that supervision had several meetings with the employee in order to correct the problem. The employee acknowledged the criticisms and expressly resolved to do better, but he didn't. This evidence gave the subjective evaluation credibility. He was terminated and replaced with a 28-year-old person. The case was tried by the jury and they awarded the plaintiff $167,320; the employer moved for a judgment notwithstanding the verdict. The lower court granted it and the circuit court in affirming stated that there was substantial evidence of poor performance so that if allowed to stand the jury verdict would be miscarriage of justice. The U.S. Supreme Court denied review. This is a good example of a case in which there was evidence of trying to correct the poor performance, so age could not have been a factor in terminating and the jury had no basis for the award.

Sometimes an employer will argue that an older worker was replaced by a younger worker to reduce costs. The courts will recognize this as a factor other than age if there would be severe economic consequences by retaining the older worker.[13]

EARLY RETIREMENT PROGRAMS

It is not a violation of ADEA if the employee voluntarily retires.[14] Most companies offer early retirement incentives to employees over 55 years and with a specified length of service (ten years or above being the most popular). Early retirement programs avoid layoffs or involuntary terminations. For this reason they have been offered more frequently during a recession than during high economic activity. In 1982, in the midst of a recession, 27 percent of the companies surveyed had made early retirement offers to their employees. However, in 1986, when there was not a recession, over 23 percent of those surveyed had offered retirement programs, which indicates that these programs are becoming popular as a personnel technique without a recession.[15] While early retirement plans are gaining wide accep-

[13]*Metz* v. *Transit Mix, Inc.*, 828 F.2d 1202 (7th Cir. 1987).

[14]29 CFR Sect. 1625.9(f).

[15]See "Early Retirement Incentives" (1987), Research Report lll.02-1, Charles D. Spencer & Associates, Inc., 222 W. Adams St., Chicago, IL 60606.

A Voluntary Retirement That Was Not Voluntary—
Case History

The following case history is an illustration of a typical problem of the aging worker.

John Doe, age 64, was for 40 years a marginally qualified administrative manager for a 250-employee manufacturing facility. As most of his work was being computerized, John realized that either he had to learn computer procedures or retire. He went to his supervisor of 20 years and requested special projects for the next year, after which he would retire, at age 65. His supervisor orally agreed. They shook hands and everybody was happy.

During the succeeding year, John trained his replacement to the limit of his ability and performed useful special project assignments with a high level of competency. In his retirement plans, John had not done sufficient financial planning to allow for inflation. Also, during the year his wife died, and working became much more interesting than a lonely retirement. John saw his supervisor and told him that he had changed his mind and wanted his old job or a similar job, and he was willing to learn the new computer procedures and considered himself more qualified than applicants being considered for a vacancy in another facility. The supervisor called the personnel director and requested advice. The personnel director consulted the legal department. The legal counsel advised that because John had a satisfactory work performance for the past 40 years, it would be difficult to convince a jury in an age discrimination suit that he was not qualified until he was given an opportunity on the new job and his performance objectively measured.

This case is a classic example of an employer making an employment decision that was considered fair to both parties without anticipating what could happen in the ensuing year. It is possible that the employer could have argued that there was an oral agreement and that the employee had to retire as agreed. However, lengthy litigation, exposure to punitive damages, employee relations consequence of an employee with 40 years of employment suing the employer, and a jury trial warranted a business decision to make retirement attractive to John. Therefore, an agreement was drafted.

tance among employers, employees also like them. Most employers underestimate the number of employees who will accept the incentive and take early retirement. However, voluntary retirement programs are not without problems, as illustrated in the case history above.

In making early retirement offers the employer often faces the loss of skills and management "know how" that cannot quickly be replaced. One way to bridge the gap between training new employees and the loss of the old is to make a consulting agreement with the early retirees. Consulting agreements are very popular, not only to bridge the gap but also to provide the retiree with additional income while the adjustment is being made from full salary to retirement income.

Waivers and/or Releases under ADEA

Almost all early retirement programs require the employee to sign a waiver or a release. The legal result is not the same. In waiver, the employee waives all rights. In a release, the employer is relieved of liability, but no rights are given up. A waiver under ADEA is enforceable in the courts if there is no showing of coercion. The EEOC will permit a waiver without its supervision if certain conditions are met.[16]

1. The agreement must be in writing, in understandable language, and must clearly waive a worker's ADEA rights.
2. A reasonable period of time must be provided for employee deliberation.
3. The waiver must state that the employee was encouraged to consult an attorney.
4. The waiver must show comprehensive efforts by the employer to compare benefits of retiring with continuing to work.
5. There should be evidence of negotiations between the parties as to terms for retiring.
6. The employee must know that the employer cannot discharge because of age and that she or he is giving up this protection by signing the waiver.

The court in *Valenti* v. *International Mill Services,* 45 EPD Para. 37628 CCH (not otherwise cited) (3rd Cir. 1987), stated the above conditions are necessary to validate a release. A sure way for enforceable waiver or release is to get EEOC approval.

These conditions are designed to assure the EEOC that the early retirement was "knowingly voluntary." Signing a waiver does not prevent the employee from filing a charge although his or her right to recover any damages may have been waived. When signing a release, the employee is prevented from filing a charge or recovering damages.

Inasmuch as the employee has the opportunity to allege coercion after the retirement plan is accepted, the employer must be cautious not to imply any form of coercion when the early retirement plan is accepted by the employee. In one case the employee stated that he would not have signed the agreement had he thought the waiver was enforceable. The court considered the testimony creditable, but enforced the waiver since the employee had consulted an attorney. The language was simple, the employer went to great efforts to explain the terms, and the employee did not attempt any different terms.[17] In *Paolillo* v. *Dresser Industries,* 813 F.2d 583 (2nd. Cir. 1987), the employees accepted the retirement plan but later sued under ADEA, alleging that they were not given sufficient time to consider. The employer contended that they had to show more discriminatory action before they could establish a prima facie case. The court said that all the plaintiff had to show was that their employment ended and they were over 40. The court was bothered by the short period of time (six days) to make a decision and that the employer had no reasonable purpose for the early retirement plan except an economic one, which was not acceptable by this court.

The rationale of this case makes the employer extremely vulnerable, since the employee doesn't have to allege any discriminatory act before the employer has to give a nondiscriminatory reason for offering early retirement to employees over 40 and make a showing that it was strictly voluntary. Any scratch of evidence that age was a factor and it was not voluntary would result in an exposure to a lawsuit. An option of early retirement or termination for whatever reason would be construed as a termination if not voluntary.[18] One court held that the employer was required to pay severance pay to employees who elected early retirement because it was paid to employees discharged as a result of reduction in force.[19] It would be a violation to give a smaller amount to those who retire at 65 than if they retired early, but not a violation of ADEA if the same amount is given early [*Harvey Karlene* v. *College of Chicago,* 837 F.2d 314 (7th Cir. 1988)]. These three cases are examples of how closely the courts will examine the facts to deter-

---

[16]Final rules on releases were published in 52 Fed. Reg. 32293, August 27, 1987.

[17]*Sullivan* v. *Boron Oil Co.,* 831 F.2d 288 (3rd Cir. 1987).

[18]*EEOC* v. *Chrysler,* 733 F.2d 1189 (6th Cir. 1984).

[19]*EEOC* v. *Westinghouse,* 752 F.2d 211 (3rd Cir. 1983), cert. denied, 469 U.S. 820 (1984).

mine whether there was any implication that the acceptance of the early retirement proposal was not voluntary.

Elements of an Early Retirement Option

Because of the exposure in early retirement plans, certain facts should be present and well documented.

1. The most important element is to draft the agreement in simple, unambiguous language.
2. Give ample inducement for the employee to retire. Some of the most popular early retirement incentives include early vesting of pension benefits, continuation of health care insurance, severance pay above the normal amount, maintaining an employee on a consulting basis, and retraining for a retirement vocation.
3. Explain what benefits the employee would receive if he or she continued working and retired at a later date.
4. Give the employee sufficient time to make the decision. Advise that she or he see a lawyer if uncomfortable about the terms.[20]
5. Get a signed statement that the early retirement option was absolutely voluntary. This is the key to avoid exposure.

Early retirement can be a useful tool in avoiding age discrimination charges, but it also can cause litigation if not properly administered.

Age and Reduction in Force

One of the areas that has been given particular attention under ADEA is termination as a result of the reduction in force (RIF).[21]

There are several reasons for this. Often the older worker's performance has not been objectively evaluated for a long period of time yet she or he continues to be employed and receives periodic wage increases. However, when it comes to RIF the employer considers the advantages in having a younger work force and looks for reasons to reduce the force by terminating the older workers. This runs head-on into ADEA. In any RIF program care must be taken to be sure that age is not a factor in selecting the employees to be terminated.

The selection of the person to be terminated cannot be subjective. There must be an objective method of selecting the most-qualified person that leaves no doubt that age was not a factor in the selection process. The courts are clear that ADEA is not a guarantee of employment beyond age 40, but "shabby employment practices" would indicate that age might be a factor.[22] Where the employer used a supervisor peer committee and a number of rating systems, which were sent to the personnel department and objectively reviewed, and some of the senior older workers were terminated, the court held that the employer had proved the nondiscriminatory basis for its decision.[23]

The most sophisticated program for RIF is found in the one used by Cargill, Inc., where three levels of management used a matrix and the human resources department was involved. The matrix was prepared to evaluate each employee. The final matrix was submitted to all department heads and division heads for approval. Nine employees were discharged, five of whom were 40 or over. The court said that the employer's action was for legitimate and nondiscriminatory reasons.[24]

---

[20]Some states require by statute that 15 days be given to rescind. In *Runyan* v. *National Cash Register*, 787 F.2d 1039 (6th Cir. 1986), the employee alleged that the waiver for ADEA was invalid. The court held it valid providing it can be shown that the employee knowingly entered into the agreement (he was a lawyer), there was no intimidation or coercion, and the employer did not unduly exercise its power over the employee.

[21]The RIF could also be a result of a merger when there are two persons for the same job.

[22]*Zick* v. *Verson Allsteel Press Co.*, 644 F.Supp. 906 (N.D. Ill. 1986).

[23]*Arnell* v. *Pan American World Airways, Inc.*, 41 EPD (CCH) Para. 36506 (D.C. S.D. N.Y. 1986).

[24]*Matson* v. *Cargill, Inc.*, 618 F.Supp. 278 (D.C. Minn. 1985).

Severance Pay as an Exposure

The principle behind severance pay is that the employee is economically supported until he or she finds another job. When employers implement this theory on older workers, it is often interpreted as discrimination against older workers. So when a company denied severance pay to all those who were eligible for early retirement, the court said this was a "heartless corporate policy" and allowed double damages.[25] Any time decisions are made that will have a disproportionate impact upon a protected class of employees, such as those over 40, there is an exposure to a lawsuit.

PUNITIVE DAMAGES UNDER ADEA

Originally the courts were reluctant to allow punitive damages under ADEA. In *Rogers* v. *Exxon Research & Engineering Co.,* 550 F.2d 834 (3rd Cir. 1977), the court said that ADEA does not authorize the recovery for pain and suffering. The legislative history of the act indicates that Congress intended to allow only compensatory damages. ADEA incorporates the enforcement powers of the Fair Labor Standards Act and therefore if willful under FLSA only liquidated damages (double the loss in wages) would be allowed. Often in punitive damages requests, the plaintiff is required to prove the violation to be a willful violation. In *Trans World Airlines, Inc.* v. *Thurston,* 105 S.Ct. 613 (1985), the Court stated that under the Age Discrimination in Employment Act (ADEA), it was willful if the employer either knew or showed reckless disregard for the statute on whether its conduct was prohibited by the ADEA. If the employer did not know that the act was being violated or did not recklessly disregard the ADEA, the action could not be willful.

---

[25]*EEOC* v. *Westinghouse,* 632 F.Supp. 343 (E.D. Pa. 1986).

Jury Awards under ADEA

No punitive damages was the rule until in *Cancellier* v. *Federated Dept. Stores,* 672 F.2d 1312 (9th Cir. 1982), the court allowed punitive damages where bad faith was shown. Since this case, the employer has had an increased exposure to punitive damages in ADEA claims. In two well-cited cases not only did the courts award punitive damages when the ADEA had been violated but also the amount exceeded one million dollars.

In *Rawson* v. *Sears, Roebuck and Co.,* 615 F.Supp. 1546 (D.C. Colo. 1985), the company discharged a 60-year-old store manager. He had worked for the company for 33 years. It was the only job he had had after returning from World War II. His performance was never below satisfactory and there was ample evidence for the jury to conclude that he was a loyal, dedicated, and productive employee. There was also sufficient evidence for the jury to conclude that he was discharged in a "callous and demeaning manner," that the method was insulting and in utter disregard for the plaintiff's rights and feelings. The plaintiff put in evidence that Sears didn't even permit him to retire with dignity by letting him resign. (We can guess he would have been agreeable to an early retirement offer.) The reason given the plaintiff for discharge was reduction in force, poor performance, failure to administer employee procedures, and mishandling of inventories; but little evidence was presented to show this. The evidence showed that the discharge was the result of a companywide plan to reduce the number of older workers in order to make room for the promotions of younger employees (a common management practice). The court said that the jury could find by the evidence that the company would reap large financial gains from employee cutbacks. The jury awarded $580,000 for lost wages, $264,410 for future loss of wages and reduction in pension plan and other benefits, and $5 million for pain and suffering. Because there was malice and wanton disregard of the plaintiff's rights and feelings, $10 million was awarded for exemplary (punitive) damages. (The plaintiff's attorney only asked for $1 million exemplary damages.) The judge in upholding the jury award stated that based on the evidence "his judicial conscience is not shocked—though his acquired cynicism has received a rather sharp blow."

In *Flanigan* v. *Prudential Federal Savings & Loan Association*, 720 P.2d 257 (Mont. 1986), the Supreme Court of Montana upheld a $100,000 award for emotional distress and $1.3 million for exemplary damages. The court acknowledged that $1.3 million was excessive, but such punitive damages were within the jury's discretion. The plaintiff had worked for the defendant for 28 years and rose from teller to assistant loan counselor. She was told that in six months her position would be eliminated and was offered the position of a teller. She took a week-long refresher course and had worked as a teller for less than three weeks when she was fired without notice. The employer in defense stated that she was a part of a legitimate reduction in force. The jury wasn't convinced, mostly because of the conflicting employer testimony. One witness testified that it was poor performance; another witness said it was a reduction in force. From this the jury could believe there was no reduction in force. The court in acknowledging that she was an employee-at-will stated that a long-time employee has an expectation of continued employment as long as work performance is satisfactory. The court states that the award was not excessive in view of the company president's stating that older employees were considered "deadwood," "old deadwood," and "ballast." The court said there was a "blatant disregard for older workers."

These cases indicate that when the jury or the court does not like the way the employer discharges, it will award large punitive damages for the abuse although the ADEA is silent on punitive damages.

AVOIDING LITIGATION

Age discrimination will be a problem for the employer in the 1990s similar to race discrimination in the 1960s. The older worker is becoming a powerful force,[26] which the employer must recognize if costly litigation and high damage awards are to be avoided. Charges to the EEOC under ADEA have been on the increase for several years and the employer must develop positive programs to stop the trend. Failure to do so will result in ADEA being the most costly and disruptive of all antidiscrimination laws.

One of the most popular methods to prevent litigation is the early retirement program. As discussed elsewhere in this chapter, the key to these programs is to obtain a voluntary decision to retire. Since it is very easy to get into court and allege coercion, the signing must be absolutely voluntary.

If the employer can show that an analysis was made of selection in a reduction of force or that performance was measured objectively and that factors other than age were used in making a decision, then litigation can be avoided. If the employer is not certain that a factor other than age can be defended, an individual agreement to voluntarily retire or a general early retirement program should be considered. Employer procedures can aid in encouraging retirement. These procedures should be designed to mitigate the impact of retiring and prevent adversity when the employee is faced with a retirement decision.

Procedures to Avoid Litigation

The following recommended procedures will aid in preventing exposure to litigation:

1. First and foremost, management must develop objective standards of performance for

---

[26]If current fertility and immigration levels remain stable, the only age groups to experience significant growth in the next century will be those past age 55. Donald G. Fowles, "A Profile of Older Americans: 1986," American Association of Retired Persons, Washington, DC 20049.

employees in all job categories and make decisions based on documented analysis of employee performance and competence. Some practitioners will claim that performances cannot be measured in certain jobs. Any human endeavor can be measured, some more easily than others. Termination policies must specifically state that failure to meet communicated standards of performance is just cause for discharge. In the past, many employers tolerated less-than-acceptable work performance from older workers who were near retirement age. This situation could always be changed by enforcement of a compulsory retirement plan.

Under ADEA this option is cut off, and the older worker must meet the performance standards like other employees or be transferred to a job that can be performed. The employer under ADEA cannot afford the luxury of a marginal worker with no option to terminate.

2. Mobility among employees must be encouraged. The assistant counsel who will not become general counsel must be encouraged to keep up broad legal training to be ready to join a small law firm when conditions change, there is a reduction in staff, or the management becomes dissatisfied. Transfers within the organization must be the first consideration.

The practice of supporting only job-related training programs backfires when early retirement is encouraged. Educational programs must be expanded in order to provide related skills for the second career or a transfer to other jobs in the organization.[27]

3. Preretirement counseling should be designed to fit the individuals' needs and not be structured to what the management thinks that they need, as many contemporary programs are. The employer should not first tell the employees what their problems will be in retirement and then offer a solution. The program should start with each employee stating what problems are anticipated and requesting aid in solution.

4. Flexible retirement arrangements should be developed with employees as much as possible. Policies should be developed on an individual basis. Phased retirement may fit some individuals (company allows employee to work three days a week and then two or one before retirement). With others, financial security is most important. For others, maintaining prestige is most important. Some employees want to work part-time; others want to be occupied or challenged, if not in their present job, in some other endeavor. Some employees fear domestic problems of being home every day. As one employee put it, "My wife said that she married me for better or worse but not for lunch." Preretirement counseling must be meaningful to the employee, and this can be accomplished only on an individual basis.

Employers who have used a factor other than age in making a decision or prevented a problem by the use of releases, waivers, or early retirement programs have been successful in reducing litigation under ADEA. As more employers adopt these policies, litigation caused by ADEA will be reduced and will become less of a problem.

---

[27]It is common to give educational financial assistance to employees only for those subjects directly related to their job. If other subjects are desired, the employee does not receive aid for tuition, and so on. This should be changed to include broader subjects in the job area.

8

REGULATION OF BENEFIT PLANS AND EFFECTIVE USE OF EMPLOYEE AGREEMENTS

Regulation of Pregnancy Disability Benefits
Reemployment Rights after Military Service
Effect of Statutes on Unpaid Leave of Absence Policy
Restrictions on Vacation Policy
Regulation of Health Care Benefits and Pensions
Effective Use of Employment Agreements

An employee benefit is something of a monetary value that is not related to work performed and paid for either in whole or in part by the employer. Health insurance, life insurance, and pensions are employee benefits when the employer is the purchaser of the plans for the benefit of the employee. Normally this type of benefit is granted by a policy decision of the employer, is not taxable, and ceases when employment terminates.[1]

Another type of benefit discussed in this chapter is payment for time not worked, such as holiday pay, vacation pay, disability leave, and in some cases leaves of absence for reasons other than medical. Usually these benefits are defined in a benefit policy statement and vested in all employees when hired or shortly thereafter. These benefits have averaged over 35 percent of payroll in annual surveys made by the U.S. Chamber of Commerce. In certain circumstances the employer does not want to treat all employees alike when it comes to terms and conditions of employment; in separating these employees from others an employment agreement is necessary. Chapter 12 will describe how the payment of wages is regulated by statute. This chapter describes how statutes have regulated employee benefits even though they were granted voluntarily by the employer.

REGULATION OF PREGNANCY DISABILITY BENEFITS

In 1978 Congress amended Title VII (Sect. 701), which corrected a Supreme Court decision that denied women pregnancy-related disabilities because they were not offered to men.[2] The amendment required the employers to include disability for pregnancy if they had an existing temporary disability sick leave or health insurance benefits program. The only exception is in the case of abortion, which could be excluded unless the life of the mother is endangered if the fetus were carried to term.

Where medical complications result from an abortion, it is considered an illness and must be covered. The amendment, however, does not prevent abortion coverage on a voluntary basis.

The amendment expands the definition of sex discrimination in employment to include all employment practices where there is discriminatory treatment due to pregnancy. The refusal to hire, promote, or transfer because of pregnancy is discriminatory and is considered a violation of the act.

The congressional intent of the amendment is clear. In all employment practices, pregnancy must be treated like any other illness. The disability period begins when the employee medically can no longer perform her duties satisfactorily and ends when she is medically able to return to work. The amendment does not require the employer to grant any more benefits for pregnancy than for any other type of disability, but they must be the same. However, the state by statute may change this, as we shall discuss next in this chapter.

State Laws Concerning Pregnancy Disability

Most states have passed laws specially prohibiting discrimination based on pregnancy or interpreting their fair employment practice laws, state constitutions, or other laws to prohibit treating pregnancy differently from illness.

Because Title VII only covers employers in interstate commerce with 15 or more employees, there is no conflict with the federal law for this group of employers. Where there is dual coverage and the state law conflicts with the federal law, the same rule applies as in all other Title VII provisions, that is,

---

[1]Section 132 of the Internal Revenue Code requires that benefits meet certain conditions before they are nontaxable. Also, under statute, insurance doesn't necessarily terminate when employment ceases. This will be discussed later in this chapter.

[2]*General Electric Co.* v. *Gilbert*, 429 U.S. 125 (1976). This case also established a legal principle used in all discrimination cases that in order for an employer's action to be sexually discriminatory it must be gender based.

the state statute can be more restrictive but not conflict with federal law or the Constitution. This sometimes comes up in the abortion section of the pregnancy disability amendment where state laws are different and can run afoul of the constitutional right to terminate a pregnancy.[3] The practitioner should be familiar with state law before drafting a policy on pregnancy disability.[4]

Generally, state laws on pregnancy disability grant more benefits than the federal law does. In addition to granting benefits for pregnancy disability, some states are giving leave to the father as well as the mother, not only for childbirth but also for adoption. This is commonly called parental leave.[5] Minnesota Statute 181.940–944 is a good example.

Difference between Pregnancy and Other Illnesses

The problem with treating pregnancy like any other illness is that pregnancy is not like any other illness. The employee has notice of the forthcoming situation. After the birth there is a natural tendency of the mother to want to be with the baby after she is physically able to return to work. In some cases it could be argued that she may not be mentally able to return to work if forced to leave the baby too soon after birth. Another problem occurs when the mother is physically able to return to work, but chooses to stay home to nurse the baby. Another difference

is that after any other illness the employee usually returns to work; this is less likely in the case of pregnancy leave. Because these differences inherently exist, the courts have had difficulty in interpreting the law according to the congressional intent of the act.

Many practitioners have difficulty in treating pregnancy like any other illness in keeping the job open until the employee returns. There is a tendency to make the policy different for pregnancy because of the large number of female employees who do not return to work after delivery; the employer has no knowledge of this unless the employee advises before the leave that she will not return to work.

At the time of leaving for pregnancy disability, the employee really doesn't know whether she will return. Individuals differ and so do facts. If the baby has "colic," maybe she will return the next week. Often the worker becomes attached to the baby and wants to remain home for a long period of time, even if she is medically able to return. In this case, she may request an unpaid leave of absence. A personnel practitioner should not accept a commitment before the baby is born but just consider the situation uncertain until after the birth and there is some indication from the employee when she intends to return to work.

Case Law on Pregnancy Disability

The first problem for the courts was the period of illness. It was obvious from the language of the statute that the period of disability cannot be arbitrary as was the practice before the act.[6] The court in one situation stated that a forced-leave pregnancy policy violated the act if leave were required when first learning of the pregnancy, but did not violate the act when it applied to flight attendants in their second and third trimes-

---

[3]*Roe* v. *Wade*, 410 U.S. 113 (1973).

[4]In *California Federal Savings and Loan Assn.* v. *Guerra*, 107 S.Ct. 683 (1987), the Court upheld a statute that requires the employer to grant four weeks of unpaid leave and job protection. Five other states and Puerto Rico have similar statutes. In *Wimberly* v. *Labor and Industrial Relations Commission*, 107 S.Ct. 821 (1987), the Court found no bar of Title VII to a Missouri statute denying unemployment compensation to a worker who leaves work because of pregnancy.

[5]For a good overview of state laws and judicial decisions on parental leave, see Mary F. Radford, *Parental Leave: Judicial and Legislative Trends; Current Practices in the Workplace*, International Foundation, P. O. Box 69, Brookfield, WI 53008–0069 (1987).

---

[6]Common practice was to force unpaid leave of absence after five months of pregnancy and require return to work within three months after birth of child.

ters of pregnancy. The court reasoned that in the later stages of pregnancy BFOQ is a defense. The court said that evidence showed that in the second stage of trimester (13 to 28 weeks) it is a medical question and after 28 weeks (third stage) there is a substantial growth of passenger safety risks to warrant the policy.[7]

Where the employer provided full costs of hospital room and 100 percent of all other medical expenses for the first $750 and 80 percent thereafter, the plan made no distinction between male and female employees, but imposed a $500 deductible on the spouse of male employees for maternity benefits in the absence of complications. The male employees complained to EEOC that they were being discriminated against because their spouses were not covered in the same manner as female employees.[8] The Supreme Court agreed, reasoning that the statute makes it discriminatory to give married male employees a benefit package for their dependents that is less than that provided to married female employees.[9]

REEMPLOYMENT RIGHTS AFTER MILITARY SERVICE

One of the first restrictions on personnel policies was the Military Selective Service Act of 1967 and its amendments that protect reemployment rights of veterans. These statutes restrict promotion, probationary periods, payment of wages, leaves of absence, and vacation policies. The purpose of the statute is to maintain the same rights as if the employee were working, although he was in the service instead.[10] The exception to this principle is where there is an hours work requirement in order to receive a benefit or where contribution to a profit-sharing plan is based on work effort.[11]

The courts take the position that the act doesn't require preferential treatment, but the employee should not lose benefits because of military service.

Probationary Period for Returning Veteran

Under the Military Selective Service Act temporary employment is excluded. The question is whether a probationary period is temporary employment.

Two circuits have considered this question and have held that the probationary employee is not a temporary employee; when the veteran returns, the probationary period by reason of seniority has been served.[12] If the purpose of the probationary period is to observe the employee's work performance for a period, then these decisions would be contrary to the employer's interests. However, the argument fails unless the employer is willing to admit that after the probationary period work performance is rated differently.[13]

Another court held that a temporary employee had reemployment rights even though he stated that after service he intended to

---

[7]*Burwell* v. *Eastern Airlines*, 633 F.2d 361 (4th Cir. 1980). Also in *National City Airlines*, 700 F.2d 695 (11th Cir. 1983).

[8]According to U.S. Bureau of Census (1986), women make up about half of the work force and 80–90 percent of them will bear children while employed.

[9]*Newport News Shipbuilding and Dry Dock Co.* v. *EEOC*, 103 S.Ct. 2622 (1983). An expansion of this case could mean that refusal of parental leave would be discriminatory since one sex is being treated differently from the other.

[10]Where the employee was serving in a two-week training camp, it was not necessary to actually work the day before or the day after a holiday in order to receive holiday pay. *Walter Myer* v. *Aluminum Co. of America*, 804 F.2d 821 (3rd Cir. 1986).

[11]In *Raypole* v. *Chemi-trol Chemical Co.*, 754 F.2d 169 (6th Cir. 1985), the court held a contribution to profit sharing was not required while an employee was in service, since the employee made no work contribution.

[12]*Collins* v. *Weirton Steel Co.*, 398 F.2d 305 (4th Cir. 1968); *Montgomery* v. *Southern Electric Steel Co.*, 410 F.2d 611 (5th Cir. 1969).

[13]The probationary period will be treated in Chapter 10.

leave. The court said that there was a reasonable expectation that his job was for an indefinite period and contemplation of changing jobs in the future does not alter this.[14]

Vacation Benefits While in the Service

Suppose that an employee exercises all vacation benefits before going into the service. On the day of return the veteran asks for vacation benefits under the seniority accumulated while in the service.[15] The act does entitle the veteran to retroactive vacation benefits while in the service; however, it does require that the time spent in the service be used to determine vacation eligibility.

The Supreme Court in considering this question in *Foster* v. *Dravo*[16] reasoned that inasmuch as the veteran accumulates seniority during military service, the veteran would be entitled to another vacation upon returning, unless there were a work hour requirement before vacation benefits could be granted. One circuit has held that where sick benefits are based on a work requirement, the veteran is not entitled to such benefits until the work requirement is met.[17]

Right to Promotional Opportunities

An employee enters the military service for four years. During that time 15 promotions occur within the organization. The veteran returns. The personnel practitioner offers the returning veteran the old job. The veteran asks to review the 15 promotions. Does the returning veteran have a right to those promotions? The Supreme Court said yes, the veteran is entitled not only to the

precise seniority status but also to improvements that one would have received without military leave.[18]

This decision has been extended by one circuit court to mean that you must allow the veteran to select the vacancy even if it requires "bumping" a nonveteran.[19]

However, there are some conditions on this right. It has to be reasonably certain that the veteran would have received the promotion if not for the military leave.[20] The Supreme Court left open in Fishgold the question of whether the employer had to inform the veteran of all the vacancies during the absence. The Eighth Circuit says that the employer does, but other circuits have not ruled on this.[21] This veteran's right can be disruptive to the seniority and training system, and the law should be carefully administered as to not deny the veteran rights but still not disrupt manpower planning and employee training programs.

General Pay Increases While in the Service

Returning veterans are entitled to certain types of pay increases granted while in the military service. These increases must be of a general type, such as group increases, cost-of-living, or longevity increases. Individual merit increases are excluded.[22] A loose compensation policy that does not define the real reason for an increase can be troublesome if the employer denies the increase to the veteran because it was a merit increase and

---

[14]*Chensa* v. *International Fueling Co.,* 753 F.2d 1067 (1st Cir. 1984).

[15]This usually happens when the returning veteran does not want permanent employment with the old employer but wants vacation time before notifying the employer of quitting.

[16]420 U.S. 92 (1975).

[17]*LiPani* v. *Bohack Corp.,* 546 F.2d 487 (2nd Cir. 1976).

[18]*Fishgold* v. *Sullivan Drydock and Repair Corp.,* 328 U.S. 275 (1946).

[19]*Goggins* v. *Lincoln of St. Louis,* 702 F.2d 698 (8th Cir. 1983). In a related situation, another court held that a veteran could turn down a lesser job without losing any rights; *Stevens* v. *Tennessee Valley Authority,* 699 F.2d 314 (6th Cir. 1983).

[20]*Tiltan* v. *Missouri Pacific Railroad Co.,* 376 U.S. 169 (1964).

[21]*Alber* v. *Norfolk and Western R.R. Co.,* 654 F.2d 1271 (8th Cir. 1981).

[22]*Hatton* v. *The Tabard Press Corp.,* 406 F. 2d 592 (2nd Cir. 1969).

in fact it was a cost-of-living increase. As mentioned in Chapter 5, all too often the reason given for a wage increase is merit but everybody is granted one, without any reference to meritorious performance. Such an increase would not come under the exclusion in the Hatton case.

Accommodation for Reserve Duty

The statute requires that veterans must be given a leave of absence when going into military service. This also applies when the reservist is called into active service, the annual two- or four-week training period, or active duty for an emergency. All such leaves of absence are unpaid unless the employer's policy states otherwise. But time off for reserve duty weekly training is treated a little differently. The employer must accommodate but not to the extent of changing the work schedule.[23]

One problem an employer sometimes faces is a reservist's request for an extended leave of absence (6 to 12 months) to enroll in an advanced school for additional training necessary to be promoted as a reservist. Since the leave for an extended period puts the employer at an inconvenience and the enrollment is voluntary, the normal interpretation is that the act does not require the employer to grant the leave. In at least one circuit the court held otherwise. In *Gulf States Paper Corp.* v. *Ingram*, 811 F.2d 1464 (11th Cir. 1987), the court said that a one-year leave for a reservist to attend a practical nursing training course was not an unreasonable burden for the employer. A replacement could be easily obtained.

EFFECT OF STATUTES ON UNPAID LEAVE OF ABSENCE POLICY

In granting unpaid leaves of absence, most employers determined cases individually,

depending on the reason for the leave and whether an employee was needed or could be replaced during the leave of absence period. In many cases this depended on the whims of the supervisor. Often one department within a facility would have a different rule from another. Most labor agreements provide for granting an unpaid leave for specific reasons such as medical or extended leave for union business. Beyond these specific reasons there is broad language in the labor agreement, which usually leaves it up to the employer when to grant an unpaid leave of absence, subject to challenge by the union.

With the present requirements of the various statutes that all employees should be treated alike, the unilateral right to grant unpaid leaves of absence is rapidly diminishing. For example, where an employee wants a leave to see his dying mother in Sweden, a leave of absence is granted by extending the vacation period. Another employee wants to see her dying mother in California; another employee has a 22nd cousin who is dying in Florida (the only relative whom he knows of); another wants to go to a religious summer camp for four months; another wants to work for passage of the Equal Rights Amendment for one year or the right-to-work law for six months. If the employer does not have some policy that is uniformly applied to all these situations, there is exposure to a violation of a statute and retaliation charges.

The court will not question the conditions under which a leave is granted but will question whether the determination of who should be allowed a leave was discriminatory. Retaliation charges can develop over a refusal to grant an employee an unpaid leave of absence under Title VII or some other statute. Sexual harassment and religious discrimination are among the retaliation charges that are alleged by a member of the protected class and often have to be defended when granting an unpaid leave of absence to one individual and not another. The employer, in view of exposure to litigation, should review the leave of

[23]*Monroe* v. *The Standard Oil Co.*, 101 S.Ct. 2510 (1981).

absence policy and if needed set a few broad guidelines for supervisors. Decisions to grant leaves of absence should not be left to the whims of the supervisor but should be uniformly applied as much as possible throughout the organization.

RESTRICTIONS ON VACATION POLICY

Granting Vacation Pay in Lieu of Time Off

In the beginning when the employer granted vacation benefits, it was considered time off with pay. The purpose of granting vacations was to grant a period of relaxation from day-to-day activities; on returning to work the employee would be a better employee. As vacations became longer, employers began to make vacation payments in lieu of time off for several reasons. One, a replacement for a long period of time was difficult and costly in quality and quantity of work performed. Second, some employees could not afford a four-week vacation trip but could afford two weeks. The employer would give four weeks' vacation pay, and the employee would take a two-week trip and work the other two weeks; everybody was happy. The granting of vacation pay in lieu of time off was extended to where an employee terminated and was paid unused vacation time if certain conditions were met at the time of termination. This caused the thinking that vacation benefits were not necessarily time off but wages for nonworking time.[24]

Enforcement of Vacation Pay as Wages

Most states have nonpayment wage statutes that permit a state agency to be used for collection of wages from an employer. Some of the states have held that because payment is made in lieu of time off, vacation benefits are wages and therefore take jurisdiction over payment of vacation benefits.

In one situation, an employee was terminated due to loss of customers. She demanded her vacation pay and sued her former employer for it. One year later the employer paid the vacation pay, but not her accumulated attorney's fees. The court ruled that vacation pay is wages and attorney's fees are due under the Nonwage Payment Statute even though the statute makes no mention of the vacation pay.[25]

Where employees went on strike, the NLRB held that they were entitled to vacation pay accrued before the strike since the employer paid one employee vacation pay in lieu of vacation time off.[26]

New Mexico is one of the states that consider vacation benefits wages. (Iowa, Montana, Connecticut, and Kansas as well as others concur.) An employee in a New Mexico bank in April told the employer that she would take her vacation in September. She quit in July and requested vacation pay in lieu of her scheduled vacation. The New Mexico State Labor Commission agreed with her. The court disagreed; the employer's vacation policy said that vacations must be actually taken and also stated that no compensation could be paid in lieu of vacation.[27] If the Deming Bank had a history of paying compensation in lieu of vacation time off and had not had an expressed policy prohibiting it, the result would have been different.

In *Aasmundstad* v. *Dickinson State College,* 337 N.W.2d 792 (N.D. 1983), the court said that an established custom of paying accrued vacation reflected expectations of the em-

---

[24]Vacation pay as wages is being claimed as back pay in discrimination cases. Some states call vacation pay wages for purposes of meeting the wage requirement for unemployment compensation benefits. In *Gray* v. *Empire Gas Co.,* 679 P.2d 610 (Colo. App. 1984), the court called a discretionary bonus wages.

[25]*Becnel* v. *Answer Inc.,* et al, 428 So.2d 539 (La. App. 1983).

[26]Thorwin Mfg. Co., 243 NLRB No. 118 (1979).

[27]*New Mexico State Labor and Industrial Commission* v. *Deming National Bank,* 634 F.2d 695 (N.M. 1981).

ployee that the employer was liable for accrued vacation pay. When telling the employee that he must take vacation time off before retiring, refusing vacation pay in lieu of time off was unjust.

The practice of granting vacation pay in lieu of time off is an employee relations decision, but the employer should be aware that it can be considered wages. Unless the policy is properly written, some courts call it wages; if wages, the employer loses discretion in how it is paid.[28]

One technique not to have vacation pay interpreted as wages is to make a distinction between the last day worked and termination date if vacation pay is granted upon termination. The period between the last day worked and termination date is vacation time off.[29]

The California court takes the position that an employee has a "vested right to vacation pay which accrues at the time of hire." The company had the usual requirement of earning vacation time during the previous year; however, the employee had to work one full year before vacation time was due. The employee was terminated after six months, into the vacation period. The court in a unanimous decision held the rule invalid and granted a prorated vacation plus 30 paid working days if denial of vacation pay was found to be willful.[30]

The Suastez decision was challenged on the basis that the Employment Retirement Income Security Act (ERISA) preempted the state nonpayment wage statute. This challenge failed[31] and the U.S. Department of Labor takes the position that ERISA does not preempt vacation plans that are paid out of general funds.

Effect of "Use It or Lose It" Policy

Vacation policies that give vacation pay in lieu of time off are in effect admitting that vacation pay is wages. The right of the employee to recover wages is often defined by a state statute that removes from the employer the right to determine under what conditions vacation benefits will be paid. To avoid vacation time being considered as wages, the employer can have a policy of "use it or lose it" and then make a distinction between last day worked and termination date. Through such a policy the employer can pay for unused vacation time at termination and still not have vacation time count as wages. The cost of the continuation of an employee on the payroll for a short period of time, in which health insurance benefits and some pension credits are continued, is minimal compared to the exposure of paying vacation pay in lieu of time off.

REGULATION OF HEALTH CARE BENEFITS AND PENSIONS

Pensions and health plans are regulated by statute. Compliance with these statutes is complicated and usually requires professional assistance. No statute requires the employer to grant employee benefits but, once granted, they restrict the employer and grant the employee additional enforcement rights that were not present before the benefits were granted.

Sex Differences in Benefits

A preceding section considered sex discrimination in pregnancy disability plans, but

---

[28]It is costly practice because vacation for many job categories is not a cost item. The employee works to get caught up before leaving on vacation and works twice as hard when returning as no replacement is made. If pay is given, it is a straight-cost item.

[29]In *Teamsters Local No. 688* v. *John Meir,* 718 F.2d 286 (8th Cir. 1983), the court called vacation benefits wages but did not require payment to strikers since the company had prorated benefits to terminees from the last day worked.

[30]*Suastez* v. *Plastic Press-up Co.,* 647 P.2d 122 (Cal. Sup.Ct. 1982).

[31]*California Hospital Assn.* v. *Henning,* 770 F.2d 856 (9th Cir. 1985).

in other benefit plans sex differences may also occur. For example, sex differences appear in pension plans because of greater life expectancy of women, benefits are greater for females for the same cost, or the cost of the plans are more than for males if the same benefit level is to be maintained for females. Where the employer required women to make greater contributions than men to the pension fund in order to receive an equal benefit on retirement because they live longer, the Supreme Court held that this policy violated Title VII.[32] The Court stated that the basic policy of Title VII is "fairness to individuals rather than fairness to classes." Although women as a class may live longer than men, some do not; for those individuals who do not, it would be discriminatory according to the court.

In a related situation, where the employer's plan allowed equal contributions but provided lesser benefits (based on greater life expectancy) the court reached the same result as in the City of Los Angeles case.[33] In subsequent discrimination cases the Supreme Court has been consistent in considering the effect on individuals rather than a class or group of employees.[34] The position of the court was reaffirmed when they had to decide whether an annuity plan that was voluntary violated Title VII. The amount of contributions was optional with the employee. The plan had three options (lump-sum, periodic payments for a fixed period, or an insured annuity plan).[35] The women received less annuity payments than the men for the same amount of contributions; however, if the other two options were selected the pay-out would be the same. The annuity

option had a smaller payment for women than men because of the use of sex segregated actuarial tables. The Court held this violated Title VII. The effect of the decision is that the use of sex segregated actuarial tables is illegal regardless of the type of plan.

Difference in Benefits Based on Age

The Age Discrimination in Employment Act gives little indication of what Congress intended as to the effect on employee benefits.

The combination of employee relations consequences, federal and state legislation, and a practical analysis[36] all indicate that there will be little distinction in benefit plan coverage based on age. The employer who gradually eliminates such a distinction, if it exists, should do so in a painless and economical way.

Requirement of Alternative Health Care Plan (HMO)

The Health Maintenance Organization Act of 1976, as amended, requires employers to include in any health plan offered to its employees the option of membership in a qualified health maintenance organization (HMO).[37] An employer that refuses or fails to comply with the act may be subjected to a civil penalty of up to $10,000 for an initial violation and a like amount for each additional month of noncompliance.

It covers all employers who have 25 employees or more and is subject to the Fair Labor Standards Act. Once the employer is contacted by a qualified HMO, the employer must offer the option either to the union that can speak for the employees or to individual employees. The HMO option cannot increase the employer's cost. The em-

---

[32]*City of Los Angeles* v. *Manhart*, 435 U.S. 702 (1978).

[33]*EEOC* v. *Colby College*, 589 F.2d 1139 (1st Cir. 1978).

[34]In *Connecticut* v. *Teal*, 102 S.Ct. 2525 (1982), they said that discrimination is an individual matter and that the fact that other employees were not discriminated against is irrelevant if the plaintiff is discriminated against.

[35]*Arizona Governing Committee for Tax Deferred Annuity and Deferred Compensation Plans, Etc., et al.*, v. *Nathalie Norris Etc.*, 103 S.Ct. 3492 (1983).

[36]Since in most organizations the executives of an advanced age are the decision makers, it is unlikely that the older worker will be treated differently on benefits.

[37]42 USC 300(e).

ployee must be willing to make up the difference if the cost is higher than the company plan.

The HMO has given the personnel practitioner little or no problems except occasionally in the communication area. Often when the employer attempts to communicate, there is a tendency to favor either its plan or the HMO. For this reason it is advisable to let the HMO organization communicate its own plan and the employer-sponsored plan be communicated by the insurance carrier or, if self-insured, by someone other than the one responsible for administration of the plan. Many states have their own HMO laws; the state regulations and laws must be reviewed when an HMO problem occurs to determine whether state or federal law applies.

Consolidated Omnibus Budget Reconciliation Act (COBRA)

COBRA (29 USC Sect. 601–608 of ERISA) provides for continued health care coverage to terminated and qualified beneficiaries. The benefits must be identical to those benefits offered to employees who have not been laid off or terminated. The purpose of the act is to prevent immediate termination of employer-sponsored group health insurance when under the terms of the plan the covered employee and dependents are terminated because of some event.

It is an amendment to ERISA and the Internal Revenue Code of 1986 and is enforced by disqualifying a violator for tax deductions of health care costs. The act applies to all employers with 20 or more employees who have group health care plans.

Certain events (called qualifying events) require continued coverage if the employee or his or her dependents or divorced spouse elects to be covered within a 60-day period of the occurrence of a disqualifying event. The employer should cover if the employee has a claim in a 60-day period but before electing coverage. Dependent children who no longer qualify because of age under the employer's plan must also be offered coverage.

A qualifying event is termination (unless for misconduct) or reduction of the employee's hours so there is no coverage under the employer's plan.[38] In the case of the employee, coverage must be continued for 18 months; for all others who qualify it must be continued for 36 months.

Coverage can be terminated (1) when the employee or dependents stop paying the premiums (which can be as high as 102 percent of the cost), (2) the employer ceases to provide a group plan to all active employees, (3) a dependent gets married to a person who is covered by another plan, or (4) the employee or dependents are covered under another group plan, including Medicare.

The plan administrator can be personally liable up to $100 per day from date of failure to give notice for continued coverage (or any other relief that the court may deem proper). This is an unusual provision since under the common law persons acting for the corporation are not held liable.

COBRA permits state plans (over half of the states have similar plans) to be more strict; if not as strict they are preempted by COBRA. The Department of Labor, the Internal Revenue Service, and the Department of Health and Human Services are authorized to issue interpretive regulations. The Department of Labor has issued Technical Release No. 86–2 which is a guideline and has a model statement to notify employees of continued coverage.

Health Care Insurance for Retirees

Nearly 60 percent of all firms with more than 100 employees offer retiree health care coverage of some sort, even after 65.[39] The issue is whether management has a right to cut benefits in the same manner as for active

---

[38]A strike is considered a qualifying event under 52 Fed. Reg. 22.716 (June 1987).

[39]See *BNA Employer Relations Weekly*, August 22, 1984.

employees. Where this has been attempted, the courts have held that once an employee satisfied the requirements for retirement his or her benefits are vested.[40] The courts have extended the principle to a situation where the employer was bankrupt. The bankruptcy court held that the rights of the retirees were vested and coverage must be continued.[41]

Cost containment health care under court decisions must begin with active employees although this may be inharmonious with good employee relations. It appears it is too late after they retire. However, the employer may limit retirees to be the same as active employees, if the plan is properly worded.

Employee Retirement Income Security Act (ERISA)

The Employee Retirement Income Security Act of 1974 (29 USC 1001 et seq. ERISA) as amended is a difficult statute to understand, and even more difficult to stay in compliance with. If the employer wants assurance that benefit plans are in compliance with ERISA, it is necessary either to seek outside professional advice or to employ a full-time specialist. Anything less results in unnecessary risks. The personnel practitioner should have a general knowledge of the law and its regulations, but time can be better spent in other problems than to attempt to become an expert in ERISA. For these reasons this section only gives an overview of the law and leaves the details to ERISA specialists.

Although the administration of ERISA is by the Department of Labor, the compliance to ERISA is through the Internal Revenue Service (IRS). All plans must be qualified plans in order to receive tax credits when contributions are made to the trust funds or payment of premiums if an insured plan. If the plan does not meet the requirements of ERISA, it is not a qualified plan and does not receive the tax deductions. Not many other enforcement procedures are necessary.

ERISA is a comprehensive statute that regulates virtually all aspects of private sector employee benefit plans and their administration.[42] It is essential for the personnel practitioner to have some knowledge of the reporting and disclosure obligations as well as a limited number of other rules.

Purposes of ERISA

ERISA was passed by Congress to solve the social problems created by private pension plans and other benefit plans such as the following:

1. When a company goes out of business, often it had inadequate funding of past service credits, which allowed only a small percentage of pension benefits anticipated.
2. Inadequate vesting provisions would often result in the employee who frequently changed jobs having no pension plan at the time of retirement.
3. The law lacked adequate control of administration of pension funds.
4. Communications to the employees of the provisions of the pension plan were often inadequate to enable the employee to understand what benefits one would receive at retirement age.

Congress, through ERISA, attempted to correct these problems by the following provisions:

1. Requiring a minimum level of funding for past service credits to better protect benefits if the company went out of business.
2. Requiring termination insurance so that if a

---

[40]See *Hoefel* v. *Atlas Tack Corp.*, 581 F.2d 1(1st Cir. 1978); *Autoworkers* v. *Yard-Man, Inc.*, 716 F.2d 1476 (6th Cir. 1983). However, the Medicare Catastrophic Coverage Act (PL 100–360) (1988) may allow employers to change their plans.

[41]*Hansen* v. *White Farm Equipment Co.*, 42 B.R. 1003 (D.C. Ohio 1984).

---

[42]For a guide on ERISA, see "What You Should Know about the Pension and Welfare Law" (Washington, DC: U.S. Department of Labor, 1978).

company went out of business, the pension credits already earned would be protected until retirement.

3. Requiring a minimum vesting provision after 10 years service; vesting must begin at age 21 and pension credits go back to age 18.

4. Permitting ready access to the federal courts when it appeared that there were improper investment and administration of pension funds.

5. Employee communication programs must meet certain standards by simplification of terms and more frequent explanation of provisions of the plans to enable the employee to have a better knowledge of the plan in order to know what she or he will receive at retirement.

Problem Areas under ERISA

ERISA regulates not only pension plans but also all types of benefit plans, such as all types of health care benefits, death benefits, unemployment insurance benefits, holiday and vacation pay, apprenticeship or other training programs, day-care centers, scholarship funds, prepaid legal services, and certain types of severance pay plans.[43] Communication of the benefit plan is also a problem for the practitioner. Sections 1022(a) & (b) and 1024(b)(1) of ERISA require that participants be furnished with a clear, timely explanation of disqualifications, ineligibility, denial, or loss of benefits. Where the administrator failed to mail an amendment to the pension participants, but stated the information was in the union hiring hall, the court said this was a violation of Sections 1022 and 1024 of the act. Even if the distribution had been adequate, the content of the notice was insufficient because it failed to explain how the amendment related to other provisions of the plan.[44]

Another problem area is where an employee is discharged and is denied certain benefits under the terms of the plan as the result of termination. If it can be shown that the discharge was solely to avoid vesting of the pension plan or otherwise deny health or pension benefits, it would be in violation of the act.[45] When an employer is considering the discharge of an employee with 9 years and 11 months of employment and that employee would be vested in pension rights in one month, a good and valid reason should be established before the termination action is taken or a pretext to avoid vesting could be alleged. The enforcement would be by the Department of Labor if the employee files a complaint.

Preemption over State Laws

The regulation of benefit plans raises the question of whether state benefit plans are preempted by ERISA.[46] The Supreme Court on two different occasions has considered the issue. It has held that if state law prohibits reduction of pension benefits while workers compensation is being paid such a law is invalid.[47] In a leading case a state law required the employer to pay disability benefits to all employees. This was contested by employers who argued that the law was unenforceable because ERISA preempted the state law. The court held that ERISA preempts state laws if they prohibit practices that are lawful under ERISA.[48] The disability plan in question was not prohibited by ERISA and therefore was enforceable.

The issue of whether ERISA preempts other state laws is in almost continual litigation. In *Metropolitan Life Insurance* v. *Commonwealth of Massachusetts*, 105 S.Ct. 2890

---

[43]*Adam* v. *Joy Mfg. Co.*, 651 F.Supp. 1301 (D.N.H. 1987).

[44]*Chambless* v. *Master, Mates & Pilots Pension Plan*, 772 F.2d 1032 (2nd Cir. 1985), cert. denied (1986).

[45]*Foltz* v. *Marriott Corp.*, 594 F.Supp. 1007 (W.D. Mo. 1984).

[46]Section 514(a) of ERISA states that ERISA shall supersede "any and all state laws insofar as they may now or hereafter relate to any employee benefit plan." The purpose of this section was to ensure employers that they would not face conflicting or inconsistent state and local regulation of employee benefit plans.

[47]*Buczynski* v. *General Motors Corp.*, 101 S.Ct. 1895 (1983).

[48]*Shaw* v. *Delta Airlines, Inc.*, 103 S.Ct. 2890 (1983).

(1985), the Court held that where state laws required mandated health care benefits they are not preempted by ERISA since they are insurance regulations.[49] ERISA does not preempt state-regulated severance pay plans. In *Fort Halifax Packing, Inc.* v. *Coyne,* 107 S.Ct. 2211 (1987), the Court upheld a Maine statute that required severance pay.

EFFECTIVE USE OF EMPLOYMENT AGREEMENTS

An employment agreement is any agreement, whether written or oral, between an employer and an employee concerning the conditions of employment. This chapter considers only the written agreement; the oral agreement has legal problems of proof that would be inappropriate to consider here. The written employment agreement sets out specific conditions of employment, but these conditions should not be interpreted as eliminating all other conditions normally granted to employees who do not have an agreement.

Need for Employment Agreements

Employers often fail to consider the employment agreement as a useful tool in administering a personnel policy. Many practitioners have the misconception that employment agreements are suited only to determine the duration of employment or job duties and are therefore difficult to enforce. In reality employment agreements are practical for any situation where the employer wants to set out certain conditions for one or more employees apart from other employees.

Suppose that the employer wants to hire a qualified manager and one of the demands of the applicant (often it is more a demand of his family) is that the four-week vacation granted by the former employer be contin-

ued. Since the employer's vacation policy is that four weeks' vacation is not granted until after 12 years of service, the policy must be violated or the applicant not hired. An employment agreement could grant the four weeks as an exception to the vacation program. Other benefits would come under the regular benefit plan. (Sometimes applicants don't want to lose higher life insurance benefits when changing jobs and an exception can be made by purchasing an insurance policy different from what other employees have.) Some practitioners feel that agreements of this type may set a precedent that makes it difficult to deny others the same benefit. This has not been the author's experience, nor can the author find any case law that supports this feeling.

Use of Employment Agreements

An employment agreement should not be used unless it changes the working conditions for the employee from what other employees have without an agreement. Here are some situations where employment agreements should be considered.

1. Where it is necessary, to define specially the rights, responsibilities, and terms of employment, including duration of those special conditions.
2. To deter acts of unfair competition while employed or after being terminated (very common).
3. Where job content exposes the employee to trade secrets or to patentable inventions.
4. To define duration of employment because of the nature of the job (athletic coaches and players, executives hired away from competitor, and so on).
5. Where employees are on commission and salary draws or have selling expenses as part of their commission (a must for this type of job).
6. To simplify proof on the part of both parties in a dispute over the conditions of employment or oral statements made at the time of employment.
7. To deal with routine matters that are often overlooked at the time of termination, such as travel advances and return of keys, records, and other company property.

---

[49]*Metropolitan Life Insurance Co.* v. *Taylor,* 107 S.Ct. 1542 (1987), which had the same result as a Michigan statute.

Provisions in a Typical Employment Agreement

Some of the usual clauses in an employment agreement are terms of employment, which state the beginning and end of the agreement but not necessarily the end of employment; a general outline of the duties, which should not be too specific; compensation, which may include special benefits; and secret information restrictions and no-compete restrictions after termination.

Confidentiality and Covenants Not to Compete

Although the employee owes a certain loyalty to the employer not to perform any acts that will adversely affect the business, it is essential that where the job content creates unusual exposure to trade secrets, the employee is contractually bound not to expose the trade secrets. Enforcement of this provision is usually against the employee and the person or corporation to whom the trade secret is revealed.[50]

Some employment agreements have covenants not to compete with the employer for a certain period after termination. These covenants are generally enforceable.

In suits concerning the validity of non-competition covenants, courts generally consider four factors: (1) Is the restriction reasonably necessary for the protection of the employer's business? (2) Does the employee have certain rights to the trade secrets? (3) Is it prejudicial to the public interest? (4) Is the employee being denied the right to make a living?[51]

Courts have refused to enforce covenants that are overly broad and/or unnecessary to protect the employer's legitimate interests. In *National Settlement Associates* v. *Creel,* 349 S.E.2d 177 (Ga. 1986), the court found that a provision which prohibited a former employee from being employed "in any capacity" was overly broad.[52] The noncompetition covenant would be valid if it prohibited the employee from using skills acquired while employed, provided they were used within the time and territorial limits of the agreement.[53]

Courts have held that restrictions must be reasonable in temporal and geographic scope. Although the courts are split on whether the time and space limitations must be defined, it is advisable to define them to avoid the issue. A three-year limitation is usually enforceable unless special conditions exist.[54]

Customers and customer lists are considered trade or proprietary information sufficient to support enforcement of a restrictive covenant.[55]

Conflict-of-Interest Clauses

Some employee agreements have special provisions that do not exist in a normal employee-employer relationship. These special provisions would not be enforceable in the absence of a formal contract or a policy that is communicated to all employees and consistently applied. One example of a special provision is a conflict-of-interest clause. This type of clause prevents the employee from engaging in any activity that would interfere with decision making or in making a judgment in performing duties on behalf of his or her employer.

Employers are often concerned about an employee who has two jobs, which interferes with job duties and performance. This is

---

[50]For further details on covenants not to compete, see "Economic and Critical Analyses of the Law of Covenants Not to Compete," 72 Geo. L.J. April 1984, pp. 1425–50; "The Law of Restrictive Covenants, Noncompetition Agreements, and Employee Loyalty—An Update," *Employee Relations Law Journal,* 9, no. 4 (Summer 1983).

[51]*Lamp* v. *American Prosthetics, Inc.,* 379 N.W.2d 909 (Iowa 1986).

[52]See also *Klick* v. *Crosstown Bank of Ham Lake,* 372 N.W.2d 85 (Minn. App. 1985).

[53]*Nunn* v. *Orkin Exterminating Co. Inc.,* 350 S.E.2d 425 (Ga. 1986).

[54]*Dorminy* v. *Frank B. Hall & Co., Inc.,* 464 So.2d 154 (Fla. App. 1985).

[55]*Instrumentalist Co.* v. *Band, Inc.,* 480 N.E.2d 1273 (Ill. App. 1985).

commonly called "moonlighting." Unless there is an overall corporate policy against moonlighting that applies to all employees, it is necessary to put the restriction on moonlighting in an employment agreement if it is to be enforceable against certain individuals.

Enforcement of Employment Agreements

Employment agreements are generally enforceable in the courts if they meet the three basic requirements of a contract: (1) offer, (2) acceptance, and (3) consideration. The offer is the conditions of employment set out by the employer. Acceptance is the employee agreeing to those conditions. Continued employment has been stated by the courts to be an adequate consideration.[56] The offer and acceptance requirement of a legally binding contract is self-serving when the applicant starts work or continues to work after an agreement is executed.[57]

Most employees will accept the obligations of the agreement if clearly defined and if the agreement is entered under amiable conditions. Accordingly, enforcement during the term of employment agreement is seldom a problem.

The starting of a new business by a manager on the employer's time and with the employer's records and equipment is not uncommon. Without an employment agreement the employer has few remedies to stop it unless disloyalty can be shown.[58]

Some jurisdictions are reluctant to enforce

covenants of noncompete, but the agreement not to disclose trade secrets is almost always enforceable; therefore, both clauses should be in an employment agreement.

Some employers do not like to use employment agreements because they feel that this limits their right to discharge for poor performance or some other legitimate reason. An employment agreement does not protect a poor performance or violation of company policies but usually describes what is expected of the employee. Where a salesperson worked harder than anyone else but did not sell anything, the court said that working hard is not enough and discharge for ineffective performance was held not to be a breach of the employment agreement.[59]

Arbitration of Employment Agreements

Some employment agreements provide for final and binding arbitration when there is a dispute over their terms. If arbitration is not specifically provided for in an agreement, the parties may still arbitrate the dispute by entering a mutual agreement to do so when the dispute occurs. The alternative to arbitration is litigation. In this situation the parties must decide whether arbitration is most desirable or whether judicial review of the dispute should be pursued. If the dispute is arbitrated, it does not have the legal exposure as in a judicial review; arbitration awards are seldom appealable.

One consideration when determining whether a disputed employment agreement should be arbitrated or litigated is that some courts have awarded punitive damages, which are rarely awarded in arbitration awards.

Arbitration serves a purpose in disputes involving small amounts of monetary damages. When large sums are involved, it is better to have the matter decided under legal procedures. An acceptable clause is one that limits arbitration to small claims such as $25,000, with court determination thereafter.

---

[56]Some jurisdictions hold that where an agreement is signed after employment, continued employment is not a consideration and other independent considerations are necessary before the contract is valid. *Modern Controls, Inc.* v. *Andreadakis*, 578 F.2d 1263 (8th Cir. 1978). Other state courts disagree; *Rollins* v. *American State Bank*, 487 N.E.2d 842 (Ind. App. 3 Dist. 1986). To be sure, state law must be researched.

[57]Under this principle a written contract is not necessary to find a contract of employment. The problem arises in unwritten contracts or oral agreements before employment of what parties understood to be the agreement.

[58]*Maritime Fish* v. *World Wide Fish*, 474 N.Y.S.2d 281 (A.D. Dept. 1984).

---

[59]*Freeman* v. *Danal Jewelry Co.*, 397 A.2d 1323 (R.I. S.Ct. 1980).

Use of Agreements with Employment Agencies

When the personnel manager needs to fill a vacancy in the skilled or managerial job category, the use of an employment agency is one way to find a qualified applicant. Relationships with an employment agency can result in legal consequences that often the personnel practitioner is not aware of. Problems and misunderstandings concerning fees, pro rata refunds when the employee is discharged or resigns, and the right to deal with the applicant privately without being "feeable" are all exposures to lawsuits when using an employment agency, as is shown in the case history below.

Another exposure is the liability incurred when the employment agency, either knowingly or otherwise, commits a wrongful act. If the agency is acting as an agent of the employer, it may be liable for the act, even if the agent is a state agency.[60]

Most of these problems can be avoided by an initial agreement between the employer

---

[60]*Pegues* v. *Mississippi State Employment Serv.*, 699 F.2d 760 (7th Cir. 1983).

and the agency that anticipates these problems and provides for their solution. A contract between the applicant and the agency often does not affect relationships between the employer and agency. There is no federal law that regulates employment agencies; only a few states have laws that regulate through licensing the relationship with the applicant. Usually the employer is not involved.

Guidelines in Drafting an Employment Agency Agreement

Where an employment agency is requested to find applicants at the high salary level jobs, an agreement should be executed (maybe a simple letter that both parties sign). The agreement should contain clauses to cover the following:

1. Fees, the amount of payment, payment dates. If a year-end bonus is paid, is that included in the annual salary for fee purposes?
2. Refunds if the employee does not work out, apart from agreement between applicant and agency. This is often detailed in the applicant's contract with the agency. Usually the employer that agrees to pay the fee has no con-

---

A Case History of a Lawsuit with an Employment Agency

The agency called the sales manager to inquire whether there was a vacancy for a salesperson. The manager stated that he was always looking for good salespersons but there was no specific vacancy at that time. On persuasion by the agency he agreed to interview an applicant. The agency orally stated that its fee was 10 percent of annual compensation if the applicant was hired. The applicant was not hired because his qualifications were not exceptional enough to hire him when there was no vacancy.

Four months later the applicant stopped to see the sales manager. There happened to be a vacancy and he was hired. The employment agency alleged that the hire was feeable since the initial interview was through its referral, the fee was explained, and the employee hired. A fee of $4500 was payable. The legal basis for the suit was an implied contract because the employer interviewed the applicant four months before the second interview, after which he was hired. The employer argued that there was no referral and too much time had elapsed. The case was settled out of court for the cost of litigation. An agreement containing time limits on referrals would have prevented this lawsuit.

tractual relationship with the agency as to re-funds except through applicant's contract.

3. Time limits on referrals. The time between referral and hiring should be agreed upon. Once the applicant is interviewed and not hired and reapplies later, should it be feeable? If so, how long?

4. A situation where the applicant is hired for a different job. The referral applicant is not qualified for the job vacancy placed with the agency but is hired for another job later. In the absence of an agreement, some courts say that it is feeable. A contract prevents litigation in this area.

5. An indemnity from liability for violations of certain laws by the agency, such as antidiscrimination laws and various state laws.

6. Requirements for the agency to follow all laws and monitor their procedure to determine if it is being done. Such laws as the Immigration Reform and Control Act make the employer liable for the employment agent's acts or omission.

If an agreement contains all or most of these clauses, costly litigation can be avoided.

CHAPTER 9

PRIVACY RIGHTS
AND DISCLOSURE
OF EMPLOYEE INFORMATION

USE OF PERSONNEL RECORDS AND REQUIREMENTS TO RETAIN

Definition and Purpose of Personnel Records

It is common practice for employers to keep individual records on each employee. These records are commonly called employee records or individual personnel files. Employee records are defined as records that contain initial application forms, results of physical examinations, interviewer's notations, test scores, periodic appraisals, transfers and promotions, disciplinary actions, releases and rehirings, wages, salaries, taxes paid, contributions, and similar items.[1] It is highly important that everything about the employee go into the employee's individual file.

The purpose of personnel records is to record information about an employee obtained during the course of employment. The fact that records are kept puts the employee on notice that there is documentation of his or her activities while employed. It also permits an audit of whether addresses are up to date, whether beneficiaries are current, and other necessary personal employee data.

Documentation for purposes of discrimination charges, unemployment compensation determination, and arbitration is an essential element of the defense. When considering whether to record or retain a fact, always ask the question: For what purpose was the fact recorded and is it necessary to retain it?

All too often important arbitration, EEOC cases, unemployment compensation or court decisions are lost because the employer fails to produce the proper evidence to substantiate a fact. Some practitioners believe that separate personnel files according to subject matter should be kept for each employee.

They suggest a general file, job performance file, medical file, and closed file where all letters of references, records of investigation, or other matters that employees should not see are filed. The justification often given for the separation of files is that sensitive information would not be given to outsiders, and further the person reviewing the file would not be able to consider irrelevant material that may be damaging in litigation or in other employee relations problems.

The reason given by proponents for keeping everything in one file is that, when segregated, relevant information is often missed; further, an employee problem is seldom categorized according to the way the data are filed and data in one file may not offer a solution to a particular problem unless all the files are reviewed. The author's experience favors the one-file concept as the most reliable method to keep employee records, except possibly certain medical records.

Requirements to Retain Certain Records

There are certain statutory requirements stating that an employer must keep records on an individual employee. The antidiscrimination laws, Occupational Safety and Health Act (OSHA), and Fair Labor Standards Act require that relevant information be available for investigation purposes and to ensure the proper administration of the laws.

The Immigration Reform and Control Act of 1986 (IRCA) requires employment records to be kept for three years or one year after termination, whichever is later. IRCA imposes a fine up to $1000 for failure to keep the necessary records. The unique part of the requirement is that the person responsible for keeping the records can be personally liable.

Record retention requirements are also indirectly found in the Consolidated Omnibus Budget Reconciliation Act (COBRA). Under this amendment to ERISA, the plan administrator can be personally liable up to $100 per day for failure to give notice of the

---

[1]Dale Yoder, *Personnel Management in Industrial Relations*, 6th ed. (Englewood Cliffs, NJ: Prentice-Hall, 1970).

right to be covered, or the court can grant such other relief as it may deem proper. This results in considerable personal liability for the plan administrator, so the incentive to keep records on notification is very real.

Under Employee Retirement Income Security Act (ERISA), records must be kept for not less than six years after the filing date of the documents. When the documents are changed the six years start all over again. Under ERISA it would be advisable to keep all current records and their respective changes.

Regulations promulgated by the agencies responsible for enforcing the antidiscrimination statutes have established record-keeping retention policies. Although compliance is not a statutory wrong but a violation of a rule, the employer should comply because the records may become the proof that an employment decision was made on a nondiscriminatory basis.

Under Title VII, job applications, resumes, payroll records, and employee personnel files must be kept for a minimum of six months or until disposition of any personnel action involved under Title VII, whichever is later. Employers of 100 or more employees are required to file the EEO-1 report annually; this gives an inventory of employees by race, ethnic group, sex, job category, and salary. Unions with 100 or more members must file an EEO-3 report, and records must be kept for one year after the report. Private employment agencies have not been subject to the Title VII record-keeping or reporting requirement except in their capacity as employers.

Government contractors under Executive Order 11246 do not have a specific record-keeping requirement except to make all their records available for compliance review. Under the Rehabilitation Act of 1973 contractors and subcontractors must retain complaints or action taken for one year. The same rule applies for contractors under the Vietnam Era Veterans Readjustment Act of 1974.

The Equal Pay Act of 1963 requires that employees' records concerning wages, hours of work, and other terms of employment (including exempt-status employees) be kept for three years, although records supporting employment decisions under the act must be kept only for two years.

The Age Discrimination in Employment Act of 1967 rules require that employment records including the employee's personnel file must be kept for one year. However, payroll information and information relating to name, address, birth date, and job category must be kept for three years. (For further record retention requirements, see "Guide to Record Retention Requirements" in 1988 Code of Federal Regulations, U.S. Government Printing Office, Supt. of Documents, Washington, D.C. 20402.)

Record Retention as a Personnel Policy

Proper personnel practice in the areas of discipline, performance appraisals, skills inventories, and so on requires the personnel practitioner to go beyond what the law requires in the area of personnel record keeping.

What records the employer should maintain is a policy as well as a legal question (except that the employer must keep all records pertaining to a charge or a complaint from the date it is filed). The employer should have records to show that company policy and procedures are complying with the law. On the other hand, too many records can be damaging in the event of a lawsuit. If the employer does not have certain information, it cannot be disclosed and a decision by the regulatory agency must be made only on the information available, which at times can be advantageous to the employer. For this reason, the employer should audit personnel records at least every three years and destroy irrelevant, immaterial, or damaging records if not required to keep them. It is also advisable to separate certain records that you are required to keep and note a destroy date. This policy will give stature to the records you retain and at the same time not subject damaging records to the subpoena process in the event of a lawsuit.[2]

Attorneys usually advocate keeping too few records for sound personnel administration. The attorney reasons that if the plaintiff wants more information, he or she can use the discovery process. Positive personnel administration dictates that only those records that are useful should be kept. If you look at all records with a critical eye, you are likely to find that you are keeping more than are really necessary.

Statutory Requirements of Disclosure

Although records are the property of the employer, certain statutes require the employer to disclose specific information for certain reasons. These reasons are usually to enable a government regulatory agency to carry out its function of enforcing the law.

Under most statutes the disclosure must be made upon request and the burden is upon the party who requests to show that they are entitled to it under the statute. Because often the disclosure of employee information causes employee relations problems, the employer may take the position that it is better to be ordered to disclose than to do it voluntarily.

Under NLRB the employer is required to give certain information. Often a labor organization that is the certified bargaining representative of the employees will request information on an employee or group of employees. The information requested must be relevant to the collective bargaining agreement or needed for the union to represent the employee properly concerning wages and working conditions and protect the collective bargaining relationship. The National Labor Relations Board and the courts have given a liberal interpretation to this general principle. However, if the information requested relates to matters not within union

jurisdiction or is of individual concern, it will be denied.[3]

Another statutory requirement to release limited employee information comes from a regulation promulgated under the authority of OSHA, which states that an employer must give access of the records to employees or their representatives and to other employees who are exposed to toxic and hazardous substances if requested.[4] The person requesting the records must show a need and have professional qualifications to interpret the information requested. The regulation requires that the medical records on exposure to toxic substances be kept for 30 years and the employee must be informed at the time of hiring and each year thereafter that such records are available.

This regulation has been reviewed by two courts, and has been judicially accepted.[5] In both cases the court required that the National Institute for Occupational Safety and Health (NIOSH) be given the information. However, the court said that the employee's privacy is a factor to be considered in the use of that information by the governmental agency.

As in other areas under antidiscrimination laws, if employee information has an adverse impact on the categories of individuals being protected, it is unlawful to use such information for making an employment decision unless a business necessity can be shown. This does not mean that background investigations are prohibited, but it does mean there must be a nondiscriminatory use and purpose for such information.

When a charge is broad and includes several allegations, information must be furnished for all the allegations. In this kind of charge the agency has considerable latitude in seeking information if the charge is properly worded. In this type of charge the em-

---

[2]See *Ramsey* v. *American Filter Co.,* 772 F.2d 1303 (7th Cir. 1985), where damaging notations on the applicant form cost the employer $92,500.

---

[3]*NLRB* v. *Holyduke Water Power Co.,* 788 F.2d 49 (1st Cir. 1985).

[4]29 CFR Part 1910.20 and 29 CFR Part 1913.10.

[5]*United States* v. *Westinghouse,* 638 F.2d 570 (3rd Cir. 1980); *E.I. duPont de Nemours and Co.* v. *Finklea,* 442 F.Supp. 821 (S.D. W.Va. 1977).

ployer has less opportunity to refuse information, and the defense of relevancy must be used with discretion.

Federal employees are protected by the Privacy Act of 1974.[6] The act requires federal agencies to permit employees to examine, copy, correct, or amend employee information. If there is a dispute on the accuracy of the information or what is to be included, an appeal procedure is provided. The act prohibits, with certain exceptions, the disclosure of information to outsiders without written consent of the employee to whom the information pertains. The agency has no obligation to inform the employee that the information exists except to publish it annually in the *Federal Register*.

Several states have enacted comprehensive privacy acts for the public sector. Other state legislatures have not gone quite as far as a comprehensive plan but have imposed certain restrictions on employee information practices in the public sector.

Although the Federal Fair Credit Reporting Act[7] regulates the activities of consumer reporting agencies, it does affect the disclosure of information by the employer where the employer engages a consumer agency to make an investigation. The employer, when using a consumer agency, must inform the employee that an investigation is being made as to character, general reputation, personal characteristics, and mode of hiring. If the employee so requests, the employer must provide a complete disclosure of the nature and scope of the investigation.

The Freedom of Information Act (FOIA) states that where a federal agency maintains a system of records, on request any individual or representative may gain access to that record if the proper authorization is shown by the representative.[8] The FOIA further provides that an individual or representative may request amendment to the record; if refused, adversary proceedings to determine the facts are triggered. Such proceedings are subject to judicial review.

FOIA's stated purpose is to require the information to be released and to inform the public; it is not for the purpose of benefiting the litigants in a lawsuit.[9] The rules and regulations in compliance with this purpose are promulgated with emphasis on disclosing information to the public.

There are exceptions under the act that an individual may examine personnel records. The federal agency may promulgate challengeable rules where revealing such information will obstruct the agency's enforcement function. If the right of disclosure is doubtful, the courts normally rule in favor of disclosure. Medical records are exempted under FOIA, but under certain conditions they can be revealed under Section 552(a) of the act.

OVERVIEW OF PRIVACY RIGHTS IN EMPLOYER-EMPLOYEE RELATIONSHIP

The protection of a person's privacy is a common law right that has been protected by the courts for many years.[10] The Restatement (Second) of Torts Section 652b states:

One who intentionally intrudes, physically or otherwise, upon the solitude or seclusion of another or his private concerns is subject to liability to the other for invasion of his privacy, if the intrusion would be highly offensive to a reasonable person.

This principle has been used in a wide variety of situations. On the issue of abortion the court had held that a state statute prohibiting it is an invasion of privacy.[11] In police investigations the officer must be careful not to invade the privacy of the accused.[12] The Supreme Court held in *Eisenstadt, Sheriff* v. *Baird*, 405 U.S. 438 (1972), that it is an

---

[6]USC Sect. 552(a), 5 CFR 297.101.
[7]15 USC Sect. 1681 et seq.
[8]5 USC Sect. 552(a)(1) (FOIA).

[9]*Cuneo* v. *Rumsfeld*, 553 F.2d 1360 (D.C. Cir. 1977).
[10]Prosser and Keeton, *Law of Torts*, 5th ed. (1984).
[11]*Roe* v. *Wade*, 410 U.S. 113 (1973).
[12]*U.S.* v. *Knotts*, 103 S.Ct. 1081 (1983).

invasion of privacy to question another person about marriage and sex life, since these are fundamental rights entitled to privacy protection. Various state laws that require safety measures (wearing of helmets by motorcycle operators) have on a case-by-case basis been held to be an invasion of privacy. In many situations, the plaintiff claims emotional distress is caused by invasion of privacy. An uninvited intrusion into a person's solitude or seclusion may also provide for an invasion of privacy claim. This is a common argument in drug and alcohol testing. As illustrated above, invasion of privacy claims are found in all walks of life. However, this chapter will be concerned only with the invasion of privacy in the employer-employee relationship.

Statutory, common law, and constitutional privacy protection has been accelerated by social legislation in discrimination, employee rights, and the availability of attorneys to pursue any and all possible indications of a violation.[13] There is also pressure on state and federal levels of the government to pass legislation to protect various privacy rights of the employee. Protection by statute is necessary, since under the common law, the employee in the employer-employee relationship has fewer rights than as a citizen. As the court said in *United States* v. *Blok,* 186 F.2d 1019 (D.C. Cir. 1951), it was a violation of privacy under the Fourth Amendment for the police to search the employee's desk, but it would have been proper for the supervisor to do so.

Employer Invasion of Privacy

Under the common law, employer invasion of privacy usually occurs when the employer commits some act that damages the employee's right to enjoy a good reputation. Public disclosure of true facts could be an invasion of privacy. An example is disclosure by the employer of information about an employee's drinking habits or failing a drug or an AIDS test. The plaintiff must prove that these facts are highly offensive and are not of legitimate concern to the public in order to recover under tort.[14]

The public not only includes persons unrelated to the employment situation but also includes supervisors and others closely related to the plaintiff. A flight attendant directed her private physician to supply the employer with information concerning her medical condition. Based on this information the employer's medical examiner waived weight limits imposed for appearance regulations and applicable to her job. The information supplied included details of contemplated gynecological surgery. The employer's medical examiner disclosed this information to her male supervisor and to her husband. She sued the employer for invasion of privacy, and the court found that it was an invasion of privacy to disclose the information to her supervisor and her husband. The supervisor had no authority to act on the data disclosed and her husband "faced no problem involving his own well-being or emergency care for his spouse"; therefore, neither recipient had a need to know. The court allowed compensatory damages but denied punitive damages and there was no evidence of malice. Unless malice can be shown in privacy cases the court will not allow punitive damages.[15] In a related case the court held that a consultation between the company physician and the employee's personal physician concerning the employee's illness did not constitute an invasion of privacy because employer conduct was motivated by concern for the employee when the information prompted a requested leave of absence.[16]

Employees in the public sector have more rights than those in the private sec-

---

[13]See "Privacy Rights Now Aired in Public," *Insight,* 44, no. 55 (February 1988), 52.

[14]*Hudson* v. *S.D. Warren Co.,* 608 F.Supp. 477 (D.C. Me. 1985); also followed in Oregon and D.C. courts.

[15]*Levis* v. *United Airlines,* 500 N.E.2d 370 (Ohio App. 1985).

[16]*Valencia* v. *Duvall Corp.,* 645 P.2d 1262 (Ariz. 1983).

tor, since they are protected by the Fourth Amendment of the Constitution. Where a police officer was discharged for living with a married woman, the court said invasion of privacy.[17] However, if the private life of the employee affects the job, the court will find that the job requirements will override the privacy right. In *Potter* v. *Murray City,* 760 F.2d 1065 (10th Cir. 1985), cert. denied (1985), the discharge of a Utah policeman was upheld when he was practicing plural marriage in violation of a Utah statute.

The courts, with increasing frequency, are finding that certain types of sexual harassment as discussed in Chapter 5 are an invasion of privacy. Other examples of invasion of privacy by the employer include but are not limited to reading mail—*Vernars* v. *Young,* 539 F.2d 966 (3rd Cir. 1975); psychological questionnaires—*Cort* vs. *Bristol-Meyers Co.,* 431 N.E. 2d 908 (Mass. 1982); and eavesdropping over the telephone—*Marks* v. *Bell Telephone Co.,* 331 A.2d 424 (Pa. 1975).

USE OF POLYGRAPH TESTS

As estimates of business losses increase due to employee theft and as drug and alcohol abuse expands, employers consider use of polygraphs or other forms of lie detector tests as a method of detecting and deterring such losses. Although this is an effective method to control losses, it does involve a certain degree of exposure.

One of the most important tasks of the personnel practitioner is to obtain valid information about a job applicant or to determine the facts when an employee is alleged to be dishonest. Applicants sometimes seek jobs not for the wages they might receive but for the opportunity to embezzle, steal, sell company secrets to competitors, or to engage in other forms of dishonesty. This type of person is often difficult to detect, and when the actions of one dishonest employee are not discovered, the example becomes a challenge to others. As a result, pilferage and dishonesty become more widespread. The obvious solution to the problem is not to hire the person in the first place or to discharge him or her when the acts are detected.

For many years the use of a lie detector test has been an available—but controversial—method of detecting dishonesty. The most common technique involves the use of the polygraph machine, but other methods have also been used, such as an intravenous injection of sodium pentothal ("truth serum"), which like the polygraph measures bodily changes that indicate whether the subject is telling the truth when responding to certain questions.

Employee Polygraph Protection Act

The Employee Polygraph Protection Act of 1988[18] was passed by the Congress "to prevent the denial of employment opportunities by prohibiting the use of lie detectors by employers involved in or affecting interstate commerce." The act includes all types of tests used, whether mechanical or electrical, or where the results are used, for the purposes of rendering a diagnostic opinion regarding the honesty or dishonesty of an employee. For those employers who are now using any mechanical or electrical means to obtain facts, or who may consider doing so in the future, this act will be limiting.

The employer is prohibited from requiring, requesting, or even suggesting to any employee or prospective employee to take any type of lie detector test. The act further prevents the employer from using or threatening to use any of the results of a lie detector test in making an employment decision. The act is enforced by the Secretary of Labor, who has promulgated rules and regulations under the act and has also prepared

---

[17]*Briggs* v. *North Muskegon Police Department,* 653 F.Supp. 585 (W.D. Mich. 1983).

[18]Public Law 100-347, 102 Stat. 646 et seq. 29 USC 2001 et seq.

a summary of the act to be posted by each employer in conspicuous places on its premises where employee and applicant notices are normally placed. (This is usually in the employment office and where employees normally come with problems, such as the personnel office.)

If an employee is discriminated against for refusing to take a test or for testifying that another employee or prospective employee was discriminated against, the act will protect such an employee from any employer adverse action. The Secretary of Labor has investigative powers and can conduct a hearing. Violation of the act has a civil penalty of not more than $10,000. This amount is determined by the Secretary of Labor, who can go to court to collect the fine or have an employee reinstated. An employee can also go to court within three years after the alleged violation and the act provides for attorney fees for the prevailing party. The waiver of employee rights and procedures under the act is specifically prohibited.

Sections 7 and 8 of the act provide for very broad exemptions that are important to note. Under Section 7, all employers in the public sector are exempt, including consultants, experts, or contractors employed by the federal government when performing any counterintelligence function.

Under Section 8 of the act, certain employers in the private sector are also exempt. If there is an ongoing investigation involving an economic loss or injury, the test can be used. (Why would any employer otherwise use it?) It also has a specific exemption for investigation of drugs. When the polygraph test is used under Section 7 or 8, the results must be used only as supportive evidence. It could be argued that most present uses of the polygraph test are exempted under these sections, except preemployment testing.

The act also has several restrictions for examiners. Only certain questions can be asked and the examinee can terminate the test at any time (which makes it strictly voluntary). The act restricts disclosure of the results only to the examinee, the employer who requested the test, or any court or governmental agency. The examinee, in writing, may permit disclosure to any other person.

The special preemption provision of the act (Section 10) provides that no state[19] or local law or collective bargaining agreement will be preempted that is more restrictive than the act. As a practical matter, most state laws are less restrictive, so the result of act will be to preempt them, except under the exemption, which will need extensive court interpretation.

After the rules are promulgated by the Secretary of Labor (for there is no time limit), it will be several years before there is court interpretation of the Employee Polygraph Protection Act of 1988. The act is devoid of the situation where the employee offers to take the test without a request from the employer, which is a common occurrence and for which a great deal of case law has been developed.[20] Whether a particular state law is preempted or is more strict is a legal determination that will take years to work its way through the courts. Federal and state courts will be involved, and in the meantime the employer has a choice of not using a polygraph test at all or being exposed to litigation. Suppose the examinee terminates the test. Must there be a good reason? Again this will be a legal battle to be settled in the future.

For the employer who still feels it is important to use the test, a policy or procedure should be developed to conform with federal and state law as much as possible, without waiting for court interpretation. However, have a lawyer review the policy or procedure as a good faith attempt to comply.

---

[19]For complete information on state laws, see Gordon E. Jackson, *The Labor and Employment Law Desk Book* (Englewood Cliffs, NJ: Prentice-Hall, 1986).

[20]See *O'Brien* v. *Papa Gino's,* 780 F.2d 1067 (1st Cir. 1986); *Kamrath* v. *Suburban National Bank,* 363 N.W. 2d 108 (Minn. 1985).

Recommended Policies for Polygraph Testing

When it becomes necessary to obtain evidence about the suspected dishonesty of an employee, the first consideration must be what techniques are allowed by federal and state law. Some states restrict the use of the polygraph test in varying degrees while others have no restrictions. No state restricts searches at the workplace and the workplace usually includes the parking lots. Both the polygraph test and search are means of obtaining evidence to determine guilt or innocence. If it is permitted by state and federal law, there is no reason why the polygraph test cannot be used. Not only is it a method of obtaining evidence, but also exposure of employees to the test may have a chilling effect on employee dishonesty. The personnel practitioner should always consider the possible effects of the use of the polygraph on employee relations. An atmosphere of suspicion may cause more harm than the test results can cure.

A policy regarding the use of the polygraph test might include the following provisions:

1. The polygraph test probably can be used in preemployment screening where the applicant is being considered for a position of trust (bank teller, safekeeping department of a hospital, and so on) under the exemptions of the federal statute.
2. If used, it will not be the sole qualifying or disqualifying factor in a preemployment evaluation but be supportive of other information.
3. For present employees a rule should be established to require that a voluntary test be only supportive in determining the facts, that an employee be a suspect before the test is given, and that there is no other way to determine the facts.
4. The polygraph test will always be used in combination with other techniques.
5. Passing or failing the polygraph test will not be considered by itself to be conclusive nor will the refusal to take the test, but in both situations the presumption of innocence or suspicion of guilt may be affected.

EMPLOYER RIGHT OF SEARCH AND SEIZURE

The employer/employee relationship must be distinguished from that of the police and a suspect who might be committing a crime. The U.S. Supreme Court on numerous occasions has restricted search and seizure under the Fourth Amendment. Surveillance by the police is restricted to what is observable—although the court allows various techniques to make evidence observable such as trained dogs, "beepers," flashlights, and the like. The law as it relates to search in the criminal sense is in place.[21]

In a police/citizen confrontation the search of lunch buckets would be a violation of Fourth Amendment rights. The employer/employee relationship is different because the employer has a legitimate interest in protecting his property and that of other employees.

Fourth Amendment Protection in the Public Sector

Would it be proper for a supervisor of a public employer to search an employee's desk when the public employee has the protection of the Fourth Amendment? The court in *O'Connor* v. *Ortega,* 107 S.Ct. 1492 (1987), said a reasonable search is permitted, but left it up to the trial court to determine what is reasonable. In O'Connor the employee had been placed on administrative leave from his hospital job pending investigation of a charge of work-related conduct. While on leave his office was searched, including his desk and files. Several items of personal effects were taken from his desk as well as work-related information, all of which were later used in adverse administration hearing. The employee claimed that the purpose of the search was to obtain evidence for the hearing, while the employer argued it was designed to inventory state property (a rather weak argument). The em-

---

[21]*Smith* v. *Maryland,* 442 U.S. 735 (1979); *Texas* v. *Brown,* 103 S.Ct. 1535 (1983).

ployee sued the persons making the search under 42 USC Section 1983, which makes employees in the public sector individually liable although acting on behalf of the employer.

The court in a five to four decision said that public employers must be given wide latitude to enter offices and should not be subject to probable cause requirements as police officers are. The standard applied was the same as in the private sector, one of reasonableness. The court said what is reasonable is decided on a case-by-case basis. Justice Scalia wrote a separate opinion and stated that any work-related search is reasonable regardless of how private or public the employee's office may be.

The significance of this decision is that even where the employee has the protection of the Fourth Amendment, his or her office may be searched. This decision gives both the public and the private employer considerable authority to make searches at the workplace.

Limitation of Searches by Labor Agreement

Privacy matters are seldom found in labor agreements since the parties choose to bargain about them on a one-by-one basis. The usual practice is that the organization makes a rule, and if the union feels that it is unreasonable, they challenge it through the grievance procedure. If the matter is not settled, then it goes to arbitration. Generally speaking, arbitrators have given management the right to search employees and their private property and have permitted disciplinary action when the employees refused. The basis for this position is that no one has a right to employment and that for this reason employment can be conditioned upon compliance with reasonable rules. The employer also has a legitimate right to prevent theft not only of property of the organization but also of property of employees. As in any arbitration situation, there is always a minority view.[22]

While most arbitrators permit searches, they disagree widely on the treatment of evidence obtained in a search. Arbitrators also differ substantially on the right of the employee to refuse search. Generally, a showing of probable cause is enough to support discipline for refusing to permit a personal search. One arbitrator held that an organization must not act in an unreasonable fashion and must have a reasonable basis for the search of lockers of employees. Such a basis might be the fact that certain property of the organization is missing.[23]

Some arbitrators require the organization to have a rule or a record of past practice before they will uphold a search. The past practice of inspecting the lunch buckets of employees who were leaving work for possible pilfered company property was found to support searching the lunch buckets of incoming employees for liquor. The search took place before a preholiday shift. Drinking on the job had been a problem on such shifts in the past.[24]

Normally employees are entitled to reasonable safeguards as far as privacy is concerned. When a security guard asked a female employee to come to a closed room where an inspection would be made by a female guard, the arbitrator held that the company took all reasonable precautions to protect the privacy of the employee and the employee had a duty to cooperate.[25]

It appears from arbitration decisions and the absence of court cases on searches and seizures that if an employer has a probable cause to search the personal property of employees at the workplace—including the parking lot—the search will be permitted.[26] This conclusion is in line with other case law and with the common law that the employee

---

[22]Detroit Gasket & Mfg. Co., 27 LA 717 (Crane 1956).

[23]International Nickel Co., 50 LA 68 (Shister 1967).

[24]Fruehauf Corp., 49 LA 89 (Daugharty 1967).

[25]Alden, Inc., 51 LA 469 (Kellcher 1968).

[26]For arbitration cases on searches, see Frank Elkouri and Edna A. Elkouri, *How Arbitration Works*, 4th ed. (Washington, DC: Bureau of National Affairs, Inc., 1985), pp. 790–91.

cannot refuse to answer questions because of possible self-incrimination, has no right to see his or her own personal files, and must reveal any information that was acquired during the course of employment.

Recommended Procedures for Searches

In order for the employer to exercise the rights granted by the common law, it is necessary to establish a policy on searches if exposure to invasion-of-privacy claims are to be avoided. Most courts will permit any reasonable search, especially if the employee is warned that it might happen. Several courts take the position that continued employment after being warned that routine searches will be made is implied consent, which would prevent any lawsuit for invasion of privacy.[27] A policy on searches should contain the following provisions:

1. The purpose of the policy is to protect company and employee interests.
2. Searches will be used only when there is legitimate reason to believe that pilferage is taking place. This includes employees' property as well as company property.
3. The employee consents to reasonable search as a condition of employment, and refusal can result in discharge.
4. In all searches personal privacy will be respected but this consideration will not eliminate the search.
5. Searches will be unannounced and routine searches will be used only where pilferage of company and/or employees' property is excessive.
6. Searches, if possible, will be conducted away from other employees and on company time.
7. Searches will be conducted on company premises; lockers and personal cars in the parking lot are considered company property and will be searched.

Search could be an invasion of privacy (which is defined as something highly offensive to a reasonable man) if not conducted

for the purpose of obtaining facts. Often the person doing the search becomes abusive and acts with malice in the attempt to get the employee to admit the wrongdoing, and a suit for invasion of privacy results. In *K-Mart Corp. Store # 7441* v. *Trotti,* 667 So.2d 6329 (Tex. App. 1984), the court held that it was an invasion of privacy to search lockers when there was no warning that lockers would from time to time be searched and that unreasonable methods were used.

Whether it be the use of a voluntary polygraph test or a search, the real purpose of the procedure is to prevent others from doing the same thing. The purpose of the policy should be made clear, that the objective is to prevent pilferage and not to find somebody guilty. The law permits the employer to use all reasonable means to protect property, whether it be the company's or that of the employee, and all management has to do is exercise the rights that the law has given it.

Sometimes management takes the position that the way to prevent pilferage is to involve the law enforcement authorities. This, in the author's opinion, is a serious mistake. The major reason is that, as we have seen, the law enforcement authorities need more proof of a violation than an employer does. All the employer needs is knowledge that the company policy was violated, but the police need substantial evidence that the employee committed the act and violated a law. If the employer accuses and the authorities fail to prosecute or the employee is found not guilty, the employer has "egg on his face" and employee relations has been dealt a severe blow. The second reason why the authorities should not be involved is that the employer's primary business is not improving society and removing all dishonest persons from the streets. The employer's concern must be work related, so the only penalty it should be concerned with is discharge.

Most employees will accept the truth but are quick to challenge any falsehood. In the past, it is not what the employer has been doing that has caused the lawsuits, but it is the way that it was done that resulted in large

---

[27]*United States* v. *Sihler,* 562 F.2d 349 (5th Cir. 1977).

awards and caused many of the employers to become "gun-shy" in exercising their court-granted rights.

COMMON LAW ON DISCLOSURE OF EMPLOYEE INFORMATION

Since litigation in the area of disclosure of information about employees has been increasing, the subject is becoming more popular in professional literature and personnel textbooks.[28]

Under present legal doctrine, personnel records (defined as all information about employees kept by an employer) are not confidential but are the property of the employer to be used at its discretion. The employee can do little to stop disclosure.[29]

Releasing information about employees is largely a consideration by the employer of who wants the information and for what purpose. The discretionary control of personnel records by the employer has often been considered by civil rights advocates, academics, and the general public as an unjust infringement on employee privacy.

With the advent of the antidiscrimination laws in the late 1960s and 1970s, certain restrictions were made on the employer in the disclosure of information about employees. This upsurge in the interest of employee privacy along with a recognition of the judicial system of individual rights has caused the employer to become aware of the employee privacy problem in the use of personnel records. The employee privacy problem has two distinct facets. On one side is the need of the employer for data on the employee for benefit packages, job placement, promotion, and compliance with government information requests. On the other hand employees have an interest in preventing unwarranted intrusions into their private lives as well as adverse consequences should certain information be released.

To avoid obsolescence, the personnel practitioner must become familiar with court decisions and statutes regarding disclosure of employee information. The use of a subpoena to obtain employee records is excluded from this discussion, as it can be used only in legal proceedings and is not normally discretionary with the personnel practitioner.

Right of Employee to Review Own Records

The well-established principle of common law that information obtained by the employer about an employee relating to the employment relationship is the property of the employer also applies to the request of the employees to see their own records.

Some states have passed laws requiring the employer to give access to the employee's own record.[30] Those states that require disclosure in the private sector usually permit the employer to remove certain information before disclosing the file to the employee.[31] These statutes should not be confused with the Freedom of Information Act (5 USC Sect. 552), which requires federal agencies to disclose information about agency activities to the general public.

Over 200 employers, both large and small, have adopted policies allowing an employee access to his or her own records. They argue

---

[28]D. J. Duffy, "Privacy v. Disclosure: Balancing Employee-Employer Rights," *Employee Relations Law Journal* (1982), pp. 594–609; Phillip Adler, Jr., Charles Parsons, Scott B. Zolke, "Employee Privacy: Legal and Research Developments and Implications for Personnel Administration," *Sloan Management Review* (Winter 1985), p. 17; William Petrocelli, *Low Profile—How to Avoid the Privacy Invaders* (New York: McGraw-Hill, 1981), p. 112.

[29]*Cort v. Bristol-Meyers*, 431 N.W.2d 908 (Mass. 1983).

[30]At least 14 states have passed such laws, including but not restricted to California, Pennsylvania, Illinois, Delaware, Michigan, New Hampshire, North Carolina, Oregon, Tennessee, Utah, Wisconsin, and Vermont.

[31]For a detailed study on access to records, see "Employee Access to Records," P/H ASPA Survey, Prentice-Hall reprint from *Personnel Management: Policies and Practices* (Englewood Cliffs, NJ: 1984).

that denying an employee access to such records is not good employee relations. Many advocates of the employee privacy doctrine state that if the employers continue to deny employees access to their own records, Congress will do something about it; it is better to establish their internal policies rather than have Congress do it.

Those companies allowing employees to see information from their own files have a policy that usually states that the employer can remove certain information that it chooses not to disclose. Normally the policy does not define the information that may be removed. Determinations are made on a case-by-case basis. Information that probably would be withheld from the employee might include consideration for promotion, the fact that an employee is suspected of violating a rule and therefore must be watched, and the scheduled elimination of the job or that of the supervisor.

It is also common to "sanitize" investigatory reports of all types, supervisors' notes, and recommendations about future salary increases.

Exposure to Liability in Reference Requests

The employer has no obligation to grant requests for disclosure of personnel records unless required by statute. At the same time almost nothing can prevent voluntary disclosure by the employer. If the employer wants to cooperate with the local law enforcement agencies or with the Federal Bureau of Investigation (FBI), it may do so. If the employer chooses not to do so, the law enforcement agency must decide on the facts that it has and whether to start court action and obtain the information by subpoena.

Where the employer decides to reveal information in the personnel file that is detrimental to the employee, the employee may sue for damages under certain conditions. This usually occurs when such facts that invade privacy under the common law are revealed to the public. The public is interpreted by the courts to mean a small group of people. If it is revealed to only one person, regardless of the seriousness of the injury, the employee has no tort action.[32]

This can best be described as follows: (1) One person knows it (no injury to one's reputation); (2) two persons know it (only a slight injury, no tort); (3) three persons know it— wrong, 111 now know it; enough know it to damage the reputation.

Under the common law of privacy, public disclosure of embarrassing private facts about a person is an invasion of the individual's interest in acquiring, retaining, and enjoying a good reputation. The violation of this interest is called defamation, which includes libel and slander.[33]

Common law invasions of privacy occur where the employer discloses information such as medical condition or drug abuse to someone who has no business need to know, as in *Bratt* v. *IBM*, 785 F.2d 352 (1st Cir. 1986).[34]

Liability for this tort usually arises when an employer communicates to a prospective employer or a credit agency information that is injurious to the reputation of an employee or former employee. Since nothing prevents an individual from filing a lawsuit, one might say that every time an employer discloses adverse information about an employee to a prospective employer, this could result in a lawsuit.

Protection by the Qualified Privilege Doctrine

Exposure for a lawsuit is greatly diminished by the common law doctrine of a qualified privilege. This doctrine protects

---

[32]*Biderman's of Springfield, Inc.* v. *Wright,* 322 S.W.2d 892 (Mo. 1959).

[33]William L. Prosser, *Handbook of the Law of Torts,* 4th ed., section 111 (St. Paul, MN: West Publishing Co., 1971), p. 737.

[34]See Suzanne Cook, "Invasion of Privacy—a 1984 Syndrome," *Industrial Management,* 29, no. 5 (September–October 1986), pp. 18–21.

the employer when revealing information about former or present employees. Privilege is defined in the Restatement of Torts as

... the modern term applied to those considerations which avoid liability where it might otherwise follow ... in its more common usage, it signified that the defendant has acted to further an interest of such social importance that it is entitled to protection, even at the expense of damage to the plaintiff. He is allowed freedom of action because his own interests or those of the public require it, and social policy will best be served by permitting it.[35]

This definition of privilege has been applied to employee records. The courts have taken the position that the public good is best served by a free exchange of information between the prospective employer and former employer as to the work habits and performance while employed. Where an employee falsified production records and the employer told other employees about it, the court said that the employer was justified in that it would discourage other employees from committing the same act.[36] However, this immunity from liability when disclosing adverse injurious information is not without limitations; an employer must take certain precautions if liability is to be avoided.[37]

Requirements of the Privilege Doctrine

As a general rule the courts will allow an employer to give information about a former employee that may be defamatory if such information is in the interest of the requesting employer and the public and the giving of information will protect that interest.[38] This is called a privilege that the courts will protect, but it is not without conditions.

1. The information must be given in good faith. Where a supervisor accused an employee of starting a competitive company and repeated other office rumors which he failed to investigate, the court awarded $19,000 in punitive damages.[39] (Punitive damages are damages that compensate above actual loss and are punishment for evil behavior.)

2. The information given must be limited to the inquiry. Asking about work habits does not require facts on personal life or information on union activities.[40]

3. The statement must be given under the proper occasion and in the proper manner. If given at a cocktail party or while playing bridge, an otherwise proper statement could be construed as invasion of privacy or libelous.

4. The information must be communicated to the proper parties and not the general public. In one case an inquiry was made by an aunt, uncle, and spouse as to an employee's whereabouts and the reason given for the inquiry was that he was accused of misappropriating company funds. The court said that it was not privileged because relatives had no job-related interest in receiving the information.[41]

5. Information requested must be related to the requirements of the job.

6. Information revealed must be true or a reasonable effort must be made to seek the truth.[42]

---

[35]Prosser, *Handbook*, 1971.

[36]*Ponticelli* v. *Mine Safety Appliance Co.*, 247 A.2d 303 (R.I. 1968).

[37]For additional information on this privilege, see Jack Turner and Terry Esser, "Reference and Background Checks: Myth and Fact," *Human Resources Management Ideas and Trends*, no. 36 (Chicago, IL: Commerce Clearing House, April, 1983); E. Dube, "Employment Reference and the Law," *Personnel Journal*, 65, no. 2 (February 1986), pp. 87–88.

[38]For good explanation see *Circus Circus Hotels* v. *Witherspoon*, 657 P.2d 101 (Nev. 1983). Also see *Humphrey* v. *National Semiconductor Corp.*, 18 Mass. App. 132 (1984).

[39]*Calero* v. *Del Chemical Corp.*, 228 N.W.2d 737 (Wisc. 1975).

[40]*Sindorf* v. *Jacron Sales*, 341 A.2d 856 (Md. 1975).

[41]*Stewart* v. *Nation-Wide Check Corp.*, 182 S.E.2d 410 (N.C. 1971).

[42]*Rady* v. *Forest City Enterprises, Inc.*, 489 N.E.2d 1090 (Ohio Com. Pl. 1986).

7. Information must be revealed without malice and bad faith.[43]

Reference checks run afoul of antidiscrimination laws only where it can be shown that the reference check was for a discriminatory purpose or information received was used in a discriminatory manner. If conclusions drawn from reference reports are biased, the result will be considered discriminatory or malicious. A minority applicant may receive a poor reference report because of poor performance on the job for a former employer. This does not necessarily mean that the applicant is unqualified for a different position and different employer. The reasons for poor performance must be considered; poor performance cannot always be used as a reason for not hiring a member of the protected class. Often the prospective employer will ask if the former employee is eligible for rehire; if the answer is negative, the person will not be hired. Relying solely on this answer may indicate a discriminatory motive in refusal to hire, if the applicant is a member of a protected class.

When the Privilege Is Lost

1. The employer did not believe that what was said was the truth or did not have reasonable grounds for this belief that it was the truth.
2. The information was given for some purpose other than business.
3. The information was not responsive to the third-party inquiry.
4. The information was given out of malice and not for a legitimate reason.

The most common reason for losing the privilege doctrine is that the information is given out of malice. Whether it is malice is a factual question determined on a case-by-case basis. In most situations the person disclosing knows whether or not it is malice, since intent is usually present.

In one case the employee was discharged under a company policy of automatically terminating everyone working a shift during which a cash shortage occurred. The plaintiff could not get employment elsewhere as the result of the termination. The court held that a qualified privilege existed; therefore, the employer was not liable unless the plaintiff could prove that there was malice. In finding that there was insufficient evidence of malice, the court said "actual malice requires proof that the statement was made with malice in fact, ill-will or wrongful notice." Here there was no evidence from which a jury could infer any motive founded on ill-will toward the plaintiff or a desire to harm her; it was merely an enforcement of a policy.[44]

Refusal to Disclose Reference Information—A Legal Paradox

Many employers have adopted a policy that information disclosed about former employees should be limited to verification of employment and the length of employment. This policy may be considered the safest to avoid lawsuits. But from an employee relations point of view it could result in the hiring of many undesirable applicants and create ill will among former employees who are refused favorable references. An employer can reduce the risk of litigation to near zero and still maintain good recruiting practices as well as good employee relations by taking advantage of the qualified privilege doctrine.

It is a legal paradox that the courts are granting immunity from prosecution and ruling that it is in the public interest to exchange information about employees to discourage hiring of undesirable applicants; at the same time many employers are unwilling

---

[43]*Bolling* v. *Baker,* 671 S.W.2d 559 (Tex. App. 4 Dist. 1984). The employer stated that the discharged employee was a liar and not trustworthy. Although this was revealed only to other employees, the court found the privilege doctrine was violated by statements made with malice and reckless disregard for the truth.

[44]*Haldeman* v. *Total Petroleum, Inc.,* 376 N.W.2d 98 (Iowa 1985).

to disclose because of the danger of being sued. Employers should be careful when taking "smart-aleck" shortcuts, such as refusing employment references or avoiding handbooks. Some of these practices make good personnel sense and will help convince the jury that the employer is dealing fairly with its employees.

It has been a common practice among employment managers to check the references of an applicant by calling the applicant's former employer and requesting specific information for preemployment purposes. Large court awards and expensive litigation, where limitations on the qualified privilege have been disregarded, have alerted many employers to the exposure to litigation to the point where they refuse to give reference information except for dates of employment and job title. If this practice continues, reference disclosures as a source of preemployment information will be as obsolete as the corner blacksmith shop.

Whether refusal to disclose employee information will have a damaging effect on the hiring of qualified applicants depends on how valid reference information has been. It has probably been as valid as other subjective selection procedures that have been common in the past. Some personnel administrators feel that the abolition of reference checks would have no effect on hiring persons qualified to perform because reference checks are not a valid method of determining an applicant's acceptability. Reference requests are somewhat unreliable unless a personal confidential relationship exists between the person requesting the information and the person disclosing the information. If a personal relationship exists, legal implications are not usually present.[45]

The only absolute protection against being sued is not to give any reference information to anybody. However, an employer that is interested in selecting qualified and stable applicants must obtain background information from some source in order to succeed. If no reference information is provided by employers concerning an applicant's qualifications or trait characteristics, then the selection process is in part a subjective one. A subjective selection process is almost certain to run afoul of the antidiscrimination laws. The refusal of former employers to give background information may also result in selection of problem applicants.

NEGLIGENT HIRING AND RETENTION

A more serious exposure to litigation exists in a new form of tort action called negligent hiring and negligent retention. This action has been created in part by the legal paradox. The courts are saying that an employer will not be liable for giving information about former employees and the employers are saying that they will be liable if they do. Is it any wonder that the courts have little sympathy for the employer when an action of negligent hiring is filed by an employee?

The action in tort of negligent hiring and negligent retention is only ten years old, with most of the cases having been filed in the last five years. It is now recognized as a cause of action in most state courts.

Negligent hiring or retention is defined as a situation in which an employer is liable to third persons for injury where the employer knew or should have known of the employee's dangerous proclivities. The employer's negligence must be the proximate cause of the injury to those persons whom the employer could reasonably expect to come in contact with the employee. The injury does not have to be personal or physical. In one case the employer was held liable for hiring a person who committed forgery and fraud.[46]

To be liable the employer must have known or exercised ordinary care to know of the

---

[45]This is one advantage in being active in local personnel associations and professional and civic organizations. You get to know the right people.

[46]*Pruitt* v. *Pavelin,* 685 P.2d 1347 (Ariz. App. 1984).

dangerous tendencies. Where the applicant had a clear record and nothing to indicate a bad record, there was no duty to check.[47] However, where the employee had a free access to customers' homes the same court held there was a duty to inquire into the applicant's background.[48]

Liability for Negligent Hiring

The employer's liability for negligent hiring will depend on the soundness of the investigation into the employee's background.[49] Important factors in the background check are the job responsibilities for which the applicant was hired and the applicant's record that indicated risk of harm to co-workers or injury to third parties.

In *Stephanie Ponticas et al.* v *K.M.S. Investments*, 331 N.W. 2d 907 (Minn. 1983), the employer hired a caretaker for an apartment building. The employee had been convicted of armed robbery, burglary, and auto theft. Using his passkey to enter an apartment, he raped one of the tenants. The court held that an employer has a duty to exercise reasonable care in hiring individuals who because of the nature of their employment may pose a threat to members of the public.

A truck driver is hired with a criminal record of violent sex crimes and aggravated sodomy of two teenaged hitchhikers while driving a truck for another employer. The defendant gave instructions not to pick up hitchhikers but the driver did, and in the sleeping compartment of the truck he raped and threatened to kill the plaintiff. The court found that it was the duty of the employer to hire competent drivers and the employer knew or should have known that entrusting a truck with a sleeping compartment to a person with a history of sex crimes was negligent hiring. There was a duty for this type of job to reasonably check the employee's

background.[50] However, where a background of an employee was not investigated the court held there was no duty to do so since there was denial at the time of hiring of any previous criminal convictions or episodes of violence.[51]

Some courts will hold that if the act was employment related the employer is liable. In *Tolbert* v. *Martin Marietta Corp.*, 621 F.Supp. 1099 (Colo. 1985), the employee was sexually assaulted on the way to lunch, and the court held that it was employment related. The employer failed to make the premises safe for the employees.

In one situation there was evidence that the employee had a drinking problem, and while drinking he assaulted a guest. The court had little difficulty in finding negligent retention.[52] Since there is an exposure to negligent retention complaints, the employer who has knowledge of dangerous tendencies has a duty to other employees to do something about it. It is not uncommon for an employee in the heat of an argument to threaten a supervisor or another employee, and if the employer does nothing about it and later the threat is carried out on another employee, there is a good possibility that the employer will be liable for any resulting injury under negligent retention decisions.

The law is, therefore, well in place that an employer has a duty to investigate applicants. If the practice by employers of not supplying information becomes universal, a greater exposure will be created than disclosing information about employees, since the court will protect under the qualified privilege doctrine but not negligent hiring. The policy of not disclosing information may eliminate a small exposure in one area but

---

[47]*Nazareth* v. *Herndon Ambulance Service*, 476 So.2d 1076 (Fla. App. 1985).

[48]*Abbot* v. *Payne*, 457 So.2d 1156 (Fla. 1984).

[49]Hire in haste; repent at leisure.

[50]*Slaton* v. *B & B Gulf Service Center*, 344 S.E.2d 512 (Ga. App. 1986).

[51]*Odom* v. *Hubeny, Inc.*, 345 S.E.2d 886 (Ga. App. 1986).

[52]*Pittard* v. *Four Seasons Motor Inn*, 688 P.2d 333 (N.M. App. 1984). See also *Gaines* v. *Monsanto Company*, 655 S.W.2d 568 (Mo. App. 1983); *Cox* v. *Brazo, et al.*, 303 S.E.2d 71 (Ga. App. 1983); *Valdez* v. *Warner*, 742 P.2d 517 (N.M. App. 1987).

create a larger exposure in another area. Failure to disclose information on applicants to prospective employers might result in all kleptomaniacs on the labor market being hired, and if an employer is not liable for negligent hiring he may be for negligent retention.

Thoroughness of the Investigation

Although there are no hard-and-fast rules on the adequacy of an investigation, there appears to be more duty imposed when jobs have a public relationship or expose the employee to opportunities to injure others. There is a greater duty to investigate for security guard or taxicab driver than for a bartender.[53] In certain jobs the risk is foreseeable, as in the case of Pinkerton's guards or a maintenance job in an apartment complex. The legal principle is that unless there is a strong reason not to do so, there exists a duty to investigate.

Hiring a Person with a Known Criminal Record

Under a federal program to provide specific skills to the unemployed, including former convicts, the employer put a convict on a work release status who had been convicted of second-degree murder and had a record of other crimes. The prisoner started his employment as a carpentry instructor but later was released from prison and allowed to live on the premises and act as security guard. While in this capacity, he sexually assaulted and murdered a twelve-year-old boy. The plaintiffs conceded that there was no negligent hiring to perform the duties as a carpentry instructor. The court in *Henley* v. *Prince*

George's County, 503 A.2d 133 (Md. 1986), agreed that there was no negligent hiring, but it was for the jury to determine whether or not it was negligent assignment of security duties. From this case as well as dictums in others, the courts will not find that hiring a criminal is negligent hiring, but it appears that there is some exposure to properly assigning the employee.

Case Law on Negligent Retention

Negligent retention is the breach of an employer's duty to be aware of an employee's propensity for malicious or violent behavior regardless of cause. The duty requires the employer to take corrective action through retraining, assignment, reassignment, or discharge. Very often a complaint will allege both. In *Cherry* v. *Kelly Services, Inc.*, 319 S.E.2d 463 (Ga. App. 1984), the court held that where a defendant's driver injured the plaintiff there was no negligent retention since the employee did not have a bad driving record. However, the fact that the employee had one prior moving violation raised an issue of whether or not there was negligent hiring.

EXPOSURE FOR DEFAMATION

A common law tort of defamation, in the employment context, is most common after the employer gives a false oral or written statement as to why the employee was discharged. In order to make out a claim for defamation the plaintiff must prove that

1. A statement has been made about him or her to another person
2. It is false or given to someone who has no need to know
3. It harms the reputation of the plaintiff by lowering his or her esteem or stature in the community or with other persons[54]

---

[53]In *Welch Mfg. Co.* v. *Pinkerton's*, 474 A.2d 436 (R.I. 1984), the court held that a police record and contacting two former employers was not enough. In *Burch* v. *A&G Associates*, 333 N.W.2d 140 (1983), the court said that a taxicab company has a higher duty to investigate than other employers. However, in *Evans* v. *Morsell*, 95 A.2d 480 (Md. 1978), the court said there was very little duty to check on a bartender. See also *Kassman* v. *Busfield Enterprise, Inc.*, 639 P.2d 353 (1981).

[54]*Stuempes* v. *Parke, Davis & Co.*, 297 N.W.2d 252 (Minn 1980). Also see W. Keeton, *Prosser and Keeton on Torts*, 5th ed., Sect. 111 (1984), p. 774; Restatement of Torts, Sect. 558 (1977).

When the qualified privilege doctrine is violated, a defamation suit is the remedy. Once the court determines that the privilege doctrine applies, the burden is on the plaintiff to show that the doctrine was violated.

In order for a statement to be defamatory it must be a personal attack upon the plaintiff and not a hearty disagreement with the plaintiff's views or a statement about an overly sensitive person. Depending upon the circumstances, a plaintiff must have some "thickness of skin."[55]

Disclosing Information to Other Employees

One of the conditions of the doctrine of qualified privilege is that information be given only to these persons who have a legitimate business right to receive it. This requirement goes to the very roots of the doctrine. The courts say that information about the reasons for the discharge of an employee should be released to other employees who have a reason to know. By so doing the employer may prevent others from making the same mistake and also being discharged. Preventing acts that will result in discharge is in the public interest. The release of information about the reason for a discharge to employees who are not exposed to the opportunity to commit similar acts can be ruled to be defamatory.

The acquisition of one organization by another is commonplace in our business culture today. Frequently such combinations leave the merged organization with two persons for only one job. Though both may be competent, one has to go. In a fairly typical case, one company acquired another with an effective date on a Friday. On Saturday, three top executives were discharged. Over the weekend all other officers and department heads were called and instructed not to go to the office on Monday morning but to attend a meeting at a nearby hotel at 8 o'clock

on Monday. At the meeting, the officers and department heads were told why the three executives were fired. Only the top management was told. Other levels of management were excluded because they did not have the same need to know since they would not be directly affected. By following this carefully thought out procedure, the organization substantially reduced the risk of litigation. If all levels of management had been invited to the meeting, the organization would have been exposed to charges of defamation.

In *Benassi* v. *Georgia-Pacific,* 662 P.2d 760 (Or. App. 1983), a general manager was discharged for allegedly having a drinking problem and using a "loud voice and considerable profanity." The employer called in all the employees and stated at a meeting, "I gathered you here to tell you why Mr. Benassi is no longer with the company. The man was drunk and misbehaving in a bar. The man had a drinking problem. Georgia-Pacific looks unkindly on this kind of conduct. It was not the first time. He had been warned." Mr. Benassi sued on the basis of this statement. The court found that there was an abuse of the qualified privilege doctrine since there was no reason to communicate to all employees in order to protect the interests of the employer.

The level of employees to whom information should be communicated should be determined by the employer, taking into consideration the likelihood that the employee will benefit from the information. When an employee was discharged for falsifying company records, the employer told higher-level employees as well as employees on the same or lower levels. In the resulting defamation suit, the court laid down the rule that communication was proper to all who have a need to know as well as those employees who would be directly affected by the discharge. In this case, the court said that all employees to whom the information was communicated had a "need to know."[56]

---

[55]*Tyson* v. *L'Eggs Products, Inc.,* 351 S.E. 2d 834 (N.C. App. 1984).

[56]*Hodges* v. *Tomberlin,* 319 S.E.2d 11 (Ga. App. 1984).

Statements That Impute Crime

Statements that impute crimes are susceptible to a defamatory meaning. In *Norman* v. *General Motors Corp.,* 628 F.Supp. 702 (D. Nev. 1986), GMC discharged the plaintiff after twelve years of employment. He sued for intentional infliction of emotional distress, alleging that GMC initiated a drug investigation with knowledge that he had not committed any offense and with a reckless disregard of whether or not he had. GMC also communicated the information about the drug investigation to the narcotic unit of the police department. The court found that the initiation of a drug investigation without a reason was outrageous conduct and, although the information was privileged, it was defamatory since the narcotic unit of the police department did not have a business right to receive it.

Statements that impute crime are not always defamatory. If properly made they come under the qualified privilege doctrine, as in the case where the employer, based on a polygraph test, had reason to believe that the plaintiff was involved in vandalism and the statement of this fact was only made to other employees. The statement was protected by the qualified privilege doctrine.[57]

Giving False Reasons for Discharge

Many organizations make a practice of "softening the record" in the case of discharges to avoid an adverse reaction on the part of the employee being terminated and to make him or her more employable. For many years it was not uncommon to avoid giving the real reason for discharge and to enter a relatively innocuous reason such as "personality difficulties"—or the more recent version, "a chemistry problem with the supervisors"—into the record. If the statements are not damaging to the reputation of the employee, there is little exposure to charges of defamation.

If the false reason is damaging to the reputation of the employee, defamation is found. In *Lewis* v. *Equitable Life Assurance Society of the United States,* 389 N.W.2d 876 (Minn. 1986), the plaintiffs submitted an expense account after returning from a business trip. The employer considered it excessive and requested them to reduce the amount. The employees refused since it was legitimate. When they again refused they were discharged and the reason given was "gross insubordination." When they applied for employment the reason was repeated to prospective employers. They could not find employment so they sued their former employer for defamation. The court ruled that the reason given was false and the employer should have known that the defamatory words would be repeated. Although the false reason was defamation, however, it was without malice and the privilege doctrine prevented damages from being awarded.

Defamation can result when a false reason for discharge is given through an interoffice communication. In one case the reason stated in an interoffice memo was "failure to increase business as a major Project Sales Representative," which was in fact untrue. Although the reason was communicated by memo only to the supervisor and CEO, the court held it was defamation, but without malice.[58] If this case is followed in other jurisdictions, any false reason for discharge is defamation regardless of to whom or how it is communicated.

It is a well-established principle that no liability results from releasing information about an employee or former employee to prospective employers as long as care is taken to follow the doctrine of qualified privilege. Where exposure to liability is most likely to occur is in a situation where the information is released to persons who are not employers or who do not have a business need to know.

---

[57]*Larson* v. *Homet Aluminum,* 449 N.W.2d 1172 (Ind. App. 3 Dist. 1983).

[58]*Frankson* v. *Design Space Int'l,* 394 N.W.2d 140 (Minn. 1986); also *Banas* v. *Matthews Intern. Corp.,* 502 A.2d 637 (Pa. Super. 1985). The court in *Rouly* v. *Enserch Corp.,* 835 F.2d 1127 (5th Cir. 1988), took the opposite view.

A vice president of engineering was discharged. He alleged that Title VII was violated and that he was discharged because of his color. In preparation for the EEOC hearing, the employer allegedly made statements to suppliers that the plaintiff was discharged because he was incompetent. The court said that such statements were not privileged and that an action for defamation could exist if the statements were false. The privilege doctrine does not extend to statements made to suppliers.[59]

Where a former employer in a telephone conversation told a prospective employer that the employee was "erratic in work hours, brought her personal problems to the office, had married another employee of the company and caused that man to have a mental breakdown," this was defamatory since some of the statements were not job related and were given with malice.[60] In *Geyer* v. *Steinbronn*, 506 A.2d 901 (Pa. Super. 1986), the court found that accusations of dishonesty or theft, even if indirect, were defamatory. The court stated this was particularly true when it involved a security employee for whom trustworthiness was an occupational requirement.

Guidelines to Prevent Exposure for Defamation

In all the cases where the court found defamation, the employer either made some assumptions without foundation or knowingly made malicious or false statements. There is a lot of difference between stating that you no longer have confidence in a person and calling her or him a liar. The fact that the qualified privilege doctrine has some restrictions does not mean that it cannot be used. The courts are telling the employer that it should be used and when used properly the employer is protected from any liability. The "bottom line" is whether the statement was intended to be damaging to the reputation of the employee or was factual with no purpose of being malicious. If the effect of it was damaging to the reputation of the employee, without malice there is no defamation. The term "poor performance" is often used as a matter of convenience and is troublesome if the employee does not in fact have poor performance.

In order to avoid exposure to defamation lawsuits the employer should

1. Have a well-defined termination policy that prevents managers and supervisors from discharging first and then looking for a reason.
2. State the facts without adjectives that may imply malice or bad faith.
3. Train managers and supervisors in the use of the qualified privilege doctrine or instruct them to let somebody who is qualified make the statements.

Often it is the attitude toward the person and not the truth of the statement that influences the court. For this reason the immediate supervisor or someone directly involved should not give the reference.[61]

RECOMMENDATIONS THAT CONSIDER EMPLOYEE'S PRIVACY AND EMPLOYER'S NEED TO KNOW

In any policy on disclosure of employee information, consideration must be given to the employee's right to enjoy a good reputation as well as the employer's concern to employ qualified and desirable people. The employer must also be concerned with the welfare of other employees. The failure to discover that the person hired is a kleptomaniac or has a history of sex crimes is not

---

[59]*Medina* v. *Spotnails, Inc.*, 591 F.Supp. 190 (E.D. N.D. Ill. 1984).

[60]*Marshall* v. *Brown*, 190 Cal. Rptr. 392 (Cal. App. 1983).

[61]For further discussion of defamation in the workplace, see "Defamation and Invasion of Privacy Action in Typical Employment Relations Situations," Lincoln Law Review, 13 (1984), pp. 1–19; D. J. Duffy, "Defamation and Employer Privilege, *Employee Relations Law Journal*, 9 (Winter 1983–1984), p. 444.

in the best interest of the employer or employees. A policy, therefore, must not discourage reference information but must be drafted in a way that reflects a real concern for the employee's privacy and the employer's need to know.

The following provisions are designed to accomplish this goal:

1. Only certain designated and trained persons should be permitted to release information. These persons should be trained in the legal requirements of disclosing employee information. The practice of allowing the supervisor to disclose reference information over the telephone should be eliminated. This practice probably was started because many application forms ask the applicant, "Who was your immediate supervisor on your former job?" If the application form asks, "Who was the immediate supervisor?" the question should be eliminated.

2. Except for dates of employment, all requests for information should be in writing. Since information should be given only to persons who have a reason to receive it, this cannot be ascertained over the telephone. Sometimes former employees seek information under disguise of a prospective employer; requiring the request in writing will eliminate this problem.

3. The firm should give out only information that is requested and is job related. When the inquirer asks the time of day, don't tell how to build a watch. If there is any doubt as to its accuracy, one should not release the information.

4. The employee should be required to consent to the release of the information requested. Although the courts hold that this is not needed, it is convenient to have this consent when the employer is being sued by an employee who consented to its release. In one situation where the employee was a member of an association, the court said that he had consented to the written cause of his dismissal through his membership.[62] The Restatement of Torts puts it this way: "Moreover, one who agrees to submit his conduct to investigation knowing that its results will be published, consents to the publication of the honest findings of the investigators."[63]

It is also good employee relations to get the employee's consent; the employee receives some satisfaction in exercising the right to determine whether certain information should be released. For example, the employee may not want disclosure of an address to a mother-in-law but may want full disclosure of all information to the promoter of an exclusive country club.

5. Information should be put in the employee's file only if it is truthful and there is a job-related or business need for it. Particular attention should be paid to records kept by persons outside the personnel office (for example, front-line supervisors or group leaders). Many problems are found in these records. Collecting irrelevant or inaccurate information adversely affects the quality of the relevant information as well as causing legal problems.

6. Information should be collected from reliable sources. Hearsay and subjective evaluations should be avoided, especially as to work performance, trait characteristics, arrest records, and results of interviews that have no other purpose except to prove somebody right.

7. The employer should refrain from giving information about performance on a specific job. This is often subjective and is not predictive of how the applicant will perform on another job. Also always express any information on performance as an opinion with a reservation.

8. The employer should be wary of giving information for background or future reference. If the recipient is not a prospective employer, the qualified privilege doctrine may not apply. It is also difficult to predict how the information will be used. This is one method to get information for use of a union for organizing purposes, for a sales mailing list, or for a sales contact.

9. Employee personnel files should be released within the company only to those who have a job-related purpose to know it. Only that information in the file that is not challengeable as to its validity and pertains to the stated purpose of the inquiry should be released.

---

[62] *Joftes* v. *Kaufman*, 324 F.Supp. 660 (D.C. D.C. 1972).

[63] Restatement of Torts, Sect. 583 (1938), p. 221.

10. Employee access to the file should be permitted but the file should be sanitized if necessary. Release of such information as comparative evaluations, mental problems, investigative interviews, and physical conditions could do more harm than good to employee relations.

11. When an employee disagrees with the information in the file, the disputed statement should be put in the file without comment in the event it becomes material.

12. The procedure should detail what, to whom, by whom, and under what limitations the information should be disclosed.

    If a practice or procedure contains most of these provisions, the employer not only will be exchanging information for the public good but will also be able to select qualified and desirable applicants objectively while enjoying good employee relations. This will also eliminate exposure to charges of negligent hiring and negligent retention.

The law does not restrict disclosure of employee information but encourages it. An employer policy or practice that respects the privacy of the employee but gives prospective employers certain accurate and non-malicious facts will prevent unwanted litigation as well as legislation that neither the employer nor the employee will like.

10
EMPLOYER'S RIGHT TO DISCHARGE

Definition and History of Employment-At-Will Doctrine
Statutes That Void At-Will Doctrine
Public Policy Exception to At-Will Doctrine
Implied Contract That Modifies At-Will Doctrine
A Discharge That Becomes a Tort
Constructive Discharge

DEFINITION AND HISTORY OF EMPLOYMENT-AT-WILL DOCTRINE

When an employer in the private sector hires an employee to work for an indefinite period, in the absence of a formal contract or union agreement, the employee can be terminated at any time without legal liability for good cause, bad cause, or no cause at all unless there is an express statutory prohibition. This general rule of the common law is stated in the American Law Reports (ALR) as follows:

Despite its sometimes harsh operation and the obvious opportunities for abuse it affords an unscrupulous employer, few legal principles would seem to be better settled than the broad generality that an employment for an indefinite term is regarded as an employment at will which may be terminated at any time by either party for any reason or for no reason at all.[1]

Under a century-old common rule, an employment relationship can be terminated at the whim of either party. As one court put it, an employee can be dismissed "for good cause, for no cause or even for cause morally wrong. . . ."[2] This is the common law doctrine of employment at will. The doctrine had its origin in the English law, where there was a legal presumption that an individual hired for an unspecified length of time was hired for a period of one year; if the employee continued to work after that year expired, the parties were presumed to have agreed to employment for an additional year. If the employee was to be terminated within the year term, "just cause" had to be shown. At least in theory, employees could rely upon the rule that their employer had to have some legitimate reason to dismiss them prior to their completion of a full year or compensate them until the expiration of one year.

When this doctrine was transferred to America, the fundamental principle of individual freedom was argued. A judicial dispute over whether the English rule should be adopted developed. Logic said that if one party could terminate employment so could the other, and this became the basis for the employment-at-will doctrine.[3] Many courts still were not accepting the doctrine and the judicial debate continued. In 1877 Horace Gray Wood (*Treatise on Master and Servant*) made an analysis of employment in the United States that contained the at-will rule and the courts were influenced. The unquestionable acceptance of the at-will rule is illustrated in the extreme case where an employee was discharged because his wife refused to sleep with his supervisor. He challenged the employer's right to discharge for this reason, but the court rejected his suit because the employment-at-will doctrine empowered his employer to discharge him at any time, even if the reason was immoral.[4] Within a short time Wood's precept was accepted by the Supreme Court in *Adair* v. *United States*, 208 U.S. 161 (1908), when the court declared a statute unconstitutional that prohibited the discharge of a railroad employee because of his union membership. The court said since the duration of the employment was not

---

[1]62 ALR 3rd 271 (1975).

[2]*Payne* v. *Western and Atlantic R.R. Co.*, 81 Tenn. 507, @ 519–520 (1884).

[3]For further reading on the history of the at-will doctrine, see Brian Hershizer, "The New Common Law of Employment: Changes in the Concept of Employment at Will: *Labor Law Journal*, 36, no. 95 (February 1985); Kenneth T. Lopatka, "The Emerging Law of Wrongful Discharge—A Quadrennial Assessment of the Labor Law Issue of the 80s," *Business Lawyer* 40 (November 1984), 1–32; the opinion of the Supreme Court of Alabama in *Comerford* v. *International Harvester Co.*, 178 So. 2d 894 (Ala. 1932); a bibliography published by the Bar Association of the City of New York called "Selected Materials of Employment at Will"; "Discharge at Will," *The Record*, 40, no. 3 (April 1985); Jay Feinman, "The Development of the Employment at Will Rule," *American Journal of Legal History*, 20, no. 118 (1976).

[4]*Comerford* v. *International Harvester Co.*, 178 So.2d 894 (Ala. 1932). See also *Tomkins* v. *Public Service Electric & Gas Co.*, 568 F.2d 1044 (3rd Cir. 1977), where there was discharge over refusal to have sexual relations with the supervisor.

specified, both the employer and the employee had equal rights to terminate for any reason.

Harshness of the Rule

With the mass migration of labor from farms to assembly lines, it became a social problem when a person's survival depended on the whims of the employer. There is little doubt that the employer-employee relationship is one of the most important relationships in life, because it affects the material well-being of every person. Although the relationship is vitally important to the quality of a worker's life, the jobs of more than 80 percent of American workers depend almost entirely on the continued good will of their employers.[5] The employer's right to terminate without a legal risk came under attack by social, economic, and legal scholars. Another concept that became popular in the employer-employee relationship was that a person had a property right in a job and that it was a social requirement that an employee should expect job security.[6]

On occasions the courts have held that an employee has a property right in a job since the job is necessary to maintain himself and his family, and therefore she or he should receive the protection of the government. The Supreme Court took this view in *Perry* v. *Sindermann,* 408 U.S. 593 (1972), when a school board failed to renew a teacher's contract and did not give an official statement as to the reason or allow an opportunity for a hearing. The teacher alleged that this denied him due process required by the Fourth Amendment. (Private sector employees do not have protection of this amendment.) The Supreme Court held that job security, whether it was expressed or implied, was a property right that could not be abridged without a procedural due process. According to the court, the existence of a tenure policy established expectations of continued employment, thereby creating a property right in the job. Although the property right in a job has been established only in the public sector, there is an indication that courts are influenced by the property right in job theory when making exceptions to the at-will rule. The influence can also come from legal theorists that argue that state and federal government should intervene in the employment relationship because employment should receive constitutional protection.[7]

Based on the history of other social problems, one would think that there would be an acceptable field for political activity. However, this hasn't happened and there are very few statutes that protect job security. When legislation fails to correct a social problem, courts relate to the problem on a case-by-case basis.

Judicial Application of At-Will Doctrine

Few legal doctrines have been more firmly established than the at-will doctrine. Under this doctrine the employer can do no wrong. Where an employee was discharged for trading in a certain store that the railroad decided to put out of business, the court said that the employer had a right to discharge even if it is morally wrong and "the law cannot compel them (employers) to employ workers, nor to keep them employed."[8] As late as 1949 a court

---

[5]Information is based on government statistics issued almost monthly. Monthly Labor Review, U.S. Department of Labor.

[6]See D. Hamermesh and A. Rees, *The Economics of Work and Pay,* 3rd ed. (New York: Harper & Row, Pub., 1984), pp. 172–74; Note, "Implied Contract Rights to Job Security," *Stanford Law Review,* 26, no. 335 (1974), pp. 367–68; P. Drucker, "The Job as Property Right," *The Wall Street Journal,* March 4, 1980, p. 2.

[7]See C. Peck, "Unjust Discharges from Employment: A Necessary Change in the Law," *Ohio State Law Journal,* 40, no. 1 (1979), pp. 25–35; "The Employment-at-Will Doctrine: Time to Collapse Another Citadel," *University of Dayton Law Review,* II, no. 2 (1985), p. 399.

[8]*Payne* v. *Western and Atlantic R. R. Co.,* 81 Tenn. 507 (1884).

held that an employer could discharge for no reason at all.[9]

With legislation concerning employees' rights, such as the Labor Management Relations Act as amended,[10] Title VII of the Civil Rights Act of 1964 as amended,[11] the Age Discrimination in Employment Act of 1967 as amended,[12] and the Occupational Safety and Health Act of 1970,[13] the courts started to take a look at this unblemished common law doctrine by listening to numerous theories asserted by discharged workers that the doctrine should have certain exceptions. Some argued that their employment was for a fixed period either expressed or implied while other discharged workers argued that the employer had an obligation to evaluate job performance in good faith and therefore could terminate only on just cause. Some employees relied more on the traditional reasons to justify their claims for relief, such as due process, contrary to fair and good faith dealing, or malicious action by the employer.

The courts in a climate of employee rights created by Congress in other areas began to favorably receive the wrongfully discharged employees' arguments and seek an exception to the common law doctrine. Because almost all these cases involve either a breach of contract or tort action, they are tried in state courts and accordingly there is a variation of law among the states.

The early 1980s was a period of the beginning of the erosion of the common law doctrine of employment at will. As one court stated, "It represents an area of the law undergoing dynamic development."[14] Aiding the erosion of the employment-at-will doctrine is the fact that the courts have awarded substantial punitive damages in cases where the doctrine is rejected.[15] As a result, employees and lawyers are more willing to pursue discharge cases that they rejected in the past. Another important fact is that the reporting of court settlements by the news media has resulted in more exposure of the employer to litigation related to discharges than at any other time.[16]

The proponents of eliminating the at-will doctrine are quick to point out that the United States is the only industrialized country that does not provide employees with some form of comprehensive protection against wrongful discharge. The just-cause provisions of labor agreements cover some employees, but union membership has failed to keep pace with the growing work force; a continually smaller percentage of workers are covered. More than 80 percent of the work force are not covered by labor agreements and have no external appeal procedure when discharged.

The employer should not be deceived into believing that the at-will doctrine has been suddenly abolished by the courts and that it must show just cause in all cases of discharge. But the employer must become aware of the rapid changes in this area of personnel law.

STATUTES THAT VOID AT-WILL DOCTRINE

The first statutory restriction of the at-will doctrine was the National Labor Relations

---

[9]*Lewis* v. *Minnesota Mutual Life Insurance Co.*, 37 N.W.2d 316 (Iowa 1949).

[10]29 USC Sect. 158 et seq.

[11]42 USC Sect. 2000 et seq.

[12]29 USC Sect. 621 et seq.

[13]29 USC Sect. 660 et seq.

[14]*Savodnik* v. *Korvettes, Inc.*, 488 F. Supp. 822 (E.D. N.Y. 1980), p. 824.

[15]For the status of the at-will doctrine from January 1980 to July 1986, see David S. Hames, "The Current Status of the Doctrine of Employment-at-Will," *Labor Law Journal*, 39, no. 1 (January 1988), 19.

[16]From 1980 to 1986, 72 percent of cases were won by employees with awards averaging $582,000. Copeland, "Revenge of the Fired," *Newsweek*, February 16, 1987, pp. 46, 47. Some notable awards are: $15 million for age discrimination in *Rawson* v. *Sears, Roebuck and Co.*, 615 F.Supp. 1546 (D. Colo. 1986); $1.3 million for age discrimination in *Flanigan* v. *Prud. Fed. Savings & Loan*, 720 P.2d 275 (Mont. 1986). These awards distort the averages. For a study from January 1979 to May 1987, see David J. Jung and Richard Harkness, "The Facts of Wrongful Discharge," *The Labor Lawyer*, 4, no. 2 (Spring 1988), 257 (American Bar Association, Chicago, IL).

Act. This act protects any union or nonunion employee from discharge when engaged in concerted activities for the purpose of mutual aid and protection of working conditions.[17] Protection from discharge because of concerted activity extends to verbal complaints about working conditions as well as dissatisfaction because of wages. Most unions when bargaining for the employee have been able to get the employer to contractually agree that an employee will not be discharged except for "just cause." This goes beyond any statutory protection. The contract terms remove the employee from the at-will status.[18]

Antidiscrimination Statutes

In the preceding chapters we have discussed the various antidiscrimination statutes that protect the employee from being discharged because of race, color, sex, religion, nationality, age, or pregnancy. Many states also add handicap, alcoholism, disability, and marital status to this list.[19] In addition to protection because of discrimination, the statutes grant protection to the employee for retaliation against any employee who exercises a right under the statute or aids others in the enforcement. The employer is often not aware of the retaliation provision since it believes the alleged discharge for discrimination is without merit and no consideration is given to the retaliation restriction. In order to have retaliation the discrimination section of the statute does not have to be violated. Of all the discrimination statutes, the protection most often used is age discrimination, with sexual harassment under Title VII running a close second. However, retaliation is the most-often-overlooked protection.

---

[17]*NLRB* v. *Schwartz*, 146 F.2d 773 (5th Cir. 1945).

[18]Researchers estimate that 140,000 unjust dismissals each year in the private sector are unprotected by collective agreements or by statute.

[19]See Gordon E. Jackson, *Labor and Employment Law Desk Book*, Part VI (Englewood Cliffs, NJ: Prentice-Hall, Inc., 1986), pp. 461–814.

Mixed Reasons for Discharge

An employee is protected if he or she is a union activist or has filed a discrimination charge under one of the various statutes, is involved in a wage dispute for a certain category of employees, or otherwise is engaged in an activity protected by statute.

If an employee violates a policy or has poor performance but also engages in a protected activity when discharged, it is called a mixed discharge. Whether the employee was discharged for the rule violation or the protected activity is always the issue before the courts. The NLRB adopted the rule that the burden of proof is on the employer to show that the discharge was not the result of a protected activity. This rule was enforced in *NLRB* v. *Wright Lines*, 662 F.2d 899 (1st Cir. 1981). However, not all courts agreed with the Wright Lines case, and the Supreme Court had to settle the issue. The court held that the board's position was reasonable. The burden is on the employer to show that the employee would have been discharged had she or he not been involved in a protected activity and that such activity did not influence the decision.[20] This principle has been consistently applied in subsequent cases.[21]

State Whistleblower Statutes

A continuation of granting employee rights in the workplace can be found in the enactment by state legislatures of "whistleblower" statutes. Although the first state whistleblower statute was not adopted until 1981, the majority of the states already have adopted the statute. These statutes apply not only to the public sector (almost all public employees are protected by whistleblower statutes) but to the private sector as well. The various statutes have some de-

---

[20]*NLRB* v. *Transportation Management Corp.*, 103 S.Ct. 2469 (1983).

[21]*Centrel Property Management* v. *NLRB*, 807 F.2d 1264 (5th Cir. 1987).

gree of uniformity, but beyond the basics they have a wide diversity. The intended objective of all the statutes is to provide protection against any adverse employment action against the employee, who for reasons considered to be in the public interest discloses violation of the law. However, the statutes also give protection to the employer in preventing false or unwarranted disclosures.

Most statutes provide a very broad protection to the employee and prohibit retaliatory action against the employee who testifies or provides information to a public body. In some states there must be an objective belief that the employer violated the law, while in others the employee must make an attempt to verify the accuracy of the information.[22] There is a wide variation in the statutes as to whom the disclosure must be made. Some require disclosure to any local, federal, or state agency, while other states require it to be made to the attorney general of that state. Various forms of notice provisions also appear in the statutes. Some require that the employer be put on notice before the disclosure, while others do not require any notice to the employer. The remedies providing for a violation also vary from making the employee whole to punitive damages. Some even provide for a criminal as well as a civil penalty.

The employer's defense against whistleblower statutes is to establish procedures and policies that require the employee to report any belief of company misconduct. This allows the company to correct any wrongdoing or to explain to the employee why the company takes such action and eliminates the need for the employee to go further. If the employee elects to go public on an ill-founded belief after disclosing to the employer, at least the employer has time to prepare a defense for the allegation in the press or public agency.

State Statutes That Require Just Cause

The first state statute to regulate discharge was passed in Montana in 1987. The act doesn't eradicate the at-will doctrine but restricts wrongful discharge suits and the amount of damages. This statute has provided other state legislatures with the initiative and example to do something about wrongful discharge suits and the damages awarded by juries.

The Montana statute states the employer may discharge at will, except where an employer discharges for reasons that are considered "wrongful." A discharge is considered wrongful:

1. If it is in retaliation for the employee's refusal to violate public policy
2. For reporting a violation of public policy (not defined in the statute)
3. If it is not for "good cause" (partially defined)
4. If the employer has violated the express provisions of its own written personnel policy

Good cause under the statute is very subjective. If the employee fails to perform job duties satisfactorily, has not served the probationary period, or is disruptive of the employer's business, or if the employer has other legitimate reasons, it is a good cause.

The statute will certainly require more judicial interpretation, but its significance is that it is a breakthrough in controlling the at-will doctrine by requiring just cause for discharge. This has the effect of eliminating the doctrine, although the statute states the opposite. "For any reason or no reason whatsoever" no longer exists under the statute. The statute benefits workers by requiring just cause for discharge and stating under what conditions they can sue for wrongful

---

[22]For the provisions in the various states, see Gregory C. Parliman, "Protecting the Whistleblower," *Personnel Administrator*, ASPA Publication, 32, no. 7 (July 1987), pp. 26–28.

discharge. It benefits employers by limiting the amount of damages the employee can receive. Most important of all, it removes the amount of damages from jury determination.[23]

PUBLIC POLICY EXCEPTION TO AT-WILL DOCTRINE

This exception, which is the most widely adopted by the majority of state courts, states that the employer should not be permitted to discipline or discharge an employee for reasons that are violative of public policy. Public policy is a broad term used by the courts as a reason for an exception to an otherwise well-accepted principle of law. Under this exception, the employee's cause of action is based on the harm that society suffers as a result of the employer's conduct. The employee is not alleging that there is an injury to himself or herself in the tort sense but to society.[24]

Some law textbooks define public policy as a private dealing that is restricted by law for the good of the community. Another definition is "whatever contravenes good morals or established interests of society."[25] Public policy is decided on a case-by-case basis and often is not defined by the court until violated. For example, the courts have said that a gambling contract, although it complies with all necessary elements of a contract, will not be enforced because it is not for the benefit or for the convenience of the public to do so. Other exceptions to principles of law are not as widely accepted as the enforcement of gambling contracts; exception to employment at will is one of them.

Where a discharge has been held to be a violation of a public policy, the reason for the discharge is probably also against a good employee relations practice. Three distinctly different reasons for discharge have been held to be contrary to public policy: first, exercising a right under a statute; second, refusing to disobey a law when requested to do so by the employer; third, disclosing the employer to authorities when the law is being violated, commonly called the whistleblower cases.

In all these situations the employee alleges that a public policy exists. When the employer refused to acknowledge the policy, the employee was discharged in retaliation for following the policy.

Litigations arising from the public policy violation concept are founded in tort law, that branch of the law dealing with civil wrongs other than a breach of contract. Tort law as applied to this concept is based on the premise that each member of society owes an obligation to every other member to be treated fairly. If public policy has been violated, the employee under this exception has not been treated fairly.[26]

Exercise of Employee Right under a Statute

A violation of an explicit provision in a statute is not considered an exception to employment at will but simply a violation of the statute, for which a remedy is provided in the statute. This straightforward situation does not warrant further consideration in this chapter.

One of the statutory rights that employers sometimes object to is the employee's right to file for and receive workers compensation benefits. The Central Indiana Gas Company

---

[23]The juries in Montana have been prone to award punitive damages in wrongful discharge cases. The most recent case before the statute was passed was in *Flanigan* v. *Prudential Savings and Loan Assn.*, 720 P.2d 257 (Mont. 1986), where $1.3 million was awarded in an age discrimination case. Some courts have ruled that the age discrimination statute does not allow punitive damages.

[24]See James A. Bryant and Michael Giallourakis, "Employment at Will: Where Is It Going and What Can Be Done?" *SAM Advanced Management Journal* (Autumn 1984), pp. 12–21.

[25]*Billingsley* v. *Clelland*, 23 S.E. 2d, 812 @ 815 (W. Va. 1895).

[26]For further explanation of public policy exception see "Employment-At-Will: Defining the Parameters," *Cumberland Law Review*, 16, no. 2 (1985–1986).

discharged an employee without a reason after she obtained a settlement on a workers compensation claim.[27] In this landmark case the court explained the reasoning behind other situations when an employee exercises a right under the statute when it said (@ 427):

If employers are permitted to penalize employees for filing workmens compensation claims, a most important public policy will be undermined. The fear of being discharged would have a deleterious effect on the exercise of a statutory right. Employees will not file claims for justly deserved compensation—opting, instead, to continue their employment without incident. The end result, of course, is that the employer is effectively relieved of his obligation.

Discharge is an employer's most common retaliation for employees' filing workers compensation claims or exercising other rights based on various statutes.[28]

Refusal to Disobey a Law

When an employee refuses to break the law and is discharged, some courts say it is contrary to public policy to force an employee to choose between violating the law and keeping a job. The most-cited case in this area is where the employee refused to testify falsely in a legislative hearing and the employer discharged him.[29] A similar result was reached where an employee refused to falsify pollution reports submitted to the state.[30]

In *Hauck* v. *Sabine Pilots Service, Inc.*, 672 S.W.2d 322 (Tex. App. 9 Dist. 1984), the court gave a good explanation on why re-fusal to disobey the law is contrary to public policy. The employee refused to illegally pump bilges into the channel. He was discharged and brought suit for damages. The court said that the state has an interest in seeing that its laws are enforced and this should not be at the expense of job security or injury to the employee. Making continued employment contingent upon the commission of a felony was a tortious violation of public policy and an exception to the at-will doctrine.

Discharge for Jury Duty Participation

Another public policy exception to the at-will doctrine is where the employee is discharged for doing jury duty or participation in a legal proceeding contrary to employer instructions. Some jurisdictions will hold that discharge for this reason is contrary to public policy. In one case an employee went to the court clerk with a letter from the employer which excused the employee, but she told the clerk that she did not want to be excused. She did not tell the employer what she told the clerk. She was discharged after serving on the jury. The court held that discharge was contrary to public policy.[31]

In another situation the employee informed the employer that he was called for jury duty. The employer said that he could get out of it by telling the court in each case that he has a "formed opinion" and therefore would be ineligible to serve. The employee refused to do this or ask to be excused. The employer discharged him on return from jury duty. The court held this to be contrary to public policy.[32]

This concept has been extended to where the person was serving on the jury and was discharged because he was gone too much, which was disruptive of the business. The discharge was allegedly for a traffic ticket, which was considered a pretext for the real

---

[27]*Frampton* v. *Central Indiana Gas Co.*, 297 N.E.2d 425 (Ind. 1973).

[28]For more information in this area, see Jean C. Love, "Retaliatory Discharge for Filing a Workers Compensation Claim: The Development of a Modern Tort Action," *Hastings Law Review*, 37 (March 1986), 551.

[29]*Petermann* v. *International Brotherhood of Teamsters*, 344 P.2d 25 (Cal. 1959).

[30]*Trombetta* v. *Detroit, Toledo & Ironton R.R. Co.*, 265 N.W.2d 385 (Mich. 1978).

[31]*Nees* v. *Hocks*, 536 P.2d 512 (Or. 1975).

[32]*Reuther* v. *Fowler & Williams, Inc.*, 386 A.2d 119 (Pa. 1978).

reason of serving on the grand jury and not being at work.[33] It is also contrary to public policy to discharge an employee because of being subpoenaed for grand jury service. The employee was to testify before the grand jury and the company was fearful of adverse testimony. The court held there was sufficient evidence to draw this conclusion and that discharge for being subpoenaed was contrary to public policy.[34]

Discharge for Whistleblowing

One of the most common public policy exceptions is where an employee complains to public officials about an employer's practice or acts that are in violation of a statute. These cases are called "whistleblower" cases and do not involve a whistleblowing statute that was discussed in a previous section of this chapter.[35]

Many employers believe that if an employee cannot be loyal to the employer, the person should be either demoted or terminated. When this occurs, there is a possibility that the employer could become involved in a whistleblower public policy exception to the employment-at-will doctrine. Loyalty, according to court rationale, is openly expressed where the employee tries to persuade the employer to comply with the law and the employer refuses. A frustrated employee discloses incriminating information to a bank examiner; the employer's response is to discharge (the employee-reported overcharges to customers were not rebated).[36]

A leading case of whistleblowing is where a driver was discharged for reporting a shipment of adulterated milk to the health authorities. An arbitrator, under the terms of the labor agreement, found that the discharge was for just cause. The court said that whistleblowing to protect the safety and health of the citizens is the type of protection that the courts must grant if the statutes are to be enforced.[37]

In order to be protected from whistleblowing there must be a good faith belief that there was an actual violation of a statute or regulation. Where an airline pilot alleged that he was discharged because he refused to fly a plane that he believed to be unsafe, the court said that in order to be protected from whistleblowing, either there must be a statute that creates the right to refuse to perform an unsafe act or the employer must violate a statute. In this case neither was alleged.[38] Some courts not only require a violation of a statute but also require that the reporting be to public officials. Where an employee reported a wrongdoing to the home office, the court said this was not contrary to public policy but was disloyalty toward the local manager.[39]

Sometimes an inspection is made to determine the violation. In *Kilpatrick* v. *Delaware Country Soc.,* 632 F.Supp. (E.D. Pa. 1986), the employee was using a solution that developed a rash on her hands and arms. Her doctor said the solution was the cause, but the employer disagreed. She reported it to the authorities, who after an inspection determined that the employer was in violation of the health statutes. The court found that the discharge for reporting a health hazard was contrary to public policy.

---

[33]*In Re Webb,* 586 F.Supp. 1480 (N.D. Ohio 1984). See also *Segal* v. *Gilbert Color Systems, Inc.,* 746 F.2d 78 (1st Cir. 1984).

[34]*Wiskotoni* v. *Michigan National Bank-West,* 716 F.2d 378 (6th Cir. 1983).

[35]For more on job protection for whistleblowing, see Thomas J. Condon and Richard Wolff, "Procedures to Safeguard Your Right to Fire," *Harvard Business Review* (November-December 1985), pp. 16–20.

[36]*Harless* v. *First National Bank in Fairmont,* 246 S.E.2d 270 (W. Va. 1978).

[37]*Garibaldi* v. *Lucky Food Stores,* 726 F.2d 1367 (9th Cir. 1984).

[38]*Buethe* v. *Britt Airlines,* 787 F.2d 1194 (9th Cir. 1984). Also see *Welch* v. *Brown's Nursing Home,* 484 N.E.2d 178 (Ohio App. 1984).

[39]*Adler* v. *American Standard,* 830 F.2d 1303 (4th Cir. 1987).

Malice and Bad Faith

A few courts have protected at-will employees when discharged for reason of malice and bad faith.[40] These jurisdictions hold that an employee must be protected from the unrestricted discretion to be discharged. Where the courts find malice and bad faith, the action must be severe and they are telling the employer that they do not like the discharge procedure.

An abusive discharge is best illustrated by the case where a restaurant owner lined up all the waitresses in alphabetical order and discharged them one by one when they would not provide information about who was pilfering food.[41]

Few employers would be this abusive and they would not be exposed to this exception to the at-will doctrine. Certainly any semblance of good employee relations policy would seem likely to avoid malice and bad faith. In actual situations, however, the employer can become involved without obvious intent or malice.

The leading case in malice and bad faith areas is *Monge v. Beebe Rubber Co.*,[42] which involves an employee who was discharged for refusing to date her supervisor. The court states that this was a breach of the contract of employment at will because it was motivated by malice and bad faith and therefore not in the best interest of the economic system and the public good.

The language in the Monge case is similar to that used in public policy exceptions. The use of the terms *malice and bad faith*, however, is adopted by some courts when they want to go further than the public policy exception. They hold that a breach of contract had occurred, defining the contract as developed by the employment relationship. Relying heavily on the Monge case, one court found malice and bad faith when an employee with 25 years of service was discharged before a customer placed a $5-million order for which the employee would have received a large sales commission.[43] Over 30 state courts have adopted the Monge decision as a public policy exception.

An early case in finding bad faith was in the case of an employee of 18 years' experience who was falsely accused of violating the employer's work rules and the employer's personnel policies. The court said that termination of a long-term employee without just cause offends an implied-in-law convenant of good faith and fair dealing. The California court took the position that an employer must establish just cause when discharging a long-term employee; failure to do so will result in punitive damages (damages that compensate above actual loss as punishment for evil behavior).[44]

If courts go as far as the California court in the Cleary case, enforcement of the just-cause provisions of labor agreements by arbitration will be replaced by litigation.[45] Bringing an action for punitive damages is much more rewarding than asking an arbitrator for reinstatement with back pay.

One employee in California discovered this when he was reinstated through the arbitration process and in a separate action the court allowed punitive damages after the arbitration award.[46]

Choosing a state court for damages rather than seeking a remedy under arbitration has been approved by the Supreme Court in *Lingle v. Norge Div. of Magic Chef, Inc.*, 108 S.Ct. 1877 (1988), where the Court held that union-

---

[40]Alaska, Arizona, California, Connecticut, Massachusetts, Minnesota, and Montana are a few states where this occurred.

[41]*Agis* v. *Howard Johnson Co.*, 355 N.E.2d 315 (Mass. 1976).

[42]316 A.2d 549 (N.H. 1974).

[43]*Fortune* v. *Nat'l Cash Register Co.*, 364 N.E.2d 1251 (Mass. 1977).

[44]*Cleary* v. *American Airlines, Inc.*, 168 Cal. Rptr. 722 (Cal. App. 1980).

[45]See Claude L. Rohwer, "Terminable-at-Will: New Theories for Job Security," *Pacific Law Journal*, 15 (April 1984), 759–83.

[46]*Alcorn* v. *Anbro Engineering, Inc.*, 468 P.2d 216 (Cal. 1970).

represented employees can sue the employer in state court over a dismissal, even when the contract provides a grievance procedure and remedies.

Courts have recognized an action for malice and bad faith in the following situations (minority view).

1. An employee alleged that his employer discharged him because he sought a smoke-free environment [*Henzel* v. *The Singer Company*, 188 Cal. Rptr. 159 (Cal. App. 1982)].

2. A marketing manager was discharged because of her romance with a manager of a rival firm [*Rulon-Miller* v. *IBM Corp.*, 208 Cal. Rptr. 524 (Cal. App. 1st Dist. 1984)].

3. A salesman alleges that he was discharged to avoid paying him commission [*Wakefield* v. *Northern Telecom., Inc.*, 769 F.2d 109 (2nd Cir. 1985)].

4. A discharge was made to avoid including the employee in a profit-sharing plan [*Mitford* v. *de Lasala*, 666 P.2d 100 (Alaska 1983)].

5. A construction supervisor was allegedly discharged prior to the payment of due annual bonuses and his share of the developer's equity in certain construction projects not completed on the date of his termination [*Cataldo* v. *Zuckerman*, 482 N.W.2d 849 (Mass. App. 1985)].

6. An employee alleges that she was discharged because of her refusal to submit to the sexual advances of her supervisor [*Lucas* v. *Brown & Root*, 736 F.2d 1202 (8th Cir. 1984)].

7. A nurse was discharged for refusing to participate in a skit with fellow workers that required her to "moon" the audience, which would violate the state statute on indecent exposure [*Wagenseller* v. *Scottsdale Memorial Hosp.*, 710 P.2d 1025 (Ariz. 1985)].

There are other courts that have rejected malice and bad faith as an exception to the at-will doctrine. In *Murphy* v. *American Home Products*, 448 N.E.2d 86 (N.Y. 1983), there was discharge for retaliation when the employee refused to engage in accounting improprieties. Other cases where malice and bad faith have been rejected include the following:

1. The employee was discharged for refusing to build facilities without government approval [*Hartley* v. *Ocean Beef Club, Inc.*, 476 So.2d 1327 (Fla. App. 1985)].

2. The employee was discharged for filing a workers compensation claim [*Evans* v. *Bibb Co.*, 343 S.E.2d 484 (Ga. App. 1986)].

3. The employee was discharged for demanding that the employer cease violating hazardous waste disposal regulations [*Phung* v. *Waste Management, Inc.*, 491 N.E.2d 1114 (Ohio 1986)].

It is apparent from the preceding cases that not all courts are in agreement. Those that reject the doctrine state that the at-will doctrine should not be violated if it is not an injury against the public. This remains the majority opinion. Those minority courts that allow an action for malice and bad faith state that there is an implied covenant (contract) of good faith and fair dealing in every employer-employee relationship and this should not be violated when a person is discharged.[47]

IMPLIED CONTRACT THAT MODIFIES AT-WILL DOCTRINE

The personnel administrator who takes pride in good employee relations would consider the foregoing exceptions as something that could not happen in his or her organization. In companies that have positive personnel policies, the common law exception of public policy, whistleblowing, and malice and bad faith is academic, but this would not be necessarily so with the implied contract exception. Positive personnel administration could increase the exposure to the implied contract exception by aggressive recruiting and promotion that result in promises being made at the time of hiring, handbooks to sell the company as a place of continuous employment, and

---

[47]*Cleary* v. *American Airlines, Inc.*, 168 Cal. Rptr. 722 (Cal. App. 1980).

salaries quoted as annual salaries, which may imply a contract of employment for one year.

The personnel administrator is the most vulnerable where in the interest of selling the company or promoting good employee relations a certain promise is made. In determining whether such a promise is an implied contract of continuous employment, the courts look at the surrounding circumstances at the time of hiring to determine whether a promise was in fact made.[48]

Where a promise is considered an implied contract, the employee must show some reliance on the promise. One example would be a long-distance move where the employee left a secure job with a competitor and at a later date was discharged without cause or where there was a reliance on a promise of a better opportunity, which never materialized.[49] Promises of this kind are not uncommon when an aggressive employment manager is operating in a tight labor market. The reason that the job does not materialize or the employee is laid off may be legitimate, but the employee is still emotionally and financially harmed.[50] In this situation the courts often allow punitive damages.

One of the more definitive statements from a court that adopted the implied contract approach is found in *Pugh* v. *See's Candies, Inc.,* 116 Cal. App.3rd 311 (1981), where a vice president of employee relations of 32 years of service was terminated. When he asked why, he was told, "Look deep within yourself." The jury determined that length of service, a series of promotions and commendations, the lack

of direct criticism of his work, and the assurance by his superior that if he did a good job his future would be secure established an implied contract and that the company violated the contract by discharge.

Quoting an Annual Salary

A fairly common practice that is becoming increasingly hazardous is quoting an annual salary in a job offer. There has always been a good selling point in using an annual salary figure since the amount looks so much larger than a weekly or a monthly figure. In recent years, however, this practice has led to litigation, and although only a few jurisdictions have considered the practice, the use of the term does result in some exposure to litigation. Courts have considered how a term reacts upon the employee rather than the intention of the person who originated the term.

In a relatively early case, the defendant hired a sales manager from another company. The defendant quoted a yearly income of $19,000 plus a 2-percent commission on sales. A few months after the sales manager was hired, he was offered a new reimbursement plan that would result in a reduction in both salary and commissions. The plaintiff refused the new offer and was discharged. The new offer was without basis or justification because no allegation of disloyalty or poor performance was made. The whole issue was whether there was an agreement for a fixed term of employment based on the annual salary quoted at the time of hire. The court said that the annual salary did create a contract for one year and that the employer was liable for one year's salary.[51]

Almost ten years later a Louisiana court concurred. In this case, the job offer was more typical. In the offer letter the defendant said

---

[48]For further reading, see Brian Heshizer, "The Implied Contract Exception to At-Will Employment," *Labor Law Journal,* 35 (March 1984), 131.

[49]Not all courts will hold that relocating forms a contract. See *Ohio Table Pad Co.* v. *Hogan,* 424 N.E.2d 144 (Ind. 1977).

[50]*Stuart* v. *Tektronix, Inc.,* 730 P.2d 619 (Or. App. 1986); *D'Ulisse-Cupo* v. *Bd of Directors of Notre Dame H.S.,* 202 Conn. 206 (1987).

[51]*Lanier* v. *Alenco,* 459 F.2d 689 (5th Cir. 1972).

This will confirm that your commission will be 10% of gross profit. You will also receive $1500 payable each two-week period, as a draw against your future sales, for a six-month period. In addition to the terms outlined, you will receive a $4000 payment up-front. As an independent contractor you will be responsible for the payment of all income taxes, social security, and medical benefits.

In hiring you we feel that you are definitely sales management material and you will be evaluated on that basis, if your performance is up to what we expect, within a six-month period.

Once again welcome to the Company. Jim and I look forward to working with you in the months and years to come. See you on January 2.

The plaintiff was terminated after one month. He sued for breach of contract arguing that he had a contract for six months and was terminated from his contract without cause prior to the expiration of the six-month period. The defendant argued that there was no contract in effect and the plaintiff could be terminated at will. The court held that the letter showed that the parties intended to create a contract for a six-month period, and the contract could not be terminated without just cause.[52]

South Dakota has a statute that states that when you quote an annual salary, it results in a contract for one year [S.D. Codified Laws Sec. 60(1)(3)].[53] This concept—that you create a contract by quoting a salary for a fixed period of time—is not the law in all jurisdictions. In fact, very few state courts have had the issue come before them. One employee tried to expand the concept by alleging that a requirement for an annual appraisal in the policy manual and hiring at an annual salary implied a fixed term of employment. The Tenth Circuit in Denver ap-

plying the Colorado law rejected the concept.[54] The court held that a statement in the policy manual was merely an expression of unilateral policy.

The problem in the use of annual salary is that it creates exposure to a lawsuit win or lose.[55] Although only a few courts have held that quoting an annual salary forms a contract for one year, why use it if you can communicate by some other language? Quoting a monthly salary does not create the same exposure and the applicant can multiply. "Annual salary" is another term that should be blocked out in the practitioner's lexicon.

Hiring Strike Replacements

The use of strike replacements will be discussed in Chapter 16, so it will only be mentioned in this section as related to implied contract. When a strike replacement is recruited and is promised that the job will be permanent (which means that it will continue when the strike is over), this becomes a contract under the implied contract theory.[56] If the person is replaced after the strike is over, she or he could sue in a state court for breach of contract. It would depend upon the state whether they would find a breach of contract.

Applicants are often promised permanent jobs in order to recruit under strike conditions. When the strike is settled the company, unless they want to face a breach of contract suit, could not bargain away their jobs. This chills the union's desire to go on strike, since their jobs are at stake when permanent replacements are hired. This is an example of the implied contract theory being

---

[52]*Roussel* v. *Blanchard,* 430 So.2d 247 (La. App. 1983). See also *Hartman* v. *C.W. Travel, Inc.,* 792 F.2d 1179 (D.C. Cir. 1986).

[53]In *Goodwyn* v. *Sencore, Inc.,* 389 F.Supp. 824 (D.S.D. 1975), the court held that an annual salary formed a one-year contract. This was before the statute was adopted.

[54]*Garcia* v. *Aetna Finance Co.,* 752 F.2d 488 (10th Cir. 1984). See also *Taliaferro* v. *S&A Restaurant Corp.,* 323 S.E. 2d 271 (Ga. 1984).

[55]In *Crawford* v. *David Shapiro & Co. P.A.,* 490 So.2d 993 (Fla. App. 1986), the annual salary concept was rejected, but in *Presto* v. *Sequoia Systems, Inc.,* 633 F.Supp. 1117 (D. Mass. 1986), the court held that the annual salary quote was an inducement to accept the job.

[56]*Belknap, Inc.* v. *Hale,* 103 S.Ct. 3172 (1983).

extended to a situation that doesn't involve discharge.

Handbooks and Policy Manuals[57]

Certain statements made in an employee handbook or a policy manual have been held to be an implied contract. The Michigan court, in a leading case, held that guidelines and the supervisor's manual were an expressed contract.[58] The clauses that were especially troublesome were where the supervisor's manual stated that an employee could be discharged only for just cause and "could work until 65 as long as he did his job."

In a companion case the employee testified that he was promised at the time of hiring he could work for the company "as long as I did my job." The court said that was a contract that changed the at-will doctrine.[59]

In one situation the handbook stated that an employee would be discharged only for just cause. When hired, the employee signed the application form, which stated that employment would be subject to the *Handbook on Personnel Policy.* Eight years later he was discharged. The court held that it was a contract; just cause had to be shown, as stated in the handbook. However, to reach this conclusion the court held that this was an expressed contract.[60]

One of the well-quoted cases after Toussaint on a handbook being an implied contract is where a loan officer in a bank was in default on his personal loan and had approved 56 out of 57 loans in violation of the loan policy. The discharge was held to be a breach of contract because the employer failed to follow the discharge procedure outlined in the handbook.

In a section entitled "Performance Review" the handbook stated:

---

[57]Only the law as to whether or not a handbook is a contract will be discussed here. The writing of a proper handbook will be given in detail in Chapter 11.

[58]*Toussaint* v. *Blue Cross and Blue Shield of Michigan,* 292 N.W.2d 880 (Mich. 1980).

[59]*Ebling* v. *Masco Corp.,* 292 N.W.2d 801 (Mich. 1980).

[60]*Weiner* v. *McGraw-Hill,* 443 N.E.2d 441 (N.Y. 1982).

Everyone wants to know "where he stands." Our performance evaluation program is designed to help you to determine where you are, where you are going, and how to get there. Factual and objective appraisals of you and your work performance should serve as aids to your future advancement.

A section entitled "Job Security" reads:

Employment in the banking industry is very stable. It does not fluctuate up and down sharply in good times and bad, as do many other types of employment. We have no seasonal layoffs and we never hire a lot of people when business is booming only to release them when things are not as active.

The job security offered by the *Pine River State Bank* is one reason why so many of our employees have five or more years of service. In return for this, Management expects job security from you. That is, the security that you will perform the duties of your position with diligence, cooperation, dependability, and a sense of responsibility.

The section entitled "Disciplinary Policy" reads:

In the interest of fairness to all employees the Company establishes reasonable standards of conduct for all employees to follow in their employment at *Pine River State Bank.* These standards are not intended to place unreasonable restrictions on you but are considered necessary for us to conduct our business in an orderly and efficient manner.

If an employee has violated a company policy, the following procedure will apply:

1. An oral reprimand by the immediate supervisor for the first offense, with a written notice sent to the Executive Vice President.
2. A written reprimand for the second offense.
3. A written reprimand and a meeting with the Executive Vice President and possible suspension from work without pay for five days.
4. Discharge from employment for an employee whose conduct does not improve as a result of the previous action taken.

In no instance will a person be discharged from employment without review of the facts by the Executive Officer.

The court did not feel that the job security provisions of the handbook were an offer of employment, nor did they put much weight on the performance appraisal section. It was considered a general statement of policy that did not constitute an offer of permanent employment, but what made the discharge wrongful is that this policy was not followed. The court found that the disciplinary policy was an offer of a unilateral contract for procedures to be followed in job termination, and when those procedures were not followed (since the executive officer did not review the discharge) the jury could find a breach of contract.[61]

The two Michigan cases and Pine River were subsequently accepted by several other jurisdictions and caused an alarm to be sounded in personnel law. Many practitioners became "gun-shy" and discarded their handbooks. As more and more states adopted the Pine River case, personnel literature became abundant. You can get advice on handbooks for any position that management wants to take.[62]

By 1985 the vast majority of the states held that a handbook was a contract, although some industrial states such as New York, Illinois and Indiana still required the written contract before the at-will status could be changed.[63] (A policy manual for the purpose of this discussion is the same as a handbook.) Practitioners became aware of another past practice that would not stand judicial scrutiny. Either the language in a handbook or manual, which was intended to provide a degree of flexibility to management in dealing with certain situations, had

to be revised or the handbook had to be discarded.

One of the reservations in changing a handbook was whether it could be changed if it is an employment contract. Employment documents can be changed. However, to be sure not to avoid exposure, the effective date of the change should be set for some reasonable time in the future. When working conditions are changed the employee should be able to have a reasonable time to find another job if he or she does not like the change.

Use of Term *Probationary Period* in Handbook

The dictionary defines *probation* as the term used for one who is being tested—a trial or evaluation period—and this is the way it has been used in personnel documents for many years. The courts never really accepted this definition. Under the Military Selective Service Act when a probationary employee went into military service and returned, the probationary period was considered to have been served even though the employee may have been tested or observed for only two weeks. One court held that the term *probationary period* does not mean temporary employment and that the returning veteran is deemed to have served the trial period while in service.[64]

Some courts are now saying that the term means more than a trial period. When used in a handbook or policy manual it indicates that once the trial period is passed, the employee has a permanent job and just cause has to be shown before he or she can be discharged. The term under this interpretation changes the employment-at-will status to a contractual relationship. How far this concept has gone was shown in a 1986 unpublished survey in Nebraska and Iowa. The majority of employees contacted stated that they expected permanent employment after serving a reasonable probationary period.

---

[61]*Pine River State Bank* v. *Richard F. Mettille Sr.,* 333 N.W.2d 622 (Minn. 1983).

[62]See John D. Combe, "Employee Handbooks: Asset or Liability?" *Employee Relations Law Journal,* 12, no. 1 (Summer 1986), 4–17.

[63]*Enis* v. *Continental Ill. Nat. Bank & Trust,* 582 F.Supp. 876 (N.D. Ill. E.D. 1984); *Mead Johnson and Co.* v. *Openheimer,* 458 N.E.2d 668 (Ind. App. 1 Dist. 1984). See *Fleming* v. *Kids and Kin Head Start,* 693 P.2d 1363 (Or. App. 1985) for majority rule.

[64]*Collings* v. *Weirton Steel,* 398 F.2d 305 (4th Cir. 1968).

One employee brought suit for breach of an oral agreement of employment. The application form stated that employment was for a definite period and could be terminated without notice. The employee argued that this statement had been changed by oral agreement. The employee admitted that her employment was subject to a 30-day probationary period and that she was terminated two weeks after hire. The court decided that the phrase *probationary employee* does not necessarily mean that the employee can be terminated at any time during the probationary period and that the employee should be allowed to prove the existence of an oral agreement. The employer also argued that under the statute of frauds, an oral employment agreement cannot be enforced because it cannot be performed within one year. The court responded that since there was a probationary period in the contract, it could be performed within one year and therefore an oral agreement would be enforceable. In this case the term *probationary period* had no effect on the rights of the employee but it destroyed the argument of the employer under the statute of frauds.[65]

A variation of this case occurred when the handbook stated that the employee would be given a trial period of three months. The employee was discharged for refusal to take a polygraph test after the expiration of the probationary period. The court said that the employee could reasonably assume that after the probationary period was successfully completed, employment would be permanent and discharge could only be for just cause. The court allowed the jury to decide whether the refusal was just cause.[66]

The Kinark case was used as authority by a truck driver who was discharged when he reported for work two hours late because of illness. He was discharged for failure to make his run on time. The employee claimed that he was not an at-will employee after completion of the probationary period and therefore could not be discharged except for just cause. The court said that even if it could be shown that a contract existed because the employee successfully completed the probationary period, there was good cause to discharge the employee.[67]

An employee can always be discharged for just cause even though he or she may be under contract. In a concurring opinion the judge stated that the majority decision accepted the employee's argument that an employment application form which stated that an employee was on probation for three months created an employment contract after the three-month period, which would require just cause for discharge.

Even when the employee has been discharged during the probationary period, some courts will hold the employer to a covenant of good faith and require proper investigation of the charges. One employer listed several charges as the reason for discharge during the 500-hour probationary period. Included in the list were "insubordination, disorderly conduct disrupting the continuity of care, violation of safety and health rules, continually getting in the way of patient care, and breach of confidentiality." These assertions were not supported by facts, and testimony showed that in fact the hospital did little investigating before discharging. Since the employee could not get a job in the health care industry after her discharge, she sued for punitive damages. The hospital argued that since she was a probationary employee, she was an at-will employee and therefore no punitive damages could be allowed for her discharge. The court disagreed. The evidence showed that at the end of the probationary period, employees did not even have an evaluation meeting with supervision, which indicated they were considered permanent. Under these circumstances the court ruled that the term probationary does not relieve the hospital of the

---

[65]*Stone* v. *Mission Bay Mortgage Co.*, 672 P.2d 629 (Nev. 1983).

[66]*Jackson* v. *Kinark Corp.*, 669 S.W.2d 898 (Ark. 1984).

[67]*Gauldine* v. *Emerson Electric Co.*, 680 S.W.2d 92 (Ark. 1984).

duty for good faith and fair dealing. The court allowed punitive damages.[68]

It can be seen from the case law cited above that the use of the term probationary offers no security to the employer in discharging without cause, in acting with bad faith, or in breaching the covenant of fair dealing. It can create an employment contract that will cancel the at-will doctrine. In the Bozeman case the employer would have had a better case if no reason for the discharge had been given. The employer could have relied upon the at-will doctrine that was at the time very alive in Montana and in most other states. The use of the term probationary period gave the employer a false sense of security that it unfortunately relied upon in its defense.

If an employee is an at-will employee before the use of the term, some courts will hold that the use of the term will not change the status. Other courts will hold that this does create a contract of job permanency. It only takes a few courts to agree with the employee to create an exposure to litigation. An attorney is more likely to take the case on a contingency basis if some authority can be cited to justify the employee's position.

In the vast majority of jurisdictions, the at-will doctrine is upheld when the employer does not create a condition that enables the courts to find an exception. The use of the probationary period creates such an opportunity. Courts have always upheld the right of the employer to discharge for poor performance. In this sense the employee is always on probation. Why limit to a specific time period?

The use of the term is an invitation to litigation. Why use it at all? There are other ways to communicate to the employee that the standard of performance is less during the first few months of employment than after a longer time. The standard of discipline, however, should be the same regardless of the length of employment—always assuming that the employee has been properly informed of the consequences of certain actions. *Probationary period,* except as the term is used in labor agreements, is another term that personnel practitioners should consider eliminating from their vocabulary.

A labor agreement is an enforceable contract, and until the employee serves the probationary period just cause does not have to be shown. For this reason it should be kept in the agreement. The labor agreement provision is one reason why the courts associate just cause with the probationary period in a nonunion situation.

A DISCHARGE THAT BECOMES A TORT

With the development of exceptions to at-will doctrine, some courts have allowed the employee to allege a tort beyond the breach of contract claim. Many of these cases arise not only when there is a wrong under the common law or under a statute but also when there is some type of emotional injury in which the plaintiff feels that recovery under the contract is not sufficient and asks for punitive damages. This type of remedy is before the courts with increasing frequency in the late 1980s,[69] especially in the areas of sexual harassment and age discrimination. Tortious conduct will be treated in more detail in Chapter 17 on management malpractice.

CONSTRUCTIVE DISCHARGE

In the simplest terms, constructive discharge may be taken to mean that when an employee apparently quits, he or she has ac-

---

[68]*Crenshaw* v. *Bozeman Deaconess Hospital,* 693 P.2d 487 (Mont. 1984).

[69]Some of the states that allow a tort for wrongful discharge are Alabama, Arkansas, California, Colorado, Georgia, Illinois, North and South Carolina, and Oregon.

tually been fired. However, the law applies a special—and much more complex—meaning to the term. Black's Law Dictionary defines constructive discharge as "that which is established by the mind of the law in its act of construing facts, circumstances or instruments; that which has not the character assigned to it in its own essential nature, but acquires such character in consequence of the way in which it is regarded by a rule or policy of law."[70] This definition has been generally followed by the courts, which, although they may from time to time state general principles for constructive discharge, apply them on a case-by-case basis. Although this legal definition has been followed by most courts, it is not generally understood by the first-line supervisor. For this reason, a termination is often recorded as a voluntary quit when in effect it is a constructive discharge and the employee has the same remedies under the law as if she or he had been discharged.[71]

Definition of Intolerable Conditions

The general guideline that the courts use in defining constructive discharge is that if an employer deliberately makes an employee's working conditions so intolerable that the employee is forced into a voluntary resignation, then the employer has committed a constructive discharge and is as liable for any illegal conduct as if he had discharged the aggrieved employee.

The original concept of constructive discharge usually involved a situation where the employer wanted to discharge an employee but was concerned about the possible legal repercussions of doing so. By making life on the job so miserable as to force a quit, the employer expected to avoid the need to discharge. Among the first cases to reach the courts were those based on charges of unfair labor practices where the employer would have "evil intent or motive" because of union activity and would set out a program to get the employee to quit.

An early case involved an employer who learned that an employee was supporting a union drive and became hostile toward her. In retaliation the employer altered the employee's method of pay—putting her on incentive rates where she was not even earning the minimum wage. She protested, but nothing was done and she quit. The court ruled that she had been fired for union activity in violation of Section 8(a)(3) of the National Labor Relations Act. The evidence in this case showed an intent or programmed action to force the employee to quit."[72]

Probably the best example of constructive discharge without specific intent involves a plaintiff who was hired as a teller. At the time of hire she was told that all employees were required to go to a staff meeting. At the first staff meeting she discovered that the agenda included a religious talk and prayer, both delivered by a Baptist minister. Being an atheist, she refused to go to the meetings. The employer countered that she must attend staff meetings and that if she objected to the devotions she could "close her ears." She still refused and the employer asked for a letter of resignation stating that she was not being fired. She charged that she was constructively discharged for reasons of religious discrimination. The court held that mandatory attendance at company prayer meetings imposed intolerable working conditions because attendance would have forced the employee to sacrifice her fundamental religious beliefs.[73]

After the enactment of antidiscrimination

---

[70]*Black's Law Dictionary*, 5th ed. (St. Paul, MN: West Publishing Co., 1979), p. 283.

[71]For further reading, see Ralph H. Baxter and John M. Farrell, "Constructive Discharge—When Quitting Means Getting Fired," *Employee Relations Journal* (Winter 1978), p. 346.

[72]*J.P. Stevens & Co. v. NLRB*, 461 F.2d 490 (4th Cir. 1972).

[73]*Young v. Southwestern Savings & Loan Assn.*, 509 F.2d 140 (5th Cir. 1975).

laws, the courts had to consider whether a violation of an antidiscrimination law created an unreasonable atmosphere sufficient to warrant a finding of constructive discharge. One of the most common situations where intolerable conditions are alleged involves inadequate or discriminatory salary increases. The charge of intolerable salary derives its legal basis from Title VII of the sex discrimination section.

One employee argued that she was constructively discharged because of intolerable conditions of sex discrimination. She had come to work for a company as a secretary and had worked her way up to the position of buyer. After 90 days as a buyer, she was given a requested increase but she was still making $130 per month less than the male person she replaced. Because of her disappointment she quit and filed a charge of sex discrimination alleging that she was doing the same work as males but was paid $130 less per month. The court cited the general rule that if the employer deliberately made conditions so intolerable that the employee was forced to quit, the employer was guilty of constructive discharge and was liable for any illegal conduct involved just as it would have been if it had formally discharged the employee. It found further that the pay arrangement did show sex discrimination but that in taking the promotion the employee had agreed to work for less money. Under these conditions the court found that a reasonable employee would not have quit because of unequal pay.[74]

Other courts have followed the Bourque precedent in holding that there is no constructive discharge even though the condition that causes the resignation is found to be unlawful. The plaintiff must prove more. He or she must show that the unlawful condition created by the employer is so offensive that the reasonable person would have found it intolerable. Failing in this

proof, the employee must continue working while seeking to remedy the allegedly unlawful practice.

Where the employee quit because the provisions of a handbook were violated, the court held that although the handbook is a contract, the employee cannot decide when there is a breach.[75] If a demotion is offered with the intent of forcing the employee to quit, the court will usually find an intolerable condition.[76] The employee is not required to show the employer's intent in order to prove constructive discharge, only that the employer knowingly permitted the condition to exist.[77]

In deciding whether an intolerable working condition exists, the court determines whether a "reasonable person in the employee's position and circumstances would have felt compelled to resign." This was the rule in the Bourque case cited above and followed in most jurisdictions. The issue in all these cases is not whether a particular employee feels that the job is objectionable or onerous but whether a reasonable person in the employee's shoes would have been compelled to resign. An employee's subjective assessment of what is tolerable is not sufficient to lead to a finding of constructive discharge.

The courts are consistent in finding that the conditions created by the employer must be more than disagreeable. If the conditions are severe enough for whatever reason, the court will find constructive discharge and will usually find that, because of the intolerable conditions, intent can be assumed.

Demotion or Transfer

An action by an employer that could lead to a claim of constructive discharge is transferring or demoting an employee. In such a

---

[74]*Bourque* v. *Powell Electrical Manufacturing Co.*, 617 F.2d 61 (5th Cir. 1980).

[75]*Ellis* v. *El Paso Natural Gas Co.*, 745 F.2d 834 (10th Cir. 1985).

[76]*Cockrell* v. *Boise Cascade Corp.*, 781 F.2d 173 (10th Cir. 1986).

[77]*Goss* v. *Exxon Office Systems Co.*, 747 F.2d 885 (3rd Cir. 1984).

claim the transfer or demotion itself is alleged to be the intolerable condition. The reason for the action is alleged to be the unlawful act. Discrimination is often claimed at the same time. The reason is that if constructive discharge is found, discrimination provides a statutory basis for claiming wrongdoing. Although antidiscrimination statutes may be violated, courts will not find constructive discharge if the condition created by the transfer or demotion is not severe enough.

In determining the severity, the court will compare the job offered with the job the employee had. The comparison will consider differences in pay and benefits, day-to-day job conditions, increased travel requirements, and similar considerations. The courts will also consider the negative effect on the employee's prestige—but this must be severe—and whether the employee was embarrassed by the employer's action. In evaluating embarrassment claims, courts seek to find out whether the embarrassment would be daily or unavoidable and whether there was a radical change in job responsibilities to warrant embarrassment.

In constructive discharge cases age discrimination is often the alleged legal basis for action. Lawyers prefer this choice because age cases are tried before a jury, and the chances that conditions will be found intolerable are better. In one such case the employee, a supervisor, was not performing her job up to standard and the employer gave her a choice between being retired or being transferred to a nonsupervisory position in the department that she formerly supervised. She chose retirement but then brought an age discrimination suit stating that she was encouraged to retire. The jury agreed. The court said that there was enough evidence to allow the jury to find that the employee was constructively discharged.[78] The employer might have anticipated that when someone is transferred to a nonsu-

pervisory position in a department that she formerly supervised very well, she would be forced to work with her former subordinates and that this would create an unreasonable condition.

A transfer sometimes can result in a breach of an employment contract. An employer entered into a written agreement with an electrical engineer specifying that he would be employed as a manager of a department. The contract permitted discharge for "just cause." After a period of time the supervisor of the employee attempted to reclassify him to the position of a sales engineer. The engineer quit and sued for breach of contract. The court held the action of the supervisor to be a breach of contract since the plaintiff was placed in the position of accepting a demotion, resigning so that he could obtain a position elsewhere, or being ultimately discharged.[79]

Alternative of Resigning or Discharge

The clearest form of constructive discharge occurs when an employer tells an employee that she or he has an opportunity to resign, but that if the employee does not do so she or he will be discharged.[80] This is a common practice of employers and the reason it is used is probably to promote good employee relations by making a terminated employee more employable. Whatever its effect on morale, the approach does open the door to possible litigation and sometimes to liability greater than would have been incurred if the employee had been discharged outright. This type of case is difficult to defend as the courts often feel that the employer has threatened the employee even though the employer may have the right to discharge.

Mr. Knee had a written contract until

---

[78]*Casola* v. *Codman & Shurtleff, Inc.*, 751 F.2d 53 (1st Cir. 1984).

[79]*Kass* v. *Brown Boveri Corp.*, 488 A.2d 242 (N.J. Super. 1985).

[80]In *Staggs* v. *Blue Cross of Maryland*, 486 A.2d 798 (Md. App. 1985), two salespersons were permitted to resign rather than being discharged. The court held this was constructive discharge per se.

1981, but in 1979 the school board asked for his resignation. He resigned and then brought action for breach of contract [*Knee v. School District No. 139 in Canyon City*, 676 P.2d 727 (Idaho App. 1984)]. The court held that the mere request to resign is not enough to justify a finding of constructive discharge. Discharge must be stated as the alternative. The fact that he had a contract would lead one to believe that he could not be discharged.

A different outcome resulted when an employee was told that she had the option of resigning or being discharged. She resigned and filed a claim for violation of handbook provisions, which in that state was considered a contract. The court not only found constructive discharge but also allowed punitive damages. The court said that the employer stands to gain from a resignation rather than a discharge because it will insulate itself from a wrongful discharge claim.[81]

An employer can be guilty of constructive discharge in encouraging early retirement. An employee who could either have taken early retirement or have been transferred under a reorganization program was told that it would be a waste of time to transfer if he preferred early retirement. He took early retirement and filed suit alleging that he was coerced into this action. The court held that in order to be considered coercion in violation of ADEA, the alternative to early retirement had to be so intolerable that a reasonable person who wanted to continue work would have refused it.[82]

---

[81]*Gates* v. *Life of Montana Ins. Co.*, 668 P.2d 213 (Mont. 1983).

[82]*Toussaint* v. *Ford Motor Co.*, 581 F.2d 812 (10th Cir. 1978).

Prevention of Constructive Discharge Claims

Employers should not assume that constructive discharge cases are the exception rather than the rule. Employees—particularly in white collar occupations—generally want to continue working and will resist being separated from their jobs. Exposure to charges of constructive discharge exist in every transfer, demotion, promotion, or termination, especially if the employee is approaching retirement age. Constructive discharge cases that are successfully argued are on the increase as the courts require less to be unreasonable. Once intolerable conditions or an unreasonable alternative have been established, the courts do not expect the employee to continue working and will consider a voluntary quit as a discharge.

An employer can take several steps to reduce exposure to constructive discharge claims.

1. Educate the supervisors. This is probably the most important defense, since the supervisor is frequently the one who seeks a way to make the employee quit.

2. Encourage the employee to accept the demotion or transfer rather than to resign. Make sure that he or she understands that the action is not intended to result in termination.

3. If you do intend to discharge the employee, be honest and open with him or her and go through with the discharge rather than give the option to resign. The employee is less likely to feel that he or she was treated unfairly, and the judge and jury will be less suspicious if the matter does end up in court.

4. Beware of resignations; always ask for a reason. This prevents the employee from later raising allegations of constructive discharge after litigation has begun. Courts give little weight to this technique.

POLICIES TO PREVENT
WRONGFUL DISCHARGE EXPOSURE

Preventing Wrongful Discharge Exposure
Writing a Handbook or a Policy Manual
The Discharge Process
The Use of Waivers or Releases

In recent years the practitioner has been given a steady diet of the exceptions to the employment-at-will doctrine. The state courts have eroded the traditional termination authority of management to terminate at will for any reason or no reason to the point where the employer believes that the right to discharge is lost. Management's concern is well founded. From October 1979 to January 1984, 51 cases were tried in state courts. The employee won in 70 percent of these cases with an average jury award of $178,184. Most of these suits were filed by professional, managerial, technical, and clerical employees who are usually not protected by an existing collective bargaining agreement. (Most agreements require "just cause" for discharge. Less than 20 percent of the work force is under a collective bargaining agreement.) It is estimated that about one half of the working force has no contractual or statutory protection from discharge. Present employees are knowledgeable of their legal rights and are not reluctant to sue their employers, when they feel that their discharge was unfair and their reputation was damaged. They read about the high awards won by other employees and are encouraged by legal advertising to have their cases assessed. It is no wonder that employers are "gun-shy" about discharging an employee.[1]

Most managers and practitioners have been exposed to the reams of literature on how the at-will doctrine has been eroded,[2] but little has been said on how to discharge under the at-will doctrine. Discharge is still a management right, but it has to be done differently from the way it has been in the past.

If a discharge is decided on by the supervisor, the personnel practitioner must take action and defend it with all available evidence to establish a legitimate reason. One can rely on an abundance of authority to defend a position provided that the proper precautions are taken before the discharge. If a manager decides to discharge, the manager will do so. The task of the personnel administrator is to advise that it be done in a way that will result in the least exposure to litigation; therefore, the personnel administrator must be notified well in advance of the discharge date.

At-will employees still exist, and the doctrine should be considered when other reasons are judicially weak, but fewer and fewer courts are adhering to the old common law doctrine.

PREVENTING WRONGFUL DISCHARGE EXPOSURE

A policy to prevent discharge exposure must start out with the audit of the application form. The wording in the form must be so drafted that it doesn't create an expressed contract unless that is what is intended. Some employers want their application form to say that it is an expressed contract and the applicant is expected to abide by its terms. Exhibit 11-1 is an example of a statement of this type.

Since employment at this point is still in the prospective, the applicant will usually not refuse to sign it.[3] Those employers who have the disclaimer in the application form state that it does not have a chilling effect on the applicant flow or obtaining good, qualified applicants. Others feel that it puts the company in a negative position at the start of the employment period.

The courts will enforce an at-will clause

[1]Jane P. Mallor, "Punitive Damages for Wrongful Discharge of At-Will Employees," *William and Mary Law Review*, 26, no. 3 (September 1985), 449–96.

[2]Sami M. Abbasi, Kenneth W. Hollman, and Joe H. Murray, "Employment at Will: An Eroding Concept in Employment Relationships," *Labor Law Journal*, 38, no. 1 (January 1987), 21; Daniel J. Koys, Steven Briggs, and Jay E. Grenig, "The Employment-at-Will Doctrine: A Proposal," *Loyola Law Journal*, 17 (Winter 1986); William J. Holloway and Michael J. Leech, "Employment Termination—Rights and Remedies," Washington, DC: (Bureau of National Affairs, 1985); Henry H. Berritt, "Employee Dismissal and Practice"(New York: John Wiley, 1984) (1985 Supp.).

[3]The experience of the employment manager is that an applicant will sign anything and remember nothing.

EXHIBIT 11-1

> The employment relationship between the employee and the employer is at-will and may be terminated at any time by either party with or without cause, unless specifically changed in writing by an authorized company representative.

in the applicant form and will usually hold that it is an expressed contract at the time of hiring. Where a handbook stated that discharge will be for just cause only, and the employee was discharged after eight years, the court held that just cause had to be shown.[4] New York is a strong at-will state, but the court held that the clause in the application form removed the employee from the at-will status.

In addition to a legal and employee relations consideration when making a decision whether or not to include an at-will clause in the application form, it must also be considered whether or not it prevents subsequent changes. Some courts hold that although the application form clearly states one thing, a later statement in the handbook or a posted memo can modify the original statement.[5] When the application form is audited and a decision is made to include language that could be interpreted to mean that it was an expressed contract, consideration must be given to foreseeable future circumstances on which the application language may have a limiting effect. Serious consideration should be given to saying nothing in an application form rather than language that will result in a contract that in the future may be troublesome.

Audit of the Interviewing Process

We have seen that a promise made at the time of hiring can result in establishing a

contractual relationship and removing the applicant, once employed, from an at-will status to an enforceable contract. However, not every utterance of the employer is binding.[6] Secondary interviews can result in forming a contract; accordingly they should be structured so promises are not made that are relied upon, since often the employee later will allege that they were broken. When the plaintiff can show that the promise was relied upon and he or she suffered damages when it was broken, there is a serious exposure to litigation.[7] Although the employer may have checklists and guidelines for interviewing, there is no assurance that they will be followed. The audit can only assure the management that such instructions exist. The instructions to the interviewers should not be specific. It is sufficient if they state that any promises made at the time of hiring will create an exposure to a lawsuit in the future in the event that those promises are not kept. Apart from the legal consequences, there is an employee relations problem of working for an employer who does not keep promises.

The Job Offer Letter

Any offer of employment above a certain level should be in writing. There are two reasons for this. The first is to avoid any misunderstanding of the conditions of employment, and the second is that in the event

---

[4]*Weiner* v. *McGraw-Hill,* 443 N.E. 2d 441 (N.Y. 1982).

[5]*Brooks* v. *Trans World Airlines,* 574 F.Supp. 805 (D.C. Colo. 1983). However other courts will hold that a subsequent statement will not modify a previous statement in an application form or handbook. *Hoemberg* v. *Watco Publishers, Inc.,* 343 N.W. 2d 676 (Minn. App. 1984).

[6]*Dumas* v. *Kessler & Maguire Funeral Home,* 380 N.W. 2d 544 (Minn. App. 1986).

[7]*Stuart* v. *Tektronix, Inc.,* 730 P. 2d 619 (Or. App. 1986).

EXHIBIT 11-2

This job offer contains entire understanding between _____ and _____ with respect to the conditions of employment. No other promises, agreements, or understandings, written or oral, not mentioned above shall be binding. No changes, additions or modifications of this letter shall be binding unless they are in writing and signed by the parties to this letter.

---

a promise was implied or otherwise understood to be a promise, it can be voided in the job offer letter.

To avoid exposure, the job offer letter should not contain a quote of an annual salary. Some courts will hold that this is a contract for one year, while others will reject the concept.[8] Since many states have not ruled on the issue, why say it? The applicant can divide and multiply. The audit must note that an annual salary is not quoted either orally or in a job offer letter.[9] The job offer letter should also contain a "zipper clause." Zip up tight any promises that may have been made at the time of the interview so it is clear that such promises were not relied upon when accepting the position.

Exhibit 11-2 is suggested language to be inserted in the job letter. The language should be as nonlegal as possible but have the necessary elements for enforcement. After the terms of employment are stated (who pays for new curtains, connecting the washer and dryer, and so on), the language in Exhibit 11-2 could be inserted. This should be the last paragraph of the letter, and when the employee reports to work, some written or at least oral assurance should be given that the letter was understood.

---

[8] *Hartman* v. *C.W. Travel, Inc.*, 792 F. 2d 1179 (D.C. Cir. 1986) held for an annual salary and *Crawford* v. *David Shapiro & Co. P.A.*, 490 So.2d 993 (Fla. App. 1986) rejected the concept.

[9] See *Presto* v. *Sequoia Systems, Inc.*, 633 F. Supp. 1117 (D. Mass. 1986), where the court held that the annual salary quote was an inducement to accept the job.

Effectiveness of a Complaint Procedure

The complaint procedure is one of the most important elements in the prevention of exposure to lawsuits in discharge cases. An effective complaint procedure will eliminate 80 percent of the exposure to wrongful discharge cases. The audit should make certain that it is used the way it was intended. Often the restrictions in the procedure chill its use; if this is the case they should be changed. The less formal it is, with liberal time limits and no restriction on what member of management the employee can express a complaint to, the more it will be used. (The Meritor Savings Bank case cited on page 88 is recalled, where the employer was found guilty of sexual harassment and the complaint procedure was useless since the employee was required to report to the person involved.) Also if a peer review or an impartial arbitrator is not provided for (assuming a nonunion facility) and the complaint procedure is not being used by the employee, serious consideration should be given to establishing a final impartial appeal procedure.

Audit of Performance Appraisals

Although an objective performance appraisal based on behavioral characteristics may appear on paper, the audit should determine how it is being used. It is much easier for a manager to be subjective than to have to verify objective data. So after a good procedure is adopted, often there is a tendency to let it fall back into subjectivity. The audit should determine whether or not the ratee has been communicated with during the appraisal period, whether the ratee understood what performance was expected, and the consequences if the standard of performance communicated was not met. This would serve as a warning to the employee of what the consequences would be for poor performance. Courts are particularly sympathetic to an employee's cause where there is documented evidence that the employee had previously received subjective favorable performance ratings and a short time later was discharged for poor performance.

Audit of Just-Cause Policy

The audit of a just-cause policy assumes that one has been established. A study of wrongful discharge cases indicates that the employer's policy must be carefully considered when discharge occurs.[10] The development of legal doctrines that make an exception to the common law employment-at-will doctrine encourages employees to file previously unthinkable claims for relief. The vague definition of public policy by the courts gives the employee free access to the courts and discourages the employer from discharging anyone except in extreme cases. Employees will file lawsuits in almost any discharge case where just cause is not clearly evident. The first question that the court will ask is the reason for the discharge. If none can be shown, the reason alleged by the employee could be an exception to the at-will doctrine.

Seldom will a wrongful discharge suit succeed when the employer adopts a just-cause termination policy and communicates to the employee the exact conditions that will cause severe disciplinary action or discharge. Where just cause is shown, the courts have sup-

ported the discharge rather than relying on the common law exceptions.

What is just cause is decided on a case-by-case basis by arbitrators whose task is to interpret the labor agreement. However, in a nonunion facility just cause must relate more to an employee relations and legal context. Fortunately we have two court decisions that give a logical definition of "just cause." In *Danzer* v. *Professional Insurers, Inc.*, 679 P.2d 1276 (N.M. 1984), the Supreme Court of New Mexico stated, "Termination for good cause is shown . . . i.e., some causes inherent in and related to qualifications of the employee or a failure to properly perform some essential aspect of the employee's job function." The author accepts this as one half of the definition of just cause. However, another court completed the definition when in *Station* v. *Amax Coal Co., Div. of Amax, Inc.*, 461 N.E.2d 612 (ILL.App. 3 Dist. 1984), the court after reviewing the decisions[11] on just cause involving arbitration under labor agreements found that "just cause includes only that conduct that an employee knows is subject to discipline." In addition the court found that statutes protecting public employees from discharge have defined "cause" as a situation where the employee's continuance in his or her position is in some way detrimental to the discipline and efficiency of the employer and where the law and sound public policy recognize that there is good cause for no longer employing the person. Not all courts have adopted the definition of the above two courts.[12]

If a court is presented with the fact that the employee was adequately informed, it is quite certain they will find "just cause." In *Conner* v. *Fort Gordon Bus Co.*, 761 F.2d 1493

---

[10]For complete survey of wrongful discharge case law from 1980 to 1986, see David S. Hames, "The Current Status of the Doctrine of Employment-at-Will," *Labor Law Journal*, 39, no. 1 (January 1988), 19.

[11]For case law on successful and unsuccessful defense of just cause, see 3 Employment-at-Will Reporter 2035 (1985), New England Legal Publishers, P.O. Box 48, Boston, MA 02101.

[12]In *Crosier* v. *United Parcel Service, Inc.*, 198 Cal. Rptr. 361 (Cal. App. 2nd Dist. 1983), the court said that "good cause was largely relative depending upon the circumstances of each case."

(11th Cir. 1985), the employee argued that the just cause was only a pretext for discrimination. The court said it was just cause as long as the standard or policy violation was the basis for the discharge and the standard or policy was communicated[13] to the employee before the violation and the employee understood it. On previous occasions the employer had only issued reprimands for violations. The fact that the employer did not issue the reprimand but discharged instead doesn't mean the discharge was sex discrimination. The just-cause audit accordingly should determine whether when an employee was discharged there was a rule violation or poor performance, that the employee was knowledgeable before committing the act, or in the case of poor performance there was an opportunity to correct. In cases where the employer has been unsuccessful in defending just-cause discharges, the employee alleges that she or he has failed to understand the consequences of committing the act.

WRITING A HANDBOOK OR A POLICY MANUAL

In the early 1950s communication was one of the most popular subjects in any management discussion. Management associations, publications, and seminar leaders discussed at length the problem of upward and downward communication. While opinions varied, the consensus of the majority of man-

agement decision makers was that the problem of downward communication could best be solved through the use of employee policy manuals or handbooks. The solution to the problem of upward communication was never quite as definite. Some managers relied on employee committees, while others depended on attitude surveys.

A rather large group of employers did nothing about the communication problem until they were threatened with union organization. Even then the usual response was to have the president write a letter to the employees. When this tactic failed and the facility was organized, the union leadership became the vehicle for communication to the employees.

In time, managements came to recognize that this too was an unsatisfactory and ineffective approach to the problem and once again the use of the handbook and employee manual became more popular. The CEO had an opportunity to write a "welcome aboard" letter to the employees. The personnel practitioner found the manual a method for informing employees of organizational rules and procedures. To the supervisor the document was a way to justify a position already taken or—if she or he disagreed with its provisions—to be ignored.

The typical handbook was loosely written with the intent of satisfying everyone. Unfortunately, it often contained language that was confusing to both management and employees. With the advent of employee rights legislation—quickly followed by lawyers' looking for material to use as an excuse for litigation—the handbook became a fertile source of ideas both for employees and for the legal profession. Since the wording frequently was designed to mean everything to everybody, it was probably inevitable that the interpretation would ultimately be left to the courts.

Need for a Handbook

The first decision to be made when writing a handbook is to decide whether one is needed. For a company of 25 employees or

---

[13]Communication in this context is best described by a situation where an employer had to get 100 percent participation in order to have a group life insurance program. One employee would not sign; the supervisor talked to him, but could not convince him; the plant manager tried without success. They reported to the president that they could not put the program in. The president talked to the employee and said, "Sign up or you are fired." The employee signed. The supervisor and plant manager were bewildered. They asked the employee why he signed when the president talked to him but refused when they tried to get him to do so. The employee's reply was, "Nobody explained it to me before."

less it is doubtful whether it is. Communications in a small organization are often made more effective by dealing with the employees directly than by trying to fit each one into a written policy. Items that are required to be put in writing can be done by a memo or a letter to the employees.

For a larger organization a well-drafted handbook has several useful purposes.

1. It is an important element in the employer's defense against equal employment opportunity charges by ensuring consistency. When the company's policies are stated in writing, agencies investigating charges give more credibility to the company's position.
2. The handbook is useful in training supervisors how to carry out the policies and ensuring some consistency in their application. This is often difficult because of the difference in philosophy of the supervisors who have wide discretion in administering policies.
3. Oral assurances as well as practices by members of management are often held by the courts to be binding, and this can be avoided by eliminating them in a handbook. Those employers who feel that a written handbook is a contract forget that oral statements or practices can also be enforced as a contract.
4. A handbook can be extremely helpful in the event of organization attempts by the union. It affords ahead of time the opportunity to set forth the policies and advantages of a union-free environment and avoids any misunderstanding or false statements of policies or benefits.

Problem Areas in a Handbook

The aforementioned advantages can be offset if the handbook is not properly drafted. When employee manuals were originally written, the legal implications of certain statements were often not even considered. The language in manuals is intended to provide a degree of flexibility to management in dealing with specific situations. This approach may have its advantages, but it may also be dangerous. A statement that "it is important that all accidents or injuries are promptly reported to your supervisor" may appear to give the supervisor some freedom

of action, but it also may incur problems that were not intended, because it is not forceful.

There is no substitute for a definitive choice of words that accurately reflects what is meant. If you don't mean it, don't write it. If there is no intention of implying permanency of employment, the use of *probationary period* should be avoided. Many handbooks have such terms as

1. "We reserve the right to . . ."
2. "Exceptions may be made for . . ."
3. "You have permanent employment."
4. "There is job security here."
5. "Fair treatment and the opportunity for promotion from within the company according to high moral standards . . ."[14]
6. Employees are classified as permanent, part time, and temporary."
7. "We request" or "We encourage you to use this complaint procedure."
8. "These rules are guidelines," or "You are encouraged to follow them."

These are all "canned" terms that could have one meaning to the employees and another to management personnel. They are also often interpreted by the plaintiff's bar in a different way from that which was intended by management. The problems arise when the courts listen to arguments by the employees and award large amounts for breach of contract. It is ironic that the courts take the position that the employee is considered to have no legal knowledge but that the employer is aware of the legal consequences of every statement. Under these circumstances the employer must consider every clause in the employee handbook not only for its communication value but also for the legal consequences if interpreted differently.

Contents of a Well-Written Handbook

The main problem with most handbooks is that they tell the employees what

---

[14]See *Mannikko v. Harrah's Reno, Inc., 630 F.Supp 191 (D. Nev. 1986).*

EXHIBIT 11-3

Whenever the employee willfully, wantonly, and adversely affects the employer's or employee's interests, it will be considered a gross misconduct that will result in immediate discharge once the facts are ascertained. The following violations will be considered gross misconduct. [List the violations—no more than fifteen; ten is better.]

the company is going to do for them. President John Kennedy's statement in his inaugural address in 1961 should be remembered when writing a handbook: "Ask not what your country can do for you—ask what you can do for your country." In writing a handbook, the employer should tell the employee what is expected of him or her and not what the employee should expect from the company. Not "we encourage" but "you shall" or "you are required." If this theme is carried out it is beneficial if the handbook is interpreted as a contract. It would be an enforceable document against the employee. It is often better to do things for the employee and not write them, since this affords more flexibility. The handbook should contain

1. Conduct that causes various degrees of disciplinary action, including "sudden death" discharge offenses. These are immediate discharge offenses where the employee has been forewarned before committing the act. The listed causes should be as specific as possible as to the conduct, but a clause should be inserted that states that discharge will not be limited to the offenses, but other offenses would require a warning unless added to the "sudden death" list.
2. Rules of conduct, including absenteeism, tardiness, leaving the work site, adherence to coffee break time, work schedules, and so on.
3. Certain safety rules and the requirement that they be followed by the employee.
4. A policy on harassment of all types, which should also be stated in a personal communication.
5. A policy on search of person and personnel property, which should be stated in a sepa-

rate communication as well as in the handbook.
6. A policy on drug testing and alcohol abuse.

Some companies include performance requirements in the handbook, while others feel this is operational and it is better to do this by department or according to job title. Whether performance requirements should be included depends upon the size of the company and upon the job category. It may be necessary to list some specific rules particular to the operation so the employees are informed what conduct is expected.

The handbook should contain a clause that defines misconduct that will aid unemployment compensation appeals and also other statutes, such as COBRA, that state an employee has no rights if discharged for misconduct. Exhibit 11-3 is an example of such a clause.

The handbook should inform the employee that from time to time management may have to change it. Exhibit 11-4 is suggested language to cover this contingency.

The employer should be assured that the employee not only has read the handbook but also understands it. Sometimes the employee will state that she or he understood it when it was presented, but after working awhile the employee found that the statements in the handbook did not correlate with actual practice and it became difficult to know which one to follow. To eliminate this argument, the handbook should contain a statement that the employee should ask questions at any time the handbook is not understood. Exhibit 11-5 is a suggested statement that should be given to the em-

EXHIBIT 11-4

> From time to time as conditions change, it will be necessary to change or add rules and procedures governing employees. Such changes will be posted well in advance of their effective date, after which time they will become a part of this handbook.

ployee at the time the handbook is distributed; after it is signed, it should be put in the employee's personnel file. The statement should make it clear the responsibility is on the employee to clear up any misunderstanding.

Disclaimer Clauses in a Handbook

Many lawyers feel that the solution to the problem of having enforceable rights created by the handbook is to include a disclaimer stating that the handbook is not a contract and can be changed at any time at the discretion of the company. Exhibit 11-6 is an example of a typical disclaimer.

If disclaimers are desired they have a better chance of being enforced if the language states

1. The handbook is not nor is it intended to be a contract of employment.
2. The handbook is not to be interpreted by the employee as a contract of employment.
3. The employer retains the right to terminate its employees at any time for any reason not prohibited by law, and employee can terminate at will.

4. The employer retains the sole discretion to modify any or all provisions of the handbook at any time for any reason. (This is often used but legally is not necessary.)

In addition to the proper language, other factors are necessary to close loopholes to prevent a disclaimer from being challenged.

1. The language must be clear, conspicuous, and easily understood (keep the legal jargon out).
2. The same language must appear in other documents, such as application forms and job offer letters.
3. There must be unambiguous evidence that the employee has received the disclaimer, has read it, and understands it.
4. Subsequent employer action and communications with the employee must establish that the employee is treated as an at-will employee.

Whether a disclaimer is legally enforceable often depends on the court. In *Castiglione* v. *Johns Hopkins Hosp.*, 517 F.2d 786 (Md. App. 1986), the court said that a disclaimer makes the handbook only a state-

EXHIBIT 11-5

> I, _____ (Social Security number), have read, understand, and have in my possession the company's policies and procedures. I agree as a condition of employment to follow the policies in the handbook, and if there is at any time something that I do not understand, I agree to ask a company representative. I further understand that this signed statement will be a permanent record in my personnel file.

EXHIBIT 11-6

> This handbook [or manual] is designed to familiarize you with the conditions of employment which the company expects you to follow. The conditions stated herein are not intended to be and do not constitute a contract of employment.
>
> or
>
> This manual [or handbook] is not intended to and does not constitute a contract between the company and its employees.

ment of the intent of the employer. This is the position of at least 26 states, as long as clear intent is shown.[15] However, a sizable minority of the courts take a different view.[16] Sometimes the courts are concerned with the superior bargaining power of the employer and will not enforce the contract without evidence of the employee's interpretation of the clause.[17] In *Helle* v. *Landmark, Inc.,* 472 N.E. 2d 765 (Ohio 1984), the court held that a disclaimer would be disregarded if oral promises were made later. Sometimes a disclaimer will not be enforced where it has the effect of giving up statutory rights, such as workers compensation or discrimination claims.

As we can see from the foregoing cases, the disclaimers are not an absolute assurance that there will not be exposure to a lawsuit. Less exposure would result from eliminating the disclaimer and writing the handbook in such a manner that its provisions were enforceable against the employee. In this case it would not be damaging if the employee attempted to enforce the handbook. If the language itself doesn't grant the employee any rights but is enforceable against the employee, it is difficult to see where there is

reason to have a disclaimer and risk the exposure.[18]

There is also an employee relations problem with disclaimers. It certainly strains the company's stature at the orientation program to go over the provisions of the handbook and at the end state that it is discretionary with the company but employees are expected to follow it. Also it may expose the company to union organization, since the employee may feel that she or he has little protection in company policies when they can be changed at will. This couldn't happen if there were a union and a labor agreement.

A disclaimer clause in a handbook from a personnel practitioner's point of view does not seem advisable but from an attorney's point of view it is the method to avoid liability for a poorly written handbook.

Audit of a Handbook

Any handbook should be reviewed at least once a year. If it has not been revised for the last three years, major changes are very likely to be in order. The review of the handbook should be made regardless of whether the state considers the handbook a legal contract. The legal principles followed in states

---

[15]*Bailey* v. *Perkins Restaurants, Inc.,* 398 N.W. 2d 120 (N.D. 1986); *Hall* v. *Central Medical Pavillion,* 654 F. Supp. 1156 (W.D. Pa. 1987).

[16]*Aiello* v. *United Airlines, Inc.,* 818 F. 2d 1196 (5th Cir. 1987).

[17]*Kari* v. *General Motors Corp.,* 261 N.W. 2d 222 (Mich. 1977).

[18]See "The Use of Disclaimers to Avoid Employer Liability under Employee Handbook Provisions," *Journal of Corporation Law,* 12 (Fall 1986), 105. For the opposite view, see "Unjust Dismissal of Employees at Will—Are Disclaimers a Final Solution?" *Fordham Urban Law Journal,* 15 (1987), 533–65.

that do consider a handbook as a contract are also good personnel principles for those states that consider the handbook a communications tool. If you have a procedure in a contract, the law says that you must follow it, but even where the law will not enforce the procedure, it is poor employee relations to promise or agree to do one thing and then do something else.

The basic principle to be followed in reviewing the handbook is to tell employees what the organization expects of them and not what the organization is going to do for them. Any procedure in the handbook that is not being followed or is not likely to be followed should be eliminated. These procedures should be guidelines for the supervisors to follow but should not be communicated to the employees as an enforceable right.

Most handbooks say too much. A handbook should state the rules and regulations that the employees must follow and the consequences if they are not followed. Progressive discipline clauses have given legal difficulties in the past because some violations should be "sudden death" violations. This information should be communicated to the employees in a way that will make certain that they know that there will be no warning or progressive discipline, just discharge. These "sudden death" violations should be limited to very serious offenses. If ten of them were listed in the handbook, that would be enough.

Management can do many things without announcing them in the handbook. A policy on absenteeism can be a guideline for management personnel to follow without being detailed in the handbook. By spelling it out in detail you lose the flexibility to deal with special situations. A promotion policy can be instituted without mention in the handbook although it will usually be found in a labor agreement. It is much easier to change a practice than to change a clause in the handbook.

The handbook should not deal with benefits, such as health insurance, vacations, and holidays, that are controlled by federal or state laws, since certain detailed communications are required that are out of place in the handbook. The tendency of the courts to treat all sections of a document alike would result in establishing the same requirements in the rest of the handbook as the required statutes in the benefit section. Another reason for keeping the benefits separate is that you can make the benefits subject to change without destroying the employee relations value of the handbook. Benefits usually are expected to be changed from time to time. Since they have always increased in the past, statements such as "these benefits effective from January 1, 19__ will remain in effect until further notice" would have little employee relations consequences as compared to "this handbook is not a contract and the organization reserves the right to alter or change the provisions at its discretion." Management has the right anyway so why make the statement? Doing so only causes employee dissatisfaction and mitigates the stature of the handbook. A good handbook may not win any prizes in legal or personnel literature, but it will tell the employees in unambiguous terms what is expected of them and what will happen if they take—or fail to take—certain actions.

The handbook still can be useful as a communication tool, but it must have a different objective than in the past and more care must be used in its language. For organizations in those states that still do consider a handbook merely a statement of organization policy, it can be a better communication tool if it is written as if it were a contract. A sincere and direct approach is better from an employee relations point of view and offers less encouragement to sue by some members of our "litigation-happy" society.

THE DISCHARGE PROCESS

Employers give a great deal of consideration to whether or not they should terminate an employee, but when the decision is finally made they give little thought to the procedure. Even in a "litigation-happy" society most terminations are never challenged in court. That is not because of how employees are discharged but because there is still a slight stigma to suing your former employer. As this stigma diminishes, there will be an increase in wrongful discharge suits unless the employer does something about it.

Generally, a discharged employee's decision to sue is not an easy one. Litigation poses fear of the unknown and the embarrassing prospect of airing a private misfortune in public. Most people have never started a lawsuit and don't know how to go about it. However, legal advertising is helping to alleviate this condition, and presumably the plaintiff's lawyer will assess the case before deciding to handle it. If the employee is angry enough, he or she can find a lawyer who will handle almost any claim. It isn't that the employee knows about the law but rather that the employee is angry and his or her only relief is to find a lawyer and try to establish some grounds for suing.

Throughout this chapter we have been talking about exposure to lawsuits, because once the employee files a lawsuit, the employer loses, regardless of whether she or he prevails on the merits. There is adverse publicity, lost time, and the distraction associated with having to defend a legal claim. The lawyer must take a great deal of the employer's time in preparing for the case, since the employer is the only one who has all the facts that the lawyer must depend upon to defend the case. This cost is in addition to the huge legal fees associated with a lawsuit. If the employer loses, usually it pays the fees for both the employee and itself. However, if the employer wins, it still usually pays its own fees. Exposure to lawsuits can be minimized if the procedure recognizes that the less provocation there is generated the less likelihood there is for a lawsuit to occur.

Proper Discharge Procedure

There are certain elements that a discharge procedure should have. The first essential element is that the discharge responsibility should be centralized in one or two persons. It should not be solely in the hands of the first-line supervision. Discharge is no longer a simple task of telling Joe he is fired. The matter should be in the hands of a person or persons who can handle the case impartially and with due regard to the rights and feelings of both the supervisor and the employee. First-line supervisors are normally charged with getting the job out and usually have little concern for the niceties of human relations when the operation is shorthanded because it was necessary to discharge someone.

The second necessary element is that the procedure should be fair and firm, and friendly, but not insensitive. For the employer it means writing off an investment, and for the employee it is the end of a source of income and it often generates a sense of insecurity. The discharge procedure should consider the impact upon the parties involved.

The third element is that the reason must be logical from the employer's point of view. An employer would not discharge somebody because of failure to say "hello" when spoken to, since that would not be a logical reason for termination. The termination must be for something that a normal employer would do and must be understandable to a reasonable person.

The fourth important element in the discharge is that a proper investigation must be made to determine the facts. An investigation should be made even when the employer is sure of the facts. There is nothing that convinces the employee more of fairness and receives more weight from a court than a thorough investigation of the facts.[19]

Causes of Provocation

One of the first things to avoid is provocation. The act of discharging is inherently

---

[19]See *William E. Hartsfield*, "Suggestions for Investigating Employee Misconduct," *The Practical Lawyer*, March 1, 1985, p. 11.

provocative, so to avoid exposure to lawsuits management must do something to mitigate it. More often than not, the merits are not as important as the way the employee was discharged. The judge or the jury may "tune out" the facts of the discharge and only hear how it was done. Some of the causes of provocation are

1. Indecisiveness, when the company behaves in a way that indicates it doesn't know whether or not to discharge. The employee is tormented.
2. Humiliation. Every employee has some worth or value to the company and at some time made a contribution. These assets should be stated as well as faults that caused the discharge.
3. Misrepresentation, which fans the flame of anger more than any other factor, especially when the employee knows that the statement is not accurate. The most common misrepresentation is a charge of poor performance after a merit increase was given a month before. Misrepresentation also indicates vulnerability, which in turn encourages aggressiveness to see a lawyer.
4. Conveying a rejected feeling. The employee has lost a job and has no place to go. If there is no union the law office is a good place for condolence. One of the biggest barriers to litigation is fear of what will happen if she or he sues. Failure to help the employee to adjust to the shock will cause this barrier to be penetrated.

Prevention of Provocation

1. Develop a concise reason for discharge. It is important for the employee to logically understand why she or he was discharged. Obscure reasons "to soften the blow" will backfire.
2. Decide upon all the severance details. There should be no ambiguities to negotiate.
3. Tell the employee who the decision makers are. If possible the decision makers should participate in the discharge process.
4. Be brief and to the point. Lengthy dissertations usually sound weak and defensive and prolong the employee discomfort.[20] One can be sensitive and still not be defensive.
5. Thank the employee for his or her contributions. This may not always be appropriate, but if this is possible the employee is less likely to be upset to the point of seeing a lawyer.
6. Offer some counseling service about finding another job. Outplacement service or advice on where the employee can sell his or her skills would be helpful to give the employee a sense of security other than seeing a lawyer.

Timing and Place of Discharge

Although there is never a good time to discharge, some times are worse than others. Some employers believe that Friday afternoon is a good time because the employee can leave without much embarrassment or undue interruption. That was formerly the most common time to discharge. In many respects, however, that is the worst time to discharge because it makes the employee angry; the weekend is spoiled—mother-in-law is coming over; there are plans to go to the beach with the children; it's your turn to have the bridge club. By Saturday morning the employee has talked to so many people justifying the ego that she or he is ready to see a lawyer. Why not on Monday morning when the children are in school, the lawyer is in court, and several employment offices are taking applications? The discharged employee can fill out a few applications and tell the family that night that she or he was discharged but already has several prospects for another job. The whole family relaxes and watches "Monday night football."

The exit interview should be held in a place where there will not be any interruption and where the manager can conclude the meeting by leaving. The place of the

---

[20]This is advisable in communicating other misfortunes. Sometimes the reaction isn't what is expected. The author once told a spouse in a brief and to-the-point statement that her husband was killed in a work-related accident an hour ago. Her reply was, "How much do I get?"

meeting should be apart from co-workers and where the discharged employee can leave the plant without contact with others. It should be as private as possible. Only those who have a need to know should be told of the discharge.

Final Steps in Discharging

A discharge is an adversity and therefore is an exposure to a lawsuit. The employer should assume that the employee will challenge it. The preceding predischarge preparation affords less chance that it will be challenged. The final steps in the process will supplement this preparation.

The first step is to suspend and allow time for investigation. This shows the employee and the court that the employer gave some consideration to the act. Suspension should be used even if it is a "sudden death" offense. There may be some question as to whether the act was committed, but even if the employer is sure of the facts suspension is a good defensive move. The suspension should be of short duration. The employee should not be left in the dark any longer than necessary. One of the virtues of the suspension technique is that it forces management to investigate immediately. In the event the employee is exonerated, the period of the suspension should be paid for by the employer; this is another reason why the suspension period should be short.

The next step is the investigation of all the facts that will establish a just cause for the discharge. Another purpose of the investigation is to consider any legal consequences of the discharge. The investigation should be well documented. Performance appraisals should be reviewed[21] and the selection procedure should be checked to determine whether there were any promises

made at the time of hiring. The handbook or the policy manual should be examined to determine whether there was any language in it that might establish a contract of employment or denote permanency of employment. After the investigation is completed, a second person who is not familiar with the case should review the file.

A Second Fresh Look

It is preferable that this audit be conducted by some person who has not yet participated in the discharge decision. However, in a small organization this is not practical so there may be some overlapping between the investigation and the audit to the extent that the same person does it. The person who is responsible for reviewing the discharge procedure should carefully evaluate and record the following:

1. Any evidence that the person was terminated for a reason that might be held to be contrary to public policy, such as refusing to commit perjury, whistleblowing, refusing to be excused from jury duty, filing a workers compensation claim, refusing to violate a professional code of ethics, or any other act that may be construed to have the public policy protection.

2. The company's handbook or policy manual to determine whether there are any statements that indicate permanency status or if there is a permanent employee classification. Does the document provide for a discharge procedure, and was it followed? Any statement in the handbook or policy manual that is not followed results in serious exposure in most states.

3. The performance appraisals to determine whether there are any inconsistencies between the performance appraisals and the reason given for the discharge.

4. The recruitment and selection procedures to determine whether there have been any promises made as to job security, promotions, or termination only for just cause.

5. Was an exit interview conducted in which more than one person participated? Were the

---

[21]See Ralph J. Baxter, Jr., "Preventive Techniques to Reduce the Risk of Wrongful Termination Litigation," Employment-at-Will on Trial, *Labor and Employment Conference Notebook*, ABA section (1986).

reasons for discharge established and clearly communicated to the employee, and if so, have they been consistent when communicated to other members of management and for use on the unemployment compensation claims? The reasons should somewhat correlate with the facts revealed in the investigation.

The Exit Interview

The predischarge information should be reviewed and applied at the exit interview. The purpose of the exit interview is to establish the reason for the discharge that will be used by all members of management and when an unemployment compensation claim is filed.[22] The important point is that the employee is told what the reason is. Some attorneys advise not to give a reason. This is acceptable in most states under the at-will doctrine. However, when the employee files an unemployment compensation claim, a reason will have to be given. If one isn't given at the exit interview, the employee's version will be given to the unemployment claims representative and the employer will immediately be put on the defensive. The ambiguity can later be used in wrongful discharge action to the detriment of the employer.

The exit interview should be structured so the employee leaves with dignity and without being emotionally upset. Two persons should participate in the meeting. Having a person just as a witness causes the meeting to be too legalistic. If both participate, then there is a built-in witness. At the exit interview the employee should be told what the employer's reply will be to reference inquiries and what position will be taken on unemployment compensation claims.

THE USE OF WAIVERS OR RELEASES

Many employers take a more legal approach in preventing discharge litigation by having the employee sign a statement at the time of hiring or sign a release at the time of termination. Although these employee agreements are usually enforced by the courts, they do not necessarily prevent litigation. [See *Pratt* v. *Brown Machine Company*, 855 F.2d 1225 (6th Cir. 1988).] They are often challenged as not being completely voluntary or not understood or because the employer has taken advantage of its superior bargaining position. As in the case of disclaimers in a handbook, they must be carefully drafted, and precautions must be taken to be sure that the employee fully understands what she or he is signing and that the language covers all claims that the employee might have, both present and future.

Employment Agreements at Time of Hiring

At-will agreements are often written in the application form and are signed at the same time that the entire form is signed. This type of clause has been used by several companies for many years and reads as follows:

In consideration of my employment, I agree to conform to the rules and regulations of XYZ company, and my employment and compensation can be terminated, with or without cause, and with or without notice, at any time, at the option of either the company or myself. I understand that no manager or representative of XYZ . . . other than the President or Vice President of the Company, has any authority to enter into any agreement for employment for any specified period of time, or make any agreement contrary to the foregoing.[23]

---

[22]Many discharge unemployment compensation appeals have been lost because several members of management give different reasons for the discharge. See also *Flanigan* v. *Prudential Federal Savings & Loan Assn.*, 720 P.2d 257 (Mont. 1986), where three managers all testified to different reasons for the termination in a wrongful discharge case.

[23]*Eliel* v. *Sears, Roebuck and Co.*, 387 N.W. 2d 842 (Mich. App. 1985) (released for publication June 18, 1986).

This clause has been enforced in most courts that have had the issue before them.[24]

Some surveys of the effect of this type of clause reveal that it chills applicants against accepting a job offer, especially when they have more than one to choose from.[25] Like disclaimers in a handbook, a signed piece of paper is seldom a substitute for a positive personnel administration. The presence of this clause could also be "fodder" for a union organizer.

When the law moved into the personnel function, the employer had a tendency to overreact; an at-will statement may not be necessary and could create certain risks.[26] Most arbitrators do not consider the clause necessary as long as the labor agreement has a "just-cause" provision. So where there is a union the clause only creates certain risks but does not necessarily protect the employer.[27]

The Use of Releases

Some companies feel that the way to stop all claims after discharge is to have the employee sign a release. This would certainly discourage a lawyer from taking a case where a release was signed, providing it was tightly worded and properly executed.

Some states require a period of time to rescind the release after it has been executed.[28] Whether it be an agreement signed separately or a release at the time of termination, there is still an exposure if the employee feels that he or she was forced into it or is angry with the employer for how he or she was discharged. The exposure exists when a release is used because there is usually a question as to whether or not it is voluntary. A further consideration is the employee relations consequences when deciding to use a release.[29]

Purpose of Discharge Procedure

This chapter may leave the impression that the discharge process is so complex that it is better not to start it but to live with the problem. The purpose of this detailed analysis is to prevent exposure to lawsuits, not to stop discharges. Anyone can start a lawsuit, but most people are not predisposed to sue. Although winning in court can be satisfying, in the real sense "the horse is already out of the barn" when a claim is filed with a court or an agency. With careful, creative, sensitive procedures, objective performance appraisals and proper discipline, most claims arising out of a discharge can be prevented. The courts and juries are telling the employer that they will not interfere with the discharge process, but they do not like the way employees are being discharged. Juries tend to overreact when the discharge is not done in a humane way using the "reasonable person" standard.

The employer that believes that employment at will is a management right is challenging the discharged employee to test the doctrine and is exposed to litigation. The

---

[24]See *Reid* v. *Sears, Roebuck and Co.,* 790 F. 2d 453 (6th Cir. 1986), *Batchelor* v. *Sears, Roebuck and Co.,* 574 F.Supp. 1480 (E.D. Mich. 1983), as well as several other Sears, Roebuck and Co. earlier cases; *Crain* v. *Burroughs Corp.,* 560 F.Supp. 849 (D.C. Cal. 1983); *Whittaker* v. *Care-more, Inc.,* 621 S.W. 2d 395 (Tenn. 1981). However, in the Reid case the court said that since the application was signed 17 years before her employment was terminated, these facts couldn't be completely ignored.

[25]See Raymond L. Hilgert, "How At-Will Statements Hurt Employers," *Personnel Journal* (February 1988), p. 75.

[26]See "The Hazards of Firing-at-Will," *Wall Street Journal,* March 9, 1987, p. 16; Raymond L. Hilgert, "Discipline and Discharge from an Arbitrator's Point of View," Proceedings of the 1986 meeting of the Midwest Society of Human Resources and Industrial Relations, Terre Haute, IN: Indiana State University School of Business.

[27]See Frank Elkouri and Edna Asper Elkouri, *How Arbitration Works,* 4th ed. (Washington, DC: Bureau of National Affairs, 1985), pp. 650–707.

[28]Minnesota Statutes Section 363.031 allows 15 days to rescind after the agreement has been signed by both parties.

[29]Unless there are unusual circumstances, the author believes releases create more problems than they solve.

employer who modifies the discharge policy and procedures to protect against some exceptions to common law employment-at-will doctrine has considerably less exposure. A policy should not be such as to prevent the employer from discharging an employee or from taking advantage of what is left of the at-will doctrine, but just-cause policies along with other procedures should not be ignored when doing so. The law makes one thing clear: The day has passed when a supervisor or a manager in an emotional state can walk up to an employee and say, "You are fired," and not be exposed to litigation.

CHAPTER
12

PAYMENT OF WAGES UNDER THE FAIR LABOR STANDARDS ACT

Coverage and Penalties
Definition of Compensable Time
Exempt and Nonexempt Classification
Controlling Overtime Costs
Definition of Independent Contractor

The problem of the proper worth of a job is as old as the employment of one person by another. Judging the worth of a job raises questions involving philosophy, economics, and sociology. From a practical standpoint the important issue is what the employer is willing to pay and what the employees are willing to accept.

Until the enactment of the Fair Labor Standards Act of 1938[1] (the act), the employer and the employee decided between themselves what compensation should be paid for services rendered. The employer developed compensation systems that attempted to reward the worker for output and for contribution to the organizational objectives, taking into consideration the supply and demand for a particular skill in the marketplace.

The act interfered with the employer-employee relationship in determining the amount of compensation to be paid an employee by requiring the payment of a minimum wage to employees and prohibited the employer from employing a person for more than a specified number of hours per week without paying time and one half of the regular rate. After the Fair Labor Standards Act, Congress passed several other statutes to control wages: Walsh-Healey Public Contracts Act,[2] Davis-Bacon Act,[3] Service Contract Act,[4] and Equal Pay Act,[5] to name a few.

The principles established under the Fair Labor Standards Act are followed by the administrator of the Wage and Hour Division of the Department of Labor in determining hours of work and related subjects under Walsh-Healey, Davis-Bacon, and Service Contract Act. Therefore, these statutes are not considered here, since they have the same administrator and have limited application. This chapter is concerned with the situations that frequently arise under the Fair Labor Standards Act and the problems involved in compliance. Minimum wage requirements under the act involve a relatively small percentage of the gainfully employed and have fewer compliance problems than other sections of the act. Therefore they are not discussed in this chapter.

It is in the areas of compensable hours, exempt and nonexempt classifications, and whether or not an employee is an independent contractor that policies and procedures can be the most cost effective. Managers often take the attitude that the law prevents them from instituting effective cost-control measures and that the statute must be accepted as a necessary cost of doing business. The Fair Labor Standards Act does restrict the freedom of the employer in the payment of wages, but it does not prevent the establishment of policies and procedures to control the costs created by the statute.

Violations under the Fair Labor Standards Act can exist for a long time before anything happens. Often the employee is content with the violation either because it is not known to be a violation or because it is more convenient (such as coming to work early and working) to ignore the requirements of the act.[6] When the honeymoon is over, the employers are caught with egg on their face. An investigation by the Wage and Hour Division of the Department of Labor for compliance can be caused by complaints from the employee, unions, or competitors. Most investigations occur through employee or union complaints. Seldom does the agency make spotchecks unless it finds a flagrant violation in one company and wants to determine if it is a practice in the industry, such as in the fast-food industry after the Burger King case. Compliance with certain provisions of the act is not difficult while in other situations it can be an employee relations

---

[1] 29 USC Sect. 201 et seq.

[2] 41 USC Sects. 35–45.

[3] 40 USC Sect. 276.

[4] 41 USC Sects. 351–58.

[5] 29 USC Sect. 206 et seq.

[6] The basic statutory limitation for liability is two years; three years for willful violations. As one manager told the author, "I have been doing it unintentionally for five years. I am already three years ahead if found wrong."

problem. Often the employer, when a violation is questionable, is willing to take the risk (for a small number of employees) of being determined in violation, such as in exempt and nonexempt classifications.

COVERAGE AND PENALTIES

The act covers employers of any enterprise engaged in interstate commerce that has two or more employees[7] and produces goods and services exceeding $250,000 (or if more than one facility, then the amount is $362,500). This definition excludes several enterprises; however, most states have enacted little fair labor standards acts that cover employees not included in the federal act. For this reason whenever an employer-employee relationship exists, it is rare that employees are not covered unless the enterprise or employees are specifically exempted by the federal or state act. Section 203 exempts enterprises such as mom-and-pop businesses where only the family is employed, and owners of nonprofit organizations not having a business purpose. Seasonal recreational establishments are also exempted under the act. State and local governments are not exempt since the Supreme Court decision of *Garcia* v. *San Antonio Metropolitan Transit Authority*, 105 S.CT. 1005 (1985).

Several types of employees are also exempted, such as professional, executive, and administrative. The determination of when an employee comes under these exemptions is discussed in a subsequent section.

If a state law is more strict than the federal law, it will supersede the federal law; otherwise, the federal law controls. Also an agreement between the employer and the employee to waive coverage is illegal, void, and unenforceable, except under "Belo"

conditions that will be treated later in this chapter.[8]

Penalties for Violation

The act is enforced by the Wage and Hour Division of the Department of Labor and carries with it a criminal penalty for willful violations. Penalty for willful violations includes fines up to $10,000 and imprisonment up to six months. In *Williams* v. *Tri-County Growers, Inc.,* 747 F.2d 121 (3rd Cir. 1984), the fact that no complaints had been filed did not mean that the employer did not intend to violate the law.

The circuit courts have been split in the definition of *willful.* The Williams case was one definition. Other courts were more liberal and stated that if the employer merely knew that the FLSA was a consideration during the time the act was being violated, it was willful. In 1985 the Supreme Court in *Trans World Airlines* v. *Thurston,* 105 S.Ct. 613 (1985), rejected this concept and defined *willful* as applied to the Age Discrimination in Employment Act as where the "employer either knew or showed reckless disregard for the matter of whether its conduct was prohibited by the ADEA." If the employer didn't know, then it could not be said that there was a reckless disregard for the statute.

The Thurston definition was adopted in *McLaughlin* v. *Richland Shoe Co.,* 108 S.Ct. 1677 (1988), to the FLSA where the Court said that the employer acted willfully if it "knew or showed reckless disregard for the matter of whether its conduct was prohibited by the Fair Labor Standards Act."[9]

It appears from the Court's basis for their conclusion in the Thurston and Richland Shoe cases that the definition of willful will apply to other statutes, and if so, the em-

---

[7]*Employee* has been interpreted to mean any individual who is "dependent upon the business to which they render service"; *Bartels* v. *Birmingham,* 332 U.S. 126 (1947); *Weisel* v. *Singapore Joint Venture, Inc.,* 602 F.2d 1185 (5th Cir. 1979).

[8]*Duplessis* v. *Delta Gas, Inc.,* 640 F.Supp. 891 (E.D. La. 1986).

[9]The court in Richland virtually put to rest all appellate court conflicts over the definition of *willful* in all relevant statutes to FLSA, Equal Pay, Walsh-Healy, and so on.

ployer would not be charged with a willful violation unless he or she knew that the action was violating a statute and made no attempt to comply. This would make it very difficult to sustain a willful violation unless the employer wanted to violate the statute or totally disregarded it. Certainly advice of counsel or serious consideration as to whether a statute was being violated would be sufficient to make any violation "nonwillful."

Where no willful violation is found, the penalty is restitutionary back pay; under certain conditions liquidated damages equaling the amount of the back pay can be awarded. That amount of back pay and liquidated damages awarded is discretionary with the court. Often in determining the damages for failure to pay overtime, the amount of overtime worked is difficult to determine. The courts have stated that in the absence of employer records, the employee's recollections of the hours worked is sufficient if reasonable.[10]

In all situations under the act the plaintiff has a right of jury trial; the successful plaintiff may obtain attorney's fees and costs from the defendant.

Many questions concerning enforcement and interpretation of the act by the Department of Labor can be found in its interpretive bulletins. Such bulletins as "What Are Hours Worked," #785; "Records to Be Kept," #516; "Overtime Compensation," #778; and "White Collar Workers," #541 are useful in understanding the division's position on the interpretation of the act. For the most part these interpretations have had judicial acceptance but cannot be entirely relied upon as law.

DEFINITION OF COMPENSABLE TIME

The act does not limit the hours that an employee can work but requires that the em-

ployee be compensated for all the time worked. It also provides that the employee must be compensated at time and one half for all hours over 40 in one work week. The act contains no definition of *work* and only a partial definition of *hours worked*. A study of the countless court cases on the subject of time worked discloses that if the employee is serving the interests of the employer, it is considered time worked under the act.

It is immaterial whether the work was requested by the employer or authorized as long as it was performed or the employer had reason to believe that the work was being performed.[11] Where work is being performed, it is difficult for the employer to plead no knowledge, because the results of the work performance or existence of it is something the employer knows about or should know with reasonable diligence. Where the employee works and the employer fails to pay for the work, there are serious problems of compliance.

Meal Periods

The act does not require payment for meal periods when employees are serving their own interests (29 CFR 785.19). Mail carriers who must remain in uniform, eat lunch in a limited number of locations, and answer occasional questions from patrons during lunch do not have to be compensated for meal periods as long as they are not required to perform substantial duties that will interfere with the lunch hour.[12]

However, in many work situations they are working on behalf of the employer. A shipping clerk is not required but chooses to remain at the desk during meal periods eat-

---

[10]*Mumbower* v. *Callicott*, 526 F.2d 1183, 1186 (8th Cir. 1975).

[11]*Handler* v. *Thrasher*, 191 F.2d 120 (10th Cir. 1951). The author once discharged an employee on Christmas day. The author knew that the employee was working overtime to keep up in his work without recording it but could never catch him. The employee never suspected somebody would be around on Christmas day to find him working.

[12]*Hill* v. *United States*, 751 F.2d 810 (6th Cir. 1984).

ing a brown bag lunch and directing the unloading of a truck while chewing on a sandwich. A secretary knits at her desk; the supervisor asks for a file. A maintenance mechanic is called to repair a machine during lunch hour. In all these situations the employer often does not pay for meal periods. Because the employee is serving the interest of the employer while eating lunch, the courts have held in these situations that the employee is not really relieved of duty and whether inactive or active all meal periods must be paid for. If the shipping clerk is active a substantial part of the meal period, all meal periods are considered time worked.[13]

Where the duties performed during lunch hour were related to the work normally assigned, the work was compensable, as held in *Brennan* v. *Elmer's Disposal Service, Inc.,* 510 F.2d 84 (9th Cir. 1975). If work during meal periods is voluntary, it is not compensable, but often there is a fine line between what is voluntary and what is not. Many assignments appear to be voluntary, but if they are refused, serious adverse consequences result, which makes them not truly voluntary.

These examples are common situations where the employer unknowingly has considerable exposure. The employer falsely reasons that since the employee is not required to work or remain at the work site and does so as a matter of convenience, or to gain employer acceptance as a good worker, it is not work time. Rest or snack periods are usually paid for as a policy matter. Under the Department interpretations, 29 CFR Sect. 785.18, if less than 20 minutes they are compensable.

However, some courts state that because employees are serving their own interests, they are not compensable[14] and do not support the Wage and Hour Division's position as stated in Section 785.18.

Where the employer relied upon a department interpretative bulletin in setting its policy on compensability of waiting time, the court in *Cole* v. *Farm Fresh Poultry, Inc.,* 824 F.2d 923 (11th Cir. 1987), stated that the bulletin was too vague and offered only broad concepts. The statement in the bulletin making breaks of more than one half-hour noncompensable was not a defense when the employees could not use the time for their own purposes. In all these situations, a bulletin or a guideline is only a position of the department, and often the courts will not not validate what the bulletin says. It is when they go unchallenged that they are often treated as the law.

Other courts enforce the regulation on the presumption that rest periods promote efficiency, which is in the employer's interest. A safer approach, if the employer does not want to pay for rest periods or snack periods, would be, if possible, to offset rest periods against other working time, such as compensable waiting time or on-call time, so total hours worked do not exceed 40. This offset has been approved by at least two courts.[15] However, this is not always possible, and employee relations problems could become prevalent. See the case history on page 211.

The leading cases on meal periods *Mumbower* v. *Callicott* and *Marshall* v. *Valhalla,* 590 F.2d 306 (9th Cir. 1979).

Call and Waiting Time

The general rule is that if an employee is completely relieved from duty and such time is long enough to enable the employee to use the time for her or his own purpose, it is not considered time worked. This often comes up where waiting time is involved. If the waiting time is part of the job, it is com-

---

[13]*Mumbower* v. *Callicott,* 526 F.2d 1183, 1186 (8th Cir. 1975). A special arrangement could be made to allow a 45-minute lunch period, deducting 30 minutes per day for the meal period and paying for 15 minutes at an overtime rate.

[14]*Blain* v. *General Electric,* 371 F.Supp. 857 (D.C. Ky. 1971); *Clark* v. *Atlanta Newspaper,* 366 F.Supp. 886 (D.C. Ga. 1973).

[15]*Mitchell* v. *Greinetz,* 235 F.2d 621 (10th Cir. 1956); *Ballard* v. *Consolidated Steel Corp.,* 61 F. Supp. 996 (S.D. Cal. 1945).

THE 10-MINUTE MEAL PERIOD—A CASE HISTORY

The employees made a deal with the manager that if they took a 10-minute lunch period they would be able to quit 20 minutes early and still work 8 hours per day. (They also had two rest periods.) After a 3-year period one employee evidently got indigestion or a nervous stomach and complained to the Wage and Hour Division.

The division took the position that under its regulations, CFR Sect. 785.18, this must be a paid period because it was less than 20 minutes. Investigation revealed that employees left their machines and went to the lunchroom for 10 minutes (one even stated that he went home for lunch). When the bell rang, then all returned to their machines. The Wage and Hour Division demanded two years' back pay (the statute permits only two years) because

employees worked 40 hours and 50 minutes per week under their interpretation. This amounted to over $12,000 for about 60 employees. The employer took the position that because employees were serving their own interest for the 10-minute meal period, it was not work time, therefore not compensable, and refused to pay the back pay. After a period of threatening litigation, the Wage and Hour Division dropped the matter. Since employees for the 10-minute period were serving their own purposes, the 10-minute period was not work time.[16]

[16]Making change for vending machines during lunch was held to be on the employee's own time and not compensable, but answering phones was compensable. *Rector* v. *Laing Properties*, 26 W.H. Cases (BNA) 1365 (N.D. Ga. 1984).

---

pensable; if the employee is free to use the time for his or her own purpose, it is not considered waiting time.[17]

A distinction must be made between waiting to go to work and being engaged to wait to go to work. If it is the latter then it is compensable. Where employees were required to wait for customer flow before going to work, the court held that this was compensable time since the employees were ready, willing, and able to go to work once they arrived at the employer's place of business.[18]

Another problem often arises when the employee is required to be on call. The usual rule is that if the employee is not required to remain on the premises but is required to leave word with the company officials or at home where to be reached, it is not consid-

ered work time while on call.[19] However, if the employee is required to remain on the employer's premises or so close to them that he or she cannot use the time effectively for his or her own purposes, it is working time on call.

Coming to Work Early

Another common exposure of an employer is where an employee comes to work well before the regular starting time. This happens when a spouse drops an employee off or with car pools, which causes the employee to get to the work site early. Being a good employee, the person performs duties before being clocked in. This is compensable work time that the employer neither stops nor approves but tolerates. Preshift work is almost always held to be compensable. Where a butcher sharpened his knives outside shift

[17]*Skidmore* v. *Swift & Co.*, 323 U.S. 134 (1944).

[18]*Brock* v. *DeWitt dba Bonanza Steak House*, 633 F.Supp. 892 (D.C. Mo. 1986). Also see *Wright* v. *Carrigg*, 275 F.2d. 448 (4th Cir. 1960).

[19]*Armour & Co.* v. *Wantock*, 323 U.S. 126 (1944).

hours, the Supreme Court held it compensable.[20]

A key case that is often cited involves employees who were required to fill out daily time and requisition sheets, assemble material to be used on the job, fuel the trucks, and pick up a daily plan before starting work at 8:00 A.M. The court stated that the test in these cases is whether the activities are an "integral and indispensable" part of the performance of the regular work and in the ordinary course of the business.[21] The work—such as fueling the trucks—does not have to be directly related to the electrical business, but it is compensable as long as it is necessary to the performance of the job and for the benefit of the employer in the normal course of business. This definition has been supported in other jurisdictions.[22]

In these situations, where employees arrive at the work site from 15 to 20 minutes early and the employer has no knowledge of whether they are working or not, the rule of thumb used by some courts is that if they arrive 15 or more minutes early, they are presumed to be working unless the employer can prove otherwise.

Travel Time

The Portal to Portal Act[23] eliminates from working time certain travel and walking time or other similar activities before or following the work day unless considered compensable by custom or practice. If travel time is integrated with work and does not involve merely getting to work, it is compensable, as those traveling on employer business or field repair crews often do.[24]

If a nonexempted employee regularly works in Chicago and is sent to Minneapolis,

travel time would be compensable[25] (deducting time between home and airport). If as a routine assignment the employee goes to Minneapolis, under certain conditions the courts may conclude that travel to Minneapolis comes under the Portal to Portal Act and travel to Minneapolis is merely a change of work site. Travel time also must be considered on a weekly basis; the employer can avoid excessive overtime due to travel by giving compensatory time off in the same work week in which the overtime was earned.

Often travel time is spent for meetings and training programs. The usual rule is that if the training program is not compensable, then the travel time is not.

Training Programs

The criterion to determine whether a nonexempt employee is to be paid for training programs is whether or not the employee is performing any significant amount of work that benefits the employer. Another important factor is whether or not the training is compulsory (related training in apprenticeship programs is excepted). Being necessary for advancement or to prevent obsolescence doesn't imply that it is compulsory. Most courts will hold that it is compulsory when the employer tells the employee that she or he must take the training or be terminated.

Another problem with formal training that the practitioner has to solve is whether or not a trainee's taking a course to get a job makes him or her an employee. If so, overtime under the FLSA if worked would have to be paid; also the IRS as to withholding and state statutes as to workers compensation and unemployment insurance coverage would cause a problem if the trainee were an employee.

The Wage and Hour Division criteria for determining whether or not a trainee is an employee have been accepted by most state and federal courts. These guidelines state that a trainee is not an employee if

[20]*Mitchell* v. *King Packing Co.,* 350 U.S. 260 (1956).

[21]*Dunlop* v. *City Electric,* 527 F.2d 394 (5th Cir. 1976).

[22]*Marshall* v. *Gervill, Inc.* 1195 F.Supp 744 (D.C. Md. 1980).

[23]29 USC Sects. 251–62, an amendment to the Fair Labor Standards Act.

[24]*DA&S Well Drilling Service* v. *Mitchell,* 262 F.2d 552 (10th Cir. 1958).

[25]*Marshall* v. *R&M Erectors, Inc.,* 429 F.Supp. 771 (D. Del. 1977).

1. The training program is similar to that which would be offered in a vocational school although the employer facilities are being used
2. The training is only for the benefit of the trainee
3. The trainee does not displace regular employees
4. There is no immediate benefit to the employer who provides the training, and training may even cause a disruption in the operations
5. The trainees are not guaranteed a job at the end of their training period
6. The trainees are informed that they will not be paid for the time spent in training[26]

The question has been raised in the airline industry where flight attendants and reservation agents are trained before hiring. Most of these programs met the foregoing criteria and trainees were not considered employees.[27]

As for training programs for present employees, the criteria are similar. The time is not compensable under Wage and Hour Division rules if

1. The session is held outside of working hours
2. Attendance is, in fact, strictly voluntary
3. The training session is not directly related to the employee's job
4. The employee does not perform any productive work while attending the meeting or training session.

EXEMPT AND NONEXEMPT CLASSIFICATION

In most companies the control of overtime costs hinges very importantly on the classification of employees into exempt and nonexempt classifications. Since often only two or three employees may appear to be wrongly classified, the Department of Labor (DOL) may take the position that certain exempt employees should be nonexempt but that compliance with regulations is a question of fact for the courts to decide (sometimes called "gray areas"). Frequently DOL will not pursue its position in the courts for one or two employees. Further complicating decisions in gray areas is the fact that employers often classify an employee exempt by job title and may consider the employee a present—or soon to become—part of management. Changing the classification may become an employee relations problem even though the change may not be allowed by a strict interpretation of the regulations.

A few basic principles and some case law may give some guidance in dealing with this troublesome problem, but in the end each company must decide to what degree it is in compliance and whether the exposure to a possible violation is great enough to justify the employee relations problems that may be caused by making the necessary changes. Some managements will take the position that in questionable areas the employee relations problem overrides the exposure, and they will wait for the DOL or the courts to tell them that they are wrong.

The Salary Test

The act specifically exempts professional, executive, and administrative employees.[28] In determining whether an employee is exempt, Interpretative Bulletin 541[29] is helpful. The Wage and Hour Division uses a salary test to determine whether an employee is included under one of the exemptions. If an employee is paid over a certain salary (this is regularly increased by the department), an employee can spend 20 percent of work time in nonexempt work and still be considered exempt. (This is called the short test.)

---

[26]On time spent on meeting, see Wm. L. Richmond and Daniel L. Reynolds, "The Fair Labor Standards Act: A Potential Legal Constraint upon Quality Circles and Other Employee Participation Programs," *Labor Law Journal*, 37, no. 4 (April 1986), 244.

[27]See *Donovan* v. *American Airlines,* 686 F.2d 267(5th Cir. 1982).

[28]Sect. 13(a)(1). Besides exemptions for white-collar employees, the act has several other exemptions, such as motor carriers, air carriers, and agriculture workers.

[29]CFR Sect. 29, Part 541.

One of the first requirements of the salary test is that the employee must be paid a certain weekly salary and not be docked for working less than 40 hours or be subject to other forms of deductions. However, the salary test alone doesn't make an executive, professional, or administrative employee exempt. In *Donovan* v. *United Video, Inc.,* 725 F.2d 577 (10th Cir. 1984), the court said that although salary level was very important, it alone doesn't make the employee exempt. The duties of the job must also be considered.

Although the salary level will often prevent an audit of those job classifications that are above the level for the particular category, changing the salary or the job title will not make the employee exempt. The key to whether an executive, professional, administrative, or outside salesperson is exempt is what type of work is being performed.

Outside Salespersons

Another exempt classification is outside salespersons. Under Section 213(a)(1) of the act they are exempted if they sell regularly or obtain orders for goods or services while off the employer's premises. Comparatively speaking, this classification is less troublesome than administrative, professional, or executive classifications because the activities can objectively be defined.

Other Considerations in Determining Exemption

Most employees tend to stress the importance of their jobs. Often when interviewed by a compliance officer, they rate their jobs at a level higher than reality, which makes them exempt, but in fact they are nonexempt (unless they are complainants who feel that they are denied overtime pay). From an employee relations standpoint, the personnel practitioner tends to classify an employee as exempt in questionable cases. Another reason the employees are often classified as

exempt is that they can control their own overtime. One way to eliminate the problem is for the employer to make them exempt and hope that it can be defended in a wage-and-hour audit. Because there are many gray areas where exempt and nonexempt classifications are being interpreted for reasons other than payment of overtime, the employer is continually exposed to violations. A business decision is often necessary on whether to take the exposure for employee relations considerations or to strictly construe the act in order to avoid the penalties of back pay.

Recommendations for Exempt Classification

The first step in an exemption policy is to assign one person the responsibility for handling exemptions. This person should be given the final authority in each case to determine whether an employee is exempt or nonexempt. Every supervisor or manager has a special interest in making an employee exempt or nonexempt; often it has nothing to do with job content.

Certain guidelines should be established and communicated to all supervisors as to exempt or nonexempt classifications in those gray areas where the risk of violation is the greatest. Job descriptions should be developed for wage and hour compliance; they should include the distinctions in Bulletin 541. As a defensive measure, one should require employees to write their own job descriptions. The job descriptions should be reviewed by the supervisor or personnel department to ensure that all the activities are included. In compliance reviews when the investigator interviews the employee, it is difficult for the employee to change a position during the interview when the employee wrote the job description originally. (There is often an incentive to change job content if the employee becomes aware of the amount of back pay and when somebody else has written the job description.) Also when the job description is in writing, made out by the employee, the compliance officer is more likely to accept it.

Most job descriptions for wage and hour compliance either are too vague or merely follow the wording of the regulations and are therefore meaningless to determine exempt or nonexempt status. The best job descriptions for wage and hour compliance are those that list specific duties and their frequency of performance. The job description should pinpoint those activities that answer whether the exempt or nonexempt requirements are met. The job description for wage and hour compliance is for the purpose of documenting management position on the exempt or nonexempt classifications and may not be applicable for other purposes for which job descriptions are used, such as hiring, promotion, and compensation.

When determining exempt or nonexempt classifications there is no exposure to violations if an employee is wrongly classified as nonexempt and paid overtime. It is only when an employee is wrongly classified as exempt that the employer has liability for overtime pay. An employee can be misclassified as exempt for a considerable time and nothing happens until the employee complains and the Wage and Hour Division investigates and takes a position. For this reason, in those gray areas it is advisable to keep a record of hours worked by exempt employees, although it is not necessary under division rules.

One reason why exempt classifications are troublesome is that in the final analysis a part of the determination is subjective. The best example of this was where a fast-food chain had all their assistant managers classified as exempt supervisors and the Wage and Hour Division claimed that they were nonexempt employees. The court gave the following rules to determine whether assistant managers were supervisors:[30]

1. They must recommend hiring and firing.

2. They must direct the work of two or more persons.

3. They have management duties.

4. They regularly and customarily exercise discretion.

Two of the four requirements are subjective; the gray areas were not eliminated. In any given situation subjective determination must be made whether management duties existed and discretion was customarily and regularly exercised.

In determining whether an employee has an exempt status, three elements are necessary:

1. More weight must be placed on job duties that are usually considered exempt and less weight placed on job title. In *Blackmon* v. *Brookshire Grocery Co.*, 835 F.2d 1135 (5th Cir. 1988), the Court held that meat department managers were not supervisors when they spent two thirds of their time cutting meat.

2. The exempt duties must actually be performed and not just assigned or expected of the employee.[31]

3. The level of compensation should be above the minimum required for exempt classification in that category.

When in doubt about an employee's status, it may be advisable to check with the local Department of Labor, Wage and Hour Division. The caller does not have to give an identification, but even if he or she does, the Wage and Hour Division does not usually follow up these calls with an investigation, since this takes an employee complaint. In addition to the interpretative bulletins mentioned elsewhere in this chapter, the *Wage and Hour Field Operations Handbook* and *Guidebook to Federal Wage-Hour Laws* are very instructive. These guidelines should be in the possession of the person who is responsible for administration of

---

[30]*Donovan* v. *Burger King*, 672 F.2d 221 (1st Cir. 1982).

[31]In *Brock* v. *Norman's Country Market, Inc.*, 825 F.2d 823 (11th Cir. 1988), the Court said time is not the only factor in determining executive duties; whether those are discretionary supervisory functions must be considered.

the act. They can be obtained at a nominal cost from the Wage and Hour Division office or the Government Printing Office.

CONTROLLING OVERTIME COSTS

One of the difficult problems for the employer in the control of overtime costs is that many times the employee's desire to earn overtime pay is stronger than any action that the employer can take. A waste control clerk or sales service expeditor can always find a reason to work overtime when money is needed to buy a new boat.[32] The first step in the control of overtime is to remove from the employee as much as possible the decision of when overtime should be worked. This can be done by a communicated policy of requiring authorization before overtime can be worked. The enforcement of the rule of requiring authorization must be by discipline; the mere promulgation of a rule is not enough. It is the duty of the employer to enforce it;[33] if the employee works the overtime, it must be paid for. The Wage and Hour Division takes the position that unauthorized overtime still must be paid if known or tolerated; the courts sustain this position.

The employer can adopt many different procedures to control the costs of overtime payments required by the FLSA. A complete approach to the problem requires consideration of individual steps to be taken in each area of exposure.

Compensatory Time Off

Because the law requires that overtime be paid only after 40 hours in one work week, compensatory time off can be given any time during the work week in order to avoid over-

time payment. Overtime hours worked in one week cannot be offset by a subsequent work week or by providing compensatory time off at a later date, unless otherwise exempt, as in the health care industry.[34]

Where the employer pays premium pay for time worked such as for working on a holiday or double time for working on Sundays, the premium pay may be excluded from the employee's regular rate and credited toward overtime pay where the employee works more than 40 hours in the work week in which the premium pay was granted. Under this rule an employee could work 42 hours in the week where double time was granted and not be paid overtime for work over 40 hours. However, this policy may cause some employee relations problems. (Many collective bargaining agreements provide that holiday pay be considered time worked for purposes of overtime.)

The Belo Contract

The Belo contract is a guaranteed wage contract made with the nonexempt employee where hours vary widely from week to week. This plan is an effective method to control overtime where the employee can control hours of work. It is widely used for field repair service, customer service jobs, and other situations where the job requires work off the premises by nonexempt employees.

The conditions necessary to qualify for a Belo contract were stated by the Supreme Court in *Walling* v. *Belo Corp.*, 317 U.S. 706 (1941). The court listed five requirements:[35]

1. The duties of the job covered by the contract must require all irregular number of hours per week. This is the key requirement. The fluctuation must not be caused by economic conditions or employer control but by job duties of the employee.

---

[32]The author once made a study of overtime for nonexempt group leaders and found that their overtime increased before they went on vacation and before Christmas.

[33]29 CFR Sects. 778.316 and 785.11 and 785.13. Also see *Lindow* v. *United States*, 738 F.2d 1057 (9th Cir. 1984).

[34]*Opinion Letter* no. 971 (Washington, DC: Department of Labor, Wage and Hour Division, March 26, 1974).

[35]This is enforceable, although an agreement to waive the provisions of the act is not.

2. Hours must fluctuate below as well as above 40 hours per week.[36]
3. The contract must pay the employee a regular hourly rate above the statutory minimum wage requirements.
4. The weekly guarantees must pay at least one and one-half times the regular rate for all hours over 40.
5. The contract cannot cover more than 60 hours a week.

Exhibit 12-1 is a Belo contract that complies with these requirements, except total hours agreed upon.

The total hours inserted in the last line must bear a "reasonable relationship to the hours an employee actually works." This is usually determined in the first contract by past overtime records. However, the actual hours worked before a Belo contract is usually greater than what is worked after the

---

[36]*Donovan* v. *McKissick Products Co.*, 719 F.2d 350 (10th Cir. 1983).

employee is paid for a set number of hours per week under the new arrangement. When the incentive to work overtime is removed by the Belo contract, the overtime hours usually decrease with no effect on job performance. To anticipate a decrease in hours by entering less than the previous average would not be in violation of the Belo requirements but may result in poor employee relations. A better plan would be to review the contract in six months or a year and base the average hours on the experience under the Belo contract.

In the second contract term, the hours could be reduced if the average shows it but should not be reduced to the average. Otherwise the employee is not being rewarded for efforts in doing the work in fewer hours.

Compliance and Overtime Control

Supervisors should be made aware that if the employee is required or permitted to work

EXHIBIT 12-1 *Belo Contract*

_____(Company Name)_____ hereby agrees to employ _____(Name of Employee)_____ as _____ at a regular hourly rate of pay of $_____ per hour for the first forty (40) hours in any work week and at the rate of at least time and one-half or $_____ per hour for all hours in excess of forty (40) in any work week, with the guarantee that _____ (Name of Employee)_____ will receive in any work week in which he or she performs any work for the company the sum of $_____ as total compensation for all hours performed up to and including (insert the total hours agreed upon; however, hours agreed upon cannot exceed 60 hours per week) hours.

COMPANY NAME
By _____

Accepted:

_____(Employee's Signature)_____

for the employer's benefit, the employee must be paid—usually on an overtime basis. When a policy is adopted that all overtime must be authorized, it must be enforced. Like any other policy, if it is not enforced, it creates an environment of false security in the belief that unauthorized overtime is not compensable.

Compliance with any statute starts with knowing the requirements of that statute. The employee relations consequences must be integrated with any policy of compliance. The decision then becomes a business decision, with consideration given to the legal exposure.

For the employer to control overtime, two strong positions must be taken. One is enforcement of a strong overtime policy that as much as possible removes the control of hours from the employee. Second, where control of overtime hours cannot be removed from the employee and exempt status cannot be justified, the Belo contract or some other pay plan should be considered. If a pay plan other than Belo is considered, it should be reviewed by the Wage and Hour Division to determine what position the division will take in the event of a compliance review.

DEFINITION OF INDEPENDENT CONTRACTOR

Employers are sometimes tempted to avoid the costs and responsibilities associated with the employer-employee relationship by claiming that those who perform certain services are independent contractors. If an independent contractor relationship is in fact established, the employer can avoid

1. The requirements of the Fair Labor Standards Act
2. The payment of unemployment compensation payroll taxes
3. The payment of Social Security taxes
4. Withholding of city, state, and federal income taxes
5. Workers compensation coverage

Obviously, there is considerable economic advantage in avoiding these statutory requirements. There is strong incentive for establishing an independent contractor relationship wherever possible, but there are also certain risks in doing so.

Risks in Independent Contractor Relationship

While the advantages are great, so are the risks if the court finds that an independent contractor is in fact an employee. No statute defines the exact meaning of an independent contractor. The interpretation is left entirely to the courts, using agency guidelines. The principal liabilities when it is determined that an independent contractor is an employee are

1. Failure to withhold under IRS regulations and therefore the employer is liable for the amount of the employee's tax plus interest
2. Overtime or minimum wages under the Fair Labor Standards Act
3. Right to join a union under the National Labor Relations Act
4. Liability to the state for unemployment compensation insurance tax
5. Failure to carry workers compensation insurance, so the employer becomes liable under the common law for a work-related injury
6. Failure to pay Social Security taxes; under IRS regulations the employer is liable for its share plus what is owed by the employee plus interest

To determine whether or not an independent contractor relationship exists, one must look to the common law, the IRS code, the National Labor Relations Board cases, decisions under the Fair Labor Standards Act, state agencies' positions on workers compensation coverage, and liability for unemployment insurance.

Most of these agencies use either all or part of the common law definition, but some put more stress on certain factors than others. For example, the NLRB looks only at the control factor, while the IRS looks to see whether or not it was a businesslike operation.

For the purposes of this section the common law guidelines will be used, but the interpretation of the agency should be reviewed before creating an independent contractor.

Guidelines to Establish Independent Contractor

The courts have said on numerous occasions that no one element establishes an independent contractor relationship. The historic base for determining whether such a relationship exists comes from the law of agency. An attempt to define the distinction between an employee and an independent contractor was made by the Restatement of the Law of Agency,[37] which stated

While an employee acts under the direction and control of the employer, an independent contractor contracts to produce a certain result and has full control over the means and methods that shall be used in producing the result. He is usually said to carry on an independent business.

To determine whether an independent contractor relationship exists, the following questions should be asked. A favorable answer to one does not make the person an independent contractor; several definitive answers are necessary, especially to 1, 2, 3, and 4.

1. Who supervises and employs the workers, and who pays Social Security, workers compensation taxes, and so on?
2. Who controls the progress of the work except for completion and final inspection?
3. Does the nature of the work imply independence?
4. Who controls how the work should be done as distinguished from what should be done?
5. Does the person perform similar work for other employers?

6. Is the work to be performed for a fixed price and for a fixed amount of services? [Make sure the number of hours is considered when determining fixed amount. *Cedotal* v. *Forti dba Bayou Truck Stop,* 516 So.2d 405 (La. App. 1988).]
7. Who invests in the equipment?
8. Is it a business including risks, profits, and losses, as compared to an employer-employee relationship?
9. If the work is defective, who pays for it?

Case Law on Independent Contractor Relationship

The Supreme Court has said that not only should an independent contractor have independence in the performance of the assigned job but initiative and decision-making authority should also be associated with the independent contractor. Otherwise an employer-employee relationship exists.[38]

The major factor in the determination of independent contractor status is the degree of control. The more control, the more likely the worker will be found to be an employee. A person who is required to comply with instructions about when, where, and how to work is ordinarily an employee. Some employees who are experienced or proficient in their work need little instruction; however, this does not put them in an independent contractor status, because the control element is present if the employer retains the right to instruct. For the purpose of determining an employer/employee relationship under the National Labor Relations Act, the board applies only the right of control test. If the person for whom services are performed retains the right of control of the end result and also the manner and reasoning to be used in reaching that result, an employer-employee relationship exists.[39]

---

[37]Restatement of the Law of Agency, 2d Sect. 220, 1958, 485.

---

[38]*NLRB* v. *United Insurance Co.,* 390 U.S. 254 (1968).

[39]In The Big East Conference, 282 NLRB No. 50 (1986), the board held that basketball referees were independent contractors. They had considerable control over which assignments they would take, they were paid by the game, and they had to pay an assessment to the college association to receive an assignment.

It is difficult not to retain the right to instruct for a person who works for the employer eight hours a day in one job and cleans the office at night or mows the lawn on Saturday. If an employer-employee relationship exists, overtime compensation is due for all hours worked over 40 unless the flat fee paid for cleaning the office exceeds what the employee would have received on a time and one-half basis under the Fair Labor Standards Act.

If an employer assumes that an independent contractor relationship exists and in fact it does not exist, the exposure in other areas is far greater than the payment of overtime. There is no insurance coverage of workers compensation for the independent contractor; if a person is hurt and an employer-employee relationship in fact existed, the employer is liable even though there is no workers compensation insurance coverage. Income tax withholding, unemployment compensation, and Social Security withholding and payments by the employer are required for an employee but not for an independent contractor. If the employer is wrong as to the relationship, the employer is liable for all payments, including the employee's withholding and Social Security payments. Because of this exposure the employer should be cautious when treating the relationship as independent contractor status.

Examples of Employer-Employee Relationship

To prevent exposure to liability where an employer assumes an independent contractor relationship exists but an employer-employee relationship legally exists, some examples may be helpful.

Where a gasoline distributor leased stations to operators, the court found that not only was the lessee an employee, but those persons whom the lessee hired were also employees of the distributor. The evidence showed that the distributor controlled the hours of operation, prices of major items, and daily management of money and took the risk of profits and loss. The court reasoned that the employees of the lessee were an integral part of the operation; therefore, they were also employees of the distributors and the lessee.[40] Other cases where the court found an employee-employer relationship are where an agent who operated a retail cleaning outlet under a contract was held to be an employee of the owner[41] and where crew leaders for a builder registered under a state law as labor contractors but were in practice employees.[42] In the Fifth Circuit a contract laborer who was a mechanic and supervisor was held to be an employee; however, where the contract laborer was a concrete subcontractor of this employee, he was held to be an independent contractor.[43]

Checklist to Create Independent Contractor

Because of the risks involved and the possibility of litigation, employers should have a very strong reason for attempting to establish an independent contractor relationship. If such a reason does exist, then it is advisable to state specifically in the agreement that

1. The only supervision will be related to result and not to method
2. The relationship is not permanent
3. Inasmuch as possible, the individual will make the investment in equipment
4. The independent contractor will be responsible for the profit or loss of the operation
5. In all other respects the independent contractor will be performing as a separate business

The "economic reality" of the relationship is the strongest element in establishing an

---

[40]*Marshall* v. *Truman Arnold Distributing Co.*, 640 F.2d 906 (8th Cir. 1981).

[41]*Donovan* v. *Sureway Cleaners*, 656 F.2d 1368 (9th Cir. 1981).

[42]*Marshall* v. *Presidio Valley Farms, Inc.*, 512 F.Supp. 1195 (W.D. Tex. 1981).

[43]*Donovan* v. *Techo, Inc.*, 642 F.2d 141 (5th Cir. 1981).

independent contractor relationship that will stand the scrutiny of the courts and the regulatory bodies. If such a relationship is intended, it must be objectively established. Careful consideration of all the elements necessary to establish the independent contractor relationship is necessary if the employer is to be on the safe side.

Creating an independent contractor status is one way to control overtime. Extreme care should be taken to make certain that although an independent contractor status was intended, an actual employee-employer relationship does not exist. Liability for uninsured workers compensation and payment of unemployment, Social Security, and withholding taxes often offsets the advantages of establishing a questionable independent contractor status. In any independent contractor status a written contract should be executed and contain the requirement of independent contractors outlined in this section. Professional advice should also be considered when establishing an independent contractor relationship that may be questionable.

CHAPTER 13

CONTROL OF UNEMPLOYMENT COMPENSATION COSTS

Historical Basis for Unemployment Compensation
Provisions of State Laws
The Use of Appeal Proceedings
Policies and Practices to Reduce Costs

The stated purpose of unemployment compensation laws is to provide benefits for those persons who are unemployed through no fault of their own. For over 50 years, unemployment compensation insurance has been considered one of the most successful social insurance programs. The major objective has a social origin, that is, to provide unemployed workers the means of getting through a temporary period of involuntary unemployment without having to turn to welfare and without having to meet the "need test" as in traditional welfare programs. Some economists also state that unemployment compensation benefits serve to aid in slowing down recessionary pressures by getting money into the business community at a time when it is most needed.

HISTORICAL BASIS FOR UNEMPLOYMENT COMPENSATION

Unemployment compensation insurance is by no means a new idea. Many trade unions at the beginning of the nineteenth century provided aid for their members forced into temporary idleness. By the middle of the nineteenth century, this type of benefit was found in England, Germany, Austria, Belgium, Norway, Sweden, and Denmark. The first public unemployment compensation insurance appeared in 1898, when the city of Ghent passed a local ordinance that supplemented the benefits provided by the trade unions. In 1911 England established the first compulsory unemployment compensation system.

In the United States, as in European countries, the beginnings of unemployment compensation are found in trade union benefit plans. Such plans appeared in the 1830's, the first established by a New York printers' local in 1831. From this period to 1937, unemployment compensation was provided either by trade unions, by joint plans arising from agreement between employers and unions, or by private voluntary plans established by individual employers.

At the beginning of the twentieth century there was a movement to establish a public compulsory unemployment compensation plan; as early as 1916 a bill was introduced in the Massachusetts legislature. More than 20 other states followed. It was not until 1932 that the first state (Wisconsin) passed a statewide compulsory plan. Some states hesitated to pass unemployment compensation legislation as it would put them at a competitive disadvantage over other states that would not pass it.

This competitive concern of the various states caused pressure for legislation on the federal level. The argument whether the states or the federal government should do it delayed action by both federal and state legislative bodies. By 1934 the federal concept had won half the battle; unemployment compensation was included in the Social Security Act. The unemployment compensation section of the act provides that the federal government would set certain minimum standards but leave it to the states to decide which type of plan best suited their needs. However, if a state had no plan or if the state law was not in compliance with the federal law, the employers would still be taxed but the tax would not be returned to the states for unemployment compensation benefits. (Needless to say, all 50 states passed laws.). These historical developments, continuing up to the present time, have influenced legislative bodies and the courts to consider the program an established employee benefit, and for this reason the laws in the various states are given a liberal interpretation by administrative agencies and the courts.

Financing of Benefits

The system is financed by two taxes, one by the states to finance state benefits paid and one by the Internal Revenue Service to finance state and federal administrative costs. In the 6.2 percent federal tax of the first $7,000 in wages paid to each employee, a credit of 5.4 percent is given to the employers for the state tax paid. This leaves .8 percent to be used to finance state and federal administrative costs and to maintain a loan fund for the states to borrow from when they exhaust their funds available to pay benefits.

State taxes are usually based on a "flexible" taxable wage base; increases in the wage base automatically follow increases in statewide wage levels. The taxable wage base ranges from $14,500 to $28,500. This may seem complicated, but the result is that the national average cost to the employer for both state and federal unemployment compensation taxes was $145 per employee in 1984. This is a decrease from the $173 per employee in 1980.[1] In all states, only the employer is taxed for unemployment compensation benefits.

Although the states are free to develop their own plan, most states follow the model plan recommended by the federal government. Also, through funding regulations the federal government retains a degree of control and forces some standardization among the various states.

PROVISIONS OF STATE LAWS

Although the federal government requires certain conformity provisions before the employer as taxpayer is granted tax credits under the Internal Revenue code, the states have considerable flexibility to design their own program. To ensure that the unemployment compensation payments are in keeping with the intent of the federal law, it is necessary for the states to establish eligibility requirements, benefit amounts, and reasons why an unemployed individual initially should be denied benefits or be disqualified from receiving further benefits.

In developing rules to determine the right to receive benefits, states have generally followed the principle that unemployment compensation is intended to provide temporary financial assistance to persons who are out of work through no fault of their own. In order to carry out the main intent of the act, state laws require eligible claimants to remain available for work and to be seeking work actively or face the loss of benefits. This requirement is loosely administered in many states.

Constitutional Restrictions

Although the federal law permitted the various states to pass their own unemployment compensation statutes, they are limited in what they can do by the U.S. Constitution. Where one state denied benefits when an employee voluntarily quit for religious reasons, the Supreme Court held that this was a violation of the First Amendment.[2] The Supreme Court also struck down a Utah statute that denied benefits to pregnant women without regard to physical capacity to continue working. The court found this a violation of the Fourteenth Amendment.[3]

The key in the Turner case was that the employee could continue to work. The court allowed the state of Missouri to deny benefits if the employee leaves the job for pregnancy and there are no openings when she is able to return. The court in *Wimberly* v. *Labor and Industrial Relations Commission,* 107 S.Ct. 821 (1987), stated that pregnancy is not a jobrelated illness and as long as pregnancy leaves are not treated differently from other illnesses it is legal to deny benefits.

The court will generally hold that a state cannot deny benefits when the employee is protected by an antidiscrimination law. In one case an employee joined a church two and a half years after employment that prohibited working on Saturdays. She informed her employer that she could no longer work on Saturdays because of her new religion.

---

[1]*Source:* National Foundation for Unemployment Compensation and Worker's Compensation (March 1987).

[2]*Thomas* v. *Review Board of Indiana Employment Security Div.,* 101 S.Ct. 1425 (1981).

[3]*Turner* v. *Department of Employment and Security of Utah,* 423 U.S. 44 (1975).

She was discharged because of her refusal to work in the jewelry store on Friday nights and Saturday. The court held that she could not be denied benefits under the state law because this would be a violation of the First Amendment, although she joined the church after being employed and worked on Saturdays until Saturday became her Sabbath.[4]

When New York gave unemployment compensation benefits to strikers, the court held that it was not a violation of any clause in the Constitution and it was within the authority of the state to do so.[5] However, in *Brown* v. *A.J. Gerard Mfg. Co.*, 695 F.2d 1290 (11th Cir. 1983), the circuit court held that unemployment compensation could not be deducted from a Title VII back pay award.

Variation of Benefit Levels

One way to instill an incentive to seek to work is to establish benefit levels that pay only a portion of the wages that an employee would have received if fully employed.

On the other side of the problem, the states want the benefit level high enough to cover the claimant's nondeferrable expenses. Usually, this is a weekly benefit equal to about 50 percent of the claimant's normal weekly wage. Other states use the claimant's average weekly wage as a guideline for determining benefits.

Some states have the absolute minimum and maximum based on the employee's weekly earnings; others determine the minimum and maximum on the average statewide annual wage. The minimum benefit requires a certain level of earnings; if an employee earns below a level, no benefits are paid.

About 14 states provide for the payment of dependents' allowances. Although there is some variation, generally a dependent must be wholly or mainly supported by the claimant or living with or receiving regular support from the claimant. All states include children, and in some states only, children and/or spouses are considered dependents. The amount of benefits is usually a fixed sum, but in a few states it depends upon the number of dependents.

In almost all states, the waiting period to receive benefits is one week, although a few states pay benefits on the first day of unemployment. All states have a maximum potential duration of 26 weeks.

Disqualifications for Benefits

All states have provisions seeking to carry out the intent of the law that benefits should be paid only to unemployed workers who are out of work through no fault of their own. The laws of the various states, in order to carry out this principle, have disqualification provisions such as voluntary quit without good cause, misconduct that results in discharge, refusal to accept suitable work offers without good cause, receipt of other payments while unemployed, involvement in labor dispute, and fraud.

Each state has certain procedures to be followed for obtaining facts involved in a disputed claim. The state agency set up for payment of compensation claims makes a determination whether the claimant is disqualified;[6] the employer or claimant may appeal and request a hearing. The decision of the hearing referee as to disqualification may be appealed to a higher reviewing authority within the department. Subsequent appeals then may be carried to the state courts unless a constitutional question is involved over which the U.S. Supreme Court has jurisdiction.

When it is determined that a claimant is disqualified from benefits, some states merely postpone the benefits for a period of time, while other states deny benefits for the entire period of unemployment.

---

[4]*Hobbie* v. *Unemployment Appeals Commission of Florida*, 107 S.Ct. 1046 (1987).

[5]*New York Telephone Co.* v. *New York State Department of Labor*, 440 U.S. 519 (1979).

[6]For further information on disqualification, see "Highlights of State Unemployment Compensation Laws," National Foundation for Unemployment Compensation and Worker's Compensation (January 1987), pp. 56–70.

All claimants, in order to qualify for benefits, must be able to work and be available for suitable work.[7] If a claimant refuses suitable work without good cause, she or he will be disqualified for benefits. Since disqualification for benefits is the provision of the law that the practitioner encounters most often, each type of disqualification will be considered separately.

Qualification of Income. Whenever the claimant is receiving any type of income, the employer should always question whether or not such income is disqualifying, since many times it is. Such income as holiday, vacation, and back pay may be disqualifying in some states. Even though the statute may not be specific as to kinds of income, any income could be considered disqualifying, since the claimant then doesn't need financial assistance. The state laws require that the claimant be unemployed and available for work, and the receipt of any income from a physical disability would raise a question as to whether the claimant is available for work. Pension payments indicate retirement from the labor market and therefore that the claimant is not available for work. The federal law requires states to reduce the weekly benefit amount of any individual by the weekly amount of a governmental or other pension, retirement, severance pay, or any other payment based on previous work of the individual.

This requirement applies only to payments made or contributed to by a base-period or chargeable employer. States may also reduce the benefits on less than a dollar-for-dollar basis in order to take into account any contributions made by the worker to the retirement plan.

Voluntary Quit without Good Cause. Benefits are paid to persons who are out of work through no fault of their own. It would therefore follow that a voluntary quit would automatically disqualify. Every state disqualifies from benefits individuals who bring about or perpetuate their own unemployment, either because they quit their job without good cause, committed work-related misconduct, or refused suitable work. Most states disqualify until minimum requirements are met for a new base period, but some states just provide for a reduction in benefits.

The issue in all these cases is whether or not there is voluntary quit without a cause attributable to the employer. Often there is a fine line between a voluntary quit and a discharge. In most states a quit is defined when the employee exercises directly or indirectly a free-will choice to terminate the employment relationship. Wherever possible, the employer should call a separation a voluntary quit, such as where the employee fails to report for work after a certain number of days. On the other hand, discharge is usually defined as an employer action that indicates to the employee that his or her services are no longer wanted. Where a supervisor had a heated argument with an employee, the employee walked away toward the door, and the supervisor said, "Keep on walking," this was a discharge. If the supervisor had let him walk through the door, however, it would probably have been a voluntary quit.[8] Quitting to avoid being discharged is usually held to be a cause not attributable to the employer and benefits are denied.[9] Also, a good personal reason is not usually considered enough of a justification to leave a job, and the claimant is disqualified.

However, a voluntary quit because of harassment or other unreasonable working conditions would be considered a good cause and benefits would be allowed. This often comes up where the claimant alleges sexual harassment. With the socialistic foundation

---

[7]In *Idaho Dept. of Employment* v. *Smith*, 434 U.S. 100 (1977), the court held that a state can deny benefits to a claimant who is attending school, but cannot if the claimant is attending night school, since she or he would be available for work.

[8]*Brown* v. *Port of Sunnyside Club, Inc.*, 304 N.W. 2d 877 (Minn. 1981).

[9]See *Boneiovanni* v. *Vanlor Investments*, 370 N.W. 2d 828 (Minn. App. 1985) for a discussion of a quit.

of unemployment compensation, it doesn't take much harassment to find that a quit was in fact constructive discharge.

Disqualification for Misconduct. This is the most common issue in disqualification proceedings. Misconduct that results in disqualification is defined as "conduct resulting in such willful or wanton substantial disregard of the employer's interests." Misconduct was first defined in *Boynton Cab Co.* v. *Newbeck*, 296 N.W. 2d 636 (Wis. 1941), and is one those rare decisions that was adopted by all the states. Often the employer confuses willful misconduct with inability or negligence. If a school bus driver has three accidents in 30 days, this may not be misconduct but only negligence, which is not disqualifying. If an employee throws paper, swears, and insults the boss, this may be misconduct but it would have to be shown that the incident was a substantial disregard for the employer's interests. The term usually means something different to the employer from what it means to the agency or appeal referee, as illustrated in the case history on page 228.

In misconduct cases the burden is on the employer to show that

1. An existing rule was violated
2. The rule was communicated to the employee prior to the violation
3. A direct causal relationship existed between the offenses committed and the discharge

It is important to remember that the longer the interval between the offense and the discharge, the less chance there is for sustaining the discharge before an appeal referee. Normally, an act is considered misconduct when

1. It is not an isolated incident (unless gross misconduct such as a felony is involved)
2. It is detrimental to the employer's best interests (usually a monetary consideration)
3. It takes place during working hours on the employer's premises
4. The employee's act disregards job duties that were previously defined and communicated by the employer.

If the act by the employee meets this definition and is well documented, it will usually be considered misconduct. However, a failure to prove misconduct doesn't necessarily mean that employer's account will be charged. If misconduct evidence is strong, the employer should argue that the cause of the separation was not attributable to the employer. The burden is then on the claimant to show that he or she did not cause the separation from employment.

In controlling unemployment compensation insurance costs, there is no substitute for clear policies that are communicated to the employee. The communication should be in such a manner that there is no doubt that when the employee commits an act of misconduct, he or she will be fully aware that if the employer learns about the act, disciplinary action will be taken. If these conditions are met, the employer will have a much easier task in showing that misconduct occurred.

THE USE OF APPEAL PROCEEDINGS

If the claimant or the employer objects to a determination made by the agency, either party has the right to appeal. Although in some cases the employer may appeal the tax liability, tax rate, or benefit overpayment, the most common type of appeal concerns rights to benefits. Issues such as ability to work, unavailability for work, or failure to accept suitable work may arise after benefits have been received, and the question of whether the employee is eligible for benefits must be considered periodically.

The appeal must be filed within a specified time, which varies from state to state. In all states the time limit allows no exceptions. The agency loses jurisdiction if the appeal is not made within the time limits, and the appeal is lost forever. Failure to file an appeal within the specified time limits is one of the most common reasons that employers lose appeals. Often the determination notice from the agency goes to the employer's Tax

INSUBORDINATION OR MISCONDUCT—A CASE HISTORY

Perhaps a case history will explain better the difference between what the employer feels is the reason for the discharge and the guidelines used by the agency.

An employee was discharged for refusing to conduct a training program. The employer requested that he conduct the program as he had done before. In his own mind, however, the employee was insecure about doing the program. He was discharged for refusing to conduct the training program, but the reason given for the discharge was insubordination.[10]

In discharge cases, the burden is on the employer to show that insubordination is misconduct and thus a disqualification for receiving benefits. In the employer's mind, insubordination was the direct refusal to follow an order that did not involve the employee's personal safety. Under this definition refusal to conduct a training program that the employee had conducted before— and with performance that the employer considered satisfactory—was insubordination.

There was a serious question as to whether

---

[10]*Insubordination* is defined as a refusal to obey a reasonable order. There is always a question of what is reasonable.

the action was misconduct under the definition used by the agency. Under case law followed in every jurisdiction, misconduct is "wanton, willful, and substantial disregard for the employer's interest." The employee was insecure about conducting the program. Did the failure to do so show a "substantial disregard for the employer's interest"? Does failure to conduct a training program result in direct economic loss to the employer? This would be difficult to show.

Under these facts the discharge could not be for willful conduct. The employee was insecure in doing the training, so his failure to train would have to substantially affect the employer's interest. This would be difficult to do because somebody else could do the training or failure to train would not cause an economic hardship.

An employer should never let the possibility of unemployment compensation benefits interfere with the decision to discharge, but once that decision has been made the method used in the discharge will sometimes determine whether the employee will receive benefits. In the case outlined above, the discharge would be most difficult to defend. Other alternatives for getting the same result would have been better.

---

or Finance department and gets put aside or the person responsible is away on vacation or sick. As a result all chances of appeal are lost. When the person regularly responsible is not available, provision should be made for a substitute.

Preparations for an Appeal

In preparing for an appeal hearing, it is important to determine what the issue is. Take the facts you developed for the claims

deputy and compare them with the reasons given for the determination. To prepare for the presentation before the appeals referee, the first step is to examine the statement that the claimant made to the agency in comparison with the one you made. If an inconsistency is apparent—as is usually the case— you must seek facts to prove the validity of your statement.

Witnesses are often required. If they are, they should be prepared before the hearing. Some referees question the claimant before you have a chance to do so. You should anticipate this possibility in preparing your case. The proceeding is mostly fact finding and is nonlegal. Formal rules of evidence usually are not observed, and seldom is any evidence excluded. When in doubt, put it in.

You can object to the remarks or evidence admitted, but it is advisable to do so in a nonlegal way. Have as many exhibits as possible. There is no substitute for having the person who made the statement come to the hearing and testify. When it is difficult to get operating people to document their actions, the best way to ensure documentation in the future is to have the supervisor testify. Frequently the testimony will induce the claimant to deny previous statements and the importance of the document becomes obvious. You then will have less problem in getting documentation from the supervisor in the future.

If you think that there are some legal arguments, it is best to present them in writing and to seek help in preparing the memorandum. If your theory is unusual, you may want to provide a short memorandum citing similar situations where the courts or the agency has held the way you are arguing. You should also take advantage of the opportunity to make a summary—called a closing statement in legal proceedings. It is not necessary to quote a lot of authority, but it is useful to the referee for you to summarize your position and the reasons you think benefits should be denied.

After the hearing, the referee will take the case under advisement and later render a decision. The proceedings are recorded either by tape or by court reporters. In most states, however, a transcript is seldom made unless the case is appealed to the commissioner level. You should always consider an appeal to the commissioner level when you receive an adverse determination that you feel is not sound. Sometimes certain witnesses were not available at the time of the hearing or certain evidence was overlooked. At the commissioner level it may be proper to ask for a remand so that the new evidence can be considered. For example, if a key person was in Florida for the winter and it was not possible to get the hearing postponed, you might have had to go ahead with the best effort you could make. If, when you got the decision, it became apparent that the testimony of the person in Florida may have changed the position of the referee, a request for a remand is in order and would probably be granted.

The hearing at the commissioner level follows the same nonlegal format as the first hearing. It is advisable to prepare a memorandum before the hearing stating your position and the reasons for the appeal. This statement should not introduce any new evidence but simply point out that based on the evidence presented, the determination of the examiner was in error. If new evidence not previously available is to be introduced, the memorandum should request a remand.

Reasons for Unsuccessful Appeals

Research by the author with hearing referees has revealed that most cases are lost not on the merits but on the way they were presented. All too often the people directly involved in the case do not testify. Witnesses are not properly instructed on what the case is all about or they don't take the task seriously.[11]

Most appeals proceedings are lost for the following reasons:

1. Witnesses do not have actual knowledge of the facts. Whenever possible the supervisor should testify on what happened. A statement by the personnel practitioner who does not have first-hand information is less effective. Usually hearsay evidence can be admitted, but conclusions and findings of fact cannot rely solely on hearsay evidence. Some direct evidence is needed to establish the facts.

---

[11]In the opinion of one commissioner's representative, the worst witnesses are from accounts, the next worst witnesses are personnel directors, and the third worst witness is the CEO.

2. Proper documentation of facts was not available at the hearing. Often employees forget what really happened, so they testify to facts that give the best case. By the time they get to a hearing, they have a fair knowledge of what favorable facts are. Often it is difficult to get a supervisor to document warnings, statements, or other action taken when dealing with the employee before termination. The best way to present the case is to have the supervisor attend the hearing where the employee forgets everything the supervisor did but remembers everything he did not do.

3. The employer fails to give a clear reason for termination. Since the employee's and employer's reason for termination is often different, the employer's reason must have strong supporting circumstances to refute the employee's statement. Often the employer gives one reason for termination when giving reference checks, another for unemployment compensation, and a third for a grievance procedure. The employer should decide on the reason for termination based on facts and not change it to fit a specific situation.

The legal structure to pay unemployment compensation benefits only where employees are out of work through no fault of their own is available to the employer; all the practitioner must do is use it properly.

Use of Attorneys in the Appeal Process

In the preceding paragraphs it has been shown that the appeal procedure is a nonlegal process, yet many employers feel more secure if an attorney represents them. The increased complexity of the appeals process has led to more of a need for representation than in the past. However, getting too legal in a process that is basically nonlegal is often fatal. As in other areas of personnel law, we must get a little more legal than in the past, but not to the extent of transferring an administrative hearing into a court setting.[12]

Even the courts recognize that nonattorneys can represent the parties before referees. In *Henize* v. *Giles,* 490 N.E. 2d 585 (1986), the Ohio Supreme Court held that nonattorneys could represent parties before referees and the Ohio Board of Review in unemployment matters. The court in reaching this conclusion noted that the informal nature of unemployment insurance proceedings, the cost to the parties of retaining attorneys, the right to judicial review, and the long-standing practice were instrumental in their reaching the decision of permitting laypersons to represent the parties.

In Colorado the Supreme Court found that representation in unemployment proceedings was the practice of law. However, the court went on to grant permission for laypersons to continue to represent the parties. It found that "as a matter of public policy, the benefits of the present system of lay representation served the best interests of the public.[13] Michigan and New Jersey also have joined the vast majority of the states that permit nonattorneys to appear before the Employment Security Commission's referee hearing as representatives of employers.[14]

One of the problems of representation is that one party may bring an attorney while the other does not. There are situations where this could be advantageous and if the other party had known she or he would have been represented by counsel. Usually the referee does not know until the hearing who is going to be represented, and this makes it even more difficult to determine whether representation is needed.

It is the author's position that in most cases the practitioner should have assistance preparing the case, but it is better for

---

[12]For a complete discussion on the use of counsel in unemployment proceedings, see *The Labor Lawyer,* 4, no. 1 (Winter 1988), 69.

[13]*Unauthorized Practice of Law Committee of the Supreme Court of Colorado* v. *Employer Unity Inc.,* 716 P. 2d 460 (Colo. 1986).

[14]For the American Bar Association position, see "Report of the Committee on Benefits to Unemployed Persons," *The Labor Lawyer,* 4, no. 3 (Summer 1988), 644.

the persons involved to present their own case than to have an attorney do so. If the case is worth spending the money on an attorney (in very few can savings justify the cost of an attorney), it is the appeal at the commissioner level at which counsel is most needed. At the first appeal level legal assistance in preparing the case is recommended, however.

POLICIES AND PRACTICES TO REDUCE COSTS

Unemployment compensation disputes all start with the termination process. Although many states have laws that disqualify the claimants from receiving benefits if they quit voluntarily, many types of resignations can result in benefits being paid. Employers often invite this result by giving an ambiguous or wrong reason for the termination. An employee who voluntarily resigns is usually disqualified from benefits if the termination results from one of the following:

- General job dissatisfaction because of
  —lack of advancement
  —low wages, or
  —too much travel
- Failure to request or return from a leave of absence
- Failure to attempt to remedy a work situation first with the employer (this is particularly damaging to the claim for benefits)
- Marital or domestic situations

The following reasons for termination are considered a good basis for benefit claims unless the state law disqualifies all voluntary quits:

- Health reasons
- The employer moves to a location outside the commuting area
- Substantial reduction in wages and/or a major change in job duties and/or hours (the validity of this reason is highly dependent on judgment about how extreme conditions are)

- Forced or requested resignation (opportunity to quit before being discharged)

As you can see from the preceding lists, one of the most difficult and important problems is being sure that the proper procedure is followed in the discharge. Supervisors often do not think about the unemployment compensation consequences when they decide to discharge an employee. This oversight is damaging since sometimes a slight change in what the employer does when discharging can make a big difference when a claim is filed for unemployment benefits.

Reporting Termination Information

Before information is reported to the agency, the reason should be well established. The reason given by the employee for a voluntary quit is often quite different from that stated after the employee decides to file a claim. When an employee is discharged, a documented statement should be given to the employee stating the reason for the discharge. Nothing weakens a case more than a showing that one party or the other changed the statement of the reason for the discharge after the claim was filed. When determining the reason, the terminology selected should be the same as will later be reported to the agency.

When a claim is filed, the agency will request separation information. The person responding to this request should first make sure that the facts stated coincide with the material available in the personnel records. When reporting separation information, give facts. Do not give conclusions. Avoid subjective terms such as *not cooperative, unsatisfactory,* and *poor worker.* They mean nothing to the person making the determination. It is also advisable to expand the reason given. For example, when reporting a voluntary quit, the reason for the quit might be

- To resume home duties
- To seek other employment

- To get married
- Dissatisfaction with the job

These are all reasons to disqualify the claimant. If the facts exist, it is wise to give a definitive reason that the agency has previously held to be disqualifying.

In discharge cases, the separation information should establish that the action was both willful and detrimental to the employer's interest. If the employee had been previously warned, give the date and a report of what was said. Stay away from vague or undocumented recollections when reporting the information. If you do not have good documentation, do not make the statement. Rely instead upon creditable supervisor testimony in the event that you have to go to a hearing.

Saying that the employee was unable to perform the job is always damaging. It is better to say that employment conditions were violated and then to specify what conditions were violated, introducing evidence that the employee was aware of the violation when committing the act. If an organization rule was violated, specify the rule, say when or how it was communicated, and show that the employee was previously warned—if such was the case.

Saying that the employee was rude to customers has very little meaning unless you can cite specific incidents. If the employee was guilty of excessive absenteeism, give the dates of warnings, state the number of times absent, and show that the number is excessive in comparison with the records of other employees.

When answering an agency request for information, remember that separation information aids in getting the proper determination from the agency and in eliminating the number of appeals. Often the person supplying the information limits the statement of information to the space provided in the form. Usually this space is not enough. When it is not, attach another sheet and use all the space necessary. The information provided in response to the initial request not only guides the agency in making a determination whether the claimant is disqualified at the first step but also is the basic information that is used in the event of an appeal.

The appeal process seeks to obtain facts that verify the original position of the employer. For this reason more time should be spent in supplying complete information in the first step than in all the others. Time spent in supplying the original information will reduce the number of appeals the employer has to attend later.

If the person supplying the information has some doubts about what should be said at this stage, he or she should get expert help. Employers sometimes seek help when there is an appeal and they feel uncomfortable in the hearing process. Often so much damaging information has been reported in the first response that no one can save the case.

The Audit of Charges

One of the areas most often overlooked in the control of unemployment compensation insurance costs is the audit of the quarterly statement where all the charges to the employer's account are listed. Even in our computer age, many errors can creep into this statement. Since all unemployment compensation state tax rates are experience-rated, finding these errors can be an important step in cost control.

Since the finance department usually pays the taxes, some employers leave the audit of the charges to them. This is a mistake since finance usually does not have the facts necessary to make the audit complete. Some of the errors to look for in an audit are the following:

1. In the extreme case a charge may be made for an individual who was not even employed by the organization.
2. If an employee has not earned enough wages during the base period, no charge should be made even though he or she may otherwise be qualified to receive the benefits.
3. Sometimes a charge to the employer's account

is made when the employee has already been disqualified. If the finance department does not receive all the terminations promptly after the appeal process is over, it has no way of knowing whether the charge is proper.

4. The appeal may be pending, in which case the account should not be charged, according to the law in most states.

5. Situations occur where the employee may be suspended for a period of time such as after being arrested and awaiting trial. Benefits should not be paid for this period unless a determination has been made.

6. Cases have occurred where benefits have been charged for a period when wages or severance pay has been paid for the same period.

7. Some states have a disqualification waiting period, but an audit may show that benefits were improperly charged for this period.

8. Situations have occurred where the employee has applied for unemployment compensation, and before a determination is made, the employer's account is charged and the claimant may or may not have received benefits.

The appeal procedure for wrong charges is very simple. Usually all you have to do is to point out the mistake, and the agency makes the correction. A hearing is rarely held over wrong charges. The law and regulations are clear on the conditions under which charges should be made. In most states the correction is made immediately and either a new report is sent or a credit notice is given. Seldom is it discovered that an account was undercharged, as this is the responsibility of the agency. If an undercharge is found in an audit, the employer has at least a moral duty to call it to the attention of the agency. In some states, the law goes beyond the moral duty.

So many mistakes occur in the experience report that people have been known to make a good income by auditing reports for various organizations and charging 10 percent of the amount saved. Organizations that have a high experience rating that puts them at or near the maximum tax sometimes do not bother to audit the report since wrong charges will not materially affect the tax rate. An audit is one way to stay at the top of the

rating. Furthermore, if the tax rate does come down for the next rating period and the practice of auditing the charges has not been established, a great deal of money may be lost. Auditing the quarterly reports should be as routine and automatic as auditing the accounts receivable or checking material received at the shipping dock.

Claim Control Programs

Most states allow the amount of tax that the employer pays to be experience-rated, with a minimum and maximum that must be paid. This allows the employer who is at or near the minimum to protect the low experience rating by paying into the fund the amount of benefits paid out. Where the employer has this opportunity it becomes extremely advantageous to keep the benefits charged to the account to the lowest possible amount. This will not happen without some affirmative action through claim control programs and personnel policies. Some suggested policies and programs follow.

1. Plan manpower needs to avoid layoffs. Often overtime is cheaper than hiring additional employees when one considers the cost of hiring and training a new employee plus fringe benefit costs (approximately 35 percent of wages) as well as unemployment compensation costs.

2. Where possible, train or hire employees who have several skills. This allows lateral or upward transfers that not only save unemployment costs but also give flexibility in work assignments.

3. Have one person responsible for the entire program, who by practice and training becomes knowledgeable in unemployment compensation rules and appeal procedures. Some employers have one person responsible for the employee's work relationship, another for the taxes, and a third for accounting procedures. This is a mistake. The control of unemployment compensation costs requires that the person who makes initial decisions or works with supervisors on employment decisions affecting costs should be responsible for the charges to the account as well as the employment decisions and appeal procedure.

4. Have the person responsible for the program

audit all charges to the account such as quarterly reports. Often wrong charges to the account are found and can be corrected by a mere protest by the employer representative who is familiar with the employees and their activities.

5. When in doubt about a determination as to whether the claimant is entitled to benefits, appeal it. Over half of all initial benefit determinations appealed by the employer are reversed by the appeal procedure. (Sometimes in the interest of good employee relations, appeals to wrongful determinations are not made.) It is also important that a determination is appealed in the event of a wrongful discharge claim. The failure to appeal weakens the wrongful discharge case, since it indicates that the discharge was not proper.

6. Hold exit interviews for all terminations where possible to attempt a mutual agreement on the reason for termination. In unemployment compensation matters, employees often have a short memory between termination and the interview with the unemployment compensation representative who determines whether benefits are to be paid.

If these procedures are followed, there will be a substantial savings in unemployment costs before the appeal procedure has to be used. If used, the employer's position can be adequately defended.

To provide income after termination, sometimes the employer will agree to pay unemployment compensation benefits. Since only the agency determines whether or not the employee is eligible for benefits, the employer cannot agree that benefits be paid unless, in reporting, it is stated that the termination was due to lay-off, which would prevent the agency from denying benefits.

Becoming familiar with the unemployment compensation procedure does not require extensive training, and the financial rewards are great. This is one area where the personnel department or other staff departments can show big savings with a little effort.[15] Once one has experience with a few cases and is exposed to various situations, knowing what to do becomes easier except in those rare cases where the practitioner should seek help. Paying more attention to this area is long overdue in most organizations.

---

[15]For several years the author had an undisclosed personal goal to save his employer four times his annual salary. Savings in workers compensation and unemployment compensation were two areas that greatly contributed to achieving this goal. Undisclosed goals of this nature afford job satisfaction when one attains them and do little harm if one fails.

CHAPTER 14

CONTROL OF WORKERS COMPENSATION COSTS

History of Workers Compensation in the United States
Living with the System
Employee Back Problems
Definition of Work-Related Injuries
Recommendations for Control of Costs

Workers compensation, like unemployment compensation, is not a new concept. Many people mistakenly think it is a twentieth-century innovation, but the purpose and intent can be traced as far back as the time of Henry I (about the twelfth century). These laws provided that if a person is on a mission for another or is sent for by another and death occurs in the course of the mission, the sender or creator of the mission is responsible for the death. Likewise in early German law a provision held masters liable for the death of their servants, and a money payment had to be made for injury.

The present workers compensation system had its origin in the German law, where in 1838 the German state of Prussia passed a law making the railroads liable for injuries to their employees, as well as passengers, unless caused by acts of God or negligence on the part of the injured employee. The first modern workers compensation was adopted in Germany in 1884; it required compulsory insurance for industrial accidents. The reason for pressure to pass such a law was a socialist movement supporting it. The Iron Chancellor, Otto von Bismarck, wanted to head off the socialist movement and pushed the law through the Reichstag.

The German approach to workers compensation was a compulsory system based on mutual association. The common law defenses of the assumption of risk, contributory negligence, and fellow-servant doctrine were too harsh for the social thinking of the late nineteenth century. The impetus was to treat workers compensation as a part of a broad social insurance system.[1]

HISTORY OF WORKERS COMPENSATION IN THE UNITED STATES

The movement to take care of the injured started in the United States at the turn of the century. It was founded on the belief that misfortunes, disability, and accidents of individuals are a social matter and the state has a duty to take care of the injured, regardless of any other facts. In 1902 Maryland passed an act providing for a cooperative accident insurance fund. This was the first legislation embodying any degree of the compensation principle. This and later laws in Massachusetts and Montana were declared unconstitutional as a denial of due process. The first real workers compensation law was passed in New York in 1910, but like the others it was declared unconstitutional.[2] This decision was met with an explosion of opposition; Teddy Roosevelt was so angry that he openly advocated the changing of the judicial system. Following this decision, states became more liberal toward the injured worker, and in 1911 Wisconsin passed the first workers compensation law that stood the constitutional test.[3] By 1925, 24 states had passed laws and the last state (Mississippi) passed the law in 1948.[4]

Basic Concepts of Workers Compensation State Laws

All workers are covered now, including maritime workers, other than seamen, who have never been covered by state laws. While economic political conditions have caused an increase in benefits and the scope of the laws, the basic concepts have not

---

[1]For a more complete discussion of workers compensation in Europe, see Ralph H. Blanchard, *Liability and Compensation Insurance* (East Norwalk, CT: Appleton-Century-Crofts, 1917).

[2]*Ives* v. *South Buffalo Railway Co.*, 94 N.E.2d 431 (N.Y. App. 1911).

[3]By 1920 nearly half of the workers were covered by some sort of workers compensation and the court rejected the employer's arguments of due process. *White* v. *New York Central Railroad*, 343 U.S. 188 (1917).

[4]The leading legal treatise is Arthur Larson, *Workers Compensation Law* (NY: Matthew Bender & Co., 1982). This is in ten volumes, but a two-volume desk edition is available. It has two supplements and has annual revisions. Other references include *Analysis of Worker's Compensation Laws*, U.S. Chamber of Commerce, revised annually; John D. Warrall, *Safety and the Work Force: Incentives and Disincentives in Workers Compensation* (Ithaca, NY: ILR Press, Cornell University, 1983).

changed. All the state laws have six basic concepts:

1. To provide benefits regardless of fault or financial condition of the employer.
2. To reduce delays caused by litigation and controversy over responsibility for the injury, thereby reducing attorney's fees.
3. To relieve public charities of the financial drain caused by occupational injuries or diseases. The legislative bodies reason that the employer is in a better position to pay for the social ills caused by occupational injury by passing the cost to the consumer than the government is through taxation (an astute political decision).
4. To encourage employer interest in reducing accidents by making the employer liable for all costs.[5]
5. To generate maximum employer interest in safety and rehabilitation through an appropriate experience-rating mechanism.
6. To promote frank study of causes of accidents (rather than concealment of fault)—reducing preventable accidents and human suffering.

There is a wide difference of opinion on whether these objectives have been achieved. However, the National Commission on State Workers Compensation Laws states that reform is needed, but the workers compensation system is fundamentally sound and a valued institution in our industrial economy. The National Commission on State Worker's Compensation Laws and a task force in the Department of Labor have both rejected proposals to replace the various state systems with one federal program, but conclude there is a need to change the state laws and make them more effective within the social insurance system.

---

[5]The cost must be excessive in relation to other costs before this arouses employer interests beyond moral considerations. In Minnesota, where costs are high, employer interests are aroused not only in safety programs but also in the political arena. The 1983 Minnesota Legislature passed a unique Workers Compensation Law (Chapter 290, 1983 *Minnesota Session Laws*) that gives the labor commissioner the power to create an incentive for employees to return to work by a two-tier system of benefits and to control insurance and medical abuses. The effect of this statute on costs is being closely watched by other states.

LIVING WITH THE SYSTEM

The administrator of a workers compensation system is told that the most important element in administration is to make the employer financially responsible for benefits. The second most important element is to supply the employer with all the necessary data to control the cost. However, one of the biggest problems the state administrator of workers compensation has is the lack of data for effective cost control. The employer must depend upon its own program for effective cost control. This program is basically establishing a relationship with the employee as well as outside sources who have a substantial influence on the employer's costs. Once the employer learns how to establish the proper relationship with other related sources, policies or practices can be instituted that will reduce the costs. These policies and practices will be recommended in the last section of this chapter after many of the problems related to the system are discussed.[6]

Treatment of Seriously Injured

When an employee is seriously injured, it is a traumatic experience. Employees react differently. Sometimes they are angry with the company, sometimes with another employee; others are not angry with anybody but are concerned about their finances. Sometimes they are worried about their ability to work again or pursue a favorite hobby. Whatever the concern, the employer should find out and relieve the injured as much as possible of the worry. Maybe the employee wants to be left alone; then direct contact after initial approach is not advisable. By working through others the same results can be accomplished. The employer should be certain that the best possible medical care is being provided, that if other financial assis-

---

[6]For control of abuses under Workers Compensation, see Bruce S. Vanner, "Cut beneath Abuse of Workers Compensation," *Personnel Journal*, 67, no. 4 (April 1988), 30.

tance is necessary, it should be obtained. The employee should have assurance that if he or she is not able to return to the old job, the employer will try to accommodate by finding other jobs or rehabilitation training for other vocations.[7]

For the seriously injured employee, some suggested employer practices are

1. To visit the hospital and assess how or through whom the employee can best be relieved of any worry
2. To contact the family; if the injured wants to be left alone, to offer help indirectly through someone else if such help is needed
3. To keep in touch with the employee, to show interest in the recovery progress, and to assure the employee of returning to the job. Accommodation, rehabilitation, possible job vacancies, and so on, should be discussed.
4. To avoid any implication that it will be necessary to obtain legal counsel at the early stage of recovery. One should explain the workers compensation law and company employee benefits. If a lawyer becomes involved, one should establish a relationship with the employee's lawyer that the company is aware of the law and will keep the matter as nonlegal as possible.[8]

Relationship with Doctor

To reduce costs successfully, the employer must have the cooperation of the doctor or doctors involved. This is sometimes difficult due to the conflict of interest with the patient-doctor relationship. The doctor

---

[7]This concern should not imply a guilt complex on the part of the employer because this would have a chilling effect on anything that the employer does for the benefit of the employee. Avoiding a guilt complex is especially important when informing the next of kin of an occupational death, if emotional and legal consequences are to be avoided.

[8]Sometimes a lawyer becomes involved in a probable third-party product-liability lawsuit against the manufacturer of the machine that caused the injury. The employer should not aid in such a lawsuit until the workers compensation case is closed, since often cooperation in the third-party suit can adversely affect the employer's workers compensation case.

often aids the employee in continuing to be paid for not working when physically able to do so. Instances of no-work slips without seeing the doctor, diagnosis of a condition over the telephone, or light-work slips that do not define light work are not uncommon and could be eliminated by an employer-doctor relationship. To establish the employer-doctor relationship, the following program is suggested:

1. The employer should inform the doctor of the physical requirements of certain job categories. This can be done on the doctor's visit to the plant site. If this is not possible, send an accurate job description of the physically demanding jobs. Often bad medical opinions are caused by the doctor's not being informed.
2. If a medical opinion is suspect as unreasonable, the employer should challenge it by sending the employee to another doctor. If the employee refuses, after informing the employee, the employer should stop the weekly compensation benefits and require that the employee return to work.
3. The employer should establish sound back-to-work procedures that are based on the physical condition of the employee and not whether it is an occupational or nonoccupational injury. A double standard of back-to-work procedures confuses the doctor on what the employer really wants. Make-work policy must be based on the physical ability of the employee to perform the job, not on protection of a safety record.
4. The employer should make every effort to keep the doctor informed about the employee's medical history and activities off the job after the injury. If the employer makes a real effort to establish a relationship with the doctor, the costs can be controlled. If the doctor seems to cooperate with the employee, the employer should use another doctor. Without an accurate medical opinion about the employee's physical condition, back-to-work programs are useless.

Relationship with Insurance Carrier

The proper relationship with the insurance carrier is extremely important, especially for small companies who do not have large legal staffs, personnel practitioners, and a security department to investigate doubtful claims.[9] If the carrier does the proper job, it can make a real contribution in controlling costs.

Many times the insurance carrier, when trying to get a new account, will stress the effectiveness of its cost control department (safety engineering). An employer in considering the selection of a carrier should emphasize how effective the carrier's claim control department is. All too often the insurance carrier's play-dead attitude in claim abuse is what the employee is seeking. A common practice is alleging that he or she slipped on the steps when going to the lockerroom before reporting to work and injured the back. The evening paper reports that the softball team that the employee was playing for won the city championship Sunday afternoon. However, there were three injuries during the game, but the names were not given. This is reported to the insurance carrier. The investigator tells the safety director that the injury probably happened while playing ball but in view of the social welfare attitude of the courts the case would be difficult to win; thus it would be wise to not contest it. Everybody is satisfied. The employee is paid compensation for a back that was injured playing ball. The insurance company is satisfied because it saves investigation and litigation costs that have been included in the premium rate. The safety director is satisfied because it is not a reflection on the company's safety program but is an uncontrollable accident.

To develop an effective relationship with the insurance carrier for claim control it is suggested that

1. When injuries are first reported to a state commission and insurance company, the employer "flag" all doubtful claims and demand that they be thoroughly investigated. In almost yearly surveys by the National Institute for Occupational Safety and Health it is reported that nationally less than 10 percent of workers compensation claims are contested. Considerably more than 10 percent of the claims should be investigated as to whether the injury occurred in the course of employment and the degree of disability alleged.

   When investigating a doubtful claim, the employer's representative should take an active part in the investigation to be assured that all pertinent facts are given to the insurance carrier and the carrier makes a thorough investigation.

2. Contested claims should not be settled by the insurance carrier unless the employer approves. Settlements often have employee relations consequences; sometimes it may be advisable to litigate although economically the case should be settled. Many lawsuits are tried on other than an economic basis.

3. Approximately 10 percent of all disputed claims should be disputed beyond the investigation stage. The employer should stay with the case to judge the quality of legal service being provided and avoid complacency on the part of the insurance carrier and its attorneys.[10]

Even though the chances of winning might be slim, forcing a disputed claim to hearing and having the employee testify to something different from what is known to be a fact by other employees has a sobering effect on other employees.

Many insurance carriers have no real interest in premium cost control. Experience-rated premiums have add-on administration costs, usually a percentage of the premium. There is seldom a direct percentage relationship between premiums and administration costs; as premium costs increase, so do profits through administration charges.

Some feel that because the employee was injured working on the employer's behalf, any program to deny the employee all possible benefits is poor employee relations. As costs increase, there is a tendency to keep the benefits lower; the other employees are

---

[9]If the employer is self-insured, *insurance carrier* as used herein should be interpreted to mean the consulting organization or whoever is responsible for claim control.

[10]The author once had an insurance company attorney drop in at 11 A.M. to prepare for a case that was to be argued at 1:30 that day. It is needless to ask who won.

being denied higher benefits level, which results in poor employee relations.

EMPLOYEE BACK PROBLEMS

The personnel practitioner or manager who has not experienced the placement or return-to-work problem of an employee with a back disability either is very new in the job or is a rare person. The back condition is sometimes caused by an injury either on or off the job, or by no injury at all. Weak backs can be found in both the young and the old and in all levels of management. Many times the employee tolerates the bad back, because his or her work doesn't require extensive use of the back. This is true in many nonphysical jobs.

Other employees do work that requires the use of the back and attempt to seek redress through statutes or employer policies. To eliminate the back problem, employers in their preemployment physical x-ray the back, and if it medically appears that the back condition will interfere with job performance, the person isn't hired. This has created a pool of unemployables because of a back condition. Applicants then allege they are handicapped and seek redress under the limited Federal Handicap Law (if a public employee or receiving public assistance), but most often they seek relief under a state law. (Over 45 states now prohibit discrimination because of a physical condition.)

The employee with a weak back or a similar recurring disability creates a complex problem in the workplace for which there is no single solution. That is probably why the problem has been around for a long time. In order to seek a solution to the problem, it is necessary to put employees in two categories: those who have a desire to work with their back condition and those who use the condition as a pretext for not working, in order to collect benefits. This section will deal with the problems the employer has had in discharging or accommodating an employee with a back condition or a similar alleged disability. It will also identify the employee who uses the condition as a pretext to seek a compensation under a statute or to get favorable job assignments, since the severity of the back condition is medically difficult to determine. The questionable employee and/or his or her attorney will allege the back condition more often than any other disability. (Tendinitis is probably the next-most-often alleged disability that is hard to prove.) These employees are often called the "plant lawyers" who become knowledgeable on how to use the law to their advantage. Their constant appearances at hearings and as witnesses in court often make them better lawyers in this area than the company counsel who spends most of his or her time on product liability, patents, and trademark or financial matters. (Every employer has had or will have in the future at least one "plant lawyer.") The solution is not hopeless; since there are only a few of these employees, something can be done about them through back-to-work procedures as well as accommodation under the law.

Discharging Employees with a Back Condition

When an employee is discharged and has a work-related injury, it is often alleged that discharge is wrongful, and the employee seeks damages beyond the state workers compensation statute under a wrongful discharge claim. It is usually alleged that the discharge is contrary to public policy because the employee was only exercising a right under the statute. Whether the injury is to the back or to other parts of the body, the courts treat the conditions the same. However, the employer often takes longer to discharge a back case than for other injuries. For this reason the issue of excessive absenteeism often is raised by the employer. Since in many states it is contrary to public policy to discharge for exercising a right under a statute and therefore an exception to the at-will doctrine, the court must determine whether the discharge was for excessive absenteeism or for filing a claim under the statute. The employer should make sure that the discharge was for a valid reason other than filing a workers compensation claim.[11]

In *Lohse* v. *St. Louis Children's Hosp., Inc.*, 687 S.W.2d 594 (Mo. App. 1985), a nurse technician injured her back while helping a patient into bed. She was ordered by her doctor not to work for three months; when she returned to work her condition recurred seven months later and she was off for another two or three months. The next year she was absent 128 days, 29 days the following year, and 34 days the first five months of the third year, after which time she was discharged. The reason for discharge was excessive absenteeism. After her discharge she filed a workers compensation claim and sued under the statute that prohibits discharge for filing a complaint under the statute. The court held that her discharge was for excessive absenteeism that was caused in part by the work-related injury. The court noted that the statute protects the employee if the reason for discharge was for exercising a right under the statute, but here the real reason was excessive absenteeism. If there is a grievance procedure under a collective bargaining agreement, the courts will normally not allow another remedy. Discharging because of the bad back does cause an exposure, and how you do it often determines whether the employee can sustain a wrongful discharge claim in arbitration.

Where the plaintiff sustained a series of work-related back injuries, after his second injury he was asked by the personnel manager to return to light duty for a short period of time and to delay filing a workers compensation claim, since in ten days the company would receive a six-month award for no lost time because of an accident.[12] After a week of light duty, he returned to his old job of fork lift operator. About a month later the plaintiff became ill at work and slipped and fell while descending stairs (a common case when the injury is not work related but the employee claims it is). Six months later he had back surgery, after which the doctor advised him he could return to work, but he was restricted to lifting objects under 75 pounds. The personnel manager disputed the validity of the last injury as being work related and said he couldn't return to work but sent him to the company doctor, who sent him back to work but restricted his lifting to 50–60 pounds. After working his job for a period of time he was discharged because he was "physically unable to perform his job classification without causing a safety hazard to himself and his fellow employees." (The employer was obviously trying to avoid another back injury.) The employee alleged the discharge was in retaliation for filing a workers compensation claim. The jury awarded $50,000 in actual damages and $75,000 in punitive damages. The court held that the jury could reasonably find malice and intentional infliction of emotional distress. It was particularly damaging that the plant manager became angry when the employee reported his second injury and questioned the validity of the injury as being work related, and that the employee had trouble getting his temporary disability payments because of the disputed claim.

The difference in the outcome of these cases is that in the Lohse case the company didn't question the validity of the claim, although the employee may have been using the back as a pretext to be off work, but just waited until there was enough absenteeism to discharge. This outcome is easily predictable with this type of employee. In Malik the company first wanted to protect its safety record and asked the employee to cooperate, which fits the game plan of a "plant lawyer." The company is creating a job and not making a back-to-work decision based on medical opinion. It is never wise to question the validity of a back case. Just act as if it is valid but take steps to eliminate the employee's game plan (once you are certain that there is a plan). To avoid exposure to lawsuits, recognize what is going on but never question openly what the employee is doing. Some

---

[11]*Moore* v. *McDermott, Inc.*, 494 So.2d 1159 (La. 1986); *Kern* v. *South Baltimore Gen. Hosp.*, 504 A.2d 1154 (Md. App. 1986).

[12]*Malik* v. *Apex Intern. Alloys, Inc.*, 762 F.2d 77 (10th Cir. 1985).

employers use a technique that says, "You and I know that you are not going back to work for some reason other than your back." This may be acceptable for a doctor, but not for an employer.

It often becomes a question of how far the employer has to go in accommodating the handicapped employee to avoid violation of a state or federal handicap law. Whether or not the injury is job related legally doesn't affect the duty to accommodate; however, from a practical matter the court may be more sympathetic to a job-related injury.

In *Carr* v. *General Motors Corp.*, 389 N.W.2d 686 (Mich. 1986), the employee was operated on for a ruptured disk and was restricted to lifting no more than 50 pounds. He requested a transfer to a job that required lifting more than 50 pounds. He was refused the promotion because of the lifting restrictions. He contended that the job only required lifting a small percentage of the time and there were other workers in the department who could lift for him; therefore the employer could accommodate without undue hardship. The court held that under the state law and the laws of most states as well as the federal law it is generally held that the employer is permitted to refuse employment to a handicapped person if it can be shown that she or he cannot perform all the duties of the job at a satisfactory standard set by the employer. The duty to accommodate is relevant only when the employee can perform the job. There is no claim for discrimination unless the person is qualified.

The situation becomes more complicated if the employee has a latent back defect. The condition doesn't prevent the employee from presently performing the job but may in the future; therefore it becomes a potential workers compensation liability. In one case the plaintiffs, both experienced over-the-road truck drivers, failed the preemployment physical. They were told about the failure one week before their probationary period was up under the labor agreement. The X-rays had revealed that one plaintiff had a

spur on his spine and the other had a condition known as spondylitis. On this basis only, they were terminated, because the company believed that their back conditions created a substantial likelihood of a disability if they engaged in heavy lifting, as is sometimes required of a truck driver. They sued under the state handicap law, stating they were terminated because of a handicap. The Human Rights Commission ordered reinstatement, back pay, and payment of the plaintiffs' attorneys' fees. In upholding the award, the court[13] found that according to the medical evidence the condition was not of any predictive value as the risk of a back injury or disability from heavy lifting. Their condition had nothing to do with the safe operation of the truck, and these were physical handicaps that entitled them to protection of the handicap law. They could perform the duties of the job, and even if the defendant could show an increased likelihood of lower back injury, it would not be sufficient to prove that in the future the employees would injure their backs. It appears where there is a latent defect of the back, very strong objective medical evidence is needed that the employee will not be able to perform the job or that injury to himself or others is unquestionably predictable.

Return-to-Work Procedures

One of the most important elements of any back-to-work procedure is development of an atmosphere in which the employer is interested in the welfare of the injured employee and that of his or her family. The employer must show some concern about the employee's misfortune. One of several ways to do this is to explain the benefits the injured is entitled to under workers compensation and how to start receiving those benefits. There is nothing that will impede a back-to-work program more than creating an adversary situation. One of the most im-

---

[13]*Rozanski* v. *A-P-A Transport, Inc.*, 521 A.2d 335 (Me. 1986).

portant aspects of recovery from any physical condition is the attitude of the worker. Nothing can happen until she or he wants to return to work.

The next step is to make sure the doctor understands the job the employee was performing before the injury or the one you want him or her to return to. No back-to-work procedure should be considered without a valid medical opinion. Often more than one opinion is needed to be assured it is medically sound and not influenced by the employee.[14] To bring an employee back to work to protect a safety record is a short-term way of creating more costs that many times creates an exposure to legal proceedings when up to that point the whole matter was nonlegal.

The next step is a good faith job offer, but the employer should be certain it is a job the employee can do. There are some basic rules that should be followed when making a job offer.

1. There must be a job available; one should not be created, nor should somebody be "bumped" unless a voluntary transfer is possible.
2. The job the employee returns to should have adequate supervision; more supervision is required, at least at first, or an injured person returning to work than of other employees.
3. The employee must be able to perform all the aspects of the job in spite of the physical condition. It does nothing for the employee's morale and creates a legal exposure if the employer does not require the same standard of performance, after a training period, as for a person who was not injured.
4. If a light-duty assignment is considered, it still must be within the employee's physical restrictions. However, it is difficult to keep the employee within those restrictions, since he or she often violates them by voluntary actions, which results in an aggravation of the condition. Light duty should be considered only where there is constant supervision or restricted activity.

---

[14]R. A. Deyo, A. K. Diehl, and M. Rosenthal, "How Many Days of Bed Rest for Acute Low Back Pain?" *New England Journal of Medicine*, 315, no. 17 (October 1986), 1064–70.

The job offer should be made once the aforementioned conditions exist, even though the compensation is not the same or there is a belief that the employee will not accept. In most states mitigation of damages will result if a suitable job offer is made. It doesn't have to be accepted. For purposes of mitigation of damages, most states define a suitable job as one that the employee can perform according to the employer's standards. It must also be within the employee's medical restrictions and restore the employee as close as possible to the economic status he or she had before the injury.

Successful back-to-work procedures restore morale in an injured employee and reduce workers compensation or health care costs and exposure to invalid claims.

Identification of the Pretext Physical Condition

When the employer has notice of a back condition, it must be treated like any other physical condition. It must be assumed that the employee is willing to return to work as soon as it is medically possible and when a job placement can be made. A bona fide effort on the part of the employer and the employee will be beneficial to both. After this effort is made and there is some indication that the employee doesn't want to return to work as soon as possible but is developing a pretext not to return to work, the employer's posture must change. The employer must always be aware that there are a few employees who are not motivated to return to work but use their physical condition as a pretext to collect benefits for not working. This type of employee becomes a professional litigator and should be handled in a way much different from that of a bona fide case.

The employer must be certain that the employee is falsely using the disability as a reason not to return to work. To treat a situation as a pretext for not working when in fact it is a bona fide condition can be disastrous both legally and in promoting good employee relations, especially if the condition is caused by a work-related accident.[15] For this reason the employer should treat all physical conditions as legitimate until there are substantial facts to indicate that the physical condition alleged by the employee is not work related.

There is a certain pattern of events that this type of employee follows.

1. The injury alleged is in the back or is a condition the extent of which is equally difficult to determine medically.
2. The exact date of the injury is not certain, but usually it occurs on Monday morning.
3. There were no employees present when the injury occurred. The incident is usually a fall or slipping in a remote place—the steps to the locker room, the parking lot, and so on. If a back injury, it could be from lifting as a regular part of the job. It is seldom the usual work-related incident that can be identified.
4. It was reported to the supervisor several days or even weeks after it happened. The employee usually states that at first the injury didn't seem to be severe enough to report.
5. The supervisor to whom it was reported is one known to forget things.
6. The employee never commits a major rule violation but does just enough for harassment of the supervision (not wearing safety glasses, filing many grievances, taking long coffee breaks, going to the men's room often, and so on).
7. She or he makes statements that are not logically true but could be true, so that an investigation is required before action can be taken.

When the incident has these elements, there is at least a suspicion that it is not work related or that the absence from work is planned. If the employee is brought back, there is a series of recurring injuries according to plan. You may have discovered the "plant lawyer."

When there is a suspect, several steps should be taken to validate your suspicion.

1. Investigate the employee's record to determine whether there is a previous pattern either with other employers or in different jobs with the same employer.
2. When in doubt, get more than one medical opinion. Usually the employee's activity will not correlate with the medically determined physical condition. The second or third opinion should be from a well-known specialist who will make a medical determination without being influenced by the employee. Based on medical analysis, the doctor should be able to detect the pretext.
3. Make every effort to accommodate even where you believe that the condition is a pretext. Avoid adversity, give the employee the benefit of the doubt, but be suspicious. (To quote a diplomatic term "Trust, but verify.") Sometimes a back heals rapidly when the employee is offered a job that is for substantially lower pay, or the conditions are not as good as a job he can do but doesn't want to. A bona fide job offer is a very effective way to heal a back condition that is medically questionable. If a good faith job offer is refused, the employer should immediately take steps to stop the benefits. Sometimes the insurance carrier will resist this, but it is the only way to bring to the surface whether or not the condition is a pretext for not returning to work.
4. Move quickly for a medical leave or termination if there is a continual effort to return the employee to work and if when she or he does return, there are recurrences of the alleged condition. This is provided that there are no vacancies for jobs in the foreseeable future that the employee is medically qualified to fill. The courts have constantly held that under workers compensation there is no obligation to treat the employee any differently from other employees. If the employee is excessively absent due to a work-related injury, he or she can be terminated like any other employee.

Sometimes the employer is reluctant to discharge an employee for absenteeism when on workers compensation. There is a fear of an allegation by the employee that the discharge is in retaliation for filing a workers compensation claim. In *Pierce* v. *Franklin Elec. Co.*, 737 P.2d 921 (Okl. 1987), the court held that "an employer who terminates an at-will employee for the sole reason that he is physically unable to perform his job duties does not commit a

---

[15]See "Hiring the Handicapped: Overcoming Physical and Psychological Barriers in the Job Market," *Journal of American Insurance* (3rd Quarter 1986), pp. 13–14.

retaliatory discharge." The overwhelming majority of the courts in other jurisdictions hold that an injured employee can be terminated for absenteeism unless it can be proven that the discharge is a pretext for filing a workers compensation claim.[16] In order to hold a retaliatory discharge, the court must find that the sole reason for the discharge was filing a workers compensation claim and a retaliatory motive must be established. This is very difficult when there is in fact excessive absenteeism or some other valid reason for the discharge, such as not being physically able to perform the duties of the job.

Although the employers have been successful in arguing that a neutral absenteeism policy or failure to perform the duties of the job provides a valid, nonpretextual reason for the discharge, many employers still do not use this method to correct a condition that cannot legally be corrected by another method. The case law is in place, all the employers have to do is use it.

(Some states have statutes that prohibit discharge while the employee is on workers compensation. In this case medical leave would be the answer.) The courts in the Lohse and Malik cases made it clear that they were following other jurisdictions when they took the position that the employer is not expected to show different treatment because of a work-related injury. If the employee is not physically able to work, the remedy is benefits under workers compensation and not special treatment at the work site.

5. Investigate all doubtful claims of disability. If the employee is at home doing physical work that medically he couldn't do when on the job and upon another examination it is found he is able to do it, he should be requested to return to work or be terminated as a voluntary quit for failure to report to work.

In these doubtful situations discharge should be the last resort. At least physical therapy should be attempted. However, it is often difficult to get employees to take physical therapy according to medical instruc-

tions. Leaves without pay are the best solution until the policy or labor agreement permits termination because of the length of the absence or failure to return to work when medically authorized.

Employees who use their backs as a pretext ("plant lawyers") will not disappear, but the numbers found in each facility will depend on how individual cases are dealt with. With proper attention and action, but always being concerned for good employee relations, the "plant lawyer" will appear less often. The Mary Hogan case (pp. 246–49) is an example of doing things wrong.

DEFINITION OF WORK-RELATED INJURIES

One of the major objections to common law and statutes that preceded workers compensation was that too much time and money were spent in litigating questions concerning the injured worker's right to benefits and the amount she or he should receive. It was expected that workers compensation laws would avoid these issues and accordingly litigation would be avoided.

In order for an injured worker to receive compensation benefits, there must be a showing that he or she was an employee of a covered employer and suffered an accidental injury in the course of employment. All of this is subject to interpretation. In addition, the employee must give timely notice to the employer or some legal excuse for not doing so. The wage basis upon which his or her compensation is based must be agreed upon, the duration of the disability must be determined, and if it is a permanent disability the degree must be medically established. In its present statutory condition, workers compensation not only fails to avoid litigation but all too often requires it. It is no wonder that the goal of reducing the cost of litigation is still far from being reached. As in other areas, litigation in the compensation system fosters additional litigation. The usual questions of evidence, procedure, identify-

---

[16]See, for example, *Slover v. Brown*, 488 N.E.2d 1103 (Ill. App. 1986); *Kern v. South Baltimore Gen. Hosp.*, 504 A.2d 1154 (Md App. 1986); *Hansome v. Northwestern Cooperage Co.*, 679 S.W.2d 273 (Mo. Banc. 1984).

MARY HOGAN'S BACK—A CASE HISTORY

In reading this case it should be noted that legal counsel was available at all times to the operating management and, after the charge was filed with the city, legal counsel was involved, except for one action—when Mary was terminated for insubordination.

The Mary Hogan case has an abundance of practical facts that involve many phases of antidiscrimination law, personnel practices, and supervisor techniques.

Workers compensation was not the issue with Mary Hogan, since the employer had accepted that the back condition was work related. However, the back condition was the source of all other problems. Her condition also made her workers compensation attorney available at little or no cost, since the extent of recovery under workers compensation would be of special interest to him. When a workers compensation claim is pending, many side personnel problems are created, and the attorney involved often influences the employee's action.

Facts Caused by Mary Hogan's Back

Paul Smith,[17] department superintendent of Acme Bag Company for the past 14 years, noticed that the conveyor belt was jammed with paper bags. He told Mary Hogan, a polypropylene (P.E.) inserter on the machine, to "get a pallet and remove the bags off the belt."

Mary replied, "I am not able to because my back is bothering me." Paul replied, "Get one that you are able to handle." Mary replied, "I will not do it." Paul said, "I think you can do it." Mary said, "No." Paul said, "You are terminated; clock out and leave the plant." Mary Hogan did just that.

Acme Bag Company is a facility of 110 employees represented by the Teamsters Union. Acme manufactures grocery bags for supermarkets and other grocery and confectionery accounts in Mill City, Minnesota, which has a population of approximately

[17]All names and places are fictitious. Only the facts bear resemblance to an actual case.

100,000. Acme Bag Company has been in operation at this location for 15 years, and 3 years ago it became a part of Standard Products Corporation, a conglomerate that operates in all 50 states and Mexico. Standard Products Corporation has an active affirmative action program both at the corporate and at the local plant levels and the Acme Bag plant had recently passed a compliance review. The Acme plant as well as the parent corporation has a good labor relations record and had no previous EEOC charges. Mary Hogan was employed by Acme in October 1974 as an unskilled worker; she worked in various unskilled positions throughout the plant during her employment.

On June 2, 1975, Mary filed a complaint with the Mill City Civil Rights Commission alleging that the Acme Company discriminated because of her sex when she was given a two-day suspension for refusing to mop the floor when males and minorities were not required to do so. (Mary did not file a grievance over the suspension.) Section 601A.7 of the city ordinance was alleged to be violated. A similar charge was filed with EEOC under Title VII; EEOC referred it to the Minnesota Civil Rights Commission, a Section 706 referral agency. The charge was investigated by the city in the summer of 1975 and dismissed on November 5, 1975.

Before the investigation by the Minnesota Civil Rights Commission and after the city had dismissed the complaint, Ms. Hogan in May 1976 amended the complaint, alleging that Acme had refused to allow her to return to light duty of lifting 10 pounds or less and that this was a violation of Title VII and state law. However, Acme had not received any medical report of Ms. Hogan's condition from July 1975 to May 1, 1976. This amendment was based on the fact that Ms. Hogan was not given the opportunity to work since August 1975. The state civil rights specialist in June 1976 discovered that Ms. Hogan had not worked since July 31, 1975 and inquired about the absence. She was told by Acme that Ms. Hogan was on a medical leave and Acme would be glad to have her return to work, providing the company doctor approved it. Acme further stated, when questioned, that the reason Ms. Hogan had not returned to work was that she had not contacted Acme stating that she was physically able to return to work and was able to perform the job in the plant that she had previously selected or that she could perform any other job.

On August 29, 1975, Acme had a medical report from the company doctor stating that Ms. Hogan was able to lift only 5 to 20 pounds. Before August 29, 1975, Ms. Hogan had signed a statement that she would perform only the job as bottom feeder and table loader, jobs that required lifting 20 to 35 pounds and 60 to 75 pounds respectively; this caused Acme to give her medical leave.

From August 29, 1975 to June 1976, Ms. Hogan had applied for unemployment insurance, which Acme contested on the grounds that the claimant was on medical leave. It was ruled that Ms. Hogan was available for work, and she received unemployment compensation. The notice to allow unemployment benefits was not received by Acme but was sent to the parent company's office, which failed to forward it. Acme would have appealed the decision.

Although the company has forms for a medical leave of absence, no medical leave was applied for by Ms. Hogan under the terms of the labor agreement. However, Ms. Hogan's status was considered a voluntary medical leave during the period of August 29, 1975 to July 12, 1976; premiums for her health insurance were paid by Acme rather than terminating her as required by the labor agreement, which stated that after three months on any leave of absence, an employee is terminated. All during this period Ms. Hogan was not considered by Acme as available for work but was not contacted to determine her status.

When Ms. Hogan was called to return to work after being contacted by the civil rights specialist on June 14, 1976, she stated that she was still under a doctor's care and would be until June 26. On June 28 Ms. Hogan inquired when she could see a company doctor; on advice of corporate counsel, the personnel coordinator arranged an appointment. The company doctor on July 2 stated that she could return to light work, but lifting 40 to 50 pounds repetitively would cause back symptoms. Ms. Hogan was notified of her physical condition, which permitted her to return to work on July 8; she agreed to return to her old job of bottom feeder on July 12, 1976 (requiring the lifting of 25 to 40 pounds).

The next day she alleged that she hurt her back. A meeting was called to determine what job Ms. Hogan could do. With the union present, she was asked what she wanted to do and she stated table loader and was returned to that job for the remainder of the day (this required the lifting of 40 to 50 pounds, which was contrary to the doctor's advice). On the following day, July 14, her husband called and stated that she hurt her back on the previous day and wanted an appointment to see another doctor. It was assumed that this other doctor would be somebody other than the company doctor; she was told that she could see any doctor whom she wanted. She requested the company doctor. It was the observance of her supervisor that when she left the plant on July 13, 1976, nothing was wrong with her back. However, an appointment was made with the company doctor for July 14.

Nothing was heard from Ms. Hogan after her physical examination until her husband called five days later and wanted to know what the doctor had found, stating that the doctor never told her the results of the July 14 examination. When told that nothing was wrong with her, she stated that she wanted to see another doctor. On July 29 she was

(*continued*)

MARY HOGAN'S BACK—A CASE HISTORY (Continued)

ordered to return to work on August 2; however, rather than return to work, she saw another doctor on August 2, who authorized her to return to work on August 3 but "no heavy lifting." She reported to work August 3 and told her supervisor that she could not load tables (a job that she said she could do on July 13, 1976, her last day worked).

As a result of her statement, a meeting was held on the same day with the union and management; Ms. Hogan requested that she be taken off table loader and be assigned to P.E. inserting. It was explained to her that this job requires lifting 50 to 70 pounds. It was a job that she had previously performed and she knew its requirements. It was also stated to Ms. Hogan and the union that she would be used on a temporary basis in other departments. Ms. Hogan performed this job until September 2, 1976, when she was discharged for refusing to get a pallet that weighted 30.1 pounds and required her only to slide the pallet to carry out the order of her supervisor, Paul Smith. The complaint of the civil rights commission was again amended, stating that her discharge was due to retaliation for filing the original complaint. As a result of the discharge, a grievance was filed under the labor agreement and the dispute was arbitrated; on August 23, 1977, the arbitrator found insubordination as the cause for the discharge.[18]

The state civil rights commission, after an investigation, determined in June 1978 (two years after the incident) that there was no reasonable cause as to the sex discrimination charges regarding the suspension for refusing to mop the floor, but there was reasonable cause to believe that Ms. Hogan was discriminated against for not returning to work during the period of August 29, 1975, to July 12, 1976, and that the dis-

[18]Arbitration decision has no bearing on the pending EEOC charge. In *Alexander* v. *Gardner-Denver*, 94 S.CT. 1011 (1974), the Supreme Court held that EEOC can consider the arbitrator's decision but it is not controlling.

charge on September 2, 1976, was retaliation for filing a complaint. The civil rights commission in its conciliation proposal demanded $9000 in back pay and reinstatement. The corporate EEOC investigator was told by the local manager that he didn't discriminate and any settlement would look like guilt. The parties were requested to attend a conciliation meeting. If this failed, the matter would go before the civil rights commission hearing examiner; an appeal from that decision would be to the district court.

Company Mistakes in Dealing with Mary Hogan

The company's major mistake after Mary Hogan was identified as an employee who was a litigator was to permit her to continue as an employee. In the interest of good employee relations the supervisor or personnel practitioner will often give the employee the benefit of the doubt and not apply a strict construction to the rules. This policy will backfire with the Mary Hogans. When the labor agreement said termination after three months, then she should be terminated. If the medical report states that she cannot do a particular job, she should not do it, but a good faith effort should be made to accommodate for other jobs. If none are available, she should not be permitted to return to work.

In Mary Hogan's case, when in August, 1975, there were no jobs that she could do, she should have been terminated under the labor agreement and health insurance should not have been paid. On July 13, 1976, when she hurt her back, she should have been taken off the job and not permitted to do other work until medically authorized.

It was not a mistake to permit her to go to several doctors, as this is permitted under most state workers compensation laws. The mistake was made when one doctor said that she could do only certain jobs and she was permitted to do other jobs that doctors said she could not do. When medical advice is conflicting, the company can take action on any one of the conflicting medical statements without being exposed to additional liability. The question of which doctor is right should not be determined before action is taken; this would be impractical. If the company acted on wrong medical advice, under most court decision and statutes there is no additional liability. In workers compensation cases under most state statutes the extent of the disability as medically determined is what the employer is liable for.

The other mistake was discharging Mary. Sending her home as being physically unfit to work would have been a better solution. The EEOC charge of retaliation is much easier for Mary to sustain than failure to accommodate. Discharge is exactly what Mary wanted. She had successfully irritated her supervisor so that his patience ran out and he discharged her, which set the company up for a retaliation charge.

Why did the company act the way it did in Mary Hogan's case? First, it thought that if it were lenient, Mary would not have a good reason to complain (this usually backfires with the Mary Hogans). Second, because Mary had been successful in irritating everybody who became involved in her case, the less adverse decisions, the less misery, until the pressure was too great so that the only way the supervisor could relieve the emotional pressure was to discharge her. The company's mistakes could have been avoided if it had bit the bullet at the early stages by termination and let Mary exercise whatever remedies were available to her.

ing a claim, when a claim can be reopened, or settling a claim have all been subjects of controversy.

Compensable Injuries

Early interpretations of an injury were limited to a traumatic physical injury, but the courts, in keeping with the socialist intent of the law, have expanded this definition to mean various nontraumatic events as well. At first the courts took the position that a disabling mental condition, a nervous disorder that is the result of a traumatic incident, is necessary to find the injury compensable, but other courts will only require a mental stimulus (for example, a shock) to make an injury compensable. Over 18 states hold that mental stress is work related, while others still require that there must be a physical trauma.[19]

---

[19]See *Kinney* v. *State Industrial Commission*, 423 P.2d 186 (Or. 1967), for a view of not requiring a physical trauma and *Lockwood: Ind. School Dist. #877*, N.E.2d 1924 (Minn. 1981), for requiring a physical trauma.

Accidental Injury

All but six states require that an injury be accidental before it can be compensable.[20] The basic element of an accident is that some part of the injury must be unexpected. In most states it is required that the injury be traceable to a reasonably definite time, place, and occasion or cause. This comes up often in heart, back, or other conditions that could happen off the job. Most courts require that the exertion is in some way unusual for the injured workers, although it may not be for other workers.

The accident requirement is also important for infectious diseases that result from unusual or unexpected events or exposure. If the disease follows the accident, it is usually considered an accident and there is little litigation over this. Some states make it compensable by statute without the requirement of an accident. Without a statute, the courts in other states have held that an unexpected

---

[20]California, Iowa, Massachusetts, Minnesota, Rhode Island, and Texas are some of the states that do not.

contraction of an infectious disease is an injury by accident. Some courts reason that the invasion of the body by microbes is in itself the injury.[21]

Injury Must Arise Out of Employment

Of all the four requirements to make an injury compensable, the requirement that the injury must arise out of employment has resulted in the most litigation and is the most common problem to the practitioner. Generally speaking, the injury must be work related and in the course of employment, which means during working hours. However, there are so many variations of this that the reader is advised to consult Arthur Larson, *Workers Compensation Law,* Vol. 1, Sect. 13 (NY: Matthew Binder Co., 1982), for a particular problem. Space permits only a limited treatment of the subject in this chapter.

One consideration is whether the job involves a risk. If the risk is personal, then it is not compensable. Where an employee was dropping off the mail on the way home from work, it was considered in the course of employment when she was hit in the face by two muggers, since this was a risk associated with dropping off the mail in the street.[22] Some courts will hold if the risk is increased by the job assignment, as compared to a non-work-related incident, it is compensable. If the employee was injured by an "act of God" (for example, lightning or an earthquake), the large majority of the courts would hold that such an injury arose out of employment if working conditions such as height or wetness increased the probability of injury.[23]

Sometimes the injury is related to the personal condition of the worker. The general rule is that this is compensable if the employment in any way contributed to the final disability by placing the person in a position where the condition was aggravated or was weakened by strain or trauma. Thus if a person had a heart attack or an epileptic seizure and fell to the floor, this would probably be held to be personal. However, if while in a high place a worker fell due to an epileptic seizure, the employment would have contributed to the final injury. It has been held, in some states, that a heart attack while having sexual intercourse is compensable if the employee was placed in a position by the employer where such activity might be expected, such as on an overseas assignment, as game warden working in the woods at night, and so on.[24]

The majority of the courts also hold that where the original injury was in the course of employment, every natural consequence that results from the injury is also compensable although there may be an intervening cause attributable to the employee's own intentional conduct. For example, if a driver runs over a child while driving in the course of employment and he subsequently gets a divorce and has a nervous breakdown, it would be a question of fact whether the incident in the course of employment caused the condition, whether the divorce was caused by the incident, or whether either one caused the mental disorder. This is a situation where it would be difficult to avoid litigation.

Definition of Course of Employment

This requirement is concerned primarily with the time and place of the injury and the activity of the employee when the injury occurred. The hard-and-fast rule would be that only an injury received during working

---

[21]*Andreason* v. *Industrial Commission,* 102 P.2d 894 (Utah 1940).

[22]*Wayne Adams Buick, Inc.* v. *Ference,* 421 N.E.2d 733 (Ind. 1981).

[23]*Whetro* v. *Auckerman,* 174 N.W.2d 783 (Mich. 1970).

[24]In *Signorelli* v. *GKN Automotive Components, Inc.* (Mich. Comp. Appeals 1982), an administrative law judge held that where an employee died while having intercourse with his secretary it was compensable, since you can't expect an employee on an overseas assignment to "stare at the walls of his hotel room."

hours would be compensable. However, in line with the socialist concepts of workers compensation, this has not been followed in all cases. Much has to do with the type of work being performed and whether there is a causal relationship between the work and the injury. Where a salesperson was returning home from a call after normal hours, the court held that this was not compensable since there is nothing unusual about a salesperson returning home after normal hours.[25] However, if this had been a person who normally quits at 4:30 and for some reason had to work an extra eight hours and got into an accident on the way home, the result may have been different. It also makes a difference if the person is an outside worker, is an inside worker, or is living on the premises. If the person is an inside worker, the course of employment starts the minute she or he steps on the premises. For an outside worker (such as a salesperson), the usual interpretation of course of employment is that when he or she leaves home the work period starts and is covered until returning. If the employee is living on the premises, most state courts will call everything course of employment except eating, bathing, sleeping, and dressing.

Because a worker is injured on the premises doesn't always mean it is compensable. If the injury is the product of intoxication or willful misconduct, fighting, unreasonable horseplay, or other conduct that substantially departs from the employment duties, it would be considered outside the scope of employment. This can also be successfully argued where the employee specifically disobeys orders. Where for safety reasons the employee was told not to climb or not to use certain equipment because he was not trained and was injured when disobeying the order, many courts will find this outside the scope of employment.[26] This is not the rule in all

states—some will hold disobedience is still in the course of employment.[27]

For application of the preceding principles in particular states the reader is advised to consult the state agency that administers workers compensation, which can be very helpful in making suggestions for policies and practices that will prevent exposure to many workers compensation claims.

RECOMMENDATIONS FOR CONTROL OF COSTS

Often the employer gets so discouraged with the socialist aspect of workers compensation interpretation of the law that he or she gives up trying to do something about it. This "play dead" attitude will not solve the problem, and it is only when the employer decides to do something about it that costs can be controlled. There are many things the employer can do. Space will permit discussing only those cost-control procedures that are considered to be the most effective.

The Delayed Recovery Syndrome

This is the situation where the employer becomes the most discouraged. The employee has a work-related back injury, has been off work for three months, and his doctor says he can come back to work, but the employee says he has a terrible pain and insists that he cannot. You meet him on the golf course, where he just made a hole-in-one, and he is jumping up and down all the way back to the clubhouse, where he buys everybody drinks and is shaking hands from the top of a table.

The first impression is that he is malingering, and maybe he is, but to treat it as such only causes adversity and litigation. It is difficult to get this person back to work

---

[25]*Ahrens* v. *Williamson Music Co., Inc.*, 287 N.W.2d 884 (Minn. 1986).

[26]*Brown* v. *Arrowhead Tree Service*, 332 N.W.2d 28 (Minn. 1983).

[27]See *Hoyle* v. *Isenhour Brick & Tile Co.*, 293 S.E.2d 196 (N.C. 1982), where the employee was killed while driving a forklift truck in violation of rules and the court held it was compensable since he was acting in behalf of the employer.

unless steps are taken to create a desire to do so. The employee is getting some kind of gain from the injury that outweighs the benefits of getting well and going back to work. Researchers call this a "delayed recovery syndrome," not malingering.[28] They claim (the author's experience confirms this) that many serious accidents are caused by internal conflicts of a personal nature, such as divorce or separation, drug or alcohol abuse, sex problems, or pending litigation, and all these factors may delay recovery. The most important thing to remember, according to research, is that delayed recovery is an emotional problem. Although it is unconscious, it is real. The golfer honestly believes that he cannot return to work but can play golf.

Stopping Malingering

Unlike the delayed recovery syndrome, true malingering is conscious avoidance of responsibility, and according to the researchers it is also rare. (This is not the author's experience, who finds malingering in more than 10 percent of all cases.) Malingering is difficult to prove, and even if you feel certain about it the wrong thing to do is to confront the employee with your suspicion. The best way is to treat her as an injured employee "with your tongue in your cheek." These steps should be tried before getting tough and terminating, which may result in an exposure to litigation.

1. Offer a suitable job that the person can medically do. Work closely with the doctor, since she will often resist. Even work with a rehabilitation consultant if a good one is available.
2. Get the person active to regain strength and psychological well-being. Most back injuries medically require only a few days of bed rest. If the employee resists, get a medical directive.
3. Limit the narcotics to only what is needed. Doctors will often be pressured into more. Most

doctors recommend the use of drugs be limited to two weeks at the most.
4. Offer relaxation training. Stress and other psychological factors can aggravate back and neck conditions. Deep breathing and other techniques can relieve this. Get the doctor involved to force the employee to do something to help in recovery.

As an employer let her know that you need her back on the job. Call or visit her during recovery and strongly encourage her to follow treatment programs. Carry a "stick in the closet"; if nothing works, then termination for being absent from work or not following medical directives is the alternative. Some type of litigation will likely follow, so be prepared for it.

Other Steps to Reduce Costs[29]

1. Monitor early, especially in the case of a serious injury. Give the employee information before he or she seeks outside help. It is too late if he or she has to see a lawyer for necessary information. Keep in touch after the first contact.
2. Get a medical assessment as soon as possible. One way to do this without being defensive is to make a sympathetic inquiry about the employee's financial welfare.
3. Give a job offer as soon as medically possible. This should not be a make-up job but one that is contributing and useful. Consider light-duty work, but only where there is not an exposure to doing other work that the employee is not physically capable of. (In sports medicine, when an athlete is injured he must keep up with normal practice that is within his capacity, although he is unable to play.)
4. Get a rehabilitation assessment where necessary. It is possible that the injured may not be able to return to the old job but can do some-

---

[28]See V. Jane Derebery and William H. Tullis, "Delayed Recovery in the Patient with a Work Compensable Injury," *Journal of Occupational Medicine* (November 1983), p. 829.

---

[29]Many of the following steps the author has practiced and found successful, eliminating the unsuccessful. They are also confirmed by studies made by various state departments who are charged with administration of workers compensation. See "Controlling Workers Compensation Costs: A Guide for Employers," Minnesota Department of Labor and Industry, 444 Lafayette Road, St. Paul, MN 55101 (1985).

thing else. It should be done within 30 days after the injury to be successful. This is an effective technique for the delayed recovery syndrome.

5. Monitor the medical aspects; this is extremely important. Medical opinion and directives are given great weight in hearings and by the courts.

If the foregoing steps do not work and you cannot think of anything else, then ter- mination is necessary and litigation is the last resort. Studies in all states have disclosed that litigation is second only to permanent and temporary disability costs in workers com- pensation cases. Many researchers believe that the biggest contributing factor to workers compensation costs is employer compliance.

CHAPTER 15

RIGHTS OF NONUNION EMPLOYEES UNDER THE NATIONAL LABOR RELATIONS ACT

Distinction between Rights of Nonunion and Union Employees
Function of the National Labor Relations Board
Definition of Concerted Activity
Refusal to Work under Unsafe Conditions
Use of Employee Committees
An Effective Complaint Procedure
Selection of a Bargaining Representative

The subject of personnel law deals with the rights of the employee and the employer. These rights are granted by statute and under the common law. Rights that employers are often unaware of are those granted to the nonunion employee under the National Labor Relations Act and its subsequent amendments, known as the Taft-Hartley Act of 1947 and the Landrum-Griffin Act of 1959. These three acts will hereinafter be referred to as the NLRA and can be found in 29 USC Sect. 151 et seq. Employee rights under the NLRA are most critical to the manager and the supervisor who are unaware of them and react defensively by disciplining or discharging the employee for exercising the rights granted to him or her under the NLRA.[1] Cases of this nature are not unique. Since 1984 the number of unfair labor practice cases filed by nonunion employees with the National Labor Relations Board (NLRB) has exceeded 16,000 each year. As the nonunion segment of the work force continues to grow,[2] employees will rely more and more upon the NLRB for enforcement of their rights.

The law is clear that the employee does not have to be a member of a union, a certified union does not have to be involved, and there does not have to be an organizing drive in existence for the employee to have protection under the National Labor Relations Act. Section 7 of the act guarantees all employees the right "to engage in concerted activities for the purpose of collective bargaining or for other mutual aid or protection." Section 7 refers "to all employees." If the employee chooses to act through a bargaining representative (commonly called a union), the right to do so is also protected by the act, or employees can represent their own interests by collective action.

Section 8(a)(1) of the act, however, prevents the employer from interfering with these protected rights by making it an unfair labor practice to "interfere with, restrain or coerce employees in the exercise of the rights guaranteed in Section 7." If the employer violates the act, the NLRB can take remedial action to make the employees affected whole or can order the employer to cease and desist from the unfair labor practice.

This chapter reviews the case law that grants nonunion employees certain rights under the act and will state what the employer can do to recognize nonunion employees' rights the same as it would in a union setting. Because the nonunion employee has the right to union representation, the complex subject of employer interference in employees' right to organize is also discussed.

DISTINCTION BETWEEN RIGHTS OF NONUNION AND UNION EMPLOYEES

When a union represents the employee and bargains collectively, the terms and conditions agreed upon become a contract between the union (as representatives of the employees) and the company. Most labor agreements grant additional rights not granted by the law or to nonunion employees. Such rights as seniority, and restrictions on promotions, layoffs, and recalls are common in a labor agreement. Also, the agreement almost always provides for a grievance and arbitration procedure, and discharge can be only for just cause, a right that a nonunion employee seldom has. This is probably the reason the discharge rate in a nonunion plant is double that in a union plant. The covered employees can sue both the employer and the union to enforce these provisions in the labor agreement.

In a nonunion setting there is no written agreement between the parties as to rights and obligations. However, policy manuals and handbooks in some states have been held to be enforceable contracts but usually are not

---

[1] In a seminar conducted by the author, over 80 percent of the managers and supervisors in attendance were unaware that nonunion employees have a right to strike.

[2] Approximately 17 percent of the civilian work force belong to unions compared to the peak of over 25 percent in 1953. Leo Troy and Neil Sheflin, *Union Resource Book,* New Brunswick, NJ: Rutgers University, 1985.

as enforceable as a labor agreement, where there is more mutuality.

Differences in Wages and Employment Practices

In a union plant, wages and benefits are determined by collective action. Often there is no logical basis for a wage level except the economic power of the union as pitted against the company ability to take a strike. The wage levels cannot be changed up or down except as provided for in the labor agreement or with union approval.

In a nonunion operation, wages are determined unilaterally by the employer, who considers the market conditions as well as other factors, such as job evaluation, merit pay plans, and job analysis. If the wages are not satisfactory to the nonunion employee she or he will quit, but if the union is involved they attempt to raise the wage level through collective action by a threat to collectively withhold their services. Another major difference as to wages is that they are not standardized in a nonunion operation. Different wage rates are usually not permitted where the union represents employees, since it is politically unadvisable for the union leadership.

FUNCTION OF THE NATIONAL LABOR RELATIONS BOARD

The NLRB is the administering agency of the National Labor Relations Act.[3] It has two main functions: the determination of appropriate collective bargaining representatives for employees and the deciding of unfair labor practice charges and, if found, providing a remedy.

This chapter and the next cite several cases that will be board orders with which the em-

ployer complied without appeal. This will be cited as Volume number NLRB No. —— (in board cases only one party is involved).[4] Where the employer refuses to comply with board orders and the board is forced to seek enforcement in the circuit court of appeals, it will be cited as any other circuit court case.

Procedure for Unfair Labor Practice Charge

If an employee or his or her representative feels that an unfair labor practice has been committed, a charge may be filed with the board. The charge is then investigated. If merit to the unfair labor practice charge is found, an informal settlement is attempted. This settlement can be made without union consent [*NLRB* v. *United Food and Commercial Workers Union*, 108 S.Ct. 413 (1988)]. If settlement fails, a formal complaint is filed as in any other legal proceeding. A hearing is then held before an administrative law judge, who gives a finding of facts and conclusions of law, and recommends an order to the board. Either party can contest this recommendation and ask the board for discretionary review of the judge's recommendation. The board may grant the review or follow the recommendation of the administrative law judge. The board has no enforcement power of its orders because its function is only to administer the law.

If either party does not agree with the order, they do nothing and the board then must go to the circuit court of appeals for enforcement of the order. The board order is argued as to whether it is proper under the law. The court either enforces or denies enforcement of the order. Appeal from the circuit court decision goes to the U.S. Supreme Court, which decides as in any other

---

[3]The board consists of five members appointed by the president with the consent of the Senate for five-year terms. They cannot be removed during their term.

[4]Some NLRB cases are cited _NLRB No. _as is reported in the services such as BNA or CCH, which means that the case was yet to be placed in the official NLRB reports. After being placed in an official volume the case number is omitted; the same case will appear as _NLRB _.

appeal whether to hear it or let the decision stand and become law of the circuit. The board does not publish guidelines or interpretative opinions like other agencies. Board law is decided on a case-by-case basis. It does, however, issue procedural rules and regulations 'for the conduct of hearings (also the NLRB *Case-Handling Manual*). Where facts are similar, the board will establish a precedent for a certain group of subjects. However, the board sometimes changes the precedent when members are changed by the political party in the White House.

DEFINITION OF CONCERTED ACTIVITY

Board statistics show that there is a continual increase of cases where nonunion employees are contesting the employer's denial of their right of concerted activity. This concerted activity is common in wage demands, safety matters, working conditions, and employee walkouts over failure to settle employee dissatisfactions. The nonunion employer that does not recognize the employee's rights to engage in concerted activity exposes the organization to violating the law and the obligation to compensate the affected employees for whatever statutory wrong was committed.

Two conditions must exist before concerted activity is protected by the act. One, the activity must be for mutual aid or protection for a group of employees. Two, employee activity must involve wages, hours, or other conditions of employment defined in the act.[5]

Where there is a group of employees involved the board has little problem in finding concerted activity. Where four employ-

ees asked to leave work early and left after being refused, the board held that this was a one-day strike and a protected activity.[6] The result would be the same if only two employees were involved.

The courts and the board give a broad interpretation on what working conditions are. Since they are determined on a case-by-case basis, some examples would be appropriate. Complaints over discriminatory hiring practices; filing complaints with government agents; circulation of petitions that express a desire for a wage increase, additional overtime, and so on; and aiding other employees in processing complaints with respect to work assignments, vacation policies, and holiday pay practices have all been held by the board to be working conditions and receive protection under Section 7 of the act.

Some of the activities that are not considered working conditions include abusive or insulting language, threatening fellow employees with violence, or other protests that are for the sole benefit of the protesters.

Examples of Group Activity

The leading case for concerted activity is where a group of nonunion employees left their jobs over the cold working conditions in the plant. The walkout took place after repeated complaints about the lack of heat at the work site. The employees were discharged for walking out and stopping production. The board held that their discharge violated Section 8(a)(1) of the act and ordered reinstatement with back pay because the employees were engaged in a protected activity to improve working conditions. On appeal the Supreme Court held that the board's order was proper because the employer interfered with concerted activity as guaranteed by Section 7 of the act and the employees' request was neither unlawful nor indefensible.[7]

---

[5]For more detailed analysis of concerted activity see Gordon Jackson, *Labor and Employment Law Desk Book* (Englewood Cliffs, NJ: Prentice-Hall, 1986), p. 53; Judith J. Johnson, "Protected Concerted Activity in a Nonunion Context," *Mississippi Law Review*, 49 (1978), 865.

---

[6]Daniel International Corp., 277 NLRB No. 81 (1985).

[7]*NLRB* v. *Washington Aluminum Co.*, 370 U.S. 9 (1962).

Where a group of employees considered a union if the employer would not change working conditions, it was an indication that they were considering concerted activity.[8] Where employees left their jobs to protest the discharge of two employees for falsifying their time cards, the court held it was a protected activity although the employer had good cause to discharge the two employees.[9]

Activity by Individual Employee

Usually, concerted activity involves two or more employees; however, it is possible that only one employee can be engaged in concerted activity. Where an employee complained of numerous safety hazards and little was done about it, the employee filed a complaint with the California Occupational Safety and Health Administration. The employer discharged the employee; the board held that although the employee acted alone, it was for the benefit of all employees and therefore was concerted activity and ordered reinstatement.[10]

In Rayglo d/b/a/ The Dirt Digger, Inc., 274 NLRB No. 157 (1985), the board held that a refusal to work overtime was a one-person strike that was protected. However, if the employee should state in the future that he would not work overtime, this would be an individual activity because he would be speaking for himself, but where there was an immediate request this affected others and was therefore protected.

Not all individual activity, however, has been held to be protected. Where a nonunion employee requested to have a witness present when signing a performance appraisal required for continued employment, the court held this was not a protected activity because the employee was not acting

for others.[11] The same result occurs where there is a violation of dress code or where job transfers are involved. If disloyalty or insubordination can be shown, it will also lose protection of the act.

The landmark case for employee disloyalty involved employees of a television station who were distributing handbills criticizing the station's quality of programs. The Supreme Court, in holding that the employer had just cause for discharging the employees, said, "There is no more elemental cause for discharge of an employee than disloyalty to his employer."[12] (The handbills being distributed made no reference to a labor dispute or improvement of working conditions.)

When an employer refused to recall an employee from lay-off because he filed an unemployment compensation claim, the board held that there was no violation. The employee was ruled to be acting in his own behalf.[13]

The Alleluia Cushion rule[14] that when benefits accrue to others from individual activity it is concerted activity was followed by the board and the courts until 1984, when the board made a precedent-changing decision in Meyers Industries, 268 NLRB No. 73 (1984). The board stated that in order to be concerted activity when an individual acts alone, the employee must be engaged with or acting under the authority of others or must have at least discussed the action with others. This drastically changed the definition of concerted activity and was immediately challenged in the courts when the board attempted to enforce it. The first court to hear the issue stated that it was a "faulty legal premise" and remanded it to the board to

---

[8]*Squeer Distributing* v. *Teamsters Local 7*, 801 F. 2d 238 (3rd Cir. 1986). In *D & D Distributing Co.* v. *NLRB*, 801 F.2d 636 (3rd Cir. 1986), there were similar facts and the same result.

[9]*United Merchandising Mfg. Inc.* v. *NLRB*, 554 F.2d 1276 (4th Cir. 1977).

[10]Alleluia Cushion Company, 221 NLRB 999 (1975).

[11]*E.I. duPont deNemours & Co.* v. *NLRB*, 733 F.2d 296 (3rd Cir. 1984).

[12]*NLRB* v. *Local Union 1229, IBEW (Jefferson Standard Broadcasting Co.)*, 346 U.S. 464 at 472 (1953). Note the Court now would probably allow handbills or pickets and not call it disloyalty.

[13]Bearden Company, Inc. dba Collins Refractories, 272 NLRB No. 113 (1984).

[14]Alleluia Cushion Company, 221 NLRB 999 (1975).

reconsider.[15] Other courts refused to enforce the Meyers rule and the board was left with a position that they could not enforce.[16] The Meyers rule was reconsidered by D.C. Circuit, who agreed to enforce the rule *Prill* v. *NLRB* (on remand), 835 F. 2d. 148 (D.C. Cir. 1987). Other courts will probably follow, so now the rule has judicial approval.

In the Meyers rule, in order to be liable for an unfair labor practice for taking disciplinary action in a concerted activity situation, the employer must have knowledge of both the existence of the activity and its concerted nature [(*Tri-State Truck Service, Inc.* v. *NLRB*, 616 F. 2d. 65 (3rd Cir. 1980)]. The employer would seldom know that the employee discussed the complaint with others or was acting under their authority.

The Supreme Court limited the rule when they held that an individual employee may act in behalf of others without discussing it when seeking to enforce a collective bargaining agreement.[17] In the City Disposal Systems case the employee refused to drive a company truck that in his good faith belief had faulty brakes. He did not discuss it with others, nor was he acting under their authority as is required in the Meyers rule. The court held that as long as there was a provision in the collective bargaining agreement that provided for a procedure over safety matters and the company didn't follow it, seeking to enforce the provision was acting in behalf of the entire bargaining unit. Therefore, it was a concerted activity.

In view of the court acceptance of the Meyers rule, the employer would be exposed to litigation if it was not followed in a nonunion setting where the action was by an individual who did discuss it with other employees or there was a provision in the collective bargaining agreement to be enforced by an individual. Individual action may not always be concerted activity, depending upon

whether others are involved, but it is better not to discipline for such activity until there is thorough investigation than to be exposed to a lawsuit. If the employer thinks it is very critical to the operation of the business to discipline for a certain activity, then it is a business decision whether to take the exposure or consider it protected activity.

Recommendations for Dealing with Concerted Activity

Employer reaction should be greater when employees walk off the job than it is when they complain about working conditions, although they both may be concerted activity. If they walk off, the employer can get replacements. It is also much more difficult to determine whether or not it is concerted activity when an individual acts as compared to when a group acts. For these reasons the facts will determine the employer's conduct.

If it is group action involving a complaint about working conditions, the employer should

1. Require that it be done on nonworking time; if it is during work time he or she could discipline. (It would be a rule violation, which would take precedence over concerted activity.)
2. Require that employees use a complaint procedure, if there is one.
3. Not retaliate because of the employee's activity.
4. Not take any adverse action, which would be an unfair labor practice. In group conduct it is almost always concerted activity unless it doesn't concern working conditions.

Recommendations When Employees Go on Strike

1. The employer must first determine whether the walkout (strike) is a protected activity.
2. If it is over working conditions, wages, or hours or for any other lawful purpose, then it is an economic strike and a protected activity. However, the employer would have the right to hire replacements and not hire the strikers until they reoffer their services and a vacancy

---

[15]*Prill* v. *NLRB*, 755 F.2d 941 (D.C. Cir. 1985).

[16]*Ewing* v. *NLRB*, 768 F.2d 51 (2nd Cir. 1985); *Garcia* v. *NLRB*, 785 F.2d 807 (9th Cir. 1986).

[17]*NLRB* v. *City Disposal Systems*, 104 S.Ct. 1505 (1984).

exists. (It is advisable that a formal request to return to work be made.)

3. If the walkout is caused by an employer's activity that under the law would be considered an unfair labor practice (defined in Section 7, 29 USC 158 et seq.), such as interfering with union membership, discharge for concerted activity, or retaliation of any kind, then the employee has reinstatement rights over any replacements hired unless the walkout was for an unlawful purpose.

4. A partial strike such as a slowdown or refusal to work overtime or perform certain reasonable tasks is not a protected activity under the act.

5. If there is any doubt whether it is a protected activity, seek legal advice before acting, since the consequences are severe.

Recommendations When Activity Is by an Individual

1. The key is whether the activity itself would affect more than one person. This is decided on a case-by-case basis, but when in doubt consider it does affect more than one employee and it is a protected activity, unless there is strong reason not to.

2. Since it is often difficult to determine whether it is a protected activity, it is advisable to suspend the employee while investigating.

3. Explain before suspending that she or he may have a legal right to act, but you first have to determine whether the employee's actions are legal. If not, there may be discipline.

4. If the individual refuses to work, it is usually considered a strike and he or she can be replaced. If it is not a protected activity, the employee can be disciplined for leaving the job.

5. When the employee leaves the job, either discipline or replacement is the employer's legal remedy, and if possible this should be explained to the employee before she or he leaves the job.

The only legal exposure that the employer has in concerted activity is if the employer does not consider it a protected activity when in fact it is, and the employer retaliates. The rights of nonunion employees to engage in concerted activity without retaliation is a well-established law. The em-

ployer, when faced with the problem, need only act reasonably—listen to the problem, investigate, and take a position as to its correction rather than try to eliminate the problem by retaliation against the employee who calls it to management's attention.

REFUSAL TO WORK UNDER UNSAFE CONDITIONS

The right of an employee to refuse to work in unsafe conditions is protected by two different statutes: Sections 7 and 502 of the Labor Management Relations Act of 1957 (LMRA)[18] and Section 11(c)(1) of the Occupational Safety and Health Act.[19]

Rights under LRMA

The refusal to work is usually expressed by walking off the job. Under the LRMA the question arises whether this is an illegal strike or one protected by Sections 7 and 502 of the act. Under OSHA the issue would be whether the employee could be discharged for refusal to work and if the discharge would be a violation of the discrimination clause in the statute.

In the interpretation of Section 502 of the LRMA the courts have stated that a refusal to work is protected by the act if there is a good faith belief with objective evidence that the working conditions are abnormally dangerous and that workers are competent to testify as to the physical conditions. Where

---

[18]LMRA Section 502 states: . . . nor shall the quitting of labor by an employee or employees in good faith because of abnormally dangerous conditions for work at the place of employment of such employee or employees be deemed a strike under this Act. Section 7 of the act gives the employees the right to strike.

[19]OSHA Section 11(c)(1) states: No person shall discharge or in any manner discriminate against any employee because such employee has filed any complaint or instituted or caused to be instituted any proceeding under or related to this Act or has testified or is about to testify in any such proceeding or because of the exercise by such employee on behalf of himself or others of any right afforded by this Act.

a fan was blowing dust and other abrasives into the workers' faces, the employer inspected the ventilation system and stated that it was operating properly. The employees were told that they would be discharged if they walked out. Despite the warning, they walked off the job, and the court held that this was a protected activity.[20]

The protection under Sections 7 and 502 of LRMA is exclusive. A no-strike clause in the labor agreement or an arbitration clause does not affect the employees' rights, although the arbitration is permitted if the labor representatives want to seek that remedy under the labor agreement.

As in other situations under the LMRA, in order to receive the protection the protest over the unsafe conditions must be such that the employee is acting in behalf of others or there are several employees affected or involved. Where the employee acted unilaterally over refusing to drive a truck that he contended was unsafe, the Supreme Court stated that as long as it was an enforcement of the labor agreement it was concerted activity and was considered a legal strike.[21]

Rights under OSHA

The right under OSHA of the employee to refuse to work under unsafe conditions is found in the Secretary of Labor's interpretation of what constitutes discrimination under Section 11(c)(1) of OSHA. The secretary's directive interpreting this section stated that if (a) the employee's fear were objectively reasonable, (b) the employee attempted to get the employer to correct, and (c) resorting to normal enforcement procedures under the OSHA were inadequate (the urgency of the situation does not allow for elimination of the danger through OSHA or any other statute), the employee then could refuse to work.

This interpretation was considered in *Whirlpool Corp.* v. *Marshall*, 445 U.S. 1 (1980). In the Whirlpool situation the employees had previously complained about the condition of a screen. An employee had fallen to his death and the company subsequently made some alterations to make the screen more safe when it became necessary to remove objects from the screen. Also the employer established a safety procedure requiring a safety net when working on the screen. The employees who had complained about the unsafe condition of the screen were ordered to perform their usual maintenance tasks on the screen without a safety net and they refused. They were ordered to go home, were not paid for the remainder of the shift, and were given a written reprimand. The Supreme Court held that in order to have a violation of 11(c)(1) of OSHA two conditions must exist: (1) reasonable belief that the employees will be placed in jeopardy of injury or death and (2) reasonable belief that there was no other alternative but to disobey the employer's order (no opportunity to go to an OSHA office or seek redress from another level of management).

The court further held that this may be termed a strike and although the employees would be protected, they would not receive pay for not working. The court also reaffirmed the rule established under Section 502 of LRMA that if a hazardous condition were found not to exist or employees were acting in bad faith, they could be discharged for insubordination.

In cases subsequent to Whirlpool, the courts will often cite Whirlpool as their authority but will not require the conditions stated in Whirlpool. Where a foreman refused to work when he believed the condition to be unsafe and, given other alternatives, he still refused to work, the court ordered his reinstatement, citing Whirlpool as authority.[22] This is an example of the court following Whirlpool although the conditions listed by the court were not present.

---

[20]*NLRB* v. *Knight Marley Corp.*, 251 F.2d 753 (6th Cir. 1958). This would be protected even though it was a violation of company and OSHA rules, according to *NLRB* v. *Tamara Foods*, 692 F.2d 1171 (8th Cir. 1982).

[21]*NLRB* v. *City Disposal Systems*, 104 S.Ct. 1505 (1984).

[22]*Donovan* v. *Hahner, Foremen, Harness, Inc.*, 736 F.2d 1421 (10th Cir. 1984).

If an employee has objective evidence of the unsafe condition, it would appear that she or he could refuse to work under the NLRA, regardless of whether the conditions under Whirlpool were met. Employers would have exposure under NLRA even where OSHA is complied with, since compliance doesn't mean they provide a safe place to work.[23]

USE OF EMPLOYEE COMMITTEES

Restrictions under NLRA

Employee discontent is often based on the lack of communications. Many labor relations experts agree that the cause of employees joining a union can be traced to a lack of communications. Some employers believe that the solution to these problems is the formation of an employee committee, since it would provide a two-way management-employee communication system and is often an effective substitute for employee representation by a union. However, if not properly constituted it can run afoul of the National Labor Relations Act, Section 15.2(5), which states:

The term "labor organization" means any organization of any kind, or any agency or employee representation committee or plan, in which employees participate and which exists for the purpose, in whole or in part, of dealing with employers concerning grievances, labor disputes, wages, rates of pay, hours of employment, or conditions of work.

Section 158(a)(2) provides:

It shall be an unfair labor practice for an employer to dominate or interfere with the formation or administration of any labor organization or contribute financial or other support to it: *Provided,* that subject to rules and regulations made and published by the Board pursuant to section 6, an employer shall not be prohibited from permitting employees to confer with him during working hours without loss of time or pay.

It is evident from the language of these two sections of the act that interpretation is needed to determine whether in a given case an employee committee is in violation of the act.

If an employee communication committee functions the same as a union, the board will find it is a company-dominated union and order that it be discontinued.

In the leading case on employee committees, the evidence showed that the committee had bylaws that were prepared by the company. The employee representatives on the committee established a procedure for handling grievances in nonunion plants. They also made proposals to management as to seniority, job classifications, job bidding, holiday and vacation pay, and so on in the same manner as a union negotiating committee. The Supreme Court held that this was clearly a labor organization under the act and was company dominated.[24]

The court had the most concern over the fact that the committee handled employee complaints. Although Section 9(a) of the act permits nonunion employees to present their own complaints to the employer, they cannot do so on behalf of other employees (unless through concerted activity) because this would be a representation situation and come within the definition of a labor organization.

The real test of whether an employee committee violates the act is whether the employer actually coerced or restrained the committee from representing the interests of the employees.[25]

NLRB Determination of Committee Status

Some of the facts that the board considers when determining whether there is a violation of the act are these:

---

[23]*United Auto Workers* v. *General Dynamics,* 815 F.2d 1570 (D.C. Cir. 1987).

[24]*NLRB* v. *Cabot Carbon Co.,* 360 U.S. 203 (1959).
[25]*NLRB* v. *Homemakers Shop, Inc.,* 724 F.2d 535 (6th Cir. 1984).

1. Did the company choose the committee members? If so, it would be a strong indication of a company union.[26]
2. How much staff assistance was given, as distinguished from control? The more control, the more likely it was a violation.[27]
3. Were committee members rotated? This is helpful because it stresses communication objectives.[28]
4. Was the committee organized after a notice that the union was organizing? This is evidence of a company-dominated union.[29]
5. Was a committee formed to discuss supervision, production, or quality circles? This would be legal because they are not subjects that unions are concerned with.

Objectives of Employee Committees

Objectives of the committee should be stated in writing.

1. The declared purpose of the committee should be for communications from management and voluntarily to management from employees.
2. Individual problems should not be discussed, but a separate complaint system should be instituted.
3. The broad problems should be in the form of communicating dissatisfaction and the employer explaining its position on employee problems.
4. Changes in working conditions such as lunch hour or wage and salary programs should be in the form of two-way communication of employees asking why and management explaining its position.
5. If employees express a general dissatisfaction, management should consider the problem and correct it or give a rational reason for not doing so.

Because an employee committee affords exposure to a violation of the act (the remedy for which is to cease and desist, in other words, discontinue the committee), it does not mean that it should not be used. If properly structured, employee committees can be a useful tool in an employee communication program and be instrumental in keeping the employees nonunion.[30]

Guidelines for Forming a Committee

1. The committee should be initiated by the employees or jointly by employees and management. (Encouragement by management is acceptable if it doesn't go too far.)
2. Committee membership should be voluntary and employees should select their own representatives.
3. Committee members should be rotated often (every six months is preferable).
4. The purpose of the committee should be stated in writing at the first meeting. Always have a graceful way to discontinue.
   a. The purpose should state that
      (1) It is a method of obtaining employee suggestions and ideas for improving operations.
      (2) It is a means for better communications between management employees.
5. The committee should agree to not discuss any antiunion animosity or in any way substitute for the functions performed by a labor union.
6. Officers should be rotated between employees and management representatives and all minutes be prepared and approved by employees and/or management representatives.
7. Wage and salary policies can be discussed so employees understand them, but no individual wages, grievances, or working conditions should be discussed.
8. The broad problems should generally be in the form of communicating dissatisfaction and the employer explaining its position on employee problems.

---

[26]*Irving Chute Co.* v. *NLRB,* 350 F.2d 176 (2nd Cir. 1965).

[27]Ripley Industries d/b/a as Missouri Heel Co., 209 NLRB No. 79 (1974).

[28]In *NLRB* v. *Scott Fetzer,* 691 F.2d 288 (6th Cir. 1982), the court said that continuous rotation of committee members was management speaking directing to its employees.

[29]Blue White Bus Co. of Watts, Inc., 198 NLRB No. 134 (1972).

[30]See Dennis J. Franiecki, Ralph F. Catalanello, and Curtiss K. Behrens, "Employee Committees: What Effect Are They Having?" *Personnel* (July–August 1984), p. 67.

9. Changes in working conditions such as lunch hour or wage and salary programs should be in the form of two-way communication of employees asking why and management explaining its position.

10. If employees express a general dissatisfaction, management should consider the problem and correct it or give a rational reason for not doing so. If such dissatisfaction is in the form of a threat or forceful demand, it should not be considered, since consideration of this type of demand is permitting the committee to be similar to a union.

11. Management should take all ideas and suggestions under consideration no matter how silly they seem.

12. The committee should meet periodically off company premises and off company time. (Often a quarterly dinner meeting at a local hotel sets up the right environment.)

Exhibit 15-1 contains the recommendations listed. It also illustrates that the committee should not have elaborate bylaws and procedures. Formal written guidelines should only be what is necessary to permit the committee to function under broad informal procedures.

The committee structured in Exhibit 15-1 of five management representatives and seven employee representatives is designed to make the committee a more effective communications device. Usually management representatives can easily communicate subjects as the information comes from one or two sources. The employee representatives have a less homogeneous group to represent; therefore, their communication problem is more difficult. There is more of a tendency to discuss wages and working conditions, which may result in the board declaring it a company-dominated union if there are only a few employee representatives.

With an unbalanced committee, the thought should be conveyed that this is not a voting situation where the majority vote will make a decision; management's being underrepresented clearly communicates this to the employees.

Pitfalls of Employee Committees

An employer who intends to use the employee committee should also be aware of the risks involved apart from the legal exposure of committing an unfair labor practice. If there is irresponsible leadership on the committee, a whole host of employee relations problems could be created.

Success of a committee is largely dependent on the trust that management can develop with the employee representatives. How well the representatives communicate to the entire employee body often depends upon how well they believe management. If distortions occur that are damaging to the business, then the committee should be discontinued.

If a large number of differences between management and the committee remain unresolved or are settled on the basis of an arbitrary management answer, a tailor-made organization is handed to a union on a silver platter. For these reasons a committee should be carefully formed before a threat of union organization.

Management can avoid these pitfalls by continual audit of the effectiveness of the committee. If there is not a harmonious relationship, it can diplomatically discontinue the committee. The advantages of an employee committee outweigh the disadvantages, however. Positive personnel administration should seriously consider employee communication committees in spite of the solvable problems that they create.

AN EFFECTIVE COMPLAINT PROCEDURE

Need for a Complaint Outlet

One of the most common causes of employee's concerted activity over working conditions is the failure of the employer to have an effective complaint procedure. There must be a place for em-

EXHIBIT 15-1 *Employee-Management Communications Committee*

The general purpose of this committee, consisting of employee and management representatives, is to promote better communications between the company and its employees.

The purpose of employee representatives shall be to communicate to management the acceptability of management policies and practices, to make suggestions for improving management-employee relationships, and to communicate generally their problems and dissatisfactions.

The purpose of management representatives shall be to communicate business conditions, customer relations, employee benefits, wage and salary policies, community and governmental problems, management policies and practices, and new developments and to represent management's position concerning general employee problems and dissatisfactions.

Selection of Committee
The committee shall consist of management representatives from production, administration, and management, except that the plant manager or employee relations representative shall not sit on the committee. Employee representatives shall be selected by the employees whom they represent; representation from different departments is desirable but not essential. There shall be a maximum of seven employee representatives and a maximum of five management representatives. Each member of the committee shall serve for no more than one year and shall not be eligible for reappointment. Vacancies shall be filled in the same manner as they were appointed.

Committee Organization
The committee shall meet at least once every three months until discontinued on request of either party. They shall elect a chair and a secretary. The chair shall be alternated from year to year between an employee and management representative. Minutes of the meeting shall be kept and distributed to all employees. The committee shall adopt such other rules and procedures as necessary to carry out its function.

ployees to go to let the steam off. After attempts to do so fail with the employee's supervisor (who often is the source of the problem), concerted activity results. Such activity usually would not be protected if a complaint procedure were available. For example, if a complaint procedure were available when co-workers protested discharge of a fellow employee, as in the United Merchants case,[31] a work stoppage would probably not be justified because

other means would be available to adjudicate the dissatisfaction.[32]

Nothing in the act prevents any employer from establishing an informal or formal complaint procedure. There are two reasons why complaint procedures avoid concerted activity. First, if the employee is offered a forum for the solution of the problem, concerted action is less likely or it would be re-

---

[31]*United Merchants Mfg. Inc.* v. *NLRB*, 554 F.2d 1276 (4th Cir. 1977).

[32]The author purposely has avoided the use of the term *grievance*. A grievance is defined as an employer action in violation of a labor agreement. A dissatisfaction or complaint is any employee concern over wages and working conditions.

stricted to a complaint procedure. Second, the employer is forced to take a position that is documented, and this often satisfies the employee. Sometimes a forum to discuss the dissatisfaction is all that is needed to satisfy the employee.[33]

Elements of Effective Complaint Procedure

There are many types of complaint procedures in union and nonunion organizations. What is effective for one organization may be ineffective for another. However, all procedures should be designed to contain the following elements:

1. The procedure should be designed so that it encourages the employee to use it. If the employee at the first instance is required to discuss the complaint with the immediate supervisor, who probably caused the problem, the procedure will not provide an outlet for the complaint. In *Meritor Savings Bank, FSB* v. *Vinson*, 106 S.Ct. 2399 (1986), the complaint procedure was ineffective because it required the employee to complain to the immediate supervisor. The Court said, @ 2409,

Moreover, the bank's grievance procedure apparently required an employee to complain first to her supervisor, in this case Taylor. Since Taylor was the alleged perpetrator, it is not altogether surprising that respondent failed to invoke the procedure and report her grievance to him. Petitioner's contention that respondent's failure should insulate it from liability might be substantially stronger if its procedures were better calculated to encourage victims of harrassment to come forward.

2. A staff person should be indirectly involved in the solution of the problem; leaving it solely up to operating management causes inconsistency.

3. The objective of settling complaints should be what's right, not who's right.
4. All complaints are real to the employee and should never be considered ridiculous, although they may be to management.

Need for Impartial Final Step

Unless a complaint procedure has a final impartial resting place, the employee will not have complete faith in its impartiality. The most valuable benefit of a union contract is the final and binding arbitration procedure of a grievance. It is something that is only found where the union represents the employees, and it is often used by the union in their organizing efforts. "If you had a union, management couldn't get away with it" is a common argument for union representation. The two impartial methods used in a nonunion setting are arbitration, similar to that under a union contract, and peer review, which has its genetic origin in the jury system. Neither of these methods is easy to sell to management because they involve giving up a traditional managerial prerogative. However, when a union represents the employees, management in almost all cases gives up that prerogative to avoid having a strike for the duration of the contract. One way to eliminate the union organizer's best selling point is to have an appeal procedure in a nonunion setting.

Arbitration in Nonunion Setting.[34] In the nonunion setting, arbitration takes many forms. Protesting employees may represent themselves or may bring friends, fellow workers, or attorneys. Some companies appoint a personnel staff person to represent the employee or have an ombudsman who, among other duties, represents the employee.

The arbitrator is selected either by the company or by a professional association such as the American Arbitration Associa-

---

[33]Many dissatisfactions or grievances are settled by permitting the employee (union or nonunion) to talk while the employer just listens. Often employees talk themselves out of the dissatisfaction.

[34]For further reading on this subject, see Richard L. Henderson, *Performance Appraisal* (Reston, VA: Reston Publishing Company, 1984), pp. 33–37.

tion or a governmental agency. Sometimes there is a panel of arbitrators, for which the employee and management each selects one and the two select the third. This often helps to correct the problem of lack of knowledge of the operation by a single arbitrator. Another problem is the question of who pays the arbitrator. If the company pays, it is difficult for the employee to understand the impartiality of the decision. If the employee is liable for one half the fee (as the union is under most labor agreements), the arbitrator, in discharge cases, is tempted to reinstate the employee so the fees can be paid. Although there is no good solution, one approach would be to have the employee pay one half if he or she wins and if he or she loses the employer pays all.

The greatest difficulty in nonunion arbitration is the lack of a definite document to provide a basis for the decision. Under a union arbitration the arbitrator is restricted to the language of the labor agreement, but a rule or policy is often vague or it is a loosely worded oral promise and it is difficult for the arbitrator to find an objective basis for a final and binding decision that would render justice to both sides.

As the concept of employment-at-will continues to be eroded, employers will resort to arbitration, at least in discharge cases, as a welcome alternative to costly court proceedings. However, some of the problems need to be worked out. The use of a panel rather than a single arbitrator would solve some of the problems, since a settlement could be worked out before the hearing that would not erode management's rights and would still do justice to the employee's position. The problems of who pays and the lack of a definitive document as a basis for a decision will have to be solved before arbitration in a nonunion setting will become popular.

Peer Review in Nonunion Setting. Many companies, dissatisfied with the little-used "open door" grievance policies, are instituting peer review boards as the final step in a complaint procedure.[35] Most of these boards consist of two management representatives and three employees. The unbalanced board with the employee representatives in the majority has resulted in management's position being upheld in over 60 percent of the cases. Evidence shows that employees are more strict with their peers than are their supervisors. Also there can be little criticism that the procedure is biased toward the company.

The peer review has been used in approximately 100 companies for nonunion employees, including such large organizations as Federal Express Corporation, General Electric Company, Citicorp, Borg-Warner Corporation, Adolph Coors Company, and Control Data. In most of the companies the employee is not permitted to use an outside representative, but the company will provide staff to help prepare the case for the employee if it is requested. This keeps the procedure informal and puts the employee in a more relaxed and a more nearly equal position.

The peer review has many advantages over arbitration in that it can be handled internally, which enables the dispute to be settled more quickly than if an outsider is involved. Since many managers want to avoid reversal by their peers, they are more careful when disciplining an employee to make sure that the procedures are followed, they are fair and open about the matter, and they give better feedback to the employee and other subordinates.

Because arbitration in a nonunion setting still has many problems that are difficult to solve, in the author's view, the peer review method will gain in popularity and is the best final step in a nonunion complaint procedure.

Exhibit 15-2 is an example of a final and binding step in a complaint procedure. It is

---

[35]For further reading on peer review, see John D. Coombe, "Peer Review: The Emerging Successful Application," *Employee Relations Law Journal,* 9, no. 4 (Spring 1984), 659; Harvey S. Caras, "Peer Review Grievance Procedure Bolsters Employee Support," *Personnel Journal,* 66, no. 6 (June 1987), 54–58.

EXHIBIT 15-2   *Complaint Procedure for Employees Not Represented by a Union*

When an employee becomes dissatisfied with the working relationship or some other problem for which a solution is desired, the employee may discuss this dissatisfaction with the immediate supervisor or with the supervisor's supervisor. If a satisfactory solution is not received at these levels, the dissatisfaction or problem shall be put in writing and submitted to the employee relations representative.

The employee relations representative shall investigate the matter and make a recommendation in writing to the manager of the department. The manager shall, after due consideration and consultation, make a determination and so inform the employee in a person-to-person meeting, by presenting a copy of the decision to the employee and sending a copy to the employee relations representative and the employee's immediate supervisor.

If the employee is dissatisfied with the manager's decision, the employee may refer it to an employee-management committee consisting of two management representatives and three employee representatives, whose majority decision shall be final and binding on both the company and the employee. This procedure shall be communicated to all employees affected; employees must be made to feel, beyond any reasonable doubt, that they will not be in any way penalized for using this procedure.

The employee-management committee shall be discontinued on 30 days' notice of either party to discontinue. Such discontinuance date shall not be effective until all pending employees' problems or dissatisfactions have been resolved.

a substitute for the type found in a union agreement, will avoid protected concerted activity, and will promote good employee relations.

In summary, the complaint procedure is an area in which personnel law has very few restrictions except to avoid retaliation liability and protect concerted activity. However, complaint procedures are an important part of effective personnel administration and an effective method to prevent litigation. The personnel practitioner and/or manager should spend considerable time and effort in developing a procedure that will work for their particular operation.[36]

---

[36]See P. M. Panken, "What Every Company Should Have: Formal Employee Complaint Procedure," *Management Review*, 73, no. 1 (January 1984), 42–45; T. J. Condon, "Use Union Methods in Handling Grievances," *Personnel Journal*, 64, no. 1 (January 1985), 72–75.

SELECTION OF A BARGAINING REPRESENTATIVE

Right to Select Bargaining Representative

The basic authority for the right of employees to select bargaining representatives is Section 7 of the National Labor Relations Act. This section provides that employees "shall have the right to self-organization to form, join, or assist labor organizations to bargain collectively through representatives of their own choosing and to engage in other concerted activities for the purpose of collective bargaining or other mutual aids or protection."

Section 7 was amended by the Taft-Hartley Act to state specifically that an individual shall have the right to refrain from any or all union activities. This was a loop-hole in the original act. Since the interpretation of Section 7 by the board and the courts is very complex and voluminous, it is only possible here to give a brief overview of the law. Important decisions concerning union-employer posture and remedies for violations are covered only briefly.

When an employer is faced with a union organizational drive, a general knowledge of the law prevents mistakes in the initial stage of organization drive. Professional advice and counsel by a person thoroughly versed in this area is advisable immediately after knowledge of an organizational attempt exists.

Steps in Selection of Bargaining Representative

If a company becomes aware of an organizational effort at its inception, it will probably be through supervisors, by loyal or ambitious employees ("apple polishers"), or by observation of some kind of solicitation. Sometimes, however, organizational efforts are kept secret, and the employer is not aware of the effort until a letter or telegram demanding recognition is received from the union. If this happens, the initial stages of the organizational campaign have passed.

As soon as the employer has notice of any kind that organizational efforts are taking place, a meeting should be called of all the employees affected and the company position clearly stated. After the initial meeting, professional advice should be obtained.

The initial organizational objective of a union is to obtain a sufficient number of authorization cards or authority (some unions use a list similar to a petition) for the union to represent the signatory employees for collective bargaining purposes. There are two types of cards, one on which the union is authorized to represent the undersigned employees for collective bargaining purposes and one on which the union is designated as the exclusive bargaining representative of the signatories and requests the NLRB to hold an election.

Various meetings; coffee parties; beer sessions; calls at the employee's home, sales parties for cosmetics, at which an organizer is present; telephone surveys by students for a term paper, whose real purpose is to discover prounion employees; and hard sell from other employees are all part of the procedure to get employees to sign authorization for representation. When the union gets 30 percent or more of the eligible employees in the job categories that they claim is an appropriate bargaining unit to sign authorizations, they may, under board procedural rules, petition for an election. As a practical matter, to ensure winning an election, most unions will not petition the board for an election unless they have 60 percent or more authorizations from those eligible to vote.

Request to Bargain without an Election

Before the union petitions the board for an election, it sometimes requests orally or in writing that the employer bargain without an election. The union states that the union represents the majority of the employees and would like to be recognized as a bargaining representative and suggests a date for the first meeting.

Sometimes the union presents the authorization forms to prove its claim of majority status. It then requests recognition and a collective bargaining meeting. The employer should not be persuaded to look at these cards or in any other way gain knowledge of who signed the cards unless it has been decided to recognize the union without an election. The courts have enforced the board's position that if the employer has knowledge of who signed the authorization form, the employer cannot later demand an election or question the majority status of the union.[37] The employer should always demand an election unless there are rare circumstances that dictate otherwise.[38]

---

[37]*Retail Clerks Union* v. *NLRB (John L. Serpa, Inc.)*, 376 F.2d 186 (9th Cir. 1967).

[38]The author as state agency representative once held an election where all voters were dues-paying members of the union but they all voted not to have the union represent them.

Signed authorizations are not always predictive of how the employee will vote. Sometimes an employee signs cards for reasons other than union representation. A person may have signed a card to get rid of the union organizer and changed his mind after hearing all the issues. The beer party may have lasted too long and the employee did not reflect his or her true feelings.[39] Once an employee signs a card, the board will not accept any testimony on why the person signed the card.[40] However, persuasion to withdraw authorization is not in itself illegal.[41]

Another reason for demanding an election is that if there is more than one union involved in organizing efforts, although management has objective knowledge of only one, recognition of one of the unions could result in an unfair labor charge by the other.[42]

If the employer denies recognition and requests the board to hold an election, the board must do so in the absence of an unfair labor practice.[43] When the board orders the election, the time and place are determined as well as the eligible list of voters. If the employer and the union agree with all the conditions, a consent election petition is signed. If they do not agree, a hearing is held and the regional Director makes a determination of the issues and then orders the election. This order is appealable to the circuit court. After the election is ordered, the campaign to influence the employees on how to vote starts.

One of the frequent issues is determination of who is eligible to vote. Often there is a dispute over confidential employees, because they must be directly involved in labor

relations policy to be confidential.[44] Another area of dispute often is close relatives of the owner or the managers. These employees are not allowed to vote under board policy, and this was upheld by the Supreme Court.[45]

When an issue of eligibility or any other issue arises, the board will order the election and permit those issues in dispute to be challenged by either the employer or the union. If the challenged ballots would change the outcome of the election, a hearing is held and the board makes a determination, on the challenged ballots that is appealable to the circuit court.[46]

Preelection Conduct

Section 8(a)(1) of the act states that it is a violation to interfere with, restrain, or coerce employees in exercising their rights under Section 7 to join or not to join a labor organization. Violation by the employer usually takes the form of threatening the loss of jobs or benefits, questioning employees about their union activities or membership, spying on union gatherings, or granting wage increases deliberately timed to discourage employees from joining or voting for the union. This should be distinguished from false and misleading statements, which are permissible unless documents are forged or otherwise deceptive.[47] However, the statements cannot be defamatory, because a suit can be brought in a state court apart from the organizational environment.[48]

The important thing to remember about conduct in representation campaigns is that coercion, promises, threats, or seeking information on whether employees are members of the union and how they individually

---

[39]Cards signed after drinking 26 bottles of beer were held to be valid. American Art, 170 NLRB No. 70 (1968).

[40]Midstate Beverages, 153 NLRB No. 14 (1965).

[41]*NLRB* v. *Monroe Tube Co.*, 545 F.2d 1320 (2nd Cir. 1976).

[42]*Hadden House Food Prods., Inc.*, v. *NLRB*, 764 F.2d 182 (3rd Cir. 1985).

[43]*Linden Lumber Div. & Summer Co.* v. *NLRB*, 419 U.S. 301 (1974).

[44]*NLRB* v. *Hendricks County Rural Electric Membership Corp.*, 450 U.S. 964 (1981).

[45]*NLRB* v. *Action Automotive, Inc.*, 105 S.Ct. 984 (1985).

[46]Election procedures are found in the NLRB *Case Handling Manual.*

[47]*NLRB* v. *Affiliated Midwest Hospital*, 789 F.2d 524 (7th Cir. 1986).

[48]*Bill Johnson's Restaurants, Inc.* v. *NLRB*, 103 S.Ct. 2161 (1983).

feel about union representation is usually held to be an unfair labor practice. One of the most common violations is where the employer solicits dissatisfaction or grievances in order to determine why employees joined the union and then corrects or promises to correct the conditions before the election. This is almost always held to be an unfair labor practice. Soliciting complaints is permissible, but promises to remedy them are unlawful.[49] Other employer conduct held to be unlawful is a statement that a plant shutdown is a possibility because the union would make it impossible to survive[50] or a company's granting an unusual number of employee loans a week before the election.[51]

Some permissible conduct includes

- Granting benefits and wage increases—a past practice[52]
- Withholding from paychecks and paying separately sums equivalent to union dues[53]
- Holding a raffle for $84 worth of groceries, stating that this was the amount of union dues for one year[54]
- Using strong persuasion to get employees to withdraw their authorization cards[55]

Unions are also held to the same standard of conduct as employers under the law. However, it is often difficult to get evidence of union conduct because of the reluctance of employees to testify against each other. Where a union waived initiation fees to those who signed authorization cards before the election, the Supreme Court held this to be unfair labor practice.[56] However, the union was within its right to give a free turkey to all employees attending a union meeting.[57] There has also been developed a large body of law on what the union and employers can say and what they cannot say, which also involves the constitutional right of the freedom of speech.

Solicitation Rules during a Campaign. One problem that often comes up when a union is attempting to organize is what degree of solicitation by prounion employees must be permitted by the employer. The general rule is that the employer must permit employees to engage in union activity during nonwork time. The Supreme Court held that prohibition of union activity during nonwork time would interfere with the employee's right to organize unless the rule is necessary to maintain discipline or production.[58]

A rule that requires permission from management for any kind of solicitation is usually held to be too broad because it could include nonwork time.[59] Another rule was struck down where all talking during work time was prohibited. The court said that such a rule was unreasonable.[60]

The Supreme Court put some restriction on solicitation during nonwork time in hospitals and health care institutions, where such activity would interfere with visitors and patient care, such as in patients' rooms and corridors. However, the court stated that solicitation in a cafeteria would not interfere with patient care or visitors.[61]

The situation that most often confronts employers is where, as a matter of good employee relations, the employer has permitted conversation or solicitation of the other subjects during work time. Then, when a union campaign takes place, the employer pre-

[49]Montgomery Ward & Co., 225 NLRB 112 (1976).

[50]W. A. Kruger Co., 224 NLRB No. 148 (1976).

[51]*Bradley Lumber Co. v. NLRB*, 128 F.2d 768 (8th Cir. 1942).

[52]*NLRB v. Otis Hospital*, 545 F.2d 252 (1st Cir. 1976).

[53]Geyer Mfg. Co., 120 NLRB 208 (1958).

[54]Buzza Cardozo, 177 NLRB No. 38 (1969).

[55]*NLRB v. Monroe Tube Co.*, 545 F.2d 1320 (2nd Cir. 1976).

[56]*NLRB v. Savair Mfg. Co.*, 414 U.S. 270 (1973).

[57]*Jacqueline Cochran, Inc.*, 177 NLRB No. 39 (1969).

[58]*Republic Aviation Corp. v. NLRB*, 324 U.S. 793 (1945).

[59]*Birmingham Ornamental Co. v. NLRB*, 615 F.2d 66 (5th Cir. 1980).

[60]*NLRB v. Chem Fab Corp.*, 691 F.2d 1252 (8th Cir. 1982).

[61]*Beth Israel Hospital v. NLRB*, 437 U.S. 483 (1978); also *NLRB v. Baptist Hospital*, 442 U.S. 773 (1979).

vents conversation or activity for union organization as well as other subjects.

The board and courts usually hold this as discrimination except where the United Fund was permitted.[62] If selling Girl Scout cookies or tickets for the Shrine circus or charity ball was permitted during work time, the employer would have exposure to an unfair labor practice charge if union solicitation were prohibited during work time after a petition for election has been filed. If the union activity were far more excessive than what had been permitted, restriction of union subjects would probably not be in violation.

The employer who had a past practice of permitting non-work-related conversation and civic projects during work time should be cautious when establishing a rule to prevent union activity during work time. Social solicitations are difficult to control, and for employee relations consequences it is better not to control them. The courts recognize that it would not be practical to prohibit all conversations of all non-work-related subjects. In *Restaurant Corp. of America* v. *NLRB,* 801 F.2d 1390 (D.C. Cir. 1986), the court held that six instances of ad hoc nonunion solicitations were not enough to show that an employer disparately enforced its facially valid no-solicitation rule against union solicitors while tolerating social solicitations among employees.

As in other situations concerning employer conduct in representation elections, the employer should receive professional advice before too much is said. However, to state that one does not want a union is always safe.[63]

Remedy for Violations during Campaign. When the board finds that the union or employer has committed an unfair labor practice, it will order a new election; if the offense is severe enough, it will order certification without an election. In order to certify a union without an election, there must be substantial proof that the company committed a serious unfair labor practice. The court said in Gissel that the employer's action must have a marked impact on employee sentiment that is expressed on the authorization forms and the election results. The employer's action, under the Gissel doctrine, must undermine the majority status of the union.[64]

However, the board takes the position that the union must make a showing that the majority of the bargaining unit has authorized the union to represent them. Without a showing of a majority status, it would not be possible for the employer to affect the outcome of the election by committing an unfair labor practice.[65]

Supervisor Conduct in Support of Union Activity

In combating union organization efforts, the most important management representative is the front-line supervisor. Supervisors' rapport with the employees gives them the greatest exposure to unfair labor practices in management's attempt to oppose the union. For this reason they must be briefed on their legal rights in representing management. Most managements assume that the supervisor will support their position, but what happens with the supervisor who supports union activity? Is there any restriction on discharging a supervisor who supports union activity? Supervisor support of union activity is not uncommon because dissatisfied supervisors will often reason that if a union represents the employees and their wages or benefits are increased, the supervisors' will also be increased.

Sections 2(3), 2(11), and 14(a) of the Taft-Hartley amendments to the act specifically exempt supervisors from the protection un-

[62]*PACECO Co., Div. of Fruehauf Corp.* v. *NLRB,* 601 F.2d 180 (5th Cir. 1979).

[63]For additional reference, see Steven C. Kahn, Barbara A. Brown, and Brent G. Zepke, *Personnel Director's Legal Guide* (Boston: Warren, Gorham & Lamont, 1984–1986 Supp.) pp. 11-2–11-52; 12-45–12-59.

[64]*NLRB* v. *Gissel Packaging Co.,* 395 U.S. 575 (1960).

[65]Gourmet Foods, Inc., 270 NLRB No. 113 (1984).

der the act. The question arises that if a supervisor is discharged for supporting union activity, is this in any way interfering with the employee's right to join a union?

Section 7 of the National Labor Relations Act does afford the supervisor some protection where the employer discharges the supervisor for

1. Refusal to commit an unfair labor practice
2. Refusal to testify on behalf of management in a board hearing involving union activity
3. Giving adverse testimony in a board hearing
4. Failure to prevent a union from organizing employees

Although Section 2(11) of the act states that the supervisors are not employees, the board and the courts have held that it is a violation of employee Section 7 rights if a supervisor is discharged for any of the foregoing reasons.[66] The court in Talladega was quick to point out that it is not extending the act to nonemployees but merely giving protection to nonemployees where their action adversely affects employees as defined by the act.

The failure to prevent a union organization must be distinguished from the situation where a supervisor does not do enough to prevent a union or where the supervisor sympathizes with the union. In *Automobile Salesmen's Union* v. *NLRB,* 711 F.2d 383 (D.C. Cir. 1983), the supervisors attended a union meeting and generally sympathized with the employees' organizational activities. The board refused to extend protection of the act to the supervisors upon discharge, stating that it was within the prerogative of management to discipline its supervisors for sympathizing with the employees' desire to join a union. The court affirmed the board's position, stating that in order to receive protection under Section 7, the supervisor's activity must directly interfere with employee rights to organize.

The act does not prevent the supervisor

from taking a vigorous role in the management campaign to prevent a union. It is where the supervisor refuses to commit an unfair labor practice or to do something such as surveillance of union activities and is discharged that is protected by the act. The discharge for the refusal is the crux of the protection.[67] If the supervisor commits an unfair labor practice, this is not protected because the action would be prohibited by the act. An employer would be enforcing the law by the discharge. When the employer discharges a supervisor for activity that has a direct impact on the employee's rights under the NLRA and it is considered an unfair labor practice, the discharge is protected.[68]

Reason for Seeking Representation

When dealing with a nonunion employee, the employer should always ask the question: Could I do this if I had a union? If the answer is no, then the planned activity should be undertaken very carefully or there will be a union to deal with some day. It is difficult to understand why employers will not develop a complaint procedure, but when a union represents the employees they are quick to give up the prerogative in the form of a labor agreement under the threat of a strike.

Employees do not request the union to represent them because they want to but because they feel that management is not listening to their problems, and this is one way to get them to do so. Management organizes employees into a union. All the professional organizer does is wait for management to make enough mistakes to cause the employees to seek representation. A knowledge of the rights of nonunion employees will keep employers from making the mistakes and at the same time promote good employee relations.

---

[66]*NLRB* v. *Talladega Cotton Factory, Inc.,* 213 F.2d 209 (5th Cir. 1954).

[67]*NLRB* v. *Miami Coca-Cola Bottling Co.,* 341 F.2d 524 (5th Cir. 1965).

[68]*Howard Johnson Co.* v. *NLRB,* 702 F.2d 1 (1st Cir. 1983).

16

RIGHTS OF UNION EMPLOYEES UNDER THE NATIONAL LABOR RELATIONS ACT

Differences between Union and Nonunion Employers
Employer Duty to Bargain
Enforcement of Collective Bargaining Agreement
Restraints on the Right to Strike
Use of Arbitration in Dispute Resolution

When the personnel practitioner looks at the title of this chapter, the thought may occur that since one does not have a union or expect to have one in the foreseeable future, this would be one chapter to skip. This would be a mistake. One of the best defenses to employee organization is for the employer always to consider whether one could make the same employment decision if a union were representing the employees.

For example, a nonunion employer in an effort to get workers to work the graveyard shift (12:00 P.M. to 8:00 A.M.) decided to pay all workers an extra four hours' pay per shift. When economic conditions changed and jobs became more plentiful, it was decided to change this expensive policy and pay only for time worked.

How can one change the policy to have the least impact on a worker's attitude? It must be done very carefully. If workers were organized, it could not be done without union acceptance, which would be unlikely. Without a union the policy change must be well communicated to the employees or the employer will have a union.

Nonunion employers should know the rights of union employees and what restrictions labor agreements contain in order to make decisions that will have the least impact on employee relations. The union should not be given the opportunity to say, "If you were represented by a union, the employer could not do this."

DIFFERENCES BETWEEN UNION AND NONUNION EMPLOYERS

Chapter 15 stated that a nonunion employee has the same rights under the National Labor Relations Act (NLRA) as an employee who is a member of a union. What difference does it make whether an employee belongs to a union? Why is there such effort by employers to keep out unions? The major difference is in the procedures. Employees represented by a union cannot individually discuss with the employer the wages and working conditions but must do so through an elected representative, which is the union. The second difference is that in a union situation a labor agreement exists that may restrict the employer in making certain employment decisions.[1]

To select a representative for the purpose of discussing wages or other conditions of employment is a right granted to the employee by Section 7 of the act. When the National Labor Relations Board (NLRB) holds an election and the majority of those voting select a union or some other organization to represent them for bargaining purposes, the employees can no longer individually represent themselves. Under the law, if the majority of those voting choose a bargaining representative, that representative must act for all the employees and all employees must go through the union with their problems.

From the employer's point of view, a third party has come between the employee and the employer. The employer no longer can grant wage increases or change working conditions without agreement by the employee representative.

When the union is certified as the bargaining agent for the employees, the employer is obligated under the law to make a good faith effort to reach written agreement as to the terms and conditions of employment.[2] Once an agreement is reached, both the union and the employer must follow it and the employee may force the union and the employer to do so through the National Labor Relations Board. Whatever rights are granted in the labor agreement are addi-

[1]There are other differences. In a union facility, the discharge rate is lower (.9 percent of total employment in a union facility and 1.8% in a nonunion facility) and the absentee rate is higher (4.2 percent for nonunion and 4.5 percent for union firms). For other nonwage effects of unions, see Lloyd G. Reynolds, Stanley H. Masters, and Colletta H. Moser, *Labor Economics and Labor Relations*, 9th ed. (Englewood Cliffs, NJ: Prentice-Hall, Inc. 1986), p. 590.

[2]For research on collective bargaining and labor relations, see John A. Fossum, *Labor Relations, Development, Structure, Process*, 3rd ed. (Plano, TX: Business Publications, Inc., 1985).

tional rights that a nonunion employee may not have, such as grievance procedures, seniority, and posting of vacancies.

This chapter describes the procedures under the law that force the employer to deal with the union as representative of the employee. It also reviews the additional rights that an employer has granted to an employee in the collective bargaining agreement.

Since the law is matured in this area and the subject is well covered in the literature and court decisions, only an informational summary will be given. Many of the cases may seem old, but they stand for a principle that has not been changed by subsequent law.[3]

EMPLOYER DUTY TO BARGAIN

After a union wins an election and is certified by the NLRB as the bargaining representative of the employees, the first real contact that the employer has with the union is the request made by the union to meet for the purpose of bargaining over wages and working conditions. The usual procedure is for the union to make several proposals to be put into a written agreement between the union and the company.[4] Under the act, the company must meet with the union for the purpose of collective bargaining but they do not have to agree to anything; however, Section 8(d) of the act requires that both parties bargain in good faith and have a sincere purpose to reach an agreement.[5]

---

[3]J. Begin and E. Beal, *The Practice of Collective Bargaining*, 7th ed. (Homewood, IL: Richard D. Irwin, 1985); Walter Galenson, *The CIO Challenge to the AFL* (Cambridge, MA: Harvard University Press, 1960); "Proceedings of the Industrial Relations Research Association, Spring 1985 Meeting," *Labor Law Journal*, 36, no. 8 (August 1985), 454–664.

[4]At these initial bargaining sessions most union proposals are the promises that the union made during the campaign of what it would force the employer to do if the employees voted for it.

[5]*NLRB* v. *Herman Sausage Co.*, 275 F.2d 229, @ 231 (5th Cir. 1960).

Bad Faith Bargaining

If there is evidence that the employer has no intention of reaching any agreement, the union can file an unfair labor practice charge; if it is found that the employer was bargaining in bad faith, the board can issue a cease-and-desist order to require the parties to bargain in good faith. Bad faith bargaining is most likely to occur when the initial contract is being negotiated. Often the employer who is still trying to recover from the shock of the loss of the representation election will be reluctant to change conditions. The employer's objective at the bargaining table is to give as little as possible, with the hope that next year the employees will see how little the union has done for them and will vote the union out or at least stop paying dues.[6]

It takes a skillful negotiator to give nothing or very little and not be charged with bad faith bargaining (this is sometimes called surface bargaining). Often there is a fine line between bad faith bargaining and saying no.[7] There is no legal definition of bad faith bargaining, since the board relies on a case-by-case basis for its decisions. What the board looks at is the total conduct of the parties at the bargaining table. This requires a subjective evaluation by the board or the courts of the parties' attitude toward intent to reach an agreement. However, it is often difficult to sustain a surface bargaining charge.[8]

Unilateral Action as Bad Faith Bargaining. Where a union is certified by the board, the employer is required by law to deal exclusively with that union as a bargaining agent for the employees. Sometimes an employer would like to give a superior employee an extra bonus or wages above the contract rate. If this is done without the union's consent,

---

[6]Under board rules, an election to decertify the union cannot be held until one year after the first election.

[7]Allbritton Communications, Inc., 271 NLRB 201 (1984).

[8]Reichhold Chemicals, Inc., 277 NLRB No. 73 (1985).

it is bad faith bargaining. The rule in plain language is "no side deals" with union-represented employees.[9]

Other conduct that may support a strong inference of bad faith bargaining is failing to give management representatives sufficient authority to bind the employer, refusal to sign an agreement already reached, withdrawal of concessions previously granted, or delaying tactics (this is tough to stop or prove). One of the problems of the board in bad faith bargaining cases is that the only remedy for the unfair labor practice is a cease-and-desist order; there is not much liability if the employer is found guilty of bad faith bargaining. The board tried to remedy this in a situation where the employer engaged in flagrant bad faith bargaining and one of the union's demands was a union shop.[10] The board in an attempt to remedy the violation ordered the company to include a union shop provision in the agreement. The Supreme Court said that such action was going beyond the intent and scope of the act. Congress never intended to give the board such powers to compel a union or the employer to agree on any contract provision.[11]

Bad faith or surface bargaining complaints usually come before the board when the employees do not want to strike but the company will not accede to their demands; the union hopes that they will be in a better position after the company is found guilty of an unfair labor practice.[12] The union reasons that the employees might be willing to strike or the employer will accede to a few more demands after being found guilty.[13]

Regulation of Bargaining Process

One of the most common situations that cause refusal-to-bargain charges is the unwillingness of either party (usually the employer) to bargain over certain subjects. This issue is important to the union because if the employer does not have to bargain over certain conditions, the employer can always refuse to discuss the situation and the union does not have the right to strike over a non-bargainable issue. The employer or the union must bargain over hours of work, working conditions, and wages because this is stated in the act. Where these subjects are involved, the court does not consider the attitude of the parties at the bargaining table, for these subjects are specifically required by the act to be discussed.[14]

Questionable Mandatory Bargaining Topics

The preceding topics are called mandatory bargaining topics, and refusal to bargain over them is per se violation of the bargaining duty.[15]

Other bargaining topics are not so clear-cut under Section 8(d); the courts must decide whether a particular subject at issue is a working condition or whether it is a management right to operate the business. The guideline used in these questionable areas is if the action taken by the company results in an economic impact on the employees, it is a bargainable subject. This comes up regularly in a situation where the company wants to contract work out to a third party rather

---

[9]Leeds Cable Div., Inc., 277 NLRB No. 14 (1985); North Coast Cleaning Services, Inc., 272 NLRB 1343 (1984).

[10]Union shop is a contract provision that requires all new employees to become members of the union within a certain period after hiring, usually 30 days. It also requires all present employees to become and remain members of the union.

[11]*H. K. Porter Co.* v. *NLRB*, 397 U.S. 99 (1970).

[12]When the employer is found guilty of an unfair labor practice, the board requires that a notice be put on the bulletin board that the employer has been found guilty to reassure the employees that in the future the firm will follow the law.

[13]This situation reaffirms what the employer should have told the employees before the election: The union can make all the promises that it wants, but the employer has to agree before any benefits are granted.

[14]Section 8(d).

[15]*Per se* as used in legal context means taken by itself; it constitutes a violation (*Black's Dictionary of Law,* 5th ed., 1979).

than have the employees do it and the labor agreement is silent on this right.

Where a company contracted maintenance work out to another company and laid off employees in the maintenance department, the court held that contracting out was a subject that the firm had to discuss with the union.[16] However, if the contracting out had not resulted in the layoff of employees, the results would have been different.[17]

The economic impact rule is not always followed where certain subjects are traditionally management concerns. Where a company for economic reasons closed part of its operation, the court held that the employer was required to bargain about the effect of the decision on the employees but not the decision itself because the plant closing was purely for economic reasons. The court reasoned that the economic burden placed on the employer in continuing the operation outweighed a benefit gained over labor management relations by the bargaining process.[18] [This is not to be confused with the Plant Closing and Mass Layoff Notification Act of 1988 (P.L. 100–379).]

The board extended this balancing test analysis to a situation where the employer would transfer or relocate bargaining unit work to a nonunion facility during the term of the contract. The board held that this was not unlawful if the employer satisfied the obligation to bargain under the contract.[19] If the parties were bargaining over the relocation, the only requirement before relocating was that the parties had to be at an impasse before the employer could relocate.[20] This position of the board is most damaging to the labor movement and has been sharply criticized by scholars of labor law.

On the other hand, where a company subsidized in-plant food services by an independent caterer, the court held that the company must bargain over the prices. The court affirmed the board's position that food services are "other terms and conditions of employment" under Section 8(d) of the act. If the employer had not subsidized the food services, it would probably not have had to bargain over such services because a subsidy is a benefit to the employees and price affects the amount of the subsidy; therefore, it is a working condition.[21]

Another frequent issue is in the benefit area, such as Christmas bonuses or turkeys at Christmas time. This situation arises where the company has a profitable year; it gives a Christmas present to the employees (turkey, ham, fruit). Next year profits are down so the firm decides not to do it. The general rule in this case is that if the bonuses are intermittently given with no consistency as to their basis, they are considered gifts; where they are unilaterally skipped after consistently being given, regardless of conditions, the courts reason that they are compensation that must be bargained over.[22] Reducing a Christmas bonus is not always a violation. Where turkeys and hams were discontinued without bargaining with the union, the board held that they were too minimal to be considered wages, but other bonuses may not be, depending upon their monetary value.[23]

Whether a particular subject is bargainable or not is important to the parties; for this reason the board and the courts hear a reasonable number of these cases. Because a subject is bargainable does not mean that the company must agree, but it does mean that the union has a right to strike over the demand. Once the employer consistently grants a benefit like a Christmas bonus, it may not be able to stop the benefit. Although this additional compensation was not bar-

---

[16]*Fibreboard Paper Products Corp.* v. *NLRB*, 379 U.S. 203 (1964).

[17]Westinghouse Electric Corp., 150 NLRB 1574 (1965).

[18]*First National Maintenance Corp.* v. *NLRB*, 101 S.Ct. 2573 (1981).

[19]Milwaukee Spring II, 268 NLRB No. 87 (1984).

[20]Otis Elevator II, 269 NLRB 891 (1984).

---

[21]*Ford Motor Co.* v. *NLRB*, 441 U.S. 488 (1979).

[22]*NLRB* v. *Wonder State Mfg. Co.*, 344 F.2d 210 (8th Cir. 1965).

[23]Benchmark Industries, 270 NLRB 22 (1984).

gained for by the union, the union can bargain over taking it away.[24]

Union Security Clauses in Collective Bargaining Agreements

After a union becomes the collective bargaining representative through a board-sponsored election, one of the first bargaining demands of the union is a security clause. These clauses, according to the union, are necessary to support the cost of the bargaining and otherwise representing the employees as their agent. It is a form of compulsory unionism or financial support that the employer must agree to before it can be enforced as part of the collective bargaining agreement. There are primarily five types of union security clauses:

1. Closed Shop. This requires union membership as a precondition of employment and continued membership as a condition of maintaining employment. The NLRA as amended by the Taft-Hartley Act no longer permits the closed shop [29 USC Sect. 158(a)(3)].
2. Union Shop. This clause requires all new employees to become members of the union within a certain period of time (at least 30 days after hire, except in the construction industry, where it is 7 days after hire) and remain members until the expiration of the labor contract. Under a union shop agreement, an employee may be discharged only when membership is available under the same conditions as other employees or when membership has been denied for nonpayment of dues or initiation fees required of other employees [29 USC Sect. 158(a)(3)]. Under this clause an employee can refuse to become a member of the union for religious

reasons. If the union expels her or him or refuses membership, the employee cannot be discharged as long as dues are tendered. As nonmembers, such employees cannot be discriminated against, but are not permitted to vote on ratification of the labor agreement to which they will be bound.[25] In a modified union shop, those who are employees at the time of agreement do not have to become members, but all new employees do. Also, under Section 14(b) of the NLRA, states are permitted by statute to prohibit union shop clauses. Over 20 states have these so-called right to work statutes.

3. Maintenance of Membership. This requires all members of the bargaining unit who are members at a specified time to remain members or who later become members to maintain their membership for the duration of the contract. Those employees who are members of the union at the time of the labor agreement have an escape period (usually from 15 to 30 days after the agreement takes effect) to resign.
4. Agency Shop. An agency shop agreement requires all employees in the bargaining unit to pay regular dues and initiation fees regardless of actual membership.[26]
5. Hiring Hall. Section 8(f) of the NLRA permits the use of a hiring hall agreement in building and construction trades. As a practical matter, the union control over employment referral requires union membership as a precondition to being referred and can be tantamount to a unlawful union shop.

ENFORCEMENT OF COLLECTIVE BARGAINING AGREEMENT

Some employers believe that they have the sole discretion in making a decision except where restricted by the labor agreement. The employer's belief is based on the theory that the firm may retain everything that it did not specifically give away in the bargaining process. If the agreement is silent about a particular subject or practice, under this the-

[24]For further references and details on the employer's duty to bargain, see Leonard E. Cohen, "The Duty to Bargain over Plant Relocations and Other Corporate Changes: Otis Elevator v. NLRB," *The Labor Lawyer*, 1 no. 3 (Summer 1985); "Proceedings of the Industrial Relations Research Association, Spring 1985 Meeting," *Labor Law Journal*, 36, no. 8 (August 1985); Brian K. Brittain and Brian P. Heshizer, "Management Decision Bargaining: The Interplay of Law and Politics," *Labor Law Journal*, 38, no. 4 (April 1987), 220.

[25]*NLRB* v. *Hersey Foods*, 513 F.2d 1083 (9th Cir. 1985).
[26]See *NLRB* v. *General Motors Corp.*, 373 U.S. 734 (1963).

ory, management has the right to act without interference from the union.

In 1960 three cases, called the Steelworkers Trilogy, went to the Supreme Court.[27] In all three cases the issue was whether the company had to arbitrate an issue not covered in the labor agreement. The Supreme Court said yes, a labor agreement cannot cover every situation and the employee has certain rights not specifically stated in the labor agreement by virtue of the employer-employee relationship. This became known as the common-law-of-the-shop theory, which was expanded into the past practice rule of labor agreements. This rule usually applies in arbitration cases where a clause is ambiguous or the agreement is silent on a particular practice. The rule as followed by most arbitrators is that a past practice is a part of the contract unless the contract clearly states otherwise.[28]

The courts have continued to follow the Steelworkers Trilogy cases and have said that a past practice is an integral part of the contract.[29] The past practice concept has been followed into nonunion situations; in discrimination cases the court or agency looks to past practice to determine whether members of the protected class are treated differently.

Changing a Past Practice

If a union employer were to change a past practice, it would be a bargainable issue if the practice is contrary to or is ambiguous in the labor agreement. For a nonunion employer it is advisable to give sufficient notice before a practice is changed. The mistake that nonunion employers usually make is that they are confronted with a glaring immediate problem where the previous practice, if followed, would result in a real economic or employee relations problem. To change the practice for that particular situation without notice is risky if the employee involved is a member of a protected class. It is also an exposure to union organization. The employer is well advised not to apply the past practice to the situation at hand and bite the bullet but give notice effective on a certain date that the practice will no longer be followed.

Duty of Union to Represent Employees

One right that a union employee has that a nonunion employee does not is to be represented and enforce the collective bargaining agreement. The Supreme Court has interpreted Section 301 of the act to mean that the individual rights of an employee under a collective bargaining agreement can be enforced in the courts. Suits can be brought by the union on behalf of the employees, by individual employees against the union and the employer, and by the employer against the union.[30] Employees can sue their union when the union does not enforce the contract against the employer. These are called fair representation cases. In a leading case, several over-the-road drivers were discharged for falsifying their expense account; when their grievance was denied before a joint Labor-Management Arbitration Committee, the employees as individuals sued the union and the employer. The basis of their suit was that the charges of dishonesty were false and that the union made no effort to investigate to determine the real facts. The court held that this was a breach of union duty to represent the employees adequately under

---

[27]*United Steelworkers of America* v. *Warrior and Gulf Navigation Co.*, 363 U.S. 574; *United Steelworkers of America* v. *Enterprise Wheel and Car Corp.*, 363 U.S. 593; *United Steelworkers of America* v. *American Mfg. Co.*, 363 U.S. 564 (1960).

[28]For discussion of past practice in arbitration, see Frank Elkouri and Edna Elkouri, *How Arbitration Works*, 4th ed. (Washington, DC: Bureau of National Affairs, 1985), Chap. 12.

[29]*Norfolk Ship Building Corp.* v. *Local 684*, 671 F.2d 797 (4th Cir. 1982).

[30]In *W. R. Grace.* v. *Rubber Works Local 759*, 103 S.Ct. 2177 (1983) the court held the contract could be enforced through arbitration even though management and EEOC had made a settlement to the contrary. The issue was over seniority.

the collective bargaining agreement.[31] The extent of liability of the union is the amount of damages caused by the union's failure to act. In *Bowen* v. *Postal Service*, 103 S.Ct. 588 (1983), the court said that the union's failure to process the grievance caused employees to lose wages and the union was liable to the extent of this loss.

The union has been held to owe a duty of fair representation to laid-off employees, employees not hired by a successor employer, employees who refuse to pay an assessment to a union, probationary employees, and those who opposed a dues increase. As the Hines case held, in deciding to bring an unresolved grievance to arbitration, the union must diligently and with vigor investigate the case thoroughly and must process the grievance. If the union gives an employee's claim only cursory attention, he or she has a right to sue the union under Section 301 of the act.[32]

Because the union is subject to fair representation charges by the employee, the union will often arbitrate weak cases rather than take the exposure to fair representation charges. This has greatly increased the use of arbitration in disputes over interpretation of the labor agreement.

Employee Rights under the Weingarten Doctrine

In its 1975 decision of *NLRB* v. *J. Weingarten, Inc.*, 420 U.S. 251 (1975), the court expanded the rights of employees as provided by Section 7 of the NLRA. The court reasoned that the employee who reasonably believes an investigatory interview will result in disciplinary action is seeking "aid and protection" against a perceived threat to his or her employment security. However, four conditions must exist:

1. The employee must request it. Employee silence is a waiver.[33]
2. The employee's right to request representation as a condition of participation in an interview is limited to where the employee reasonably believes the investigation will result in some kind of disciplinary action. (This would include a mere warning.)
3. The exercise of the right may not interfere with legitimate employer prerogatives. This means that management's investigative process can't be interfered with; management determines the rules of the interview process.[34]
4. The employer has no duty to bargain with the union representative who is attending the interview. However, the representative has the right to participate in the interview. The employee may consult with his or her representative prior to and during the meeting.[35]

Litigation over whether or not the doctrine applies seems to be a useless expense, since the same result could be accomplished by some other means. Either do not have the interview and make a decision on the facts that are available or get the facts by some other means.

The question of the remedy for violation has been before the board and the courts several times. After considerable litigation, the law has settled down to where reinstatement is allowed only if the general counsel can establish a prima facie case for reinstatement and concerted activities were not involved; otherwise a cease-and-desist order is issued. If the employee was sus-

---

[31]*Hines* v. *Anchor Motor Freight, Inc.*, 424 U.S. 554 (1976). The author had a related experience. He found 25 maintenance employees drinking in the local bar. He recommended discharging five of the least productive workers. The union objected, since there were others in the bar. The author told the union that if they would disclose the names, he would discharge them too. This was the end of the grievance because the union did not want to investigate further. In this situation the Hines case would apply for the five workers discharged.

[32]*Taylor* v. *Belger Cartage Service, Inc.*, 762 F.2d 665 (8th Cir. 1985). See also *Carpenter* v. *West Virginia Flat Glass*, 763 F.2d 622 (4th Cir.1985).

[33]*Prudential Insurance Co.* v. *NLRB*, 661 F.2d 398 (5th Cir. 1981).

[34]Manville Forest Products Corp., 269 NLRB No. 72 (1984).

[35]*NLRB* v. *Texaco, Inc.*, 659 F.2d 124 (9th Cir. 1981).

pended for just cause, then she or he could not be reinstated, since the court reasoned that the employee would have been fired whether the doctrine was violated or not.[36] The violation of the doctrine does have serious consequences, because under the labor agreement there would be other, more serious problems than violation of the doctrine if the employee were not discharged for just cause.

Extension of Doctrine to Nonunion Employees. The board originally took the position in Materials Research Corp., 262 NLRB No. 122 (1982), that the Weingarten doctrine applied to nonunion as well as union-represented employees. The court granted enforcement of this policy.[37] Later the court vacated its enforcement order upon request of the board and remanded to the board with an opportunity to change. In *Sears, Roebuck and Co.*, 274 NLRB No. 55 (1985), the board changed its position and stated that the Weingarten doctrine did not apply to unrepresented employees because it would be contrary to the exclusivity principles of the NLRA. The courts have not accepted this. The court in *Slaughter* v. *NLRB,* 794 F.2d 120 (3rd Cir. 1986), said the doctrine applied to nonunion employees. However, since this case, the board has consistently reaffirmed its position and refuses to apply the doctrine to nonunion employees. From the Slaughter case, the board now has a doctrine that they cannot enforce. The employer who would refuse representation to a nonunion employee could have considerable exposure to litigation. The best policy would be to allow the representation under the conditions of the Weingarten doctrine or not have the interview at all. To trigger litigation over a matter that can be resolved by some other means would seem not to be the most advisable approach.

RESTRAINTS ON THE RIGHT TO STRIKE

None of the parties to a labor dispute likes a strike because the consequences fall most heavily upon the union members and the company. For this reason there is a built-in incentive for the negotiators to avoid strikes. Management doesn't like the loss of revenues, customers, market share of their products, or community goodwill that results from a strike. Likewise, unions and workers don't take lightly the loss of wages and benefits, the family problems, and the poor public image that may result from the strike.

Because of the consequences of a strike, it is the threat of a strike that forces concessions and compromise in the negotiation process. Often more is gained by the threat than by engaging in the strike. It is for this reason that the right to strike under the NLRA, as opposed to the threat, is used very sparingly. From 1971 to 1980, only 2.6 percent of the workers in the United States were involved in a strike. In 1986 the number of strikes involving 1000 or more workers was only 69.[38] The state of the economy is not the only factor affecting strikes; economic strength and tactics by either side to force a compromise or an agreement also play a leading role.

Use of Strike Replacements

The law permits the employer to operate during a strike by the use of replacements.[39] The replaced strikers are placed upon the preferential hiring list. After they have communicated an unconditional request for

---

[36] This was first decided by the board in Taracorp Industries, 273 NLRB No. 54 (1984) and reaffirmed in *Communication Workers of America* v. *NLRB,* 784 F.2d 847 (7th Cir. 1986).

[37]*E.I. duPont deNemours Co.* v. *NLRB,* 733 F.2d 296 (3rd Cir. 1984).

[38]See *Monthly Labor Review,* U.S. Department of Labor, Bureau of Labor Statistics. See current issue for years after 1986.

[39]*NLRB* v. *Mackay Radio & Tel. Co.,* 304 U.S. 333 (1938).

reinstatement, they are entitled to receive their jobs back or substantially equivalent work as a vacancy occurs. The employer must recall all qualified strikers on the preferential hiring list before hiring new employees to fill vacancies.[40] Subsequent to the Mackay Radio case, the main issue at the bargaining table was what to do with the replacements after the strike was settled. A condition of the union for a settlement was to terminate the "scabs." Often the employer would agree, reinstate the strikers, and terminate the replacements. However, in the leading case of *Belknap, Inc.* v. *Hale,* 463 U.S. 491 (1983), the Supreme Court allowed the terminated replacements to bring a cause of action in a state court when they were promised permanent jobs when hired as strike replacements. This ruling opened the door for the employer to offer permanent jobs during the strike that could not be changed through bargaining, as a condition of settling the strike. Belknap only applies where the replacements have been clearly offered permanent jobs. This gave the employer a strong bargaining position before the strike. The union would threaten a strike and the employer would say, "Go ahead and we will hire permanent replacements." The threat of replacements to sue for breach of contract is being assigned great weight by union negotiators, and the members, knowing they may not get their jobs back, are reluctant to strike. The use of replacements has for years been seen by the employer as not being effective, but, with the Belknap decision, it is now used as a threat in bargaining that can be carried out. Business is also discovering that an increasing number of employees will cross the picket line rather than lose their jobs to replacements.[41] Further, the employer is discovering that replacements can be trained in a short time for skilled jobs.

To further strengthen the employer's bargaining position, one court has held that replacements can be used for a lockout that is motivated by legitimate business reasons. In Local 825 Operating Engineers, 829 F.2d 458 (3rd Cir. 1987), the court said that the lockout itself was not antiunion and it was not destructive of employee rights as long as no antiunion action was taken.

The strikers on the preferential hiring list retain their seniority when they return to work and cannot be placed below the replaced employees who refused to strike.[42] However, under certain conditions the union, to settle the strike, can agree to no seniority for the returning strikers.[43]

Often when union members return to work during the strike, the union will invoke provisions of the union constitution and fine the members. To avoid this, members crossing the picket line give notice to the union that they wish to be "financial core" members. The board in Carpenters Local 470, 277 NLRB No. 20 (1985), held that this was lawful; as long as the dues were tendered they could return to work without being fined under the union constitution.

The use of replacements will be a continuing employer response to the strike threat, and when a strike occurs the replacements will be effective in bringing striking workers back to the job. As one replacement said to a picket, "If you don't want your job, I do." This means that the use of a strike to force economic demands has diminishing effectiveness.

Although the effectiveness of a strike has diminished, the right to appeal to the public has not. In *Edward J. DeBartolo* v. *Florida Gulf Coast Building Construction Trades Council,* 108

---

[40]*NLRB* v. *Fleetwood Trailer Co.,* 389 U.S. 375 (1967); *Laidlaw Corp.,* 171 NLRB 1366 (1968) enf'd 414 F.2d 99 (7th Cir. 1969), cert. denied, 397 U.S. 920 (1970).

[41]In 1984 approximately 2500 employees returned to work at McDonnell Douglas after it began advertising for permanent replacements in the 17th week of the strike.

[42]*NLRB* v. *Harrison Ready Mix Concrete,* 770 F.2d 78 (6th Cir. 1985).

[43]This is now before the Supreme Court in *Trans World Airlines* v. *Flight Attendants,* Docket #87–548, and should be decided in the 1988–1989 term.

S.Ct. 1392 (1988), the Court held that the union had the right to distribute handbills at a shopping mall because of a labor dispute between the union and a construction company hired to build a store at the mall.

Restrictions on Strikers' Conduct

The right to picket during a strike is protected by the act, although the act does not expressly say so. It is inferred from the right to engage in concerted activities for the purpose of collective bargaining or other mutual aid and protection under Section 7 of the act. However, the right is conditional. The strike must be lawful and picketing must be peaceful.[44] Picketing in an unlawful strike will result in the strikers losing their employment status, and accordingly they will not have the right of recall when the strike is over. An unlawful strike would be picketing for a closed shop, a secondary boycott, or for the purpose of inducing the employer to enter into a "featherbedding" arrangement.

Violence can also result in denial of reinstatement rights. Violence during a strike can take several forms other than physical contact. Insulting language directed at the employer (a threat like "I am going to kill you") has been held to be violence and a reason to deny reinstatement.[45] Verbal threats to a nonstriker that his family will be harmed are sufficient to deny reinstatement.[46]

It is not necessary to be an employee of the facility being picketed, since Section 2(9) of the act defines a labor dispute to include "any controversy regardless of whether the person stands in proximate relation of employer and employee." This means that a union can hire professional pickets if it so desires. As a practical matter usually the pickets are either employees or members of the union employed elsewhere.

Enforcement of No-Strike Clause

The law permits the employee to enforce the labor agreement against the union and the employer. It also permits the union to sue the employer or the employer to enforce the labor agreement against the union. The employer enforcement of the agreement against the union usually appears in a situation where the union authorizes a strike in violation of a no-strike clause in the agreement. Under the Norris-La Guardia Act of 1932, the courts are prohibited from granting injunctions for strike activity. But where there is a no-strike clause, the question is whether it can be enforced in view of the Norris-La Guardia Act. Until 1970 no-strike clauses could not be enforced because the Supreme Court held that the Norris-La Guardia Act superseded the contractual no-strike clause,[47] which prevented the use of an injunction to stop a strike.

However, in certain situations the court partially reversed itself; in 1970 it held that a no-strike clause can be enforced provided the labor agreement contains a mandatory grievance adjustment or arbitration clause. The court reasoned that a no-strike clause is a trade-off for an arbitration clause; therefore, the union must arbitrate rather than go on strike.[48] In subsequent cases the court has made it clear than an arbitration clause is a prerequisite to issuing an injunction to enforce a no-strike clause. Where employees went on strike in sympathy with other employees from another company, the court held that such a strike could not be enjoined because the strike was not over a dispute of the employer in the labor agreement but in support of others not subject to arbitration.[49] This case reaffirms the court's posi-

---

[44]*Brotherhood of Railroad Trainmen* v. *Jacksonville Terminal Co.*, 394 U.S. 369 (1969).

[45]Clear Pine Mouldings, Inc., 268 NLRB No. 173 (1984).

[46]*Newport News Shipbuilding and Dry Dock Co.* v. *NLRB*, 738 F.2d 1404 (4th Cir. 1984).

[47]*Sinclair Refining Co.* v. *Atkinson*, 370 U.S. 195 (1962).

[48]*Boys Market* v. *Retail Clerks Union*, 398 U.S. 235 (1970).

[49]*Buffalo Forge Co.* v. *United Steelworkers of America*, 428 U.S. 397 (1976). This was a five to four decision.

tion in the Boys Market case that the decision is narrow; the Norris-La Guardia Act is by no means dead.

USE OF ARBITRATION IN DISPUTE RESOLUTION

The courts have stated that arbitration is a preferred method to settle disputes under a labor agreement. It has been declared that it is a federal policy to encourage the inclusion of grievance and arbitration clauses in the collective bargaining agreements.[50] The judicial policy of favoring arbitration in the resolution of labor disputes was first outlined in three landmark decisions of the Supreme Court, frequently referred to as the Steelworkers Trilogy. In one case the court compelled arbitration where the arbitration clause in the contract did not relate to the particular grievance.[51] In the second case the court held that the NLRA made arbitration awards enforceable in the courts.[52] In the third case the court compelled arbitration of a dispute although there was no arbitration clause in the collective bargaining agreement.[53]

The Collyer Doctrine of Referral to Arbitration

The right to arbitrate a dispute arises only from an agreement between the employee representative and the employer. The board takes the position that whenever possible it will refer an unfair labor practice to arbitration, providing the parties agree to arbitrate and the interpretation of the contract is the basis of the dispute. This is commonly known as the

Collyer doctrine for the board decision in Collyer Insulated Wire, 192 NLRB No. 150 (1971). The board later took the position that it would defer all cases to arbitration that could be settled under the labor agreement.[54] However, at least one court felt that the United Technologies position was not permitted by the NLRA and stated, in *Taylor* v. *NLRB,* 786 F.2d 1519 (11th Cir. 1986), that if the charge was an unfair labor practice as defined by the act, the board could not defer to arbitration but must hear it.

Whenever possible, the employer should assert the Collyer doctrine when unfair labor charges are filed. Arbitration is a faster way to settle the dispute and much more economical. Also, by referring it to arbitration, often the dispute is resolved without any arbitration, since either party may feel it is better to settle than to arbitrate.

Determination of Arbitrability of a Dispute

Sometimes the dispute is over whether the contract requires the issue to be arbitrated. The logical solution is to let the arbitrator decide the arbitrability of a dispute and if it is so decided he or she goes on and arbitrates the dispute. The Supreme Court, relying upon the Steelworkers Trilogy cases, said in *AT&T Technologies Inc.* v. *Communication Workers of America, et al.,* 106 S.Ct. 1415 (1986) that it was up to the courts, not the arbitrator, to determine whether an issue should be arbitrated. The court stated that it is a judicial question whether the parties have ever agreed to arbitrate the issue. Most agreements state that "all issues over the interpretation of this agreement must be submitted to arbitration." This case makes it advisable for the parties to be more specific in the collective bargaining agreement on what is and what is not subject to arbitration. Under the AT&T case failure to do so will only result in litigation.

---

[50]Approximately 95 percent of all labor agreements contain arbitration clauses.

[51]*United Steelworkers of America* v. *Warrior and Gulf Navigation Co.,* 363 U.S. 574 (1960).

[52]*United Steelworkers of America* v. *Enterprise Wheel and Car Corp.,* 363 U.S. 593 (1960).

[53]*United Steelworkers of America* v. *American Mfg. Co.,* 363 U.S. 564 (1960).

---

[54]United Technologies, 268 NLRB No. 557 (1984).

Enforcement of Arbitration Awards

Arbitration is not judicial process: There are no standard rules of evidence or procedure and one arbitrator is not bound by another's decision. Most arbitrators ignore previous decisions of others except to justify a position they have already taken. Reliance on prior decisions could reflect on the arbitrator's ability to decide the case on its merits.

Arbitration awards have no bearing on the employee's right to sue under a statute. As the court put it in *Alexander* v. *Gardner-Denver*, 94 S.Ct. 1101 (1974), in holding that an arbitration award does not prevent the employee from bringing a lawsuit under Title VII, "the specialized competence of arbitrators pertains primarily to the law of the shop not the law of the land."

The law enters into arbitration only when the award is challenged in the courts.[55] Arbitration awards are challenged because of

1. Fraud, misconduct, or gross unfairness by the arbitrator (rare)
2. Fraud by one of the parties affecting the result (very rare)
3. Failure of the arbitrator to stay within the contract (common)
4. Violation of public policy of the award (narrowly used)

Normally the courts are reluctant to reverse arbitration awards, since arbitration is a nationally recognized method to settle labor disputes and, further, the parties have agreed that the award will be final and binding. The two most compelling reasons to overturn an award are (1) when the arbitrator exceeds his or her authority by substituting judgment for that of the parties, and (2) where the award is contrary to the clear language of the contract.

Overturning of Awards by Courts

The Supreme Court stated in *United Steelworkers* v. *Enterprise Wheel*, 363 U.S. 593 (1960), "He may, of course, look for guidance from many sources, yet his award is legitimate only so long as it draws its essence from the collective bargaining agreement."

Where an arbitrator ordered that an employer must hire 39 employees who had been laid off from another brewery, the court said in *Miller Brewing Co.* v. *Brewery Workers*, 739 F.2d 1159 (7th Cir. 1984), that since there was no authority in the contract that would permit rehiring those workers with unsatisfactory work records, the arbitrator exceeded his authority, "although the interpretation of the contract is none of our business."[56]

Another reason for overturning an arbitration award is the arbitrator's substituting his judgment for that of the parties to the contract. This often happens when the contract limits the right to challenge a disciplinary action after the facts are determined. In *Riceland Foods* v. *Carpenters Local 2381*, 737 F.2d 758 (8th Cir. 1984), the arbitrator mitigated the discipline for a rule violation when the contract said that the arbitrator was limited to determining if the rule had been violated and not if the discipline was proper.[57]

Violation of public policy is another reason the courts will not enforce an arbitration award. In *W.R. Grace and Co.* v. *Rubber Workers Local 759*, 103 S.Ct. 2177 (1983), the Su-

---

[55]For further information on arbitration, see Robert Coulson, *Labor Arbitration—What You Need to Know* (NY: American Arbitration Association, 1978); Frank Elkouri and Edna Elkouri, *How Arbitration Works*, 4th ed. (Washington, DC: Bureau of National Affairs, 1985); Ken Jennings, Barbara Sheffield, and Roger Wolters, "Arbitration of Discharge Cases: A Forty Year Perspective," *Labor Law Journal*, 38, no. 1 (Jan. 1987), 33.

[56]See *Frederick Meiswinkel, Inc.* v. *Local 261*, 744 F.2d 1374 (9th Cir. 1984) where the arbitrator exceeded his authority.

[57]See also *Devine* v. *Pastre*, 732 F.2d 213 (D.C. Cir. 1984); *Morgan Services* v. *Local 323 of Amalgamated Clothing Textile Workers*, 724 F.2d 1217 (6th Cir. 1984).

preme Court stated that the courts may not enforce any collective bargaining agreement that is contrary to public policy. Since public policy is a vague term, it is often difficult to determine what is contrary to public policy. However, awards have been vacated as being contrary to public policy where a truck driver was reinstated despite the fact that his discharge had been for drinking on the job.[58] The award was held to be contrary to public policy where an employee was found guilty of graft and the arbitrator held that discharge was not for just cause since he agreed to pay money back.[59] In another case the award was contrary to the principles of labor law.[60]

The Supreme Court in *United Paper Workers* v. *Misco,* 108 S.Ct. 363 (1987), stated that there were insufficient facts to warrant the discharge, that the arbitrator should not be second-guessed by the courts. To create a public policy basis for setting aside an award, it must be shown that the policy is clear and explicit regarding laws or legal precedents, rather than a generalized notion of public interest. Violation of a public safety statute would be an example. See *Stead Motors of Walnut Creek* v. *Automobile Machinists Lodge No. 1173,* 843 F.2d 357 (9th Cir. 1988). The Court did not say that public policy could not be used as a basis for setting aside an award, but what it did say is there must be little doubt that a public policy exists, before the arbitrator as the trier of fact will be interfered with.

It is more common in the 1980s for the courts to overturn arbitration awards than at any previous time since the Steel Trilogy cases in 1960. Slightly less than half of the awards that were contested in the last decade have been reversed. There is no reason to believe that this trend will not continue. The most common issue in arbitration under the contract is discharge.[61] It is in discharge cases that the arbitrator often goes beyond the labor agreement, especially where those agreements only allow the arbitrator to determine the facts and not determine whether the penalty justifies the offense. It is desirable for both parties to include such a clause in the contract to prevent some arbitrators who do not believe in "capital punishment" from exceeding their authority by reinstating the employee.[62]

After Misco, some legal scholars believed that this was the end of arbitrators' decisions being overturned for public policy reasons. In many situations it is difficult to show that a clear public policy exists when over the years court decisions in other areas have been very vague in defining public policy.

One sure way to keep arbitrators from reinstating employees discharged for what the company may believe is contrary to its own public policy is to put a clause in the contract limiting the arbitrator's authority to fact finding only. Specifically, take away the right to prescribe a remedy (see Exhibit 16-1). In *S.D. Warren Co.* v. *United Paperworkers' International Union, AFL-CIO,* 846 F.2d 827 (11th Cir. 1988), the court, in overturning the arbitrator's award, held that the arbitrator had no authority under the contract to reinstate an employee who violated the rule of possession, sale, or use of drugs on company property. Whether the case came under Misco, as the union argued, was never an issue. In Misco, the company did not specifically reserve the right in the labor agreement to discharge for a rule violation, and in this respect, S.D. Warren was different from Misco. In S.D. Warren the court decided that the arbitrator, having found that

---

[58]*Meatcutters Local 540* v. *Great Western Food Co.,* 712 F.2d 122 (5th Cir. 1983).

[59]*U.S. Postal Service* v. *Postal Workers,* 736 F.2d 822 (1st Cir. 1984).

[60]*Carpenters Local 1478* v. *Stevens,* 743 F.2d 1271 (9th Cir. 1984).

[61]Federal Mediation and Conciliation Service, Arbitration Statistics (FY 1985), report that half of all referrals for a panel are for discharge disputes.

[62]For information on arbitration of discharge cases, see Thomas R. Knight, "Impact of Arbitration on the Administration of Disciplinary Policies," *The Arbitration Journal,* 39, no. 1 (1984), 53.

EXHIBIT 16-1   *Suggested Clause to Limit Arbitrator's Authority in Discharge*

> The following offenses are deemed sufficient cause for discharge, and are subject to arbitration only to determine the facts of whether the offense was committed. Once facts are established the discharge can be invoked. [List "sudden death" offenses, such as possession of firearms and drugs, sleeping, and violation of certain safety rules.]

a drug violation had occurred as charged, was prevented under the contract from upholding the discharge.

A clause making the arbitrator a fact finder only is not too difficult to negotiate if the company is reasonable and somewhat limits the offenses that are "sudden death" discharges. Possession, sale, or use of drugs certainly would be one of them. Possession of firearms, stealing company or employees' property, to name a few others, would be reasonable to negotiate. The union is not interested in keeping undesirable employees any more than the company is, but as rep-

resentative of the employee they must to some extent legally rely upon the arbitrator to define just cause unless it is already defined in the contract.

There is always an exposure that the employee will file a fair representation charge with the NLRB when the decision of the union is subjective.

Since arbitrators' decisions are difficult to overturn, the best approach is to limit their authority in the labor agreement. This should be a part of every collective bargaining agreement and should be on the company's agenda at the next bargaining session.

MANAGEMENT MALPRACTICE

Use of the Term Malpractice
Malpractice in Management
Sexual Harassment as a Form of Malpractice
Individual Liability When Acting in Behalf of Employer
Failure to Provide a Safe Place to Work
Prevention of Exposure to Malpractice

USE OF THE TERM *MALPRACTICE*

Malpractice in the Professions

The oldest and most common use of the term *malpractice* is in the medical profession where the doctor is negligent in the treatment of the patient. This is usually considered professional conduct that is below what is expected of a doctor, which also includes judgment. The law requires professional competence of a doctor when he or she undertakes to treat a patient.

Malpractice suits are also common in the legal profession where because of the attorney's failure to act, the client loses some rights or is denied monetary recovery. Legal malpractice also occurs when the attorney gives advice without adequate research and such advice adversely affects the client. For example, if the attorney tells a client that she or he does not have a legal basis to sue when upon research the law is clear that there is a remedy, this would be malpractice. If the attorney had used care and researched the problem before advising the client, the advice would be poor judgment, which is not legal malpractice.

Malpractice suits against accountants, consultants, and other professionals are on the increase, but far from approaching the frequency of those against the medical profession. However, attorneys are catching up to doctors in the frequency of lawsuits.

Malpractice in Business Relationships

Management malpractice can be related to business conduct other than the treatment of employees. Customer mistreatment, unethical conduct between competitors, tax fraud, ruthless pricing practices, or fraud in dealing with the public are all examples of management malpractice that doesn't involve the employee. In one situation a lower court found that malpractice was committed by the clergy when the pastor of a church described heaven to a 24-year-old man who had suicidal tendencies as a very nice place, a natural thing for clergy to do. The family sued the church and collected damages for malpractice when the person committed suicide. The case was appealed and at this printing still is being litigated.

MALPRACTICE IN MANAGEMENT

The concept of management malpractice in dealing with employees is different from that in business conduct. The term refers to conduct that is not necessarily negligent or incompetent but includes acts that are unacceptable in our society. The court in *Belanoff v. Grayson*, 471 N.Y.S.2d (A.D. 1st Dept. 1984), characterized it as "conduct that exceeds all bounds usually tolerated by society." Lawsuits for management malpractice are becoming more frequent. Some lawyers have a lucrative practice representing employees in malpractice suits when they are terminated. When this type of case does go to court and the employers lose, they pay awards that average above six figures, plus the employee's attorney's fees.[1]

Legal malpractice can occur when management uses what it believes is an effective way to correct unacceptable conduct of the employee and to train him or her in a manner to ensure that such conduct will not recur. The problem arises when the law decides that the techniques used are not acceptable to our society. What may be legitimate conduct to management may not be legitimate to a jury.

This chapter will examine this relatively new area of management liability and give some insight into those management practices that the courts say society will not accept. To prevent malpractice in management it is first necessary to know what it is and then to know the legal consequences when a "short fuse" manager takes action

---

[1]See Craig R. Waters, "The New Malpractice," *Inc.* (June 1983), p. 136.

involving an employee. Although malpractice exists in other areas in business, this chapter will deal only with the employer-employee relationship.

Malpractice Defined

Management malpractice is conduct that has serious consequences on the employee's personal or physical well-being. This new area of management liability is presently very small, but its growth is being aided by other rapidly expanding areas of employee rights and enforcing social responsibility on employers. The courts are taking the position that the employer-employee relationship carries with it certain legal obligations. This position is supported by statutes as well as by common law. The National Labor Relations Act requires the employer to refrain from certain activities affecting the employee's right to join or not to join a union. Financial protection for job-related injuries is provided under the workers compensation laws of the various states. The Equal Pay Act requires employers to give equal pay for equal work without regard to sex, and Title VII states that an employer cannot make any employment decision that is based on race, color, nationality, or sex.

All these statutory rights have strengthened the belief that an employee has a property right in his or her job. This property right is being expanded so rapidly that in some situations, a person cannot be discharged without a just cause. This erosion of the common law employment-at-will doctrine is resulting in the elimination of another management prerogative that forms the basis for malpractice.

Change in Employee Attitude

Another important development in the employee relations field is the change in the attitude of the dissatisfied employee. Formerly a dissatisfied employee grumbled for a while, looked to a union for help, or even-

tually quit. Today employees use the various agencies established to hear complaints such as the NLRB, EEOC, or the union, or they may go to an adventurous attorney to start a private lawsuit and receive large monetary awards from management through the jury system rather than rely upon the relief provided by statute.

Almost all malpractice suits are actions in tort and differ from the breach of contract suits common in wrongful discharge cases. The successful prosecution of malpractice action requires a showing of more extreme action by the defendant but also results in the awarding of higher damages. In supporting a claim of emotional distress it is usually necessary to show intent, but in other malpractice actions the courts only require evidence that the plaintiff was injured by the defendant's unreasonable conduct.

Examples of Malpractice Lawsuits

A common form of management malpractice is where the employee alleges intentional infliction of emotional distress. This is sometimes called "a contemptuous tort" and is a common allegation in discharge cases. In this type of case the employee alleges that the employer's conduct was intentional and/or reckless and contrary to what a civilized society should tolerate. The effect upon the employee must be severe, and since this is a new area of law, we are not yet sure how severe. Refusing to allow an employee (who was hypersensitive) to take a tranquilizer when being questioned for theft was held in *Tandy Corp.* v. *Bone*, 678 S.W.2d 311 (Ark. 1984), to be intentional infliction of emotional distress because the employer had knowledge of the employee's condition.

Where the employer ridiculed, threatened, humiliated, and sexually harassed the employee, the court found a tort of outrageous conduct.[2] The court in another situ-

_____
[2]*Wing* v. *JMB Management Corp.*, 714 P.2d 916 (Colo. App. 1985).

ation found that the employee's refusal to date the son of the owner resulted in harassment, which subjected the employee to extraordinarily difficult and onerous working conditions and was a cause of action to be submitted to the jury.[3]

Wrongful Employment Action but Not Malpractice

An example of a case where the action was not severe enough to be malpractice is where in *Moye* v. *Gary,* 595 F.Supp. 738 (S.D.N.Y. 1984), the supervisor called an employee a "fag" and a "poor woman." In *Morrison* v. *Sandell et al.,* 466 N.E.2d 290 (Ill. App. 1983), a co-worker put human waste in a file drawer that the plaintiff was about to use. The court held that the conduct was not severe enough and was an "isolated incident that lacked duration." Another example of conduct not severe enough to find emotional distress was where in *Vinson* v. *Linn-Mar Community School District,* 360 N.W.2d (Iowa 1984), a former employer was guilty of defamation of character by malice and mistruths, for which damages were awarded, but the court held that this was not an act that was "atrocious and utterly intolerable in a civilized community."

In another case, the court agreed that the employee may have

- Suffered embarrassment by his wrongful discharge when he had to tell acquaintances that he was unemployed
- Stayed awake at night worrying about employment
- Had unsteady nerves
- Been depressed most of the time
- Avoided social contact with his friends
- Experienced fear about meeting financial obligations

- Gone to a physician as well as a psychologist regarding stress
- Had no self-confidence when meeting prospective employers

The court did not consider these effects severe enough, however, to maintain a claim of intentional infliction of emotional distress for the wrongful discharge. It held that the law intervenes only when the employer's action is "so severe that no reasonable man could be expected to bear it."[4]

Where the discharge was because the employee refused to stop dating a co-worker, the court held discharge was not severe enough conduct to warrant emotional distress even though the discharge caused severe distress.[5] This rule was also adopted in Missouri where the employer—before the discharge—said "Dammit, you've done it again" and commented that she "doesn't know a goddamn thing." The plaintiff alleged that she suffered "severe mental pain, anguish, embarrassment, shock, fright, humiliation and distress and had stomach problems and loss of sleep" as the result of the employer's conduct at the time of her discharge. The court noted that the employer's conduct, although not above reproach, could not be characterized as so extreme and outrageous as to be considered a tort. It further stated that employees must necessarily be hardened to a certain amount of rough language and certain other facts that are inconsiderate and unkind. Although the plaintiff suffered mental stress, it was not sufficient to allow recovery.[6]

The successful prosecution of an emotional distress claim requires the plaintiff to show more extreme action by the defendant than in other malpractice cases. In supporting an allegation of emotional distress it is usually necessary to show intent, but in other malpractice actions the courts only require

---

[3]*Lewis* v. *Oregon Beauty Supply Co.,* 714 P.2d 618 (Or. App. 1986). Also see *Beye* v. *Bureau of National Affairs,* 477 A.2d 1197 (Md. App. 1984), rev. denied; 484 A.2d 274.

[4]*Eklund* v. *Vincent Brass and Aluminum Co.,* 351 N.W.2d 371 (Minn. App. 1984).

[5]*Patton* v. *J.C. Penney Co.,* 719 P.2d 854 (Or. 1986).

[6]*Rooney* v. *Super Markets, Inc.,* 668 S.W.2d 649 (Mo. App. 1984).

that the plaintiff was injured by the defendant's unreasonable conduct.[7]

SEXUAL HARASSMENT AS A FORM OF MALPRACTICE

Distinction from Violation of Title VII

Sexual harassment as a tort (when one person injures another) that will allow punitive damages occurs when the employee alleges that failure to submit to sexual advances results in emotional distress or is an invasion of privacy. This claim by the plaintiff differs from sexual harassment under Title VII in that jury trial is allowed. Back pay and being reinstated to the job are not the relief asked, but punitive damages (a monetary punishment for a wrong) are requested, which are determined by the jury and are always greater than back pay.

The court explained the difference between statutory violation and common law very well in *Lucas* v. *Brown*, 736 F.2d 1202 (8th Cir. 1984). This involved an employee who refused to submit to sexual advances and alleged that she was discharged for that reason. In dismissing a Title VII claim because it was not filed within the time limits, the court allowed the employee to recover punitive damages on the basis that the discharge was a violation of public policy. The court stated that "a woman invited to trade herself for a job is in effect being asked to become a prostitute." The court allowed damages for intentional infliction of emotional distress because "in light of the nature of the employment relationship and the power of the employer" punitive damages would be justified. The courts that allow recovery beyond Title VII for mental anguish and physical symptoms of distress state that back pay and reinstatement would not adequately compensate the employee. This was the reason that mental anguish was allowed in *Holien* v. *Sears, Roebuck and Co.*, 677 P.2d 704 (Or. 1984),[8] which had the effect of allowing a tort recovery in a wrongful discharge.

In some situations the evidence will not permit a violation of Title VII, but the employer still can be liable for sexual assault. A District of Columbia court in *Clark* v. *World Airways*, 24 F.E.P. Cases (BNA) (D.C. D.C. 1980), held that the evidence would not allow a Title VII action because the company president never made submission to sexual favors a condition of employment. However, there was sufficient evidence for a jury to find that the president had sexual relations with the plaintiff and while doing so he was serving his employer. The court found that the act was in the course of employment because the employer provided the opportunity for the offensive conduct and it was an outgrowth of the employment situation.

Not all courts will hold that sexual harassment is malpractice for which jury trial and punitive damages are allowed. When a fashion director with high performance ratings was discharged allegedly for refusal of sexual favors, the court, in *Wolk* v. *Saks Fifth Avenue, Inc.*, 728 F.2d 221 (3rd Cir. 1984), held that the remedy was under Title VII and would not permit an action for tortious conduct. A Florida court said that mere sexual harassment conduct was not outrageous enough to allow an action for punitive damages.[9]

Sexual Harassment as Invasion of Privacy

Sexual advances are considered an invasion of privacy under certain conditions. This

---

[7]For further reading on emotional distress, see "Intentional Infliction of Emotional Distress in the Employment-at-Will Setting: Limiting the Employer's Manner of Discharge," *Indiana Law Journal*, 60, W.D. 2 (1984-1985), 365–88.

[8]See also *Ball* v. *Cracking Good Bakeries*, 777 F.2d 1497 (11th Cir. 1986), where the court allowed claim for malpractice. Also see *Ford* v. *Revlon, Inc.*, 734 P.2d 580 (Ariz. 1987), and *O'Connell* v. *Chasdi*, 400 Mass. 686 (Mass. 1987), where court found emotional distress in sexual harassment complaints.

[9]*Ponton* v. *Scarfone*, 468 So.2d 1009 (Fla. App. 2 Dist. 1985).

offense has more potential exposure to law-suits than the infliction of emotional distress. The reason is that the case law is more advanced. In *Eisenstadt, Sheriff v. Baird,* 405 U.S. 438 (1972), the U.S. Supreme Court held that in questioning an employee about marriage and her sex life, these are fundamental rights entitled to privacy protection. When questioning about sex with her husband, accompanied by sexual advances, there is a likelihood that this would be an invasion of privacy for which damages would be determined by a jury, as was the case in *Phillips v. Smalley Maintenance Services,* 711 F.2d 1524 (11th Cir. 1983). The court in these cases held that questioning about a person's sex life is an invasion of privacy, whereas touching or other sexual advances are not an invasion of privacy but only a violation of Title VII.

The problem of sexual harassment in the workplace is not going to be completely solved in the near future. Sexual advances are difficult for some people to control. Management's exposure to litigation very often will extend beyond Title VII. Not all courts agree that sexual harassment can result in a tort, but there is presently enough case law to make the exposure troublesome for the employer. Why be concerned about whether sexual harassment is malpractice? Just have strict enforcement of a nonharassment policy.

INDIVIDUAL LIABILITY WHEN ACTING IN BEHALF OF EMPLOYER

In this era of legal scrutiny of management activity, the question is often asked whether the personnel practitioner, the manager, the supervisor, or any other member of management can be held personally liable for actions taken in behalf of the employer. In an unpublished survey of management personnel by the author, respondents were asked whether they believed they could be held personally liable when acting in behalf of their employer. Almost 80 percent wrongfully thought that they could be held per-sonally liable, but few knew the circumstances that might lead to personal liability.

Managers run the risk of personal liability in several different areas of activity, such as price fixing under antitrust laws, misuse of funds or company property, and conflicts of interest. Most directors of any organization, whether profit or nonprofit, have potential personal liability when acting in behalf of the organization. Officers of corporations are often asked to participate in community activities, which they do on company time and company expense accounts. They could be liable under certain circumstances. Many officers are exposed to information that makes them "insiders" for security transactions. They could be personally liable under some conditions in this area.

Due to space limitations, this section will discuss the exposure only in the treatment of the employee. However, administrative management working with legal counsel might be well advised to inform members of management who participate in other areas to seek independent advice to determine the extent of their personal liability.

Corporate Veil Protection

The general rule is that in absence of intent, deceit, or fraud the manager is not liable for mere mistakes or errors in judgment when acting in behalf of the employer. The courts take the position that a corporate veil of immunity protects the manager from personal liability. There have been rare incidents where employees have caused this corporate veil to be penetrated and the courts have found the manager individually liable to the employee when acting in behalf of the employer.[10]

Although court decisions where the manager has been held individually liable are rare and the corporate veil of immunity still prevails, unawareness of the exposure may lead to abuses that will have the effect of making lawsuits against managers as popu-

---

[10]*Emmert* v. *Drake,* 224 F.2d 299 (5th Cir. 1955).

lar in the future as malpractice suits against doctors and lawyers are today. Where the employer intermingled personal assets with corporate funds and failed to pay wages and benefits, and then dissolved the corporation, NLRB held the owner personally liable.[11]

Cases of Liability of Company Officers

Unless an officer participates in deceit or fraud, the courts will not find individual liability. However, where corporate officers knowingly permitted the company to violate the Wage Payment and Collection Act to deny employees their wages, the officers were held individually liable for the unpaid wages when the company filed bankruptcy. The court said in *Mullins* v. *Venable,* 297 S.E.2d 866 (W.Va. 1982), that the officers had a duty to see that the corporation obeyed the law. As a general rule the courts will inflict a greater degree of responsibility on officers than on other members of management. In a situation similar to the Mullins case, the corporate officers had a substantial interest in the corporation and were directly involved in decisions affecting the employees' compensation. They were held personally liable under the Fair Labor Standards Act for failure to pay minimum wages and overtime during the last week of existence of the corporation.[12] In considering the liability of an officer, the court will look to see if he or she was acting in good faith, within his or her authority, and using the proper degree of prudence and diligence. When a manager attempted to hide assets to avoid paying back pay for wages due, the court said the corporation is the alter ego of the manager, who became personally liable.[13] Where corporate officers acting in behalf of the corporation caused damages by willful participation in fraud and deceit, they were held personally liable.[14]

Where a stockholder-employee asked if he could inspect the corporate books and was discharged instead, the court allowed a claim against the officer and director of the corporation for inducing the corporation to discharge the employee and in doing so not acting for the benefit of the corporation.[15] The corporation was not held liable because it had a right to discharge under the employment-at-will doctrine. Normally, officers are not held personally liable for discharge since most courts hold that it is within their supervisory duties to act in behalf of the corporation. In the Campbell case discharging the employee was not the cause of liability, but refusal for him to see the stockholders list is what caused the personal liability.

Personal Liability under Antidiscrimination Laws

When claims against supervisors or managers for personal liability are brought under the discrimination statutes, the courts have refused to entertain them. When the employee wants to sue a manager, rather than relying upon a discrimination statute she or he will sue for a tortious injury under the common law.

Management personnel are often named in discrimination suits for reasons other than personal liability. The plaintiff may wish to have a member of management available to negotiate a settlement or for establishing the ultimate liability of the employer. Once the purpose is achieved, the managers are usually dropped as defendants.

There is nothing in the contents or legislative history of Title VII or most other antidiscrimination statutes that indicates that Congress intended managers or other employees to be personally liable. Title VII refers to only three kinds of entities: employers, employment agencies, and labor unions. When defining employers, the courts adopt the National Labor Relations Act definition,

---

[11]*Las Villas Produce,* 279 NLRB No. 120 (1986).

[12]*Donovan* v. *Agnew,* 712 F.2d 1508 (1st Cir. 1983).

[13]*Donovan* v. *Burgett Greenhouses, Inc.,* 759 F.2d 1483 (10th Cir. 1985).

[14]*Lentz Plumbing Co.* v. *Fee,* 679 P.2d 736 (Kan. 1984).

[15]*Campbell* v. *Ford Industries,* 546 P.2d 141 (Or. 1976).

which states that an employer is anyone who is not an employee. In *Silver* v. *KCA, Inc.*, 586 F.2d 138 (9th Cir. 1978), a supervisor made a remark about an employee, calling her a "jungle bunny." A co-worker overheard the remark and became indignant and demanded an apology. The apology was made to the indignant employee but two days later the co-worker was discharged. She sued, alleging that her termination was a violation of Title VII, since it was the result of her opposition to the supervisor's remark about her black co-worker. The court said that the opposition to a remark made about a co-worker to another employee is not a violation of the act unless the remark is directed at an employment practice. Title VII was not intended to stop discrimination by private individuals—reprehensible as that may be—but the intent was to eradicate discrimination by employers against employees.

The courts have consistently found the employer and not the offender liable under other antidiscrimination statues. This was true in *Martin* v. *Easton Publishing Co.*, 478 F.Supp. 796 (E.D. Pa. 1979),[16] even when the manager was not acting in behalf of the employer when he discriminated under the Equal Pay Act. The court said that "no additional relief can be obtained from individual defendants and no purpose will be served by retaining them in litigation for equal pay."

Liability under the Civil Rights Acts of 1866 as Amended

The Civil Rights Act 1866 and its 1971 amendment are specifically antidiscrimination statutes, since they were passed to enhance the Thirteenth and Fourteenth amendments of the Constitution. The statutes proclaim that all persons have the right to enforce contracts and have equal benefit of all laws regardless of their color. In effect, these two early statutes bar intentional discrimination because of race but got little attention in the courts until 1968. They grant all persons the right to redress a wrong. Section 1983 of the 1871 statute says, in effect, that any person who acts under the color or authority of any statute, ordinance, or regulation and causes injury to another or deprives that person of his rights, privileges, or immunities secured by the Constitution shall be liable to the party injured. This statute has the effect of making all persons in the public sector or those persons acting under the authority of a law personally liable for their acts. Where the directors of a nonprofit corporation operated a swimming pool with public funds, the court held them personally liable when they denied blacks admission.[17]

In recent years this statute has been used extensively in finding public officials personally liable when performing their duties under the authority of a statute, ordinance, or regulation. In a leading case of *Vinard* v. *King*, 728 F.2d 428 (10th Cir. 1984), an employee handbook of a municipally owned hospital stated that a permanent employee could not be discharged without cause. The personnel director of the hospital discharged an employee without a hearing. When the employee brought suit, the court held that the action of the director was a violation of Section 1983 (1871 amendment) and the Fourteenth Amendment. The court allowed punitive damages against the director as a municipal official but not against the hospital because this was a municipal organization that couldn't be sued. See also *St. Louis* v. *Praprotnik*, 108 S.Ct. 915 (1988), where the court held that the city could not be sued by an employee.

The U.S. Supreme Court has endorsed personal liability of a public employee in *Smith* v. *Wade*, 103 S.Ct. 1625 (1983), where a prison guard placed the plaintiff in the same cell with another inmate who the guard knew was dangerous. The plaintiff was beaten by his cellmate, and the court allowed punitive

---

[16]See also *Padway* v. *Palches*, 665 F.2d 965 (9th Cir. 1982).

[17]*Tillman* v. *Wheaton-Haven Recreation Assn.*, 517 F.2d 1141 (4th Cir. 1975).

damages against the guard. This has been extended to state judges. In *Forrester* v. *White,* 108 S.Ct.538 (1988), a judge was personally liable under Section 1983 of the U.S. Code when making an administrative decision involving the discharge of a probation officer; he was immune only from judicial activity.

The courts strictly follow the requirement that the defendant must be acting under the authority of a regulation or a statute. The court did not accept the plaintiff's argument that since the defendant used the name "Kentucky Fried Chicken," the manager was liable, since he was acting under the authority of the state when he used the name of the state in the business title.[18]

Personal Liability under Antitrust Statutes

The antitrust statutes most often used for personal liability are the Sherman and Clayton Acts. All the various antitrust regulations basically state that any act that restricts competition is illegal. Section 2 of the Sherman Antitrust Act states that every person (a corporation is considered a person) who shall make a contract or engage in any combination or conspiracy declared illegal under the act is guilty of a felony. A violation shall be punished by a fine not exceeding one million dollars ($1,000,000) if the act is committed by a corporation, and if by any other "person," not more than one hundred thousand dollars ($100,000) or imprisonment for a term not exceeding three years or both at the discretion of the court. This section unequivocally imposes personal liability on any member of management, when acting for the benefit of the corporation, as well as on the corporation.

To be in violation the acts or omissions must result in restricting competition and the facts must show implied or actual intent. In the past, courts have given jail sentences to individuals although in most cases the sentences have been suspended or the defen-

dants have been required to perform some community service. In an early case (which the Supreme Court refused to review) where there was clear intent to violate the Sherman Act, the court sentenced eight officers and management personnel to from 20 to 60 days in jail.[19]

The personnel practitioner has the most exposure to antitrust liability when making wage or cost surveys with competitors. These information requests present an exposure that must be recognized. Surveys run afoul of the antitrust laws when the reason for obtaining the information is to formulate future policies as to costs, wages, working conditions, and benefits in order to conform with those of their competitors. This, according to the U.S. Justice Department, has the effect of lessening competition. This is what happened when nonunion stockbrokers sued the New York Stock Exchange for conspiring among its members to reduce their commissions. The court held in *Cordova* v. *Bache & Co.,* 520 F.2d 1231 (2nd Cir. 1975), cert. denied (1976), that this exchange of information was a violation of the antitrust laws because it resulted in collusion to fix commissions. In a situation that was settled out of court, but established rules for surveys, the Women Organized for Employment alleged that the purpose of the salary surveys in the San Francisco Bay Area was to keep female wages and benefits below the competitive levels. This case was filed as *Goodspeed* v. *Federated Employers of the Bay Area.* The Justice Department, in an out-of-court settlement, stated that surveys among competitors are in compliance with the Sherman Act if certain conditions are met.

Since intent has to be shown to prove an antitrust violation, getting approval from legal counsel for a survey with competitors is important. Although the cases involving surveys are few in number, the Antitrust Division of the Justice Department and activist groups are ready to challenge any question-

---

[18]*McCarthy* v. *KFC Corp.,* 667 F.Supp. 343 (D.C. Ky. 1985).

[19]*U.S.* v. *American Radiator and Standard Corp., et al.,* 338 F.2d 201 (3rd Cir. 1967).

able survey. Participants in salary surveys are in compliance if the following conditions are met:

1. Report only aggregated information.
2. Publish no data as to future intentions.
3. Avoid surveys that have fewer than ten participants.
4. Avoid discussions with competitors where there is agreement to pay certain rates for certain jobs. This is a sure violation.

Court interpretation on surveys as to antitrust violations is rare; most survey cases have been settled out of court. Whether a salary survey is within the antitrust laws is a matter to be determined by legal counsel.

Labor unions are specifically exempted from antitrust laws under both the Sherman Act and the Clayton Act. Section 20 of the Clayton Act states that neither unions nor their members can be considered "illegal combinations in restraint of trade."[20] Unions lose their antitrust immunity when the activity is designed to control the marketing of goods and services or limit competition for goods and services.[21] They can also lose their exemptions where they coerce nonunion groups to join the union or where they conspire with employers to hire only union contractors.[22] Unions also have no standing in suing their employer under antitrust when the employer diverts work from union to nonunion contractors.[23] Normally labor-management relations are not regulated by antitrust laws nor are they intended to infringe upon the authority of the National Labor Relations Act.

Extent of Liability under Other Statutes

The plan administrator under the Consolidated Omnibus Budget Reconciliation Act

(COBRA), who is usually a personnel director, can be held personally liable up to $100 per day from the date of failure to give notice to the employee or dependents of the right to be covered by the employer's group insurance.

Under the Employee Retirement Income Security Act (ERISA), the fiduciary can be personally liable for violations, but this usually is an outside professional.

The Immigration Reform and Control Act of 1986 (IRCA) imposes civil, criminal, and equitable liability on any employer or an individual acting in behalf of an employer who recruits, hires, or employs an undocumented alien or those persons unauthorized to work in the United States. It also imposes a personal liability if an individual fails to keep records.

Personal Liability for Unsafe Conditions

Everyone who has worked in safety programs knows that injuries can occur despite the best efforts of the safety director and other members of management. In most lawsuits involving personal liability for unsafe conditions, the corporate veil of immunity has been upheld. Most courts will not even allow the employee to sue the employer for an injury, since the workers compensation statute is the exclusive remedy. Since no one wishes to face even the remote threat of personal liability, the safety practitioner often overreacts to any potential danger. However, there are some indications that the "safety net" of immunity has been pierced and a slight exposure of personal liability does exist for failure to provide a safe place to work. Section 17(e) under the Occupational Safety and Health Act (OSHA) makes individuals criminally liable under the act when it is shown that they knowingly and intentionally violated the act.

Safety officials or managers have an exposure for lack of professional responsibility in failing to provide a safe place to work if up-to-date techniques are not used to prevent accidents. This exposure is still embryonic but may grow rapidly, particularly if the existence of the exposure is ignored.

---

[20]*United States* v. *Hutcheson,* 312 U.S. 219 (1941).

[21]*Allen-Bradley Co.* v. *Electrical Workers (IBEW) Local No. 3,* 325 U.S. 797 (1945).

[22]*Amalgamated Meat Cutters Local 189* v. *Jewel Tea Co.,* 381 U.S. 676 (1965).

[23]*Associated General Contractors* v. *Calif. State Council of Carpenters,* 103 S.Ct. 897 (1983).

Employer Indemnification for Employees Acting in Employer's Behalf

Managers who perform their duties in good faith and carry out corporate policy sometimes become insecure if they feel that employees or unsuccessful job applicants will sue them as individuals. The employer, to eliminate this problem, often agrees to indemnify the person acting on behalf of the company for the losses, thereby encouraging the innocent manager to resist meritless suits or unjust charges and to induce competent persons to accept responsible positions.

Some states have statutes that require the employer to indemnify if the corporate bylaws are silent, providing the manager acted in good faith and had no reason to believe the act was unlawful. Most state courts permit some form of indemnification, which includes expenses, settlement costs, judgments, and fines, providing the manager acted in good faith and reasonably believed that she or he was acting in the best interests of the company. This principle was endorsed by the U.S. Supreme Court in *Burks* v. *Lasker,* 441 U.S. 471 (1975).

When liability insurance coverage is used to indemnify the manager in discrimination lawsuits, it usually is not effective, because there is a well-settled rule that a contract to indemnify a person for damages caused by intentional misconduct is against public policy. The question in all these cases is whether there was intentional misconduct in violation of a statute. Since the courts will not allow personal liability under Title VII, indemnification is a moot question under that statute. In other discrimination statutes, however, such as Equal Pay, Age Discrimination, and Pregnancy Disability Act, whether there was misconduct or intent is an important question for indemnification coverage.

Sometimes the court will not permit indemnification because of the nature of the offense. In *Kryriazi* v. *Western Electric Co.,* 647 F.2d 388 (3rd Cir. 1981), the plaintiff was allowed to recover from the employer under Title VII for sexual harassment by her co-workers and supervisors. She was allowed to bring a separate action in state court against her supervisor for maliciously interfering with her employment. The corporate immunity veil was pierced and the supervisor was held personally liable. The court prevented the employer from paying the damages because this would not correct the abusive conduct.

Recommendations for Avoiding Personal Liability

We have seen that except in the case of an individual acting under the authority of a statute as a public employee or committing an antitrust violation, the general rule is there is no personal liability for persons acting wrongfully in behalf of the employer. However, there are enough exceptions to this general rule and the consequences are so catastrophic that it is worthwhile for members of management to take reasonable steps to avoid possible exposure.

The most important factor to prevent exposure is to recognize that the possibility does exist in rare situations. The second point is that the standard of behavior must be what is acceptable in our society. Everyone should know what that standard is, but individuals sometimes get trapped into an organizational philosophy that is either obsolete or otherwise out of step with contemporary thinking on how employees should be treated. When other employees or the company participates in activity that may result in personal liability, evidence of lack of participation is the best defense. This question frequently comes up in antitrust violations which provide for personal liability. If employment decisions are reasonable and participation documented, there is little chance of personal liability. The documentation should include the date of the decision and a brief synopsis of the facts and events surrounding the decision. The manager should not rely upon indemnification insurance because this is of little help where intent is shown or implied and if the act is contrary to what is accepted by society.

Employee-related litigation has made a small start in attempting to obtain damages from the manager or officer involved in an employment decision. Being aware of the trend and taking the necessary preventative steps will permit the manager to accept the responsibility along with the liabilities of the job without fear of the tragedy from personal liability.

It should also be noted that there is a trend in Congress to make the individual liable for a violation. COBRA and IRCA, to name a couple of laws, were passed in the late 1980s.

FAILURE TO PROVIDE A SAFE PLACE TO WORK

Workers Compensation Exclusion

Employers have more immunity from malpractice charges for failure to provide a safe place to work than for most other employment actions. The main reason for this immunity is that workers compensation statutes provide an exclusive remedy in all but four states (West Virginia, Ohio, Pennsylvania, and Texas). In *Blankenship* v. *Cincinnati Milacon Chemicals*, 433 N.E.2d 572 (Ohio S.Ct. 1983), the court found an exception when the employees became ill because of exposure to toxic chemicals and the employer knew or should have known of the condition but failed to take corrective action. The court held the employer guilty for failure to provide an injury-free environment because this was outside the scope of the Workers Compensation Statute.[24] In *Granite Const. Co.* v. *Superior Ct. of Fresno*, 197 Cal. Rptr. 3 (Cal. App. 5 Dist. 1983), the employer was indicted criminally for manslaughter in the death of seven employees who died when their platform cable snapped.[25] In Texas, Virginia, and Pennsylvania the employer must be indifferent to employee welfare and safety in order for the corporation to be liable outside of the work-

ers compensation laws. Some courts require intent to harm to take it outside of workers compensation laws.[26]

There is constant pressure from organized labor, some government authorities, and college professors to change the corporation protection under workers compensation laws.[27]

The Future of Malpractice for Unsafe Conditions

Although under present court decisions the risk of corporate or personal liability for failure to provide a safe place to work is almost nonexistent, courts have shown an increasing tendency to hold employers liable both financially and criminally for work-related deaths. In the future they may be held liable for malpractice for failure to use up-to-date techniques, follow regulations, or use accepted practices that prevent accidents. The real issue is going to be whether there was a negligent disregard for the safety of the employees. Failure to act in a reasonable manner and not be sensitized to the vulnerability could change the present low level of exposure.[28]

PREVENTION OF EXPOSURE TO MALPRACTICE

Management malpractice lawsuits have their roots in the medical, legal, and professional

---

[24]Ohio by statute passed in 1986 allowed a tort action under the Workers Compensation Law so that it is no longer an exclusive remedy.

[25]See "Civil and Criminal Law Liability Exposure of the Safety Professional," *Professional Safety* (April 1987), p. 10.

[26]Frank W. Lancianse, "Is Exclusive Remedy in Jeopardy?" *Occupational Hazards* (December 1983), p. 45.

[27]See Arthur J. Amchan, "Callous Disregard for Employee Safety: The Exclusivity of the Worker's Compensation Remedy against Employers," *Labor Law Journal* (November 1983). Also see "Forecast 1984," *Occupational Hazards* (December 1983); Robert Mc Clory, "Murder on the Shop Floor," *Across the Board* (June 1986), p. 31.

[28]For further reading in this subject, see George A. Peters, "Safety Law in Historical Perspective," *Professional Safety* (Oct. 1986), p. 46; Charles R. Goerth, Esq., "In Search of Justice in Injury Liability Law," *Occupational Health and Safety* (Jan. 1983), p. 38; Frank Lancianse, "Criminal Charges Loom over Workplace Fatalities," *Occupational Hazards* (Dec. 1984), p. 43.

areas. Although management malpractice lawsuits are not as common as in the professional groups, they are about to explode in the management area as they did in the medical area a few years ago. Intentional infliction of emotional distress is yet to be defined in the employer-employee relationship. *Breach of public trust* and *covenant of good faith and fair dealing* are still terms that are legally vague. However, the increasingly common use of these terms by employees means that the employer's exposure to litigation by employees is rapidly growing. Some attorneys are now advertising their "unjust dismissal services." The advertisement encourages employees to make an appointment without obligation to learn whether they have a cause of action.

The present indications are that management malpractice litigation will get worse, and no legislative relief is on the horizon to change this trend, as there is in product liability and medical malpractice. This increasing trend of exposure to litigation can only be stopped by management action before adverse case law is developed by bad facts. Progressive management should develop low-key policies and procedures now rather than wait to experience the ordeal of a malpractice lawsuit before doing something about it.

The first step the employer should take to avoid being a target for malpractice suits is to decide what acts are believed to be malpractice and then establish policies and procedures to prevent such acts. Policies should not interfere with the profitability of the operation but where possible should be more strict than what is required under existing law, since what is not outrageous conduct today may very well become so in the future. Each year it seems that more "reasonable acts become unreasonable."

Drafting Policies on Malpractice

Policies on malpractice should be somewhat different from other policies because of the catastrophic consequences of a lawsuit. They should be a directive from the CEO and not guidelines allowing the option of following them or not. The only committee you need to draft such policies is the chief operating officer and legal counsel. Indemnification should be granted only when the policy is followed and discharge is the result when it is not. Discharge of the employee who violates a policy is always a good defense for the corporation, since it shows a good faith effort to enforce.

Recommended Policies to Prevent Malpractice

The purpose of the policies is to make the employee aware that an exposure exists in these various areas and to communicate the requirement that they be complied with. The following policies are recommended.

1. Each member of management above a certain level should be required to become familiar with the term *malpractice*. This could be done internally along with other training.
2. A strong policy against harassment should be drafted to comply with Title VII. If this is enforced, there would be little need to have any policy to prevent for invasion of privacy or for emotional distress except to inform that such an action is possible in certain situations.
3. An antitrust policy should be drafted requiring strict compliance and stating that corporate and personal liability is provided under the law. The policy should be silent on personal liability in other areas unless the operations are under 1866 or 1871 statutes. Then the policy should make it clear the personal liability is permitted under the statute.
4. The policy should allow only a few persons who understand the qualified privilege doctrine to release information. Whether externally or internally, information should be released only to those persons who have a business reason to receive it.
5. The policy emphatically should require all members of management to follow an established procedure on discharges.

Malpractice in Discharge, Negligent Hiring, and Negligent Retention

The most common management actions that result in malpractice are discharge, negligent hiring, and negligent retention, although other situations such as sexual harassment can be troublesome.

The most important action to prevent malpractice is the establishment of a discharge procedure. Such a procedure should go beyond that which is designed to prevent wrongful discharge for a breach of contract. The compliance procedure, exit interviews, investigation, and a joint decision to discharge should be in place under the wrongful discharge policy. To prevent malpractice in discharge, all that is required is compliance with the discharge policy or establishing one if there isn't one in existence. If there is an objective performance appraisal that will stand judicial scrutiny and those acts that will result in discharge are properly communicated to the employee, there is little exposure to malpractice in the discharge process.

For prevention of negligent retention exposure, there should be a rule that requires a co-worker to report all incidents that indicate that the employee has dangerous tendencies. Management should provide for treatment, but suspension until cured, for alcoholics and drug addicts where there is some indication that their condition causes dangerous activities. In certain industries action can be taken before it affects their work. As for negligent hiring exposure, we are not sure how much investigation is required to prevent a lawsuit, but what we do know is that at least the police records should be checked as well as any questionable work history information. Reference information that relates to performance, absenteeism, and tardiness is of little value in determining the character of the applicant.

Malpractice exposure should not be a serious management problem. If progressive management establishes policies and procedures that prevent employment actions that are not socially acceptable behavior and takes steps to ensure that all members of management comply, the increased trend to management malpractice suits will subside.

Management should not depend upon others to solve the malpractice problem. Lawyers can only do so much. They must depend upon convincing testimony and facts created by management. As has so often been said, "Bad facts make bad law."

CHAPTER
18

THE LAW AND THE PERSONNEL FUNCTION IN THE 1990S

Federal Laws Most Encountered in Personnel Management
Direction of Antidiscrimination Laws
Labor-Management Relations
Direction of Personnel Law in Discharge
Predictions in Other Areas
High-Priority Tasks in the 1990s

This book has discussed the most recent legal intrusions on the personnel function. It is evident by court decisions and statutes that the law does not interfere with personnel administration in carrying out its function. To the contrary, it has caused the personnel practitioner to eliminate many subjective practices that did not always contribute to the profits of the organization. The changes that the laws have forced upon the personnel function in the 1970s and 1980s will not stop in the 1990s, but the law has matured and the gray areas will continue to decrease. Employers and employees alike have become more sophisticated in using the law to accomplish their objectives. Where past lawsuits have been in lower-level jobs, in the future there will be more adversity in the upper levels of management. Since there is no longer a social stigma in suing your employer, policies and procedures will become more sophisticated to avoid exposure to the law. Management resistance to the new laws experienced in the 1970s is rapidly fading as they are learning to live with the law, and legal counsel is becoming better trained in employee relations. Employees in the 1990s will be more reluctant to sue when employers better understand the law. Management in the 1990s will develop a painless way to economically live with the law when making employment decisions.

The personnel practitioner in the 1990s, to avoid obsolescence, must be alert when employees use their newly acquired rights, and advise management how to minimize exposure to litigation and still not interfere with organizational goals.

FEDERAL LAWS MOST ENCOUNTERED IN PERSONNEL MANAGEMENT

In the 1990s the laws that we have been discussing in the preceding chapters will not go away. The only thing that will change is their application to different sets of facts. There is one thing certain in employee relations— management will continually be tested by employees as to their enforcement of policy, compliance with existing laws, and decision making in those areas where there is no policy or law.

Since the personnel practitioner will be living with these laws in the 1990s, it may be beneficial at this point to review them. Exhibit 18-1 lists the laws most frequently encountered by personnel management. From time to time personnel management will have other laws to consider, but it will be so infrequent that it does not warrant the space to discuss them.

DIRECTION OF ANTIDISCRIMINATION LAWS

In the early 1970s most discrimination cases dealt with race. Many of the basic principles that apply to sex, age, and religion were developed in racial cases. There is considerable maturity in the law in racial discrimination. Employers know what is required to validate a test, what is meant by the labor market area, what is required for a prima facie case, what are acceptable recruiting practices, that the law permits the employer to hire the best-qualified applicant, and that there is no obligation to maximize the hiring of minorities. These principles were developed in racial discrimination cases.

Age, Handicapped, and Sex Issues

In the early 1970s budgets of the regulatory agencies were used to resolve the immediate problem of racial discrimination. Age and sex cases were brushed aside. In disputes under ADEA, the Department of Labor until 1979 was the enforcement agency, with a small budget; in the case of sex, the EEOC was too busy with racial problems. Many of the women's rights groups were using their resources and energy in an unsuccessful attempt to get the Equal Rights Amendment to the Constitution passed. The conditions that prevented active enforcement of age and sex cases in the 1970s will not be present in the 1990s,

EXHIBIT 18-1

Date	Name	Description
1866 1870	*Civil Rights Act* *(Sect. 1981 U.S. Code)*	All persons are protected by same laws regardless of race.
1931	*Davis-Bacon Act*	Requires federal construction contractors to pay prevailing wage rates.
1932	*Norris-LaGuardia Act*	Cannot use injunction to prevent a strike.
1935	*National Labor Relations Act*	Government intervention in labor-management matters, encourages union growth.
1938	*Fair Labor Standards Act as amended*	Sets minimum and overtime rates and time and one-half after 40 hours for all employers in interstate commerce.
1947	*Taft-Hartley Act* *(amendment to National Labor Relations Act)*	Permits states to pass right-to-work laws, promotes free choice in accepting or rejecting union membership.
1959	*Labor Management Reporting and Disclosure Act (Landrum-Griffin Act, amendment to National Labor Relations Act)*	Gives employees more rights against union leaders. Eliminates sweetheart contracts. Requires disclosure of union financial affairs.
1963	*Equal Pay Act*	Requires same pay for women as for men doing similar work under similar working conditions.
1964 1972	*Civil Rights Act* *Amended (Title VII)*	Prohibits job discrimination based on race, color, religion, sex, or national origin.
1967 1978	*Age Discrimination in Employment Act Amended*	No job discrimination based on age for persons over 40 years of age.
1967	*Veterans Reemployment Rights as amended (Military Selective Service Act)*	Requires employer to grant leaves of absence for military duty.
1970	*Executive Order 11246*	Federal contractors or subcontractors prohibited from job discrimination based on race, color, sex, religion, or national origin.
1970	*Occupational Safety and Health Act*	Employer in interstate commerce must comply with federal health and safety standards; permits state administration.
1973	*Health Maintenance Organization*	Requires employers to offer employees optional health insurance coverage where available as an alternative to company plan.
1973	*Vocational Rehabilitation Act*	Government contractors must take affirmative action to employ and advance qualified handicapped workers.
1974 1984	*Employee Retirement Income Security Act (ERISA)* *Amended*	Requires vesting in pension plans, insures pension funds, and requires employee communication.
1974	*Vietnam Veterans Readjustment Assistance Act*	Government contractors shall take affirmative action to employ and advance qualified Vietnam-era veterans.
1978	*Pregnancy Discrimination Amendment to Title VII*	Requires equal treatment for all employment practices with respect to pregnancy, childbirth, or related medical conditions.
1986	*Consolidated Omnibus Budget Reconciliation Act (COBRA)*	Requires employer to offer to continue health insurance to terminated employees.

EXHIBIT 18-1 (Continued)

Date	Name	Description
1986	Immigration Reform and Control Act	Makes employers liable when hiring undocumented aliens.
	Various State-Laws	Include workers compensation, unemployment benefits, fair employment practices, polygraph tests, handicap discrimination garnishments, and so on. The mention of the state laws is only to remind the reader that they exist; often they close the loopholes left by the federal laws.
1988	Polygraph Protection Act	Bans polygraph tests in employment. However, there are many exceptions.
1988	Plant Closing and Mass Layoff Notification Act	Requires employer to give 60 days' notice of mass closing or layoff.

especially in the sexual harassment area, where the first application to Title VII was in 1978. Few cases of age discrimination were ever brought to court although the violations existed.

The older worker no longer has a stigma for suing the employer. In the past persons in lower-level jobs were bringing discrimination lawsuits that consisted mostly of younger workers who were not protected by ADEA. As the stigma of suing the employer diminishes, middle- and upper-level management, almost all over 40, will use the ADEA by hiring an attorney and going directly into court. Their financial resources will permit this, rather than depending on a governmental agency. This makes the employer extremely vulnerable to age discrimination litigation.

Too few employers have a measurement of performance that will pass judicial review. What other reason is there to terminate an employee of 30 years' service except performance or policy violation (which is rare with middle and upper management)? If performance is the reason for discharge, the measurement must be objective and uniformly applied to the extent that a jury will accept. Age cases also have a practical problem in

that one does not see many young people on the jury. Furthermore, can anyone imagine going before the U.S. Supreme Court and arguing that an employee is too old to perform the job, without extremely convincing evidence?

The employer's problem with ADEA was increased when Congress lifted the mandatory retirement age of 70. Where many employers could "coast" with the problem until age 70, this option is no longer available. The only solution to the problem of the older worker (other than poor performance or rule violation) is voluntary programs or, in the case of the small company, making a private deal. In the 1970s the most popular cases were race, in the 1980s sex discrimination. In the 1990s, with the baby boom now including persons over 40, the most exposure will be in age discrimination. A group of practitioners have already developed programs to cope with ADEA. One of the most popular is early retirement incentives.

Such incentives include

• Pension benefits vesting early or more fully
• Continuation of health care benefits in retirement

- Generous severance pay policy
- Retraining for a retirement vocation, or providing out-placement aid
- Maintaining an employee on a consulting basis

The key to these programs is to obtain voluntary decisions to retire.

Releases and early retirement plans are an effective way to avoid litigation under ADEA. However, certain precautions should be taken when using them.

1. An adequate period of time should be given to rescind.
2. There should be adequate monetary incentives, beyond the existing policy.
3. The employer should request the employee to have an attorney look at the document.
4. There should be a statement that the signing was absolutely voluntary.

Where the employer is not sure that a factor other than age can be defended, voluntary retirement programs will be used more often. Each year the employer is winning a larger percentage of age discrimination cases by using some factor other than age or preventing the problem by the use of releases or early retirement programs. This trend will continue, and in the next decade the employer will solve the age discrimination problem by one of two options: Using either a factor other than age or voluntary retirement.

In the sex discrimination area, most of the original antidiscrimination law as to hiring, promotion, or transfers has matured to the point where the employer knows what the law is. However, sexual harassment under Title VII is a continuing problem. Since the Meritor case we know what it is but have to find a way to stop it.

In sexual harassment problems, members of women's groups are active in correcting this form of sex discrimination, which is similar to what occurred in the racial discrimination area in the early 1970s. Over one third of all law students are women.[1] Women are not only accepted in great numbers by law firms (over 16 percent of the practicing bar are women); but also, to the surprise of some male attorneys, they are becoming good trial lawyers. Because of the influx of women into the legal profession, women employees are more comfortable going to a woman lawyer with their problems; as with all lawyers they are anxious to take the case. The employer of the 1990s must prepare for an increase in sexual harassment cases and establish policies and procedures that will prevent litigation in this area.

Sex Discrimination in Wages

The wide difference in compensation between the sexes for the same work still remains unsolved. The traditional method of job evaluation and equal pay legislation has failed to correct the problem. Wage levels established by the marketplace have received judicial acceptance by the majority of the courts, and as more women come into the marketplace, wage differentials in many job categories will be greater. The violation of the equal pay law will continue until there is complete job integration.

In the next decade women in the work force will become more dominant in our society. The number of women in the work force will exceed the 1988 figure of 7 out of 10. They will, with increasing frequency, occupy top echelon jobs. As they enter top jobs in the 1990s they will become very effective professionals and entrepreneurs. Women have not been deeply influenced by assumptions and practices that have been used in the past to deny them a place in management. These perceptions will not work in the future. Women have the social incentive to succeed, and doing well means more to them,

---

[1]When the author first went to law school, there was one woman in his class of 125 students. When asked what she was doing in law school, her reply was "to marry a lawyer." She did in her junior year and never returned.

because as women they must prove that they are better than or as good as men. This is no easy task when traditionally they have been considered inferior.

There is a light at the end of the tunnel in job integration to solve the equal pay problem. Other methods have failed. Comparable worth was a fad of the 1980s that was doomed at the outset. You cannot compare one job with another by job evaluation when the wage level of one job was not determined by job evaluation. Although comparable worth is legally dead, some state legislatures are trying to revive it. The result of this legislation is to raise the compensation level of female jobs. This will only start a "seesaw action" in the future when the males again decide to rely on the marketplace for their wage levels. Politically, legislation in the comparable worth area is advisable, but it cannot be relied upon to solve the equal pay problem in the future. This does not mean that wage differentials should be accepted by management; it just means that more effective methods should be used.

The Handicapped Worker as a Future Problem

This area has a potential exposure in the 1990s. An increasing number of physical conditions and abuses are considered a handicap by most state laws. This is one area where state law will dominate personnel law, although a federal law is inevitable. A person who is physically handicapped doesn't pose a problem if a reasonable attempt is made to accommodate. Employers in the 1990s will have learned from their mistakes of the 1980s and will be more objective when attempting to accommodate. There will be more tryouts and fewer subjective suppositions that the employee cannot do a certain job. The argument that accommodation affords a danger to others and to the employee will be used with more discretion.

It is in the areas of drug and alcohol abuse that the more serious problems prevail. The employer can have a policy, but its effect is to drive the activity underground, which causes a more serious problem when it surfaces. A policy alone will not solve the problem; help is needed from the co-workers as well as employee treatment that is designed to kill the desire. The employer in the 1990s must recognize that the problem will not go away and a constant vigilance is necessary. No one approach will solve it.

In the 1990s there will be an increasing number of companies that have a smoke-free environment. A smoke-free environment at the workplace should be a goal. Although sufficient medical evidence doesn't exist to judicially accept the fact that passive smoke is a health hazard, medical opinion is coming close.[2] There is enough worker opposition to smoking in the workplace to make it advisable for the employer to eliminate the smoking problem by creating a smoke-free workplace.

The employer who does as little as possible about the AIDS problem will have the least number of scars in the future. There is no relief in sight for an employer solution. Medically AIDS cannot be acquired in a work-related activity. Most states hold it is a handicap under their handicap laws. Except for high absenteeism in the final stages, AIDS does not interfere with performance on the job. All these facts lead to the conclusion that the employer has no need to know if a person has AIDS.

The employment problem arises when a co-worker refuses to work with a known or alleged AIDS victim. Educational programs will give some degree of security, but if the employee has already made up his or her mind, ignoring medical facts, then there is little the employer can do. The AIDS problem is a temporary one that will be solved when a vaccine is found. This is predicted to be within the next five to six years. In the meantime the employer should go into a holding action and deal with each situation on an individual basis, except to continually

---

[2]See "The Consequences of Involuntary Smoke: A Report of U.S. Surgeon General " (Washington, DC: U.S. Department of Health, (1986).

educate the employees. Transfer, co-worker pressure to terminate, and voluntary quit of co-workers are all considerations. One of the problems with educating the employee is that the media and the government are attempting to educate the public, and this may be contrary to the employer's best interests. It is for this reason that a management educational program must be continual and current.

Discrimination for Religion

This area of discrimination is continually being tested. Religious belief is strong motivation that will not be compromised without a fight. In the next decade there will be some refinement of what is considered well-settled law. Employers know that they must accommodate, but only a minimum effort is required. The courts have also settled the issue that the employee does not choose accommodation and any reasonable accommodation satisfies the law. What is reasonable will be determined on a case-by-case basis. However, the courts will continue to respect any religious discipline that is acquired before or during employment. The employer's defense is a bona fide attempt to accommodate and not to question the religious belief or the employee's dedication to it. Except for some refinements there will be little change in the 1990s in this area of personnel law.

Employment of Aliens

Congress has made it clear that it is the responsibility of the employer to stop illegal aliens from crossing our borders. The Immigration Reform and Control Act has not removed the acquired rights of undocumented aliens to be protected by anti-discrimination laws or any other statute. If an employee is an undocumented alien the law is saying that there will be no relief until he or she goes home, and the employer is liable if she or he does not send the alien home, unless citizenship or a work permit is acquired. It is saying to the employer that all that is asked is showing of an intent to comply with the spirit of the law.

Compliance with the Immigration Reform and Control Act will not be a problem in the future, but it will be another added routine administrative task for which the personnel practitioner is responsible.

LABOR-MANAGEMENT RELATIONS

There will be little increase in unionization in the 1990s. The best-educated prediction is that labor will continue to lose a percentage of the work force. The previous 25- to 30-percent level will not be achieved in the foreseeable future. The 15- to 20-percent level is more realistic.[3] However, the heavy concentration of union membership in auto, paper, steel, aerospace, entertainment, mining, construction, transportation, and communications will continue.

The Changing Image of Unions

To attract new members, unions are offering a variety of nontraditional benefits. Such benefits include

1. Credit cards requiring no annual fee and charging 12-percent interest
2. Free 30-minute legal consultations and document review and a 30-percent discount on subsequent legal charges from a national panel of attorneys
3. Supplemental group insurance.
4. Low-cost travel, such as on airfare, hotels, and car rental discounts

Union members will be able to enjoy these benefits as associate members, which will be a quasi-union membership and will not be included in the bargaining unit. Associate members will not be subject to strikes or reg-

---

[3]See Paul G. Engel, "Labor in Retreat," *Industry Week* (July 8, 1985); John G. Kilgour, "Decertifying a Union: A Matter of Choice," *Personnel Administrator*, 32, no. 7 (July 1987), 42. Also, see Kirkland Ropp, "State of Unions," *Personnel Administrator*, 32, no. 7 (July 1987), 37–64; William J. Usery, Jr., and Douglas Henne, "The American Labor Movement in the 80's," *Employee Relations Law Journal*, 7, no. 2 (Autumn 1981).

ular dues, nor will they be under the labor agreement grievance procedure.

Unions in their organizing efforts will continue to wait for any management action that breeds discontent. Wages and benefits are no longer a big concern for employees, but layoffs, discharges, and fairness in working conditions will still be important.

Unions will continue to be active in enforcing antidiscrimination laws and safety or health laws. Governmental enforcement agencies will not be able to relax in their enforcement activities as long as union pressure continues.

The major change in union activities will be an abandonment of the traditional collective bargaining and grievance representation. Studies show that members are no longer interested in seniority issues, nor do they want to strike, the very foundations that unions grew from in the 1950s and 1960s.[4] In the 1990s unions will have associate memberships that do not become involved in strikes or seniority problems. The union will represent the individual as an agent. The representation will be in many areas other than the traditional working conditions. In such areas as discrimination, workers compensation, unemployment compensation, and OSHA where laypersons are permitted to represent others, union professionals can become experts as employee representatives in the same manner as they have acquired expertise in arbitration. The newly educated union leader will be more effective as a representative in areas other than working conditions, wages and seniority problems, for which formal education is not needed and in some respects is a handicap. The leader who rose through the ranks from a worker to a union leader is being replaced by the educated activist.

Ineffectiveness of the Strike Weapon

In the 1990s the effectiveness of the strike as a technique to achieve economic gains will continue to diminish. This was once a powerful weapon to pressure the employer into submitting to almost any demand. As a union leader once told the author, "We have to decide how much we will take from the employers this year." The employer has found a way to combat the strike weapon by the use of replacements. (They can also be used in case of a legal lockout.) The right to hire replacements and deny the strikers reinstatement until a vacancy occurs has existed for many years but was not used until the middle 1980s when the Supreme Court in *Belknap, Inc.* v. *Hale,* 103 S.Ct. 3172 (1983), held that under certain circumstances a strike replacement had an employment contract that was actionable in a state court when replaced by the striker after the strike was settled. Employers have been surprisingly successful in the use of strike replacements. Many workers were convinced that the employer could not operate without their skills. The striking workers were overwhelmed when they found out the employer could. For many years employers, too, did not think it was possible, but their success in use of replacements has grown to the extent that highly talented professional football players can be replaced when they go out on strike.[5] The threat of the use of replacements at the bargaining table not only will give the employer a superior bargaining position but also will cause the membership to accept the employer's position. When the power to strike is gone, it will be difficult for the union to hold their membership unless there is representation in other areas.

Organized labor problems of survival will also be increased in the 1990s by the changing of the complexion of the work force. The union-represented workers are not only declining in numbers,[6] but their militancy has

---

[4]"The Changing Situation of Workers and Their Unions," a report by the AFL-CIO Committee on the Evolution of Work (February 1985).

[5]In the strike of the National Football League in 1987, replacements weakened the bargaining position of players to the extent that it was settled without granting of the major demands that caused the strike.

[6]In 1979 unions represented 24 percent of the work force, in 1985 18 percent, and in 1987 17 percent. (Washington, DC: U.S. Department of Labor, Bureau of Labor Statistics, 1988).

also disappeared. They have become middle-class workers who are concerned with individual achievements rather than collective action.[7]

The Rise of the Nonunion Worker

Another substantial change in labor management relations in the 1990s will be the increased use of the National Labor Relations Act by nonunion workers. They will become more aware of their rights under the act. The realization that they do not have to belong to a union to be protected under the act will cause many problems for the employer in the 1990s who often does not realize that nonunion employees have protection of the act. Since the workers have rejected the union as a place to go for relief, they will turn to the board. Employer concern that concerted activity has the same protection for the nonunion worker as for the union worker will be on the menu in the 1990s to protect the employer from liability under the act.

DIRECTION OF PERSONNEL LAW IN DISCHARGE

The erosion of the employment-at-will doctrine will continue in the 1990s to the point where most states will grant either the public policy or the implied contract exception. Just-cause legislation on the state level has started in Montana; this will spread to other states in the 1990s. It will force more employers to adopt a just-cause policy of their own before their state legislature does it for them.

Importance of the Handbook or Policy Manual

The handbook or policy manual will play an increasing role as a contract in the 1990s. Employers will have to change the tradi-tional handbook to either make it a contract or put in a disclaimer. The disclaimer or release will have limited popularity. If the employer discovers that this false security will create more problems than it will solve, their use will cease. A disclaimer will not be a substitute for a poorly written handbook in the future. The handbook of the future will tell the employees what is expected of them and not what the employer will do for them. It will cease to be a document to sell the company to the worker and will be a document to enforce the company policies and procedures. In the future, management as well as the employee will have to follow the handbook provisions. It will be in a nonunion setting what the collective bargaining agreement is in a union facility.

PREDICTIONS IN OTHER AREAS

Remedies in Tort Actions

The most serious change in personnel law in the 1990s will occur in the area of punitive damages as a result of malpractice. The theory that a violation should make the employee whole is rapidly changing. Members of the plaintiff's bar will seize every opportunity to bring an action for punitive damages rather than to rely on the remedy provided in statutes. Most statutes were passed on the theory that a violation is a statutory wrong for which the plaintiff should be made whole. The trend in punitive damages can be stopped through policies and procedures that respect the law and a humane treatment of the employees. In sexual harassment cases and under the ADEA, the plaintiff feels that a greater wrong is done for which he or she wants money, so rather than going under the statute, the plaintiff sues under the common law doctrine of tort.[8] If the court finds

---

[7]For further explanation, see Peter F. Drucker, "The Rise and Fall of the Blue Collar Worker," *The Wall Street Journal*, April 22, 1987.

[8]See *Ford* v. *Revlon, Inc.*, 734 P.2d 580 (Ariz. 1987), where the court allowed damages for infliction of emotional distress in a sexual harassment case because the company took no action after a complaint. See also *O'Connell* v. *Chasdi*, 400 Mass. 686 (1987), for the same result.

that the statute is not an exclusive remedy, the case will be allowed to go to the jury, which can award punitive damages rather than the remedy under the statute.

The plaintiff's bar will push malpractice suits and huge awards to their very limits. The movement to limit the size of the awards by statute will continue in the 1990s. By the middle of the decade many states will have statutes limiting the liability. When a doctor has to pay up to $200,000 for malpractice insurance, it becomes a social problem that the politician will do something about. The correction of the abuse for the medical profession will also apply to such other areas as legal malpractice and management malpractice. Montana has already started putting a limit on wrongful discharge suits. This will be extended to sexual harassment, age discrimination, and many others before the end of the decade.

Under the Employee Retirement Income Security Act[9] (ERISA), the practitioner or manager can, by terms of the statute, be individually liable for a violation. This was followed by the Consolidated Omnibus Budget Reconciliation Act[10] (COBRA), and later the Immigration Reform and Control Act[11] (IRCA) also contained a provision for individual liability. These three major acts in personnel law all made the individual personally liable for violation of a particular provision. In the 1990s the Congress, in an effort to have a built-in enforcement provision, will include individual liability. The personnel practitioner must not in the future rely upon the "corporate veil" for protection when a particular provision of a statute is violated.

Trends in Workers Compensation

The high cost of this insurance will in the future cause the employer to institute cost

control programs the same as cost containment in the health care field. In the 1990s there will be more deductibles and back-to-work incentives similar to the health care area. Because it is a social insurance program, it is highly unlikely that there will be any co-insurance. The cost of insurance will become competitive among the states, and in this respect, changes will become political.

Iowa, Michigan, and Minnesota have incentives built in the law for both the employee and the employer to control costs. This will spread in the 1990s to more states. There will be more pressure to reduce litigation in workers compensation because this is one objective of the state laws that has badly failed.

There will be a deregulation of the insurance industry that will cause open competition, and then the insurance companies will be interested in claim control in the same way as they have been selling their services because of the lost control programs.

Unemployment Compensation in the 1990s

In the future there will be more revisions of the tax rate, so those industries that have the highest unemployment will be paying higher taxes. This will be done by lowering the minimum and increasing the maximum tax. Because of higher taxes, employers will be more concerned with reducing their costs and therefore will become more skilled in presenting their appeals. However, the use of legal counsel will increase in cases where the stakes are high. The employer will insist that the only benefits that the employees should receive are when they are out of work "through no fault of their own" and are available for work while receiving benefits. As more case law is developed in the areas of voluntary quit and misconduct, employers will better understand it. They will develop policies and practices that will clearly define misconduct. The definition of voluntary quit will be clearly communicated to the employees so there is no misunderstanding.

---

[9]29 USCA Sect. 1001 et seq.

[10]P.L. 99–509, Title X (1986).

[11]P.L. 99–603, also known as Simpson-Rodino Act (1986).

When an employee acts in a certain way it will be considered a voluntary quit.

An Increase in Written Policies

In the 1990s more companies will have written policies than in the past. The larger the organization the more need for policies. These policies will be for the purpose of preventing exposure to lawsuits and defending them if the matter goes to litigation.[12] In most cases policies already exist in some form, but all too often they are in a form that the courts will not accept. Policy revision in the 1990s will get the attention of management when

1. There are attempts by the union to represent the employees
2. A lawsuit is started because of absence of policy
3. Present policies are in conflict with state or federal law
4. The organizational structure has changed so much that the old policies are no longer effective

In some areas, such as sexual harassment, drug testing, searches, and discharge, policies are essential to avoid liability. In other areas policies are desirable for communication to the employees. The policy manual or handbook in the 1990s will be more carefully written. They will avoid such phrases as "We reserve the right"; "Exceptions may be made for _____"; "You have job security here." The use of policies by managers to justify a position already taken or to disregard the policy if it is contrary to that position will cease in the 1990s. All provisions of the policy will be followed by supervisors or there will be a lawsuit and then the policy will be followed.

Relationship with Legal Counsel

The personnel practitioner in the 1990s must have enough knowledge of the law not only to keep legal costs and damages at a minimum but also to be able to carry out the personnel function as economically as before employee rights legislation. The legal counsel, to be of service to the personnel practitioner, must be more discreet in giving legal advice in the 1990s. Counsel must do a better job of understanding employee relations consequences of a decision. There may be many policies with which legal counsel does not agree but which are legally sound. "On advice of counsel" must be legal advice and not policy advice on personnel matters unless specifically requested.

The personnel legal counsel of the 1990s must say no[13] less often and assess the exposure to taking a certain action to keep the wheels turning. Saying that a particular employment decision is not legal is easy and safe because the exposure of being proven wrong is almost eliminated if followed, and it does not take much research. An employment decision must be made. One with the least legal exposure should be forthcoming from the legal counsel.[14] There is a duty on the personnel practitioner to demand useful legal advice on how to do something, not that it can't be legally accomplished. If such demand is made without success, then a change in legal counsel should be considered.[15]

The legal counsel of the 1990s must be aware of personnel practitioner problems and understand that although there may not be the best evidence to discharge an employee to prevent a wrongful discharge lawsuit, the

---

[12]See "An Ounce of Prevention," *Inc.* (Oct. 1984), p. 153.

[13]When this author was a corporate legal counsel and was called to give an opinion on a problem, the answer was no, it could not be legally done. The practitioner then reminded me of a directive I had written while a personnel executive two years previous directing the requested action. This author's answer was, "Then I was in personnel; now I am legal counsel and I say you can't legally do it."

[14]As the author's superior once said in mild reprimand, "Mismanagement is better than no management at all."

[15]This is sometimes difficult where there is in-house counsel. The best effort is probably to complain to the supervisor, who uses best political judgment on how to correct the situation.

manager is going to discharge the employee regardless of the legal advice. The task of legal counsel is to advise on the best way to do it to prevent a lawsuit.

Managers are not going to let the law or the courts run the operation; the job of the legal counsel and personnel practitioner is to advise the most legal way to do it.[16] The personnel practitioner must insist on legal advice that tells how to do it, not that one cannot do it, if economically effective use of legal counsel is to be accomplished.

HIGH-PRIORITY TASKS IN THE 1990S

The strains and stresses of the employment relationship are evident in the preceding chapters. The employer within its ability directly or indirectly must take action. Nothing will happen unless action is taken and priorities for this action are set.

This book has an abundance of recommendations to relieve the stress and strain of the employment relationship and suggestions either to prevent litigation or to defend lawsuits. If all were adopted, the personnel practitioner would do nothing else but write and administer policy changes. It would be unrealistic to expect that such recommendations would fit all organizations and all situations. It is, therefore, appropriate at this time to recommend five of the most important actions to be taken that will prevent litigation and not interfere with the objectives of the organization to make a profit or perform a service. They are

1. Measurement of performance
2. Uniform policy administration
3. Adoption of a termination policy
4. Development of criteria to determine a qualified worker for employment and promotion
5. Establishment of a complaint procedure

---

[16]The author once was legal counsel to a manager who always got in trouble with the law. When asked why he did things that tested the law, he replied, "You are smart enough to get me out of it."

Measurement of Performance

If there is only one opportunity to change procedures in the 1990s, the measurement of performance will reap the highest rewards. In the 1990s malpractice will be a major source of litigation. One way to stop this trend is to have valid performance appraisals. For every law mentioned in this book, an almost absolute defense to alleged violations would be poor performance. Poor performance is often stated as an affirmative defense but fails when scrutinized by the courts. In some categories, measurement is easy, in others more difficult; but any human endeavor can be measured. In some job categories the measurement may not be as accurate as the courts would like, but any degree of objectivity is better than a completely subjective measurement. In reviewing the large number of cases cited in this book, the author failed to find any court decision where the employer's defenses of poor performance that objectively measured performance were not accepted by the courts. Unfortunately, too few employers have a valid procedure to measure performance; for this reason the defense fails when used.

Uniform Policy Administration

In the 1980s uniform administration of policies and procedures was essential to avoid litigation under the antidiscrimination laws. In the areas of leaves of absence, promotion, vacation, merit pay, absenteeism, and so on, policies were often different between departments or job categories and in some cases between nonexempt and exempt employees. Because of the external audit caused by employee rights laws, court interpretation, and the demand for information by employees when filing a complaint for an alleged violation of the law, information about practices in other parts of the company cannot be kept from the employees. The word *discrimination* became so popular in the 1970s and 1980s that any different treatment of one employee from another was considered discrimination with a potential lawsuit. This caused employee demand for information about company practices. In the 1990s uniform policy administration will be the order of the day from a cost-conscious CEO.

Adoption of Termination Policy

This is the third most important policy to be adopted. The day is gone when the supervisor, while in an emotional state and with shaky hands, goes to the work site and says, "You're fired." Employers must adopt a just-cause policy for discharge before legislation and the courts do it for them. If adopted by the employer, the policy should coordinate with other policies and goals of the organization. If just-cause requirement is passed by legislatures, it will be unlikely to fit the employer's procedures. If required by the courts, it will fit a certain set of facts and will result in case-by-case litigation.

There are enough decisions by the courts to know what just cause means. Just cause is the violation of policy or warning for poor performance when the employee has knowledge that the violation would result in discharge. The adoption of a just-cause policy by the employer should be a gradual program starting at certain job levels or job categories and expanding with experience. In a nonunion plant the blue-collar worker should have a just-cause policy. The policy in the beginning does not have to be any more than communication of the reasons for discharge and a procedure to determine the facts. Many employers feel that adoption of a just-cause policy would eliminate any defense that the common law employment-at-will doctrine affords. This is not necessarily true. The policy could adopt the exceptions to public policy, malice, and bad faith, but not implied contract. Since the United States is the only industrialized country that does not have a legislative just-cause policy, it is essential that it is kept that way and employers adopt one of their own to suit the needs of both employees and the employer.

Employment and Promotion of Best-Qualified Worker

In the early 1970s some employers believed that the new employment laws required them to hire or promote unqualified workers and they had lost their right to determine the best-qualified workers to hire or promote. No court decision ever said that this was the law; however, some regulatory agencies did. Court decisions such as Furnco and Burdine have cleared up the problem of the best-qualified worker. In the 1990s the employer will benefit from these landmark decisions.[17]

Since employers often fail to adopt a policy of qualified worker through fear of either not meeting affirmative action goals or litigation under Title VII, the 1990s will afford the opportunity for them to change this, and it therefore rates as a high-priority procedure.

Establishment of a Complaint Procedure

Although it is listed last, the complaint procedure is one of the most important elements in the prevention of lawsuits, especially in discharge cases. In a nonunion setting it is often the most difficult to sell to top management. They do not want to give up the sole right to discharge, but when a union represents the employees, it is one of the first items that management agrees to be put in a collective bargaining agreement.

The two most important provisions in any complaint procedure are that the employee is allowed to complain to any member of management and that there is a final appeal procedure, either peer review or an impartial arbitrator. Without these two elements the procedure has only very limited effectiveness in preventing exposure to litigation.

---

[17]*Furnco Construction Co.* v. *Waters*, 438 U.S. 567 (1978); *Texas Department of Community Affairs* v. *Burdine*, 450 U.S. 248 (1981).

For those employers who have a complaint procedure with a final impartial review, the complaint procedure could be the major reason for fewer wrongful discharge cases or no union representation.

Employers who do not have a complaint procedure with an appeal provision will have one once their employees are represented by a union and a collective bargaining agreement is signed. Also, management's failure to have a complaint procedure is all too often paid for by large attorney's fees and/or unreasonable jury awards. In either event the complaint procedure is a small price to pay for the consequences of not having one.

The Personnel Function and the Law

During the period of the original printing and revision of this book there isn't a relationship in the United States that is not experiencing stress—relations between men and women, between the employer and the employee, between husband and wife, between executives and their boards, between unions and their members, and between management, employees, and legislative branches of governments. These strains on social and political relationships are evident in the preceding pages. In the 1990s employer and employee will become aware of this stress and, within their ability, directly or indirectly relieve it. There will be more consideration for the other person's point of view, and restraints in all areas will decrease. Power will be exercised only to relieve the stress and not to create it. Failure in the 1990s to do something about this situation will be a substantial loss for the personnel function.

Personnel work in the 1990s should continue to be exciting. One can consider questions on the application form that are meaningful, merit increases that reward performance, tests that will predict performance on the job, performance appraisals that will actually rate performance, uniform criteria for discharge, not having to defend the supervisor's subjective judgment of hiring and promotion, and employees knowing their rights.

The personnel function will become one of the most important functions of management. By hiring qualified applicants the company will grow. Poor performance when objectively measured is always correctable and accordingly does not prevent growth. The work force will take an interest in the company growth and with high-quality people, stock options, profit sharing, and other incentive plans will be easily sold to the board of directors as an effective means to accomplish organizational goals.

The law is in place; the merging of the law and personnel function is basically completed. Since the personnel function has an added ingredient of the law it has become more professional and very exciting. As a result of the new ingredient, the practitioner has more responsibility and in some cases is overworked.

As we close out the twentieth century and enter into the twenty-first, the personnel function has made a complete cycle. From its very beginning it was a necessary management function that was considered administrative. It is now not only administratively necessary but also a cost-control function. Exposure to lawsuits not only is an abortion to good employee relations but also is necessary for survival, especially for a small company.

The author's only regret is that he is not beginning his career in personnel and law — what fun it would be! The students—those starting in the field as well as present practitioners—are to be envied. It is only the passive, obsolete personnel practitioner, his or her legal counsel, and those of us who are ending our careers in personnel law that are to be pitied.

APPENDIX

Casename	Casedata
Aasmundstad v. *Dickinson State College*	337 N.W.2d 792 (N.D. 1983), *134*
Abbot v. *Payne*	457 So.2d 1156 (Fla. 1984), *161*
Adair v. *United States*	208 U.S. 161 (1908), *169*
Adam v. *Joy Mfg. Co.*	651 F.Supp. 1301 (D.N.H. 1987), *139*
Adler v. *American Standard*	830 F.2d 1303 (4th Cir. 1987), *176*
Agis v. *Howard Johnson Co.*	355 N.E.2d 315 (Mass. 1976), *177*
Ahrens v. *Williamson Music Co., Inc.*	387 N.W.2d 884 (Minn. 1986), *251*
Aiello v. *United Airlines, Inc.*	818 F.2d 1196 (5th Cir. 1987), *198*
Albemarle Paper Co. v. *Moody*	422 U.S. 405 (1975), *30, 49*
Alber v. *Norfolk and Western R.R. Co.*	654 F.2d 1271 (8th Cir. 1981), *132*
Alcorn v. *Anbro Engineering, Inc.*	468 P.2d 216 (Cal. 1970), *177*
Alden, Inc.	51 LA 469 (Kellcher 1968), *154*
Alexander v. *Gardner-Denver*	94 S.Ct. 1011 (1974), *248, 286*
Allbritton Communications, Inc.	271 NLRB 201 (1984), *276*
Alleluia Cushion	221 NLRB 999 (1975), *258*
Allen v. *City of Mobile*	466 F.2d 1245 (5th Cir. 1972) cert. denied, 411 U.S. 909 (1973), *113*
Allen-Bradley Co. v. *Electrical Workers (IBEW) Local No. 3*	325 U.S. 797 (1945), *298*
Amalgamated Meat Cutters Local 189 v. *Jewel Tea Co.*	381 U.S. 676 (1965), *298*
Ambrose v. *U.S. Steel*	38 EPD ¶3561 (CCH) (D.C. Cal. 1985), *87*
American Art	170 NLRB No. 70 (1968), *270*
American Federation of State and County and Municipal Employees v. *State of Washington*	770 F.2d 1401 (9th Cir. 1985), *102*
American Postal Workers Union v. *Postmaster General*	781 F.2d 772 (9th Cir. 1986), *64*
American Tobacco Company v. *Patterson*	102 S.Ct. 1534 (1982), *111*
Andreason v. *Industrial Commission*	102 P.2d 894 (Utah 1940), *250*

TERMS AS USED IN THE TEXT

Adverse impact. A term used interchangeably with *disparate impact*, which alludes to group discrimination.

Applicant pool. A technique to have qualified candidates available when a vacancy exists. Often used in affirmative action programs.

Belo contract. A guaranteed wage contract for nonexempt employees that, under certain conditions, is permissible under the FLSA.

Bona Fide Occupational Qualification. As defined in Sect. 703(a)(e)(1) of Title VII, means that it is in compliance to discriminate because of sex if sex is a qualifying factor to perform all the duties of the job.

Business necessity. A decision that is reasonably necessary for the safe and efficient operation of the business.

Collyer Doctrine. Position of the NLRB that wherever possible a dispute should be arbitrated rather than processed by the board as an unfair labor practice.

Common law. As distinguished from statutes, it is a body of law that derives its authority from customs, rules of action, and decrees of the courts enforcing such customs and rules. It is the unwritten law of England, statutory and case law of the American colonies before the American Revolution.

Comparable worth. A wage theory that requires equal pay for comparable work even if job content or job categories are different.

Compensatory damages. Damages that compensate for actual loss caused by the defendant's wrongful act or omission of an act.

Complaint. When used in nonlegal context it is an employee's disagreement over a management policy or action concerning working conditions or wages.

Concerted activity. A protected activity under the NLRA where a group of employees are involved in an activity concerning work conditions or where an individual action affects working conditions of others or she or he is acting in behalf and under authority of others.

Constructive discharge. When an employer creates conditions that a reasonable person cannot endure so she or he quits, but the action is treated by the courts as a discharge.

Contemptuous tort. A form of malpractice where intentional conduct by the employer is contrary to what civilized society should tolerate.

Defamation. A written or oral statement that has the effect of damaging the reputation or social stature of another person.

Deposition. A pretrial discovery procedure whereby testimony is given under oath outside of open court.

Dictum. Court language in a decision that does

not relate specifically to the issue. The statement, remark, or observation that is not necessary in deciding the issue.

Discharge.   An employer action that indicates to the employee that his or her services are no longer wanted.

Discrimination.   Where there is different treatment in violation of a statute.

Disparate impact.   A situation where as a result of a qualifying criteria the persons protected by statute are disproportionately selected as compared to groups who are not included in the protected class. (Usually if under 80 percent, it is considered a disparate impact.)

Disparate treatment.   Where an employee is treated less favorably than other employees in violation of a statute.

Employee benefit.   Something of a monetary value to the employee that is not related to work performed and is paid for either partially or wholly by the employer.

Employer.   Anyone for whom an employee works.

Employment-at-will.   A common law doctrine that an employee can be terminated for good cause, for no cause, or even for a cause morally wrong.

Equal work standard.   A term used in applying the Equal Pay Act to determine whether two jobs performed by persons of different sex have equal skills, and have equal responsibility, and require equal effort under similar working conditions.

Exposure to litigation.   A potential lawsuit that has sufficient facts to incite an attorney to represent the employee on a contingency.

Financial core member.   Where a union member cannot be disciplined for crossing the picket line during a strike as long as she or he tenders dues to remain a member of the union.

Gray areas.   An uncertainty as to the application of a statute or legal principle.

Grievance.   A procedure under a labor agreement where the employee alleges that the agreement is not being followed.

Hostile environment.   Conduct permissible by the employer whereby an environment is created that is offensive and abusive to a reasonable person. This is most often used in sexual harassment situations.

Insubordination.   Where an employee refuses to obey a reasonable order from the employer.

Interrogatories.   Written questions asked in a discovery procedure to a party having information of interest in the case.

Just cause.   Used in connection with discharge where the employee has been informed that a certain rule violation or poor performance will result in discharge.

Legal paradox.   Where courts grant immunity from liability for disclosing employee information and employer refuses because of fear of being sued.

Liquidated damages.   Statutory damages based on actual loss but increased two or more times to compensate for a violation of the statute.

Litigation-happy society.   That urge to sue everybody regardless of whether there is merit to the offense.

Lodester.   A court-approved method of determining reasonable attorney fees.

Management malpractice.   Where the conduct of the employer toward the employee is such that it exceeds the bounds that society will tolerate.

Manager.   An employee who directly or indirectly manages the work of others.

Mixed discharge.   Where an employee is engaged in a protected activity and in an unrelated action violates a rule or policy or has poor performance.

Moonlighting.   Where an employee has two jobs that may be competing with each other.

Negligent hiring.   The employer is liable for injury to third persons where employer knew or should have known of an applicant's dangerous tendencies, and employer's negligence was the proximate cause of the injury to those persons that employer could reasonably expect would come in contact with the employee.

Negligent retention.   Where employer is aware of or should have been aware of an employee's dangerous propensity for violence or maliciousness (regardless of the cause) and did not do anything about it.

Per se.   As used in legal context, without any other facts, it is a violation.

Personnel documents.   All information kept by an employer that is received about an employee in the course of employment.

Practitioner.   A person who has part-time or full-time responsibility for all or part of the personnel function.

Prima facie case.   There are sufficient facts for the action to prevail until it is contradicted and overcome by other evidence.

Protected activity.   An employee activity that is protected by statute from retaliation by the employer.

Protected class. That group of individuals who are protected from discrimination by a federal, state, or local statute.

Punitive damages. Monetary damages above the actual loss, which are given for punishment for wrongful behavior.

Qualified privilege doctrine. Where under certain conditions the employer is immune from liability when disclosing employee information to another person who has a business right to receive it.

Quid pro quo. Something for something. As used in the text, giving one thing of value to one person for another thing considered valuable to another person.

Reasonable accommodation. An effort on the part of the employer to give consideration for job placement to an employee as required by statute.

Red circle rate. Where an employee retains the rate of his or her old job when performing a job that has a lesser rate.

Retaliation. An adverse action by an employer against an employee for exercising a right under a statute.

Statute of Frauds. A statute that provides that an enforceable agreement must be in writing unless it can be performed within one year.

Subpoena. A court order directed to a person to appear at a certain time and place and give testimony on a certain matter.

Subpoena duces tecum. A court order to appear as a witness and bring certain documents related to the issue at trial.

Sudden death discharge. A discharge where the employee has been warned that when she or he commits the offense immediate discharge is mandatory.

Summary judgment. A motion to dismiss the action because there is no genuine issue of material fact to be determined by a judge or jury.

Summons. A document that commences a civil action or proceeding that asserts jurisdiction, states the wrong done against the plaintiff, and requests certain relief.

Supervisor. A person who directly supervises the activity of others.

Tort. When one person causes injury (physical or otherwise) to another, for which a court will allow a civil action.

Undue hardship. The result from accommodating that affects the employer to the point that no accommodation is necessary to comply with a statute.

Use it or lose it. A term used in connection with vacation time off. You take the time or lose it.

Voluntary quit. When an employee exercises directly or indirectly a free choice to terminate the employment relationship.

Weighted application blank. A structured method for determining which characteristics will predict job success.

Weingarten Doctrine. The right of an employee to have representation in an investigative interview.

Writ of Certiorari. A discretionary device used by the U.S. Supreme Court to choose cases it wishes to hear.

INDEX